Critical Essays on

MAXINE HONG KINGSTON

CRITICAL ESSAYS
ON
AMERICAN LITERATURE

James Nagel, General Editor
University of Georgia, Athens

◆ ——————————

Critical Essays on
MAXINE HONG KINGSTON

—————————— ◆ ——————————

edited by

LAURA E. SKANDERA-TROMBLEY

G. K. Hall & Co.

New York

G. K. Hall & Co.

1633 Broadway
New York, NY 10019

Library of Congress Cataloging-in-Publication Data

Critical essays on Maxine Hong Kingston / edited by Laura E. Skandera-Trombley.
     p.   cm. — (Critical essays on American literature)
     Includes bibliographical references and index.
     ISBN 0-7838-0036-3 (alk. paper)
     1. Kingston, Maxine Hong—Criticism and interpretation. 2. Women and literature—United States—History—20th century. 3. Chinese Americans in literature.   I. Skandera-Trombley, Laura E.
II. Series.
PS3561.I52Z63   1998
813'.54—dc21   98-30772
                                           CIP

For my son,
Nelson Edmond Trombley Jr.
"Sparkey"
I love you so

Contents

◆

REVIEWS OF *TRIPMASTER MONKEY*

ESSAYS ON *TRIPMASTER MONKEY*

General Editor's Note

◆

This series seeks to anthologize the most important criticism on a wide variety of topics and writers in American literature. Our readers will find in various volumes not only a generous selection of reprinted articles and reviews but also original essays, bibliographies, manuscript selections, and other materials brought to public attention for the first time. This volume, *Critical Essays on Maxine Hong Kingston,* is the most comprehensive gathering of essays ever published on one of the most important contemporary writers in the United States. It contains a sizable gathering of early reviews, a broad selection of more modern scholarship, and a number of special features, including a new interview with Kingston. Among the authors of reprinted articles and reviews are Anne Tyler, Bharati Mukherjee, Caroline Ong, Amy Ling, and King-kok Cheung. In addition to a substantial introduction by Laura E. Skandera-Trombley, there are also two original essays commissioned specifically for publication in this volume—new studies by David Leiwei Li on *The Woman Warrior* in historical context and Jeanne R. Smith on the theoretical aspects of *Tripmaster Monkey.* We are confident that this book will make a permanent and significant contribution to the study of American literature.

JAMES NAGEL
University of Georgia

Publisher's Note

◆

Producing a volume that contains both newly commissioned and reprinted material presents the publisher with the challenge of balancing the desire to achieve stylistic consistency with the need to preserve the integrity of works first published elsewhere. In the Critical Essays series, essays commissioned especially for a particular volume are edited to be consistent with G. K. Hall's house style; reprinted essays appear in the style in which they were first published, with only typographical errors corrected. Consequently, shifts in style from one essay to another are the result of our efforts to be faithful to each text as it was originally published.

Introduction

LAURA E. SKANDERA-TROMBLEY

Maxine Hong Kingston is a writer of luminous prose who, with the publication of her three books, *The Woman Warrior* (1976), *China Men* (1980), and *Tripmaster Monkey* (1989), has indelibly changed American writing as well as challenged and transformed critical scholarship about it.[1] While the body of Kingston's work is compact (three book-length works in 13 years in addition to several journal articles), her place as an important American author is well established.

Kingston conveys through contemporized myth, autobiography, memoir, history, fiction, magic realism, fact, and biography the zeitgeist of what it means to be Chinese American in a frequently hostile and antagonistic white America. Her brilliance lies in her ability to create unforgettable characters such as *The Woman Warrior*'s Fa Mu Lan, the mythic woman warrior; Maxine Kingston as the troubled, powerful narrator; and Kingston's mother, the indomitable Brave Orchid. The physically diminutive Brave Orchid, singularly the most captivating of Kingston's many characters, conveys a strength that often borders on the fantastic. Brave Orchid is the overwhelming presence in *The Woman Warrior* to whom everything in the narrative continually responds.

Kingston also constructs scenes that are extraordinarily visual in nature; indeed, her ability to create tableaux results in descriptions that are almost painterly in their effect. Two examples can be found in the books *China Men* and *Tripmaster Monkey.* In *China Men,* grandfather Ah Goong risks his life—he dangles over the Sierra Nevada mountains in a wicker basket, setting dynamite charges to clear the way for the construction of the transcontinental railroad. Thrown in relief against this mountainous backdrop, the tiny figure of the grandfather defiantly yells to the valley floor below, "I am fucking the world."[2] The verbose and manic Wittman Ah Sing invites the world, in *Tripmaster Monkey,* to come watch and participate in his one-man show. By the third evening, after the one hundred and eight bandits climb into the sky to become stars, Wittman finishes his wild ride with a furious, staccato-paced monologue, and the reader is finally left breathless by the trip.

Over the past 20 years, a plethora of articles have been published focusing on Kingston's three book-length works, and there have been significant comparative studies of Kingston and other ethnic writers. In addition, essays and studies have used Kingston as the starting point for a concentration on pedagogical materials, genre, textual and historical examinations, and language. Also of interest are a number of foundational overviews of Asian American writing, strategies for reading, and comprehensive bibliographies. All of Kingston's books have successfully transgressed disciplinary boundaries (a phenomenon all but unimaginable just a few years ago) and are studied at the college level in anthropology, history, sociology, politics, women's studies, and literature classes.

The Woman Warrior has been cited by the Modern Language Association as the most widely taught work by a contemporary writer on college campuses today, and this popularity has undoubtedly been aided by the publication of a number of fine teaching-resource articles and books. Foremost among these tools is Shirley Geok-lin Lim's indispensable *Approaches to Teaching Kingston's The Woman Warrior* (1991). This edition is part of the Modern Language Association's Approaches to World Literature series. In part 1 of this exhaustive volume, Lim has included an explanation of editions and anthologies of Kingston's work and a summary of secondary texts useful in explaining the cultural and historical background of *The Woman Warrior.* Part 2 includes an introduction to the edition, a statement by Kingston, and a collection of fine critical articles by Sau-ling Cynthia Wong ("Kingston's Handling of Traditional Chinese Sources"), Patricia Lin ("Use of Media and Other Resources to Situate *The Woman Warrior*"), Kathryn VanSpanckeren ("The Asian Literary Background of *The Woman Warrior*"), Robert G. Lee ("*The Woman Warrior* as an Intervention in Asian American Historiography"), Vicente F. Gotera, (" 'I've Never Read Anything like It': Student Responses to *The Woman Warrior*"), Judith M. Melton ("*The Woman Warrior* in the Women's Studies Classroom"), James R. Aubrey ("Woman Warriors and Military Students"), Kathleen A. Boardman ("Voice and Vision: *The Woman Warrior* in the Writing Class"), Paul W. McBride ("*The Woman Warrior* in the History Classroom"), Marlyn Peterson and Deirdre Lashgari ("Teaching *The Woman Warrior* to High School and Community College Students"), Marilyn Yalom ("*The Woman Warrior* as Postmodern Autobiography"), Joan Lidoff ("Autobiography in a Different Voice: *The Woman Warrior* and the Question of Genre"), Colleen Kennedy and Deborah Morse ("A Dialogue with(in) Tradition: Two Perspectives on *The Woman Warrior*"), Victoria Myers ("Speech-Act Theory and the Search for Identity in *The Woman Warrior*"), Gayle K. Fujita Sato ("*The Woman Warrior* as a Search for Ghosts"), Cheng Lok Chua ("Mythopoesis East and West in *The Woman Warrior*"), and Timothy Dow Adams ("Talking Stories/Telling Lies in *The Woman Warrior*"). There is an extensive bibliography and listing of films, video productions, and recordings.[3]

In "Dragons, Ghosts, and China Dolls: Chinese American Women's Writing in the Canon and the Classroom," published in the Fall 1995 issue of *Transformations,* Laura Skandera-Trombley writes about her rewarding experiences teaching Chinese American literature at a midsize, state-funded rural college; in addition to the narrative, she provides a lengthy bibliography, resource list, course syllabus, semester outline, ground rules for the course, and exams. Suzette A. Henke's essay, "Women's Life Writing and the Minority Voice: Maya Angelou, Maxine Hong Kingston, and Alice Walker" (1995), is included in *Traditions, Voices, and Dreams: The American Novel since the 1960s;* the collection is intended as a textbook for courses on the contemporary American novel. For individuals considering teaching *The Woman Warrior,* Shirley Geoklin Lim offers the practical guide for " 'Growing with Stories': Chinese American Identities, Textual Identities" (1996). Lim divides her piece into two sections: The first half provides background materials, including Edward Said's *Orientalism* (1978) and Judy Yung's *Chinese Women of America: A Pictorial History* (1986), and classroom and teaching strategies as well as writing and discussion assignments. A selected bibliography lists related work, best criticism, other sources, and video and films. Jennie Wang's provocative 1996 article, "The Myth of Kingston's 'No Name Woman': Making Contextual and Intertextual Connections in Teaching Asian American Literature," calls for a reexamination of how to teach The *Woman Warrior.* Wang's view is that teaching the work as a multicultural text is problematic in that it is an American girl's story about growing up in the land of her birth.[4]

What makes Kingston distinct from other contemporary authors is not just the soaring quality of her writing but her high visibility and her willingness to take on her critics in both articles and interviews. Since 1977 she has given dozens of interviews, the latest of which is published in this critical edition. Kingston is extremely candid in many of her interviews in discussing her writing, her family, and future projects. In her earliest interview with Susan Brownmiller, when asked if *The Woman Warrior* is fiction or nonfiction, Kingston responds, "I guess I do think it's closer to fiction, but whatever sells. . . ." In a 1983 interview with Arturo Islas, Kingston rejects the idea that she is a racial representative in her writing. In her view, African Americans have already surmounted the problem of diversity of expression that Asian Americans are still confronting. In a 1989 *Boston Globe* interview, Kingston remarks that it is impossible for Chinese Americans to assimilate because it is impossible to disappear into the mainstream; she maintains that the healthy solution is for Americans to recognize that the United States is a multicultural country composed of multicultural people.[5]

Kingston has been the subject of an award-winning documentary, "Maxine Hong Kingston: Talking Story" (1990), and has narrated the audio versions of *The Woman Warrior* and *China Men* (1993). In 1990 she was interviewed by Stephen Talbot, coproducer of "Talking Story," who describes the making of the documentary and provides a well-written, concise overview of Kingston's career and controversies. Particularly entertaining are his observations of Kingston's mother, Brave Orchid.[6]

Kingston has also become a significant presence in cyberspace. It is a sign of our technologically networked times that a quick internet search results in 419 "hits" associated with Kingston. Included among this multitude of web pages are posted dissertations, articles, and journal announcements about her or mentioning her. There is also an invitation from Kingston to join the National Women's History Project; various Asian American reading lists; several college-level course syllabi; an advertisement for posters of great Asian Americans; a hypertext reading of *Tripmaster Monkey;* and, most intriguingly, a band of women calling itself "The Kingston Group" inviting the web crawler to check out its interpretations of Kingston's oeuvre.

Maxine Hong Kingston was born in central California in the city of Stockton on October 27, 1940, the year of the Angry Dragon, a first-generation daughter to well-educated Chinese immigrant parents, Chew Ying Lan and Tom Hong. In China, Kingston's mother had graduated from medical school and her father had been brought up to be a scholar. Her father named his daughter Maxine after a blonde woman who was lucky at cards at the gambling den Tom Hong managed in Stockton. The Hong family eventually totalled eight with the subsequent births of two daughters and three sons. As a child Kingston worked with her parents and siblings in Stockton's New Port Laundry, which the family owned. English was her second language; her first was Say Yup, a Cantonese dialect. By age nine her proficiency in her second language had improved to the extent that she began composing poetry in English.

Numerous scholarships enabled her to attend the University of California at Berkeley, where she first enrolled as an engineering major. Eventually Kingston gravitated to English literature, although she found that studying literary criticism did not prove to be a boon to her own creative writing. In 1962, the year of her graduation, she married thespian Earll Kingston, a fellow English classmate. Two years later, she returned to Berkeley to earn her teaching certificate. During this period of the sixties Berkeley was the epicenter of the Days of Rage and the activist peace movement. By her own admission, Kingston was profoundly influenced by the politics of that era, and echoes of that time continually surface in her writings. Kingston moved to Hawaii in 1967 with her husband and their young son, Joseph, where she taught English, creative writing, and mathematics for several years at the high school and college level.[7]

Kingston's first book, *The Woman Warrior: Memoirs of a Girlhood among Ghosts,* was published in 1976 and became an immediate best-seller, with over half a million paperback copies sold to date. It was lauded by the literary establishment and won the National Book Critics Circle Award for the best nonfiction book of 1976. That year Kingston also won the Anisfield-Wolf Race Relations Award; a year later she won the *Mademoiselle* Magazine Award.

In 1979 *Time* magazine cited *The Woman Warrior* as one of the top 10 nonfiction books of the decade, and in 1980 Kingston received a National Endowment of the Arts Writers Award and in addition was recognized as a Living Treasure of Hawaii, the first Chinese American to be so honored. In an interview with Timothy Pfaff in 1980, Kingston talks about being honored by a Honolulu Buddhist sect.[8]

Kingston's works have had a profound impact, both positive and negative, on many disparate individuals, including sinologists, feminists, male Chinese American writers, genre critics, literary critics, and ethnic studies academics. While preparing for the publication of her first book, Kingston and her editor asked Frank Chin, author of the plays "Chickencoop Chinaman" and "Year of the Dragon" and coeditor of the anthology *Aiiieeeee! An Anthology of Asian American Writers* (1974), for his endorsement. Chin declined because in his view autobiographies by Asian Americans were simply bids for white literary and popular acceptance.[9]

This controversy over genre first voiced by Chin has continued to haunt Kingston since the publication of *The Woman Warrior*. Because Kingston continually conflates, deconstructs, and problematizes standard conceptions of genre categories, critics and particularly reviewers have been hard-pressed to determine the nature and, interestingly, the acceptability of her work as an ethnic writer. Henry Allen, in his *Washington Post* review, writes that Kingston captures female Chinese American life "in a wild mix of myth, memory, history and a lucidity which verges on the eerie."[10] Clearly if *The Woman Warrior* is read strictly as autobiography, the text becomes immediately resistant to the reader. As Kingston points out in the interview included in this edition, "Those people who tried to read it as autobiography had to get information off the flap of the book. . . . And they never really noticed that I hardly appear in the book. I am just the observer of the people's shenanigans."

Kingston and Chin's initial disagreement has become what has been called "a full-blown cultural debate."[11] In the 1991 edition of *The Big Aiiieeeee!*, Chin claims that Kingston's work perpetuates stereotypes of Chinese Americans: "Every Chinese American autobiography or work of autobiographical fiction . . . has been written by Christian Chinese perpetuating and advancing the stereotype of a Chinese culture so foul, so cruel to women, so perverse, that good Chinese are driven by the moral imperative to kill it. . . . The autobiography is not a Chinese form."[12]

A practicing Buddhist, Kingston has repeatedly refuted Chin's statements, declaring in the interview published here,

> You know, what I wish that people could appreciate, they could see [is] that what I'm doing is riding that border between fiction and nonfiction. You know we have a land of fiction and there is a land of nonfiction; there's a border in the middle. Well, what I'm doing is making that border very wide, and I am taking into consideration I am writing about real people and these real people

have powerful imaginations. They have minds that make up fictions constantly, and so if I was going to write a true biography or an autobiography I would
have to take into consideration the stories that people tell. I tell the dreams
that they have and then when I do that, that border becomes so wide that it
contains fiction and nonfiction and both going toward truth.

For all of the distance between Kingston and Chin, it does look as
though both are locked in a continuing response to each other. Upon the publication of *The Woman Warrior,* it appeared that part of what Chin had warned
against, a racist commodification and appropriation of Kingston's work, did
surface in numerous reviews.

Three of *The Woman Warrior*'s earliest reviews are reprinted in this edition.
John Leonard's laudatory piece published September 17, 1976, in the *New York
Times Book Review* is seen by many as responsible for creating the book's initial
enormous surge of publicity. Diane Johnson's 1977 review in the *New York
Review of Books* unintentionally set the stage for the airing of some major dif-
ferences between European American and Asian American critics as well as
between female and male critics. If nothing else, Johnson is culpable because
of her generalizations and assumptions regarding Chinese Americans, which
Jeffery Paul Chan seizes upon in his reply to her. Chan, coeditor with Frank
Chin of *Aiiieeeee!,* takes strident issue with Johnson's remarks concerning
Chinese Americans while negatively critiquing Kingston's writing. Unwilling
to allow Chan the last word, Johnson then takes issue with him and defends
both her review and Kingston's writing. Johnson defines *The Woman Warrior* as
memoir. Nan Robertson, in her 1977 *New York Times* review (included in the
"Family/Style" section), describes *The Woman Warrior* as a "memoir-fantasy."[13]
In the three reviews and one exchange republished here, the debate over
Kingston's work was formally begun, and it continues some two decades later.

In 1982 Kingston was moved to write a formal response in reaction both
to Chin's remarks and to the multitude of book reviews *The Woman Warrior* had
garnered. Kingston states in "Cultural Mis-readings by American Reviewers"
that she "did not foresee . . . the critics measuring the book and me against the
stereotype of the exotic, inscrutable, mysterious oriental. About two-thirds of
the reviews did this."[14] "Cultural Mis-readings by American Reviewers" provides an excellent summary of the best reviews (as well as many of the most
offensive ones) and functions as Kingston's critique of the publishing establishment (including her own publisher), popular press reviewers, the academic
milieu, and male Chinese American critics. A 1991 review by Elizabeth Baer
demonstrates the growth by certain reviewers in the years since the book's initial publication. Baer argues that in *The Woman Warrior* Kingston has provided
the reader with a postmodern paradigm to study cultural differences and that
she writes at "the site of cultural confrontation."[15]

The Woman Warrior has inspired a watershed of scholarly articles.
Throughout the criticism several reoccurring topics emerge: genre combin-

ing, authenticity of subject matter, and male/female/ethnic autobiography. The first published article on Kingston is Woon-Ping Chin Holaday's 1978 article, "From Ezra Pound to Maxine Hong Kingston: Expressions of Chinese Thought in American Literature"; Holaday observes that while China was an idealized abstraction for Pound, for Kingston it is a hard, often brutal reality drawn from her personal experience. Deborah Homsher's essay *"The Woman Warrior,* by Maxine Hong Kingston: A Bridging of Autobiography and Fiction" (1979) examines form and observes that the issues of distance in the book go beyond the topic and influence the narrative structure. Patricia Lin Blinde's 1979 essay, the first to focus on Kingston's mixture of genres, describes the text as a "collage" that functions to rework Chinese folk tales and the author's own life history. Another early piece of criticism is Jan Zlotnik Schmidt's "The Other: A Study of the Persona in Several Contemporary Women's Autobiographies" (1980). Schmidt tries to fit *The Woman Warrior* within Simone de Beauvoir's conception of "the Other" in relation to male-authored autobiographies.[16]

Two other essays published in 1980 examine autobiography and Kingston's manipulation of it. Suzanne Juhasz discusses in "Towards a Theory of Form in Feminist Autobiography: Kate Millet's *Flying* and *Sita;* Maxine Hong Kingston's *The Woman Warrior*" the differences between male- and female-authored autobiographies. Millet's writing is seen as developing the "concept of dailiness" as a structural principal, and Kingston's style is viewed as coming from "fantasy, the life of the imagination." Lynn Z. Bloom's "Heritages: Dimensions of Mother-Daughter Relationships in Women's Autobiographies" interprets the daughter in the text as an autobiographer in the act of reinventing herself in the role of the mother and thus assuming a position of power.[17]

In the second of what would be many articles devoted to Kingston's fiction published by the *Journal of the Society for the Study of Multi Ethnic Literature of the United States (MELUS)*, Cheng Lok Chua examines how the original dream of economic mobility for Chinese immigrants has transmogrified as successive generations evolved from sojourners to native-born Americans (1981). Amy Ling's 1981 article, "A Perspective on Chinamerican Literature," also in *MELUS,* offers the first concise summary of topical issues in Asian American literature. She provides a brief history of Chinese immigrants in America and describes Frank Chin's attempts to identify an authentic Chinese American voice. Ling coins the term "Chinamerican" due to her unhappiness with the conventional term "Chinese-American," and she describes the power of the hyphen and the power that is gained by removing it.[18]

In 1982 Diane Johnson expands in book form, and to some extent repeats, her now infamous 1977 book review. A 1982 comparative study of Lin Yutang, Louis Chu, and Maxine Hong Kingston by Cheng Lok Chua discusses how the original immigrant dream of economic success has changed and expanded. Kingston's act of self-creation is confusing, according to Amy Ling in her essay "Thematic Threads in Maxine Hong Kingston's *The Woman*

Warrior" (1983–1984). Ling views Kingston's work as part of a movement that is revitalizing contemporary literature. Margaret Miller covers familiar territory in her 1983 discussion of the Chinese knot as a metaphor for Kingston's difficulty in sorting out the strands of her identity.[19]

A number of provocative articles relating to questions of gender and ethnicity were published in 1985. Linda Hunt's " 'I could not figure out what was my village': Gender vs. ethnicity in Maxine Hong Kingston's *The Woman Warrior*" finds Kingston's double bind emblematic of the position that she occupies, namely as both an insider (identifying strongly with her ethnicity) and an outsider (rebelling against her cultural dictums). Veronica Wang describes Kingston's search for self-realization in her essay "Reality and Fantasy: the Chinese-American Woman's Quest for Identity" and argues that for Chinese American women to attain a sense of self, they must confront their reality and reject all external authority to allow their own voices to speak. Suzanne Juhasz traces how despite superficial similarities between the two texts, *The Woman Warrior* and *China Men* employ decidedly different narrative patterns. Paul John Eakin contends in "Self-Invention in Autobiography: The Moment of Language" that like Saul Friedlaender and Jean-Paul Sartre, Maxine Hong Kingston realizes that self-invention is determined by a dialectical interplay between the person and her culture.[20]

Victoria Meyers comes to grips with narrative technique in her 1986 article, "The Significant Fictivity of Maxine Hong Kingston's *The Woman Warrior*"; Meyers concludes that through utilizing speech act theory it is possible to determine that Kingston's reworking of language is a continuing process because "multiplicity is Kingston's point." A Chinese professor, Zhang Ya-jie, responds to Kingston's writing and admits that as an ethnic Chinese she was initially offended by what she perceived as Kingston's rewriting of history; however, she came to realize that the story was an American one and that she was basing her assumptions on her own upbringing (1986). Once again Kingston's narrative structure—her mélange of genres and styles—is addressed, by Marjorie L. Lightfoot in "Hunting the Dragon in Kingston's *The Woman Warrior*" (1986).[21]

The year 1987 produced a bumper crop of articles and books about Kingston. In "No Lost Paradise: Social Gender and Symbolic Gender in the Writings of Maxine Hong Kingston," Leslie Rabine analyzes Kingston's writing to reconcile "insights of symbolic and social feminism." Evocative of Helene Cixous and Luce Irigaray, Rabine claims that Kingston's writing violates gendered dichotomies and renders them into irresolvable gender differences. Another essay dealing with gender is Joan Lidoff's "Autobiography in a Different Voice: Maxine Hong Kingston's *The Woman Warrior*"; Lidoff states definitively that gender affects genre and cites studies by Nancy Chodorow and Carol Gilligan to support her thesis. In *Boundaries of the Self: Gender, Culture, Fiction,* Roberta Rubenstein examines the symbolic meanings associated with auditory ability, the act of naming, and language. Although

Rubenstein's book deals primarily with fiction, Rubenstein includes Kingston, asserting that her works straddle, challenge, and remake the boundary between fiction and nonfiction. Linda Morante discusses the familiar issue of narrative silence in her *Frontiers* article and connects silence in *The Woman Warrior* with the process of self-creation.[22]

Autobiography was also frequently discussed in 1987 criticism. Kim Chernin's *In My Mother's House: A Daughter's Story* and *The Woman Warrior*, identified by Jeanne Barker-Nunn in her *Women's Studies* article as autobiographies, substantially differ from male-authored texts in their portrayal of history and its relation to the narrator. Sidonie Smith includes a chapter on *The Woman Warrior* in her *Poetics of Women's Autobiography*, because "no single work captures so powerfully the relationship of gender to genre in twentieth-century autobiography." Smith identifies *The Woman Warrior* as a postmodern work in that it is self-reflexive—an autobiography about female-authored autobiography. Shirley K. Rose examines the myths that emerge from autobiographies of literacy acquisition in "Metaphors and Myths of Cross-Cultural Literacy: Autobiographical Narratives by Maxine Hong Kingston, Richard Rodriguez, and Malcolm X." An early comparative study between Margaret Atwood's *Surfacing* and Kingston's *The Woman Warrior* as contemporary female bildungsroman is done by Mara E. Donaldson in *Heroines of Popular Culture*, and the final publication for 1987 is Reed Way Dasenbrock's important *PMLA* article where he discusses "explicitly multicultural texts" that are also "implicitly multicultural." Writing in response to R. K. Narayan's *The Painter of Signs*, Kingston's *The Woman Warrior*, Rudolfo Anaya's *Bless Me, Ultima*, and Witi Ihimaera's *Tangi*, Dasenbrock concludes that a multicultural text is one that not only contains overt multicultural themes but also is written for readers who represent a range of cultures.[23]

Five important essays appeared in 1988 devoted to issues of silence, gender, and autobiography. King-kok Cheung, in " 'Don't Tell': Imposed Silences in *The Color Purple* and *The Woman Warrior*," notes that both these books begin with parental injunctions against speaking out and that the protagonists in each proceed to tell their stories as a means of self-preservation. Cheung concludes that for these two writers silence is ended not by assimilating into the mainstream but rather "by rendering their distinct voices." In "Autobiography as a Sociolinguistic Resource," April Komenaka contends that the bilingual-bicultural autobiographer can provide important insights to ethnolinguistic issues by presenting them within the context of maturation. Joanne S. Frye takes issue with Suzanne Juhasz in her essay "*The Woman Warrior*: Claiming Narrative Power, Recreating Female Selfhood." Frye disagrees with Juhasz that Kingston's fantastic, novelistic form signals a withdrawal from reality; instead, she argues that Kingston is creating her own vision of the self and is realistically affirming that self within a societal context. David Leiwei Li notes insightfully in his *Criticism* essay that the timing of *The Woman Warrior*'s publication, coming during a period of feminist and new historicist theory, has a great deal to do with how the book has been framed in terms of critical responses. Li argues that these responses are inadequate and recommends that Kingston's representations of race and gender are "embodied in the broader categories of culture in relation to which the individual defines or dissolves his/her identity." In "Emigrant Selves: Narrative Strategies in Three Women's Autobiographies," Sarah Gilead studies Laura Ingalls Wilder's Little House series, Isak Dinesen's *Out of Africa,* and Kingston's *The Woman Warrior* using polarized pairs of concepts that structure the narrative and serve to project an image of the self.[24]

An important step forward in the evolution of Kingston criticism comes with the publication of Malini Schueller's 1989 article, "Questioning Race and Gender Definitions: Dialogic Subversions in *The Woman Warrior.*" For the first time Kingston's writing is investigated from neither a feminist viewpoint nor an ethnic studies stance; instead, Schueller approaches it in terms of revealing the interstices between the two—in other words, exploring the conjunctures and relationships between female and ethnic identity. In *Literature and Medicine* (1989), Alfred S. Wang contends that the language describing treatments and ailments serves to express Chinese and Chinese American intercultural encounters over previous generations and that these encounters can alter or intensify personal identity. Kingston's narrative strategy is discussed by Bobby Fong in *Biography* (1989); he notes that Kingston's narrative structure is circular instead of linear—the personal growth on the part of the narrator is toward not autonomy and independence but rather "reattachment to familial and cultural patterns," and the past is constructed from recollections by the mother. Michael S. Duke's 1989 edition, *Modern Chinese Women Writers: Critical Appraisals,* contains two essays on Kingston. The first, by Lucien Miller and Hui-chuan Chang, compares Kingston's *The Woman Warrior* to Eileen Chang's "The Golden Cangue." The second essay, by Joseph S. M. Lau, discusses moments of what he terms "exorcism," where Kingston negotiates her selfhood as a Chinese American woman.[25]

In *Amerasia Journal* (1990) Deborah Woo revisits the controversy concerning how Kingston's work is emblematic of the dilemma that confronts writers of color in that ethnic writers who appeal to a general audience will simultaneously create controversy among their ethnic group regarding representativeness. The prolific King-kok Cheung published two essays in 1990; the first, "*The Woman Warrior* versus *The Chinaman Pacific:* Must a Chinese American Critic Choose between Feminism and Heroism?," responds to the friction between male and female Chinese American literary camps. Cheung writes partly in response to the movement founded by Frank Chin to create a "heroic tradition" based on outlaw bands and philosophers and notes that while this movement is "recuperating a heroic tradition," women academics and authors are in the midst of "reassessing the entire Western code of heroism." Cheung's second article, "Self-Fulfilling Visions in *The Woman Warrior* and *Thousand Pieces of Gold,*" examines the issue of creating a positive identity by comparing the two texts as vehicles of "self-invention." Robert Lee in *The*

New American Writing: Essays on American Literature Since 1970 (1990) hails Kingston as a "passionate witness" to the history and traditions of China as well as to the emphasis on the present and future in America.[26]

Two articles invoking the figures of the ghost and the trickster were published in 1991. Gayle K. Fujita Sato, in "Ghosts as Chinese-American Constructs in Maxine Hong Kingston's *The Woman Warrior*," reads the text as distinctly Asian American by showing how the figure of the "ghost" designates a particular as well as a shared Chinese American existence. In Sato's view, Kingston represents her life as a totality even though she differentiates what is experientially "Chinese" and what is "American." Bonnie TuSmith suggests interpreting Kingston as less of a social documentarian and more as a "creative artist" in "Literary Tricksterism." In doing so, the reader should view the autobiographer as purposely adopting a strategy of "narrative ambiguity" in order to tell her tale; by reenvisioning the text and the writer in this manner, TuSmith recognizes Kingston as a "trickster" sine qua non. Gloria Chun discusses the origin of *The Woman Warrior*'s nonfiction autobiography classification in "The High Note of the Barbarian Reed Pipe: Maxine Hong Kingston" (1991). Chun discovers that Kingston's editor, Chuck Elliot, thought the text would sell better if it was labeled as nonfiction autobiography; Elliot noted, "It could have been called anything else." Helen M. Buss and Donald C. Goellnicht both discuss theory in relation to readings of *The Woman Warrior.* Buss recommends in her 1991 *Auto/Biography Studies* article that formalist and poststructural theory can be useful in reading female-authored autobiography. Goellnicht asks in a chapter published in *Redefining Autobiography in Twentieth-Century Women's Fiction* (1991) if Western academic feminist theory is adequate to multicultural writing as embodied by Joy Kogowa and Maxine Hong Kingston. In his 1991 *College Literature* article, Martin A. Danahay explores issues of resistance and accommodation through readings taken from *I Know Why the Caged Bird Sings, The Woman Warrior,* and *Hunger of Memory.* Danahay suggests that what may be perceived as resistance from one perspective will, when placed in a larger context, actually be an adjustment to hegemony.[27]

Perhaps the two best articles of the early 1990s are Lee Quinby's "The Subject of Memoirs: *The Woman Warrior*'s Technology of Ideographic Selfhood" (1992) and Sau-ling Cynthia Wong's "Autobiography as Guided Chinatown Tour? Maxine Hong Kingston's *The Woman Warrior* and the Chinese-American Autobiographical Controversy" (1992). Quinby examines the "is it fiction or is it biography" brouhaha and traces how the five "memoirs"—she resists efforts to label Kingston's work as autobiography—combine to construct "a new form of subjectivity"—what she terms "ideographic selfhood." Quinby argues that while experience cannot be separated, or unmediated, it is marked by "a knot of significations." Sau-ling Wong reviews the authenticity, genre status, and representative nature debate and determines that these issues represent the "heart of any theoretical discussion of ethnic American autobiography. . . ." Wong asserts that the lively exchange between Johnson and Chan raises some important theoretical points. At no step, Wong notes, does the "ignorance of white readers" not appear to be taken for granted, and the prospect that this readership might "learn to read the allusions . . . just as generations of minority readers have learned to read the Eurocentric canon, is never once raised."[28]

In "The Tradition of Chinese American Women's Life Stories" (1992), Shirley Geok-lin Lim first responds sharply to the "male misreadings" she finds evident in the 1974 edition of *Aiiieeeee!* before providing an extremely valuable history of the literary tradition of Chinese American women's life stories. Patricia Chu summarizes some of the past critical controversies concerning *The Woman Warrior,* listing Kingston's detractors—Frank Chin and Jeffery Paul Chan—as well as her defenders—Elaine Kim, Sau-ling Wong, and King-kok Cheung—in her essay for *Diaspora* (1992). Khani Begum, in "Confirming the Place of 'The Other': Gender and Ethnic Identity in Maxine Hong Kingston's *The Woman Warrior*" (1992), discusses the motif of the quest and how Kingston's protagonist Maxine must negotiate two cultures in order to develop her selfhood.[29]

King-kok Cheung reasons in her illuminating 1993 comparative study, *Articulate Silences: Hisaye Yamamoto, Maxine Hong Kingston, Joy Kogawa,* that of the three women authors she examines, Kingston is most demonstrative regarding her feminist beliefs. In contrast to Yamamoto and Kogawa, Cheung finds Kingston's silences ringed with power. Kingston's feminist strategies work, Cheung argues, to disrupt the dichotomy of the silenced female and in doing so create a world devoid of gendered dichotomies and "monocultural imperatives." Shirley Nelson Garner also discusses Kingston's use of silence in "Breaking Silence" (1993) and finds that her decision to speak is the core of the text. Garner links Kingston's equation of silence with insanity and how speech enables her to retrieve her sanity. Also published in 1993 is Bonnie TuSmith's insightful *All My Relatives: Community in Contemporary Ethnic American Literatures.* In the section dealing with *The Woman Warrior,* TuSmith includes an expanded version of her 1991 article "Literary Tricksterism." In her *Biography* article (1993), Sue Ann Johnston offers the term "fictive autobiography" and claims that Kingston creates her own "idiolect" that incorporates both a "mythic, three-dimensional reality represented" by an imagined China and a "flat literal reality" associated with America.[30]

The year 1994 produced a number of valuable articles on *The Woman Warrior.* Lauren Rusk's "Voicing the Harmonic Self: Maxine Hong Kingston's *The Woman Warrior*" examines three dominant themes: the suppression and power of women, the power and necessity of speech, and the ways in which art is and can be interaction. Rusk concludes that for Kingston, art is performance, and the audience is invited to act as a collaborator in completing meaning. *MELUS* published Ruth Jenkin's essay in which she reasons that women writers use elements of the supernatural as a rhetorical strategy to destabilize androcentric cultural norms. Jenkins sees both Kingston and Isabel Allende as using the supernatural, taking the form of ghosts and spirits, to create a narrative distinct from that promoted by Western, patriarchal cultures. Bonnie Melchior continues and expands the ongoing discussion of autobiography in her article "A Marginal I—The Autobiographical Self Deconstructed in Maxine Hong Kingston's *The Woman Warrior.*" Melchior asserts that Kingston deconstructs the autobiographical form (and by relation the masculine ideology affiliated with it) by "problematizing its assumptions about the nature of the self and the nature of 'fact.'" Catherine Lappas in *College English Association Critic* takes issue with Sidonie Smith's contention that "memory leaves only a *trace* of an earlier experience that we adjust into story." Instead, Lappas contends that Leslie Marmon Silko in *Storyteller* and Kingston in *The Woman Warrior* neither suppress nor forget but actively utilize the "trace" to create narratives that reflect their ethnicity.[31]

In her superb 1995 piece, "Maxine Hong Kingston and the Dialogic Dilemma of Asian American Writers," Amy Ling thoughtfully investigates the sometimes treacherous place that the Asian American writer occupies. Ling identifies that such writers as Kingston become targets when they write. If Kingston desires to be understood by a popular audience, then she is compelled to provide cultural and historical information until that happy day when Asian American experience and culture is taught as mainstream United States history. Yet choosing to write for the larger audience, Ling maintains, is an act that can "place the multicultural writer in a visible and vulnerable position." Marlene Goldman's essay, included in *International Women's Writing: New Landscapes of Identity* (1995), declares that Kingston creates a model for an "experimental treatment of the novel form." Goldman classifies the work as "postmodern" and traces how it "maps" the sometimes jarring intersections that occur between two disparate cultures. Kingston's China visit is recalled by Sandra Kumamoto Stanley in a 1995 *CEA Critic* essay. When in China, Kingston realized that Chinese young people were discovering the roots of their collective memory through her works. This revelation is particularly ironic in view of Frank Chin's accusation that Kingston is a purveyor of the "fake" rather than the "real." Sheryl A. Mylan's chapter in *Women of Color: Mother-Daughter Relationships in 20th Century Literature* (1996) draws upon Edward Said's *Orientalism* and discusses how elements of Orientalism surface in Kingston's portrayal of her mother. Mylan charges that Kingston's framework for characterizing her mother exhibits a Western monocultural perspective, and this perspective, Mylan surmises, might be what attracted such criticism from Frank Chin. A less successful study is Sämi Ludwig's *Concrete Language: Intercultural Communication in Maxine Hong Kingston's* The Woman Warrior *and Ishmael Reed's* Mumbo Jumbo (1996), which traces patterns of intercultural communication. Ludwig contends that both Reed and Kingston are concerned with intercultural interaction and "with the concepts by means of which such encounters are perceived and controlled."[32]

Perhaps an accurate way to describe Kingston's writing and the critical reception of it is as a series of intersections that almost appear to have an active element of synchronicity in their timing. With the publication of *The*

Woman Warrior at what some would identify as the height of the women's movement, Kingston's work was widely embraced by feminist theorists and academicians. In an interview with Donna Perry in 1993, Kingston responds that when *The Woman Warrior* was first published, she didn't consider herself a political writer, although she does now. What Kingston means by political has less to do with Marxist literary theory than with wanting to affect contemporary politics and desiring to change the world through "artistic pacifist means." With the publication of *China Men* in 1980, Kingston appeared almost to anticipate the recovery and publication of Chinese American history that occurred during the decades of the 1980s and 1990s.[33] For *China Men* Kingston won the National Book Award for nonfiction and was named the 1981 Asian/Pacific Women's Network Woman of the Year; also in 1981 she was awarded a Guggenheim Fellowship.

When Kingston's first two books were published, in the late 1970s, the rise of feminist scholarship and the initial efforts to expand the canon of American literature meant that her work found a ready audience. In many ways, timing is everything. Interpreting Kingston's texts as overtly feminist in topic and theme is by no means the only way in which they can be appreciated; her writing has also coincided with the rise of ethnic studies and theory. In the interview published in this edition, Kingston rejects the notion that writers should cater to what is popular or marketable: "I just think that is really not a very good strategy to write towards the market. . . . I encourage students to write whatever they want, whatever comes from inside, and then you send it out and you change the market." And while Kingston's work has been readily accepted by some, she also was and continues to be heavily criticized by other groups. In a very real sense, Kingston's work has become, to quote Elaine Kim, a "crucible" for Asian American issues.[34]

After replying to critics of her work in her essay "Cultural Mis-readings by American Reviews," Kingston responded again in her prose. In her third book, *Tripmaster Monkey,* at the conclusion of his play, the protagonist, Wittman Ah Sing, reads the reviews to his audience and tells them, "Don't be too easily made happy. Look. Look. 'East meets West.' 'Exotic.' 'Sino-American theater.' . . . What's to cheer about? You like being compared to Rice Krispies? Cut it out. Let me show you, you've been insulted." Wittman offers to his audience, "I am so fucking offended. Why aren't you offended? Let me help you get offended."[35]

Reviewers, among them Bharati Mukherjee, suspected the ghost of Chin again in *Tripmaster Monkey.* Although Kingston denies it, Chin is viewed by some as the model for Wittman Ah Sing. Wittman is a fast-talking fifth-generation playwright living in Berkeley during the 1960s. According to Jeslyn Medoff in 1991, "Wittman is not meant to be admirable or likable at all times; his male chauvinism and egotism are often unattractive. Some reviewers have taken issues with Wittman's . . . anger, complaining of his 'harangues' and 'manic monkey talk.' "[36] *Tripmaster Monkey* has been called the "*roman a clef* of the Asian-American literary world," and Kingston received the PEN West award in fiction for it.[37] One interpretation maintains that Kingston ventures a peace offering to Chin in the book because by its conclusion the warlike Wittman evolves into a life-affirming pacifist.

This dispute between Chin and Kingston regarding form has been partly responsible for her works coming under the scrutiny of sinologists, most notably Fredric Wakeman. Wakeman, in his 1980 piece on *China Men* for the *New York Review of Books,* echoed some of Chin's objections in taking issue with Kingston for what he contended was her freehanded rewriting of Chinese myths: "*China Men* is a mixture of myth, history, and recollection. Of these, the myths seem at first the most striking element, and they become the most perplexing." Wakeman concludes that "precisely because the myths are usually so consciously contrived, her pieces of distant China lore often seem jejune and even inauthentic—especially to readers who know a little bit about the original high culture which Kingston claims as her birthright." Chin's disapproval with Kingston's taking license with classical Chinese myths is, predictably, much more blunt: "In *The Woman Warrior,* Kingston takes a childhood chant, 'The Ballad of Mulan' . . . and rewrites the heroine, Fa Mulan, to the specs of the stereotype of the Chinese woman as a pathological white supremacist victimized and trapped in a hideous Chinese civilization."[38]

Kingston's responses both to Wakeman and Chin and to other critics who question her rewriting of Chinese myths have been consistent and strong. In a pointed reply to Wakeman, Kingston retorts that he "is a scholar on what he calls the 'high tradition,' and so he sees me as one who doesn't get it right, and who takes liberties with it. In actuality, I am writing in the peasant talk-story Cantonese tradition ('low,' if you will), which is the heritage of Chinese Americans. Chinese Americans have changed the stories, but Mr. Wakeman compares our new stories to the ancient, scholarly ones from the old country and finds them somehow inauthentic."[39] Kingston has always maintained that she is "experimenting" with her writing and tries to blend myths, fiction, and nonfiction. Kingston questions, "Who knows whether the stories are 'real' or not?"[40] Kingston has always advocated that Chinese Americans must create their own myths: "I don't claim I'm an archivist preserving myths, writing the exact, original version." Instead, Kingston's task as she views it is to write "a living myth that's changing all the time."[41]

With the publication of *China Men,* critics continued to be disconcerted by Kingston's mixing of genres. Once again interweaving Chinese legends and folklore, Kingston also includes autobiographical passages and history. This combining caused Phyllis Quan, in her review for the *Los Angeles Times,* to comment that "the cohesion and vitality of myth of the first half" is lost because Kingston interrupts the narrative with her section "The Laws," "a somewhat rude but informative overview of the immigration and naturalization policies affecting Chinese people." Kingston's response to Quan was that "the mainstream culture doesn't know the history of Chinese-Americans. . . .

That ignorance makes a tension for me. So all of a sudden, right in the middle of the stories, plunk—there is an eight-page section of pure history. . . . It really affects the shape of the book, and it may look quite clumsy. But on the other hand, maybe it will affect the shape of the novel in the future."[42]

Clara Claiborne Park, in her 1980 piece for the *Hudson Review,* concentrates on what she terms the "harsh richness" of *China Men*'s prose and, in a charged historical leap that would infuriate Chin, decides that for all of America's faults, it has "been kinder than [China], even to Chinese Americans." Mary Gordon, in her 1980 *New York Times Book Review* piece, while calling *China Men* a "triumph," finds the tale of Kingston's Vietnam veteran brother a "disappointment." In a 1981 review in the *Journal of American Ethnic History,* Edith Hoshino wonders if Kingston, in writing *China Men,* wasn't influenced by Chin, who labeled her upon the publication of *The Woman Warrior* as a "yellow pochahontas dumping on yellow men." Patricia Lin Blinde, in her 1981 *Amerasia Journal* review, states that *China Men* establishes Kingston as a premier fabulist. Linda Kauffman, writing for the *Georgia Review* in 1981, likens Kingston's prose to Faulkner's fiction with her "creation of a cosmos in miniature." Kauffman views *The Woman Warrior* and *China Men* as two texts inextricable from each other and suggests they work best when seen as parts of a unified whole. Kingston commented on why she made the decision to separate *The Woman Warrior* and *China Men* in an interview with Paula Rabinowitz in 1987. Kingston felt that her men's stories appeared to interfere with the "feminist point of view. So I took all the men's stories out, and then I had *The Woman Warrior.*"[43]

The publication of *China Men* engendered considerable debate among critics in part because of Kingston's continued experimentation with genre definitions, but also because she was offering a characterization of the Chinese American male experience. Linda Ching Sledge in her 1980 *MELUS* article refers to the debate regarding Kingston's accuracy in portraying Chinese American life and culture. She makes the interesting point that although Kingston's detractors have made their charges, their views have yet to be supported by critical methods of inquiry, literary theory, or substantive analysis of Kingston's work. Sledge finds *China Men* so true to historical fact that it can function as a casebook. Elaine Kim establishes a new context for viewing Asian American writing in her 1981 *Amerasia Journal* article, where she observes that unlike male Asian American authors who do not depict Asian American women with much depth, female Asian American writers have consistently provided balanced portrayals of men. Kim views Kingston as exemplary in demonstrating her concern with both male and female Asian Americans as well as attempting to define what it means to be Chinese American in *The Woman Warrior* and *China Men.* In her highly informative "Developing Ties to the Past: Photography and Other Sources of Information in Maxine Hong Kingston's *China Men*" (1983), Carol E. Neubauer writes on the unreliability of memory and Kingston's reliance upon photographs, traditional legends, newspapers, diaries, and legal records in her book *China Men*. Patti Pao, in "Male Stereotypification in Maxine Hong Kingston's *China Men*" (1983), charges that Kingston creates a "negative, . . . incomplete image of Chinese men" in *China Men*. Pao takes issue with Elaine Kim's observation that the men are portrayed as heroes.[44]

Alfred S. Wang's assertion in his 1988 *South Dakota Review* piece is that if "properly read" *China Men* is a synthesis of generations of Chinese American men who managed to claim a share of the American dream. Wang claims that in *China Men* the savage history of America's treatment of Chinese men is dealt with honestly and profoundly for the first time. In his 1990 essay for *American Literary History,* David Leiwei Li sees *China Men* as Kingston's challenge to "the problematic democratic nationalism of the canonical paradigm" and that she "endeavors to write into the existing canon the possibilities of change within the canon itself." Li finds that the cross-cultural mixture in *China Men* assures the work is both accessible and compelling to a general audience. E. San Juan Jr. positions *China Men* within his larger discussion of an agenda for Asian American writers. In "Beyond Identity Politics: The Predicament of the Asian Writer in Late Capitalism" (1991), San Juan calls for Asian American writers to "problematize the eccentric 'and/or' of their immigrant, decolonizing heritage and of their conjunctural embeddedness in the world system." Quin-yun Wu, in a 1991–1992 *MELUS* article, offers a "typical" Chinese reading of *China Men*. Wu opines that *China Men* should be classified as historical fiction in that through Kingston the chronicle of Chinese American men is "preserved in a breathing monument, simultaneously history and fiction." Joseph Fichtelberg proposes in "Poet and Patriarch in Maxine Hong Kingston's *China Men*" (1992) that while Kingston writes within what Henry Louis Gates Jr. identifies as a signifying tradition—"the reproduction of dominant literary models with a distinct, often ironic difference—Fichtelberg views her work in *China Men,* to paraphrase Julia Kristeva, as not only reversing her culture's tropes but traversing them. In "Tang Ao in America: Male Subject Positions in *China Men*" (1992), Donald C. Goellnicht declares that statements that appear to contest one another in Kingston's writing are not only antithetical to her work but, in his view, essential to understanding it. Goellnicht's intention is to concentrate on Kingston's "double-edged antiracist, antisexist sword wielded by the narrator."[45]

In *The Literature of Emigration and Exile* (1992), Shu-mei Shih follows the theme of exile as represented in the 18 fragmented segments from *China Men*. In characters such as Bak Goong, Ah Goong, and BaBa, Kingston demonstrates the physical movement between China and America; however, Shih claims that exile also describes Kingston's particular brand of storytelling. Patricia Linton's " 'What Stories the Wind Would Tell': Representation and Appropriation in Maxine Hong Kingston's *China Men*" (1994) views the core of *China Men* as a story of alienation and reclamation that occurs on two levels, "the individual and the social." Mary Slowik's "When the Ghosts Speak:

Oral and Written Narrative Forms in Maxine Hong Kingston's *China Men*"
maintains that what is at the heart of the work is not just the question of
breaks in "historical continuity" but the larger issue of whether immigrant
history can indeed be reclaimed. Slowik proclaims *China Men* a seminal work
in the canon of multicultural literature because Kingston identifies the locus
of where oral and written traditions merge and "where pre-literature and
post-literature stories can question and ultimately free each other." Her
search, as LeiLani Nishime terms it in her article "Engendering Genre:
Gender and Nationalism in *China Men* and *The Woman Warrior*" (1995), is less
concerned with trying to locate Kingston's "'authentic' voice" within the
genres she incorporates in her writing than it is with examining how she
manipulates these forms to meet her "own ends." Nishime acknowledges that
Kingston's works raise questions regarding the role genre plays in "defining
both gender roles and Chinese-American identity." Kingston's reshaping of
genre, in Nishime's view, enables her to create a space where she can incorporate discussions of nationalism and community as well as delve into questions of identity.[46]

In some quarters a critical sigh of relief might have been heard upon the
publication of *Tripmaster Monkey,* Kingston's first full-fledged work of fiction,
described by one reviewer as a blend of "magic realism . . . with the hard-
edged black humor of flower-epoch comic writers and performers—a little bit
of Lenny Bruce and a whole lot of Gabriel García Márquez."[47] Even though
reviewers might have been reassured regarding the text's genre, the book's
portrayal of its protagonist and the Chinese American experience still generated considerable commentary. After *Tripmaster Monkey*'s publication, Edward
Iwata, a San Francisco writer, charged that "no white critics got it."[48]

Tripmaster Monkey garnered numerous reviews in 1989, and many of
them were mixed. In her *New York Times* review, Michiko Kakutani calls
Tripmaster Monkey's plot "vague" and describes the narrative as a picaresque
form. Kakutani adds that readers may grow impatient with Wittman's "long-
winded style." Bharati Mukherjee, in her *Washington Post* review, lauds
Kingston's character, the Walt Whitman reincarnate, fifth-generation
Chinese American, Wittman Ah Sing. She also quietly notes that Wittman is
written in the angry young man tradition of another California writer, drama-
tist Frank Chin. Departing from Mukherjee's largely enthusiastic take is Anne
Tyler's review, "Manic Monologue." Tyler is admittedly exhausted at times by
the fast-paced tempo of the narrative, yet she concludes that the novel is a satisfying read and has both "bite and verve." Herbert Gold, in the *Chicago
Tribune,* describes *Tripmaster Monkey* as a combination of magic realism and
black humor, concluding that Kingston's energy makes the book a kind of
"hefty Chinese nouvelle maxi-cuisine stew." In her *Boston Globe* piece, Gail
Caldwell contends that the difficulty with *Tripmaster Monkey* is that Kingston
devotes too much of the book to the main character's interior story; she concludes that while the story is "finely wrought," it does not hold the reader's

attention. Le Anne Schreiber's *New York Times Book Review* article describes Wittman Ah Sing's voice in the book as a "racket" of noise and that she misses the "precise, sinewy . . . beautiful voice of the author." Gerald Vizenor, while positive in his *Los Angeles Times* review of *Tripmaster Monkey,* does find Kingston's diction awkward and concludes that even though ironies in language are exposed, intimacies seldom are. Priscilla Montgomery in the *Washington Times* defines *Tripmaster Monkey* as a comic epic and rejects descriptions of the text as evocative of magic realism. Montgomery assumes that Wittman would not be offended if she referred to his story as "reminiscent of a fine silk robe, elaborately embroidered"; in fact, she might be best directed to Elaine H. Kim's "Asian American Writers" so that she might learn that indeed he would.[49]

Other reviews from 1989 reveal as much about the reviewer in some cases as about Kingston's writing. Ray Mungo in *USA Today* pronounces Kingston a "first-rate novelist" and counts each chapter as a "theme song, with Wittman Ah Sing performing as vocalist/revolutionary in racist America." Gail Boyer's review, "One American's Heavy Load of Chinese Ancestry," observes that at times the reader felt she was being "force-fed facts about Chinese culture"; however, when the text goes from monologue to dialogue "it is riveting." Patricia Holt, while recognizing the novel's "wild brilliance," concluded in her *San Francisco Chronicle* piece that the narrative often is "deliberately (and successfully) offensive." Margarett Loke, in the cleverly titled "The Tao Is Up," offers a retrospective of Kingston's career combined with interviews of Kingston and her spouse and a brief positive review of *Tripmaster Monkey.* Writing for the *Atlanta Journal Constitution,* Anne Whitehouse makes the interesting point that it is as though Kingston is writing a contemporary "Journey to the West" and that the work is a reconciliation of sorts, not of East or West but of West and West.[50]

John Leonard, Kingston's initial great supporter writing for the *Nation,* says that Kingston's *Tripmaster Monkey* is "less charming" than her first two works but "more exuberant." Instead of sending Mozart, Leonard claims, Wittman radiates rock and roll. In a piece for *Ms,* Pamela Longfellow characterizes *Tripmaster Monkey* as "wonderful and awful" and objects to Kingston's lecturing tone at the end of the work. Longfellow, a Native American who admittedly is a great admirer of Kingston, says, "I know what you mean, I don't need speeches." D. E. Pollard states that *Tripmaster Monkey* provides fresh evidence that a novel "does not have to have a story." Yet he concludes in his *Far Eastern Review* article that to read the book one must have an education due to the "proper nouns, acronyms, and Sino-American terms." Nicci Gerrard, in the *New Statesman and Society,* calls Wittman Ah Sing an "extraordinary and unforgettable creation." Gerrard adds that the first section of the book is "bitter repetitious paranoia." Charlotte Painter, in the *San Francisco Review of Books,* concludes that Kingston in *Tripmaster Monkey* shows Americans' "soul-destroying racism as we've never seen it before, subtle, slippery, all-pervasive." Caroline Ong shares Anne Tyler's ambivalence in the *Times Literary Supplement,* and she charges Kingston with self-indulgence in Wittman's effusive allusions to literature and the media. While Ong admires what she describes as Kingston's extremely "loose narrative style," she criticizes the way in which the narrative is neatly resolved. David Leiwei Li's commentary in *Amerasia Journal* allows that "Kingston has once again superbly expressed her interest in the community with her word-magician sleight of hand." Li views the book as another "test flight," with no easy answers to difficult questions.[51]

Three book reviews were published in 1990. Gerald Vizenor elaborates in *American Book Review* on his earlier review published the preceding year in the *Los Angeles Times.* Charles L. Crow finds misleading the book jacket's blurb that Kingston's third book is a novel, in that it implies delineated genre distinctions while her work is about blurring the categories that mark autobiography, essay, and fiction. Crow's review in *Western American Literature* calls the book the "most complex exploration to date of the forces at work to deprive Asian Americans of their sense of identity. . . ." (86). Tom Wilhelmus, in "Various Pairs," calls *Tripmaster Monkey* the most impressive novel of the season, "familiar and exotic, not long but imposing and encompassing." According to Wilhelmus, Kingston's works give "voice to the anxieties of difference."[52]

Strangely, while *Tripmaster Monkey* attracted many reviews, there is scant published criticism addressing Kingston's latest work. Patricia Lin insightfully comments in her essay "Clashing Constructs of Reality: Reading Maxine Hong Kingston's *Tripmaster Monkey: His Fake Book* as Indigenous Ethnography" (1992) that the critics' hurry to try to fit Kingston's latest work within preestablished genre constructs, as happened with *The Woman Warrior,* risks diminishing some vitally important aspects. Lin argues that reading *Tripmaster Monkey* as an "ethnographic enterprise of the postmodern era rather than a novel," as the cover instructs the reader, "is based on the premise that it 'anthropologizes' rather than novelizes the United States." Malini Schueller argues in 1992 that Kingston and Amy Tan, in *Tripmaster Monkey* and *The Joy Luck Club,* affirm a "politics of resistance and difference and thematize the construction of a Chinese-American identity." Both works, Schueller maintains in *Genders,* emphasize the social constructions of gender and ethnic identity. The difference between the two authors is that while Kingston uses the conception of ethnic identity to subvert the notion of cultural origins, Tan demonstrates how constructions of cultural origins are multiple and complex. John J. Deeney discusses the transformation of the characters set against cultural stereotyping in "Of Monkeys and Butterflies: Transformation in M. H. Kingston's *Tripmaster Monkey* and D. H. Hwang's *M. Butterfly*" (1993–1994). Deeney discusses the transformation struggle in the first two sections of his article, and the final section includes responses to these works from readers of different ethnic backgrounds.[53]

The elusive hyphen is the subject of Isabella Furth's fascinating "Bee-e-een! Nation, Transformation, and the Hyphen of Ethnicity in Kingston's *Tripmaster Monkey*'" (1994). Furth identifies the hyphen as the central trope of multicultural theory and rejects efforts by individuals to authenticate Kingston's writing "to some sociologically verifiable ethnic reality" as attempts to exoticize her work. Furth insightfully observes that Wittman's self-identity constitutes itself not around a shifting hyphen "but in and around a radically untotalizable space." Wittman's play is seen by Furth as an example of destabilizing a unitary vision to instead embrace "a protean, unquantifiable one, which cannot be apprehended from any individual perspective"; Furth recommends misreading *Tripmaster Monkey* as "our only choice is also our only chance." Debra Shostak's "Maxine Hong Kingston's Fake Books" (1994) provides an excellent context for reading Kingston's oeuvre. Shostak contends that Kingston's writing works to "complicate our understanding of what constitutes memory, how memory can document the past, and how the past itself is plural. . . ." Shostak makes vital points concerning the question of identity and concludes that "identity originates in one's knowledge of personal and group history . . . the multiethnic person defines him- or herself in part by what he or she is absent from. In general, memory is *about* absence."[54]

Articles written in 1995 focus on Kingston's use of language, her continuing "war" with her critics, and Walt Whitman's influence. How Chinese American women writers position themselves in "linguistic/cultural borderlands" through their language usage is the question Victoria Chen asks in *Women and Language*. Chen points out that in Amy Tan and Maxine Hong Kingston's works, one can identify the instability of cultural identity for Chinese American women. Jennie Wang's informative *MELUS* essay interprets *Tripmaster Monkey* as Kingston's declaration of war on reviewers and critics who persist with racist readings of her books. Throughout *Tripmaster Monkey* Kingston dares the reader to accept a character with an Asian last name as an "all-American hero." James T. F. Tanner in another *MELUS* publication asserts that the plot of *Tripmaster Monkey* is subordinate to Wittman's song of himself, with an interior monologue strongly reminiscent of Whitman's "Song of Myself." In comparing the two it is possible to discern an interesting cultural interaction between Whitman and Kingston. Tanner concludes that Wittman has "absorbed and internalized the democratic message of America's greatest poet." Kingston's use of parody is examined in A. Noelle Williams's "Parody and Pacifist Transformations in Maxine Hong Kingston's *Tripmaster Monkey: His Fake Book.*" Williams sees parody deliberately employed by Kingston in *Tripmaster Monkey* as a defensive mechanism to ward off some of the "antagonisms" between the feminist and ethnic communities induced by her earlier work.[55]

Kingston has frequently commented on *Tripmaster Monkey* in interviews. In 1983, Kingston talks to Phyllis Hoge Thompson about her struggles to blend her fictional character with real-time events. Kingston believes that fiction "can be 'truer' than nonfiction." In a conversation with Marilyn Chin published in *MELUS* (1989–1990), Kingston relates that the chapter in *The Woman Warrior* where her mother and her aunt drive to Los Angeles to reclaim the aunt's bigamist husband followed the format of an "I Love Lucy" plot. In *Tripmaster Monkey,* Kingston feels that the disappearance of the narrator marked "artistic" and "psychological" improvement for her. Interviewed by Shelley Fisher Fishkin in 1991, Kingston maintains that her intention is to create a new model of drama in *Tripmaster Monkey,* a nonviolent one. Kingston asks writers to "imagine" the possibility of a powerful, nonviolent woman and man and suggests that the imagining is the first step to creating them. In a 1996 *Transition* interview with Michele Janette, Kingston relates that in *China Men* she was struggling with trying to write about men and calls the book "a feat of empathy and imagination." In *Tripmaster Monkey,* with her character Wittman Ah Sing, Kingston tried to answer her question of what is a Chinese American man.[56]

As for Kingston's upcoming book, entitled *The Fifth Book of Peace,* she is still defiantly playing with genre. In the interview included in this edition, Kingston tells her readers: "So just look for a large section in there of nonfiction. Then there's gonna be this whole section where Wittman and Taña appear, I don't know how critics will categorize it. It's very different from the other books in that—fiction and nonfiction not mixed either, it's like a sandwich. That's the way I see it. There's a nonfiction section at the beginning and at the end, and the middle part is Wittman and Taña. They're putting together a peace sanctuary." Kingston mentions her upcoming work in an earlier interview. In a 1995 interview with Neila C. Seshachari, Kingston discusses how her upcoming book will be a book of endings that were omitted from her three previous works. In her new work Kingston intends to show how a war veteran can return home and become a peaceful, nonviolent, "feminine human being."[57]

Most recently Kingston's writing has come under fire by ethnic-studies academics who have termed her work "assimilationist." There is a certain irony in a writer who was viewed as a destabilizing iconoclast upon publication of *The Woman Warrior* now being critiqued for her supposed conformity. Once again one hears the echoes of Chin, although rather than an objection to form, the concern now appears to be content, the author's intentions for her audience, and the audience's reaction. In a 1996 interview with Eric James Schroeder, Kingston criticizes what she calls a "movement" that is looking for one version of history; she terms it "traditionalism, retro-thinking, fundamentalism."[58] In the conversation published here, Kingston comments on the current critical imbroglio: "I am also caught in all these, I don't know what they are, they're wars. Ethnic wars. Because there's actually disagreement between the disciplines, and some people are very personal, and ethnic-studies people have an idea about one being appropriated or assimilated, which they don't consider a good thing. It is very shocking to me when students come in—students have come in from ethnic-studies classes during office hours—and they ask me, "Are you an assimilationist writer?" Then where do I begin looking at the assumption behind that question and talk about what literature is? It bothers me when books are read for political messages and with an absence of looking at the aesthetic reason."

Over the past two decades Kingston has given a multitude of interviews in which she discusses and sometimes defends her writing. It is clear that Kingston is not just involved in what she writes but also cares very deeply about how it is perceived, and that if in her view there are misperceptions, then it is her duty to try to clarify matters. For Kingston, to use her words, "there's a life that's not the text," yet it is clear that this life is greatly intertwined with her writing. In short, the critics can expect that if they comment on her writing, it is certain that she will comment on theirs.

A number of excellent books offer foundational overviews of Chinese American writing and strategies for reading. Elaine H. Kim's seminal text, *Asian American Literature: An Introduction to the Writings and their Social Context* (1982), offers seven chapters: "Images of Asians in Anglo-American Literature," "From Asian to Asian American," "Sacrifice for Success," "Portraits of Chinatown," "Japanese American Family," "Chinatown Cowboys and Warrior Women," and "Multiple Mirrors and Many Images." In "Chinatown Cowboys," Kim performs critical readings of Kingston's *The Woman Warrior* and *China Men.* A full bibliography is also included. Another indispensable text is A. LaVonne Brown Ruoff and Jerry W. Ward's *Redefining American Literary History* (1990). This cutting-edge volume (at the time) includes chapters by Shirley Geok-lin Lim, "Twelve Asian American Writers: In Search of Self-Definition"; Amy Ling, "Chinese American Women Writers: The Tradition behind Maxine Hong Kingston"; and Linda Ching Sledge, "Oral Tradition in Kingston's *China Men.*" Amy Ling's extraordinary *Between Worlds: Women Writers of Chinese Ancestry* (1990) should be required reading for those interested in a concise, informative text offering historical and cultural backgrounds on China, Chinese immigrants, and Chinese Americans. It offers a fascinating chapter on the lives and writings of the Eaton sisters, Sui Sin Far and Onoto Watanna; a political and historical perspective on America's views of China; the issue of Chinese American identity as examined through the works of selected Chinese American writers, including Kingston; and issues of racism, sexism, and colonialism as portrayed in Chinese American writing. Included is an extremely helpful and informative annotated bibliography of women writers of Chinese ancestry who have published prose in the United States. Shirley Geok-lin Lim and Amy Ling's informative *Reading the Literatures of Asian America* (1992) is essential reading for those readers interested in Kingston, and, more broadly, current scholarship in Asian American literature. The foreword is by Elaine H. Kim and the essays focusing on Kingston include King-kok Cheung's " 'Don't Tell': Imposed Silences in *The Color Purple* and *The Woman Warrior;* Donald C. Goellnicht's "Tang Ao in

America: Male Subject Positions in *China Men*"; David Leiwei Li's "The Production of Chinese American Tradition: Displacing American Orientalist Discourse"; and Patricia Lin's "Clashing Constructs of Reality: Reading Maxine Hong Kingston's *Tripmaster Monkey: His Fake Book* as Indigenous Ethnography."[59]

In *Mules and Dragons: Popular Culture Images in the Selected Writings of African-American and Chinese-American Women Writers* (1993), Mary E. Young studies the responses of female African American and Chinese American writers to stereotypes that inhabit American cultural history. In chapter 5, "Sui Sin Far to Amy Tan," Young provides a helpful history of Chinese American women's writing. Taking the title of her book from two terms derived from passages in Kingston's *The Woman Warrior*, Sau-ling Wong's fine *Reading Asian American Literature From Necessity to Extravagance* (1993) is a study of themes in Asian American literature and part of the movement to reposition Asian American literature within the canon of American literature. Wong discusses *China Men* and *Tripmaster Monkey* and reprints her 1988 *MELUS* article, "Necessity and Extravagance in Maxine Hong Kingston's *The Woman Warrior:* Art and the Ethnic Experience," in chapter 4. In the *MELUS* essay Wong responds to the charges made by Jeffery Paul Chan and Benjamin R. Tong that Kingston is an ethnic sellout. Wong defends Kingston on the basis that demanding orthodoxy, as Chan and Tong appear to do, is to adhere to a limited view of literature, resulting in a reduction of the life one is trying to portray. A recent publication by Yan Gao, *The Art of Parody: Maxine Hong Kingston's Use of Chinese Sources* (1996), offers a study of Kingston's "transplantation of Chinese sources, her metamorphosis of Chinese stories into American tales" (1). One can hear echoes of her dissertation, and the text is limited in that, as the author admits in the introduction, it was written before several seminal articles and books were published that unquestionably would have added depth and scope to the subject. Jeanne Rosier Smith's study, *Writing Tricksters: Mythic Gambols in American Ethnic Literature* (1997), views the figure of the trickster as "profoundly cross-cultural." Smith expands upon past scholarship by viewing the lines of contact and intersections between cultures and how the trickster facilitates these negotiations. Smith includes Kingston's *The Woman Warrior* and *Tripmaster Monkey* in her discussion.[60]

For those interested in published bibliographies on Kingston and Asian American writing in general, see Elaine H. Kim's excellent article "Asian American Writers: A Bibliographical Review" (1984), where she provides annotated bibliographical sections on social context for Asian American literature, discusses critics of Asian American literature, reviews first- and second-generation Asian American autobiography, and examines contemporary concerns in Asian American literature. A 1985 *ADE Bulletin* contains Amy Ling's article providing a brief history of Asian American literature as well as some of the critical controversies and a selected bibliography of Asian American literature. King-kok Cheung and Stan Yogi's helpful *Asian American Literature,*

An Annotated Bibliography (1988) lists bibliographical and reference works, anthologies, journals and periodicals, and primary sources for Chinese American literature in prose, poetry, and drama. There is also a secondary-source listing for books, theses, and dissertations on Chinese American literature and a bibliographic listing of articles and interviews.[61]

Before closing, I would like to include a brief note on this edition. The leadoff piece, a wide-ranging and provocative conversation between Maxine Hong Kingston and the editor, includes Kingston's reactions to her critics, the genre debate, and the current status of the American literature canon. The conversation took place shortly after Allen Ginsberg's death, and Kingston briefly describes their friendship and the impact of his death upon her. The selection of previously published scholarship for this Critical Essays volume was a welcome though particularly difficult task. The guiding principle was to select the best essays, while another important criterion was to choose reviews and articles that represent some of the debates that are a hallmark of Kingston's career. Happily, the two considerations have not proven to be mutually exclusive. Beginning with the first reviews of and essays on *The Woman Warrior* to those written about *Tripmaster Monkey*, it should become clear to the reader that Kingston forces critics to reconceptualize their means of critical analysis to process the kind of innovative, provocative work that she produces.

Groundbreaking essays by such seminal critics as King-kok Cheung, Sau-ling Cynthia Wong, and Amy Ling are included as well as important articles by Debra Shostak, Lee Quinby, Donald C. Goellnicht, Mary Slowik, and LeiLani Nishime. Two original pieces were commissioned from David Leiwei Li and Jeanne R. Smith, both of whom have recently published books discussing Kingston's writing. David Leiwei Li's essay, "Re-presenting *The Woman Warrior:* An Essay of Interpretive History," provides a valuable chronicle of the controversies and power contestations that have occurred since that book's publication. Li contends that at the heart of the debate is "the definitional struggle of 'Asian America,' its geopolitical location in and cultural relevance to the construction of the United States," and he advances the challenging thesis that Kingston's popularity and wide literary acceptance began with her deliberate adoption and usage of familiar American Orientalist discourse. Jeanne R. Smith's essay, "Cross-Cultural Play: Maxine Hong Kingston's *Tripmaster Monkey,*" contends that discussing a multicultural work requires "culturally specific, flexible, border-crossing analysis," a methodology for which at present there is no model. *Tripmaster Monkey,* in Smith's view, is representative of an author in the act of creating theory with her fiction.

I made the editorial decision to select book reviews from both popular press and scholarly journals to give the reader a sense of the differing kinds of coverage Kingston has received. Since Kingston is such a widely read contemporary author, she has been reviewed in literally just about every kind of print media, from the *New York Times Book Review* to the *Far Eastern Economic Review* to the Chattanooga *News-Free Press*. The reader can therefore see how she is viewed by both scholarly reviewers and her fellow writers.

No matter the combination of genres Kingston employs in her writing, all of her works deal with the recurring subject of asserting one's right to belong in America. Whether the character is a first-generation Chinese American woman, a Chinese immigrant in Hawaii or the American West, or a fifth-generation Chinese American man, her works repeatedly explore the relationships the protagonist(s) have with themselves, their immediate family and the European-American society they have inherited and that has inherited them. Regarding her intention for her readership, Kingston states, "I want my audience to include everyone. . . . I do believe in the timelessness and universality of individual vision. It would not just be a family book or an American book or a woman's book but a world book, and, at the same moment, my book."[62]

Judging from the abundance of scholarship on Kingston's works, criticism that appears only to be increasing with the passage of time, it looks as though Kingston has been successful in reaching her world audience. Kuan Yim, the Buddhist goddess of mercy and the narrator of *Tripmaster Monkey,* eloquently sums up the current state of Kingston studies: "Life is ultimately fun and doesn't repeat and doesn't end."[63]

Kingston is here to stay.

The final stage of completion for this volume was greatly complicated by a move from New York to Iowa. Simply put, I could not have finished without the assistance of the following talented individuals: Holly Chambers and Keith Compeau, reference librarians at the State University of New York at Potsdam; at Coe College, my secretary, Eddi Krug; Harlene Hanson, library reference assistant; Pat Gossman, academic secretary; and Betty Rogers, head of library reference. Richard Doyle, director of academic computing services, thank you for the Mac "loaner." Doris Gitzy, I am indebted for your blocking time and so capably managing my often hectic schedule. To James Nagel, general editor of this series, goes a special note of appreciation for his kind patience and invaluable advice. My profound gratitude goes to Maxine Hong Kingston, who so graciously allowed me to interrupt a busy teaching day to come and interview her for several hours. Our conversation was truly enjoyable and marked by a great deal of laughter. As always, my best regards to Michael Kiskis, who listens (and listens) and makes me laugh. I would like to express my deepest thanks to my beloved parents, Mary and John Skandera, for their lifelong support and unfailing good humor. Finally, I must recognize my husband, Nelson Trombley, for without him the sun would lose its shine.

Notes

1.   (New York: Alfred A. Knopf, 1976); (New York: Alfred A. Knopf, 1980); (New York: Alfred A. Knopf, 1989).

2.   133.

3.   (New York: Modern Language Association).

4.   *CEA Critic* 6.2, 17–34; ed. Melvin J. Friedman and Ben Siegel (Newark: Univ. of Delaware Press), 210–36; *Teaching American Ethnic Literatures: Nineteen Essays,* ed. John R. Maitino and David R. Peck (Albuquerque: Univ. of New Mexico Press), 273–91; *CEA Critic,* 59.1 (Fall 1996), 21–32.

5.   "Susan Brownmiller Talks with Maxine Hong Kingston," *Mademoiselle* 83 (March 1977), 149, 210–11, 214–16; *Women Writers of the West Coast Speaking of Their Lives and Careers,* ed. Marilyn Yalom (Santa Barbara: Capra Press), 11–19; D. C. Denison, "The Interview: Maxine Hong Kingston," 18 June, 3.

6.   Joan Saffa, director and editor, Joan Saffa and Stephen Talbot, producers (NAATA), 60 min.; (excerpts) American Audio Prose Library, 52:50 min.; *San Francisco Chronicle,* 24 June, 6–17.

7.   Biographical information is from the following sources: *Contemporary Authors,* ed. James G. Lesniak and Susan M. Trosky (Detroit: Gale Research, 1993), 206; *1990 Current Biography Yearbook* (New York: H. W. Wilson, 1991), 360; *Who's Who in America, 1997* (New Providence, N.J.: Marquis Who's Who, 1996), 2312; Stephen Talbot, "Talking Story: Maxine Hong Kingston Rewrites the American Dream," *Image* (*San Francisco Examiner*), 24 June, 1990, 6–17.

8.   "Talk with Mrs. Kingston," *New York Times Book Review,* 15 June, 1, 24–27.

9.   (Washington: Howard Univ. Press, 1974).

10. *Contemporary,* 207.

11. Edward Iwata, "Word Warriors," *Los Angeles Times,* 24 June 1990, 4.

12. (New York: Meridian), 11.

13. "In Defiance of 2 Worlds," C21; "Ghosts," (February 3), 19–21; "The Mysterious West," *New York Review of Books* (April 28, 1977), 41; "Diane Johnson replies," *New York Review of Books* (April 28), 41; "Ghosts of Girlhood Lift Obscure Book to Peak of Acclaim," (February 12), 26.

14. *Asian and Western Writers in Dialogue: New Cultural Identities,* ed. Guy Amirthana-yagam (New York: Macmillan), 55–65.

15. "The Confrontation of East and West: The Woman Warrior as Postmodern Autobiography," *Redneck Review of Literature* 21 (Fall 1991), 26–29.

16. *The Iowa Review,* 10.4, 93–98; *MELUS* 5.2 (Fall 1979), 15–24; "The Icicle in the Desert: Perspective and Form in the Works of Two Chinese-American Writers," *MELUS* 6.3 (Fall 1979), 51–71; *CEA Critic* 43.1, 24–31.

17. In *Women's Autobiography: Essays in Criticism,* ed. Estelle C. Jelinek (Bloomington: Indiana Univ. Press), 221–37; *The Lost Tradition: Mothers and Daughters in Literature,* ed. Cathy N. Davidson and E. M. Broner (New York: Frederick Ungar), 291–303.

18. "Two Chinese Versions of the American Dream: The Golden Mountain in Lin Yutang and Maxine Hong Kingston," 8.4, 61–70; 8.2, 76–81.

19. "Anti-Autobiographical: Maxine Hong Kingston, Caroeth Laird, and N. Scott Momaday," *Terrorists and Novelists* (New York: Knopf), 3–13; "Golden Mountain: Chinese Versions of the American Dream in Lin Yutang, Louis Chu, and Maxine Hong Kingston," *Ethnic Groups* 4.1–4.2, 33–59; *Tamkang Review* 14, 155–64; "Threads of Identity in Maxine Hong Kingston's *The Woman Warrior,*" *Biography* 6.1, 13–32.

20. *MELUS* 12.3 (Fall 1985), 5–12; *MELUS* 12.3 (Fall 1985), 23–31; "Maxine Hong Kingston: Narrative Technique and Female Identity," in *Contemporary American Women Writers:*

Narrative Strategies, ed. Catherine Rainwater and William J. Scheick (Lexington: Univ. of Kentucky Press), 173–90; *Fictions in Autobiography: Studies in the Art of Self-Invention* (Princeton: Princeton Univ. Press), 181–278.

21. *Biography* 9.2 (Spring 1986), 112–25; "A Chinese Woman's Response to Maxine Hong Kingston's *The Woman Warrior,*" *MELUS* 13.3–13.4 (Fall–Winter 1986), 103–7; *MELUS* 13.3–13.4 (Fall/Winter 1986), 5–66.

22. *Signs* 12.3 (Spring 1987), 471–92; *A/B: Auto/Biography Studies* 3.3 (Fall 1987), 29–35; *Boundaries of the Self: Gender, Culture, Fiction* (Urbana: Univ. Illinois Press), 164–89; "From Silence to Song: The Triumph of Maxine Hong Kingston," 9.2, 78–82.

23. "Telling the Mother's Story: History and Connection in the Autobiographies of Maxine Hong Kingston and Kim Chernin," *Women's Studies* 14.1, 55–63; (Bloomington: Indiana Univ. Press); *MELUS* 14.1 (Spring 1987), 3–15; "Woman as Hero in Margaret Atwood's *Surfacing* and Maxine Hong Kingston's *The Woman Warrior,*" ed. Pat Browne (Bowling Green, Ohio: Popular Press), 101–14; "Intelligibility and Meaningfulness in Multicultural Literature in English," 102.1 (January 1987), 10–19.

24. *PMLA* 103 (March 1988), 162–74; 69, 105–18; *Faith of a (Woman) Writer,* ed. Alice Kessler-Harris and William McBrien (Westport, Conn.: Greenwood Press), 293–301; "The Naming of a Chinese American 'I': Cross-Cultural Significations in *The Woman Warrior,*" 30.4 (Fall 1988), 497–515; *Criticism* 30.1 (Winter 1988), 43–62.

25. *Criticism* 31.4 (Fall 1989), 421–37; "Lu Hsun and Maxine Hong Kingston: Medicine as a Symbol in Chinese and Chinese American Literature," 8, 1–21; "Maxine Hong Kingston's Autobiographical Strategy in *The Woman Warrior,*" 12.2, 116–26; "Fiction and Autobiography: Spatial Form in 'The Golden Cangue' and *The Woman Warrior,*" (Armonk, New York: Sharpe), 25–43; "Kingston as Exorcist," (Armonk, New York: Sharpe), 44–52.

26. "Maxine Hong Kingston, the Ethnic Writer and the Burden of Dual Authenticity," 16.1, 173–200; *Conflicts in Feminism,* ed. Marianne Hirsch and Evelyn Fox Keller (New York: Routledge), 234–51; *Biography* 13.2, 143–53; "Ethnic Renaissance: Rudolfo Anaya, Louise Erdrich, and Maxine Hong Kingston" (New York: St. Martin's Press), 139–64.

27. *Haunting the House of Fiction: Feminist Perspectives on Ghost Stories by American Women,* ed. Lynette Carpenter and Wendy K. Kolmar (Knoxville: Univ. of Tennessee Press), 193–214; *Literature Interpretation Theory* 2.4, 249–59; *Journal of Ethnic Studies* 19 (Fall 1991), 85–94; "Reading for the Doubled Discourse of American Women's Autobiography," 6.1 (Spring 1991), 95–108; "Father Land and/or Mother Tongue: The Divided Female Subject in Kogawa's *Obasan* and Hong Kingston's *The Woman Warrior,*" ed. Carol L. Snyder (New York: Garland), 119–34; "Breaking the Silence: Symbolic Violence and the Teaching of Contemporary Ethnic Autobiography," 18.3 (October 1991), 64–80.

28. *De/Colonizing the Subject: The Politics of Gender in Women's Autobiography,* ed. Sidonie Smith and Julia Watson (Minneapolis: Univ. of Minnesota Press), 297–320; *Multicultural Autobiography: American Lives,* ed. James Robert Payne (Knoxville: Univ. of Tennessee Press), 248–79.

29. *American Women's Autobiography: Fea(s)ts of Memory,* ed. Margo Culley (Madison: Univ. of Wisconsin Press), 252–67; " 'The Invisible World the Emigrants Built': Cultural Self-Inscription and the Antiromantic Plots of *The Woman Warrior,*" 2.1 (Spring 1992), 95–115; *New Perspectives on Women and Comedy,* ed. Regina Barreca (Philadelphia: Gordon and Breach), 143–57.

30. (New York: Cornell Univ. Press), 74–125; *The Intimate Critique: Autobiographical Literary Criticism,* ed. Diane P. Freedman and Olivia Frey (Durham, N.C.: Duke Univ. Press), 117–25; (Ann Arbor: Univ. Michigan Press); "Empowerment Through Mythological Imaginings in *The Woman Warrior,*" 16.2 (Spring 1993), 136–46.

31. *Constructions* 9, 13–30; "Authorizing Female Voice and Experience: Ghosts and Spirits in Kingston's *The Woman Warrior* and Allende's *The House of the Spirits,*" 19.3 (Fall 1994), 61–73; *Biography* 17.3 (Summer 1994), 281–95; "The Way-I-Heard-It-Was-Myth, Memory and Autobiography in *Storyteller* and *The Woman Warrior* (Silko and Kingston)," 57.1 (1994), 57–67.

32. *Bucknell Review* 39.1, 151–66; "Naming the Unspeakable: The Mapping of Female Identity in Maxine Hong Kingston's *The Woman Warrior*," ed. Anne E. Brown and Marjanne E. Gooze (Westport: Greenwood Press), 223–32; "Ethnicity and Ethnography: The Artist's Fiction as Cultural Artifact in the Works of Maxine Hong Kingston," 58.1 (Fall 1995), 17; "The Mother as Other: Orientalism in Maxine Hong Kingston's *The Woman Warrior*," (Austin: Univ. of Texas Press), 132–52; (New York: Peter Lang).

33. *Backtalk: Women Writers Speak Out* (New Brunswick, N.J.: Rutgers Univ. Press), 171–93; Ronald T. Takaki has written extensively about Asian American history and culture since 1979: *Iron Cages: Race and Culture in Nineteenth-Century America* (New York: Knopf, 1979); *Pau Hana: Plantation Life and Labor in Hawaii, 1835–1920* (Honolulu: Univ. of Hawaii Press, 1983); *From Different Shores: Perspectives on Race and Ethnicity in America* (New York: Oxford Univ. Press, 1987); *Strangers from a Different Shore: A History of Asian Americans* (Boston: Little, Brown, 1989); *A Different Mirror: A History of Multicultural America* (Boston: Little, Brown, 1993).

34. "Word," 3.

35. (New York: Vintage, 1990), 307–8.

36. "Maxine Hong Kingston," *Modern American Women Writers* (New York: Scribner, 1991), 257.

37. "Word," 1.

38. "*Chinese Ghost Story,*" (August 14), 42–43; *Big,* 3.

39. *Contemporary,* 209.

40. "Word," 4.

41. "Word," 5.

42. *Contemporary,* 209.

43. "Ghosts on Gold Mountain," 33.4 (Winter 1980), 589–95; "Mythic History," (June 15, 1980), 24–27; "Legends of Chinese America," 1.1, 84–90; "*China Men,*" 8.1, 139–43; "*China Men,*" 35 (Spring 1981), 205; "Eccentric Memories: A Conversation with Maxine Hong Kingston," *Michigan Quarterly Review* 26 (Winter 1987), 177–87.

44. "Maxine Kingston's *China Men:* The Family Historian as Epic Poet," 7.4, 3–22; "Visions and Fierce Dreams: A Commentary on the Works of Maxine Hong Kingston," 8.2, 145–61; *MELUS* 10 (Winter 1983), 17–36; *Critical Perspectives of Third World America* 1.1, 267–74.

45. "Maxine Hong Kingston's Reclaiming of America: The Birthright of the Chinese American Male," 26.1 (Spring 1988), 18–29; "*China Men:* Maxine Hong Kingston and the American Canon," 2.3 (Fall 1990), 482–502; *American Literary History* 3.3 (Fall 1991), 542–65; "A Chinese Reader's Response to Maxine Hong Kingston's *China Men,*" 17 (Fall 1991–1992), 85–94; *Autobiography and Questions of Gender,* ed. Shirley Neuman (London: Frank Cass), 166–85; *Reading the Literatures of Asian America,* ed. Shirley Geok-lin Lim and Amy Ling (Philadelphia: Temple Univ. Press), 191–214.

46. "Exile and Intertextuality in Maxine Hong Kingston's *China Men,*" ed. James Whitlark and Wendell Aycock (Lubbock: Texas Tech Univ. Press), 65–77; *MELUS* 19.4 (Winter 1994), 37–48; *MELUS* 19.1 (Spring 1994), 73–88; *MELUS* 20.1 (Spring 1995), 67–82.

47. *Contemporary,* 210.

48. "Word," 1.

49. "Being of 2 Cultures, and Liking and Loathing It" (April 14), 3; "Far-out West" (April 16), 1; *New Republic* 200 (April 17), 44–46; "Wittman at the Golden Gate" (April 16), 1; "Playing Fast and Loose with a Playwright" (April 16), B51; "The Big, Big Show of Wittman Ah Sing" (April 23), 9; "The Triumph of Monkey Business" (April 23), 1; "On Swinging between the Branches of Two Cultures" (April 24), E7, 9.

50. "The Adventures of a Hip 'Tripmaster' " (April 28), D6; "One American's Heavy Load of Chinese Ancestry" (April 30), C5; "Monkey Business" (April 30), 1; *New York Times Magazine* (April 30), 28, 50, 52, 55; "*Tripmaster Monkey: His Fake Book:* A Transformation in Life and Fiction" (May 7), 4.

51.   "Of Thee Ah Sing." 248 (June 5), 768–72; "Monkey Wrenched" (June 17), 66; "Much Ado About Identity," 1465 (July 27), 41, 44; "Wittman Ah Sing," 2 (August 25), 28; "In Search of a Voice," 14 (Summer 1989), 15–16; "Demons and Warriors," (September 15–21), 998; *Tripmaster Monkey: His Fake Book,* 15.2, 220–22.

52.   "Postmodern Monkey," 11 (January 1990), 17, 22; *"Tripmaster Monkey: His Fake Book,"* 25.1, 85–86; *Hudson Review* 43 (Spring 1990), 147–54.

53.   *Reading the Literatures of Asian America,* ed. Shirley Geok-lin Lim and Amy Ling (Philadelphia: Temple Univ. Press), 333–48; "Theorizing Ethnicity and Subjectivity, Maxine Hong Kingston's *Tripmaster Monkey* and Amy Tan's *The Joy Luck Club,"* 15 (Winter 1992), 72–85; *MELUS* 18.4 (Winter 1993–1994), 21–39.

54.   *Modern Fiction Studies* 40.1 (Spring 1994), 33–49; *Memory, Narrative, and Identity: New Essays in Ethnic American Literatures,* ed. Amritjit Singh et al. (Northeastern Univ. Press).

55.   "Chinese American Women, Language, and Moving Subjectivity," 18 (Spring 1995), 3–7; *"Tripmaster Monkey:* Kingston's Postmodern Representation of a New 'China Man,' " 20:1 (Spring 1995), 101–14; "Walt Whitman's Presence in Maxine Hong Kingston's *Tripmaster Monkey: His Fake Book,"* 20.4 (Winter 1995), 61–74; *MELUS* 20.1 (Spring 1995), 83–100.

56.   "This is the Story I Heard—a Conversation with Maxine Hong Kingston and Earll Kingston," *Biography* 6.1; "A *MELUS* Interview: Maxine Hong Kingston," 16.4 (Winter 1989–1990), 57–74; "Interview with Maxine Hong Kingston," *American Literary History* 3.4 (Winter 1991), 782–91; "The Angle We're Joined At," 71, 142–57.

57.   "An Interview with Maxine Hong Kingston," *Weber Studies* 12.1 (Winter 1995), 7–26.

58.   " 'As Truthful as Possible': An Interview with Maxine Hong Kingston," *Writing on the Edge* 7.2 (Spring 1996), 83–96.

59.   (Philadelphia: Temple Univ. Press); (New York: Modern Language Association); (New York: Pergamon, Press); (Philadelphia: Temple Univ. Press).

60.   (Westport: Greenwood Press); (New Jersey: Princeton Univ. Press); (New York: Peter Lang); (Berkeley: Univ. California Press).

61.   *American Studies International* (22 October), 41–78; "Asian American Literature: A Brief Introduction and Selected Bibliography," 80, 29–33; (New York: Modern Language Association).

62.   "Cultural," 64–65.

63.   103.

INTERVIEW
◆

A Conversation with Maxine Hong Kingston

Laura E. Skandera-Trombley

LST: Your mentioning [Fredric] Wakeman brings me to the first thing I wanted to ask you, which is how does it feel to be canonized and yet, it seems to me, under attack for the changes that you have created? *Woman Warrior* is so widely taught and anthologized, but it seems to me that there is a real backlash going on right now to the broadening of the canon, and you seem to be in the middle of this in a certain sense.

MHK: I have all kinds of ambivalent feelings. I feel honored, and I feel honored appropriately, when I see that my work is in English and American literature classes and I feel that I've been, well, canonized. But I am also caught in all these, I don't know what they are, they're wars. Ethnic wars. Because there's actually disagreement between the disciplines and some people are very personal, and ethnic-studies people have an idea about one being appropriated or assimilated, which they don't consider a good thing. It is very shocking to me when students come in—students have come in from ethnic-studies classes during office hours—and they ask me, "Are you an assimilationist writer?" Then where do I begin looking at the assumption behind that question and talk about what literature is? It bothers me when books are read for political messages and with an absence of looking at the aesthetic reason.

LST: It also seems that one set of dichotomies is being replaced by another set.

MHK: Yeah, true, right.

LST: There seems to be a changing of the guard, and you still don't come out well. That when you are operating under those circumstances the choices are either/or. And if you are trying to create something new and something that's inclusive and you don't fall into those categories, then the assumption is that somehow you haven't been successful, rather than you are doing something that's entirely new and maybe we should look at it in that light.

MHK: Yeah, what I hope is that my work will change criticism and not critics trying to cut my work up in order to fit their critical theories. You know, even when I'm politically correct, or even when they look at it and say she's politically correct, it still isn't right. I was very concerned when *The Woman Warrior* came out right at the height of the feminist movement, and everyone saw my work as being the epitome of a feminist book. I felt really mad about that because that's not all that it is.

LST: Right, but at that time for that particular group it may have hit a category that they were looking for, which I don't think exists anymore. I think that the criticism has grown since then. But I did notice when I was reading through all the criticism, deciding which ones I was going to choose for the edition, that people had a tendency to view your works, and I think particularly I found this with *Tripmaster Monkey,* in extremely narrow ways. That there was one focus that they were going to have and they would go with this—either it was a meeting of the east and west, or it was jazz, or it was contesting the canon and so forth, and all of the rest of the text would be left out.

MHK: Yeah, that's right, but I think that's happened with all of my work. From the very beginning, of course, they wanted to figure out how to categorize it. And so there were lots of reviews and papers just figuring out what genre it was, and that kept them from looking inside the book for a long time. In fact, every review in Great Britain had to do with "this is neither one thing nor another."

LST: Yeah, where do we put it?

MHK: Yeah, and no review looked at anything else but genre. I felt like there was a door that said, or a chute of some kind, that said fiction or nonfiction. And since it couldn't go down either chute, it never made its mark in Britain until a few years went by and it was reissued and relaunched again. By that time they had gotten over what genre it was, and we could get on with it. But then every single book, that happens to me. *China Men* is listed in the Dewey Decimal system under California history.

LST: That's interesting. I wouldn't have thought to do that.

MHK: Then it gets reviewed as California history, or it gets reviewed as Wakeman did, as a Chinese book. But what's been wonderful is that it doesn't stay in those categories. I've seen it in African American studies. *Tripmaster Monkey* was taught at Harvard in an African American–studies course, and I think they were connecting it up with the signifying monkey. And then in anthropology, my works are in anthropology, which ethnic-studies people see as a real insult because it's not art. It's studying other people in an anthropological sense. And then it's in sociology and Chinese writing, and so it's O.K. because my work is in so many categories that essentially it has not been categorized.

LST: Well, that's probably why they have such difficulty in terms of literary criticism, because it does cross. And when you have generations trained as new critics, how do you place this? Because even now, for example, I was reading a review of *Bone* where the reviewer says essentially, "Nothing much happens but I like the text." And I thought, there's an extraordinary amount of things happening here, but one of the difficulties that people have is they come without a sense of historical or cultural knowledge. But then the question is, what do you do with this text? You can break it down in terms of new criticism, but I think that people have realized, then, what does that leave you?

MHK: I've always been very aware that I'm writing for the common reader, and I've felt that I had to fill in historical material, so it has always been a challenge to me how to give expository information gracefully.

LST: Right, without the tour.
MHK: Yeah.

LST: The Jade Snow Wong kind of tour of "this is where I am and what I represent at this particular point."
MHK: Although I think she does it gracefully too, because stuff happens. It's not as if she stops everything in its tracks while she gives you the exposition.

LST: I think she was and has continued to be treated rather harshly by critics.
MHK: I do too. Very harshly. Too harshly.

LST: And again, there is a question of recognizing the times when she wrote that text and her necessity for doing that.
MHK: The 1940s, now come on! They are using sixties and seventies standards. Even politically they were attacking her politics. I mean, this is World War II.

LST: This is a time when *Look* magazine is printing racial characteristics so you can determine who the enemy is. I think she's been very hard hit; however, with the criticism that I've read about you, there still seems to be a struggle, not just in terms of where do you rest as far as assimilationist and nonassimilationist, but also there's that struggle with genre.
MHK: You know, what I wish that people could appreciate, they could see that what I'm doing is riding that border between fiction and nonfiction. You know, we have a land of fiction and there is a land of nonfiction; there's a border in the middle. Well, what I'm doing is making that border very wide, and I am taking into consideration I am writing about real people and these real people have powerful imaginations. They have minds that make up fictions constantly, and so if I was going to write a true biography or an autobiography I would have to take into consideration the stories that people tell. I tell the dreams that they have and then when I do that, that border becomes so wide that it contains fiction and nonfiction and both going toward truth.

LST: Right, but the border that you are talking about, where those two meet, that becomes reality.

MHK: Yeah, yeah, yeah, what a wonderful way to put it.

LST: Whereas the critics to me seem to be fairly simplistic. They have an almost platonic view of truth and fact. There's truth and untruth.

MHK: Yeah, and then when they try to understand culture, such as Chinese culture or Chinese American culture, then if they have a platonic idea of Chinese American culture all they can do is find, they either find that I have examples of it, or they find that I have mistakes.

LST: Exactly, that this isn't the myth and so forth. I come from a family where we tell stories all the time. And when we are telling the stories we know that in a sense they are family fables. And they are based somewhere, somehow on something that happened once.

MHK: Then you appreciate and understand that every time you tell it, it's different.

LST: Absolutely.

MHK: And you have every right to change it, and it changes according to your personality and circumstances and who you are telling the story to.

LST: Absolutely.

MHK: And stories and myths stay alive when they change like that. That is being alive. But when they are frozen in one version, that's when they die. It just frustrates me a lot when critics don't understand that. But Chinese critics are like that, too. They're even worse because they *know* what the version is, the true version, and what we're doing in America is fake.

LST: But I wonder about people like that. Because when we're sitting around the table telling these stories we know that we are building on the story and that it's changing and that we are not telling the absolute facts of the story. I wonder if there are people who don't engage in that.

MHK: English departments emphasize the text. I mean, the text is sacred. The text is the bottom ground from which everything takes off. And you and I were both trained like that. And for people who did not have a strong storytelling tradition at home, then they have no antidote to this idea of everything is text. Something is real if it can be documented. And so critics forget, we're actually encouraged to forget that, you know, there's a life that's not the text. There are lives of all those people that are in the book, there's the life of the author, and then of course you hear it in English departments: you know there isn't an author, there isn't a biography, we don't need to look at the biography, nor do we need to look at the historical circumstances. And of course I understand we have to read carefully and figure out exactly what the book says, but this is at the expense of the reality of the writer.

LST: It's very limiting in what you take from the text. I had written a biography on Twain and I was sending it out, and I tried to give a sense of the cultural and historical background. My focus was on how women affected Twain and his thinking and his fiction. One reviewer was just furious and said, this is a history book, this isn't a biography. Because there is a very strong sense, that certainly my students have, that if you are going to write about life it should be in a linear fashion, a clear-cut linear fashion.

MHK: Yeah, yeah, yeah. Life is ordered here.

LST: Exactly. Yeah, that A goes to B to C. And they became very frustrated when you begin to contest that, which is what you do in your work. Life becomes a circle and where does it start, what's real, where did I invent this, where did someone else invent this and I participate in this? Maybe that is part of the frustration, where some of the confusion comes in, is it an autobiography, is it nonfiction, how do we deal with this?

MHK: Those people who tried to read it as autobiography had to get information off the flap of the book.

LST: It's funny finally because they compare. They actually do a comparison/contrast.

MHK: And they never really noticed that I hardly appear in the book. I am just the observer of the people's shenanigans.

LST: In *Tripmaster Monkey* I was thinking that here you have such a wonderful mixture of world literatures, and one of the ways people are taught, particularly in American literature or English literature, is that the two are exclusive of other literatures. You have the Norton anthology of American literature.

MHK: And then there's the one with women, and the one with African Americans.

LST: All very carefully separated. I was wondering, after reading *Tripmaster,* what would your anthology look like? How would you construct an anthology that actually could take the reader to the point of where we are in terms of America? What would you suggest?

MHK: *Tripmaster Monkey* is practically my anthology, isn't it? I use so many titles. Now of course a well-read person would read from all kinds of cultures and in different languages, too. I expect you can read *Tripmaster Monkey* as an anthology. There's a whole list in there of California, western writing, which I think is neglected by the establishment, you know, New York being at the other end. . . . I mention western all the way, too. And then I have the great Chinese epics, and I keep thinking how could any well-read person not include those with the *Iliad* and the *Odyssey* and the *Aeneid.*

LST: It almost seems as though you're tricking the reader.

MHK: Yes, that's right. Come on, there's the other half of the world. And then I have Rilke, it's so multicultural. I teach a course here, "Reading for Writers," and I think that I encourage them to read in a way that they constantly take into consideration how a book was written, what were the circumstances of the writer, how much money did he have, how much time did he or she have trying to get this work done, how do you find the energy and time to write it? Here's Norman Mailer, he wrote this huge book in six weeks, now how did he do that? How did Virginia Woolf get her five hundred pounds? I taught *David Copperfield* as Dickens's autobiography. He calls it an autobiography. And so it's the becoming of a writer, so how does he do it? And I'm comparing what he's writing with what he's living constantly.

LST: That will help chip away at these romantic myths that exist about writers and art and how [inspiration] comes to them and maybe gives people a sense about how gruesome it can be.

MHK: And then I teach my own work so that I could . . . you know, it's not conjecturing. I can tell them exactly how I came to each section and what inspired me to write this, why did I write that, how did this come to me? I am really working against that idea of pure text.

LST: I think that is something I have come to against all of my training. I tell my students I have rejected everything I was taught at this point.

MHK: Yeah, yeah, yeah.

LST: At the same time I live with knowing that there are those who think I have done a terrible thing. But that's all right. You still see these strange divisions, it's almost as though there's these walls around America when you have American literature here and then world literature's over here, maybe in another department, and there's no sense of the synchronicity that actually occurs and that one is not separate from the other.

MHK: I just heard somebody from the ethnic-studies department here who said that she's really thinking of quitting her job here, where everything is so categorized, and going to UCLA, where they have a literature department.

LST: I don't know if the ideal exists yet in academia. I don't think so.

MHK: No, no.

LST: All the periodicals are still so specialized, and the conferences now are becoming increasingly focused. You have these tiny symposiums that take place now. Where on the one hand, it's good that this is happening because we are now paying critical attention to texts that in the past were ignored, but also there's the sense of fragmentation.

MHK: You know the use of the term "world literature," it was really wonderful when the Berkeley Repertory Theatre put on *The Woman Warrior,* the play, and it was *Woman Warrior* and *China Men* and it was a magnificent, huge play. And the director, Sharon Ott, kept talking about world theater, and a world theater would be Brechtian and Shakespearean and Chinese opera and jazz and ballet and kung fu, and she managed to fuse all the elements, and she named it world theater. And she talked about the movement that she might want an actor to make, and it should have a certain emotional response. And one of the actors, actually it turned out three of the actors, had actually built railroads. One was from Vietnam, who actually built the railroad in Vietnam. And these actors were able to say, this is how you make that movement in dance or in work, and then they would show that movement and then she would incorporate it. And I said, "Oh, my gosh, she was right, this is world theater." And you know, theatrical people also look at texts and they use the same criticism—don't deviate from the text, really look at what it is, trust the text. But then you also have to work in this other dimension, of the actual physical body moving, the music and all that. I was really happy that they were able to arrive at this idea of world theater.

LST: I saw the production of *Woman Warrior* in Los Angeles.

MHK: Oh good, I'm glad you saw it.

LST: I just loved it and at the same time I thought, how is the audience taking this?

MHK: Yeah, yeah. I think the audience was getting it because audiences grew as the play went along. And I know there were lots of people who hadn't read anything and there were some people going to the theater for the first time, so they didn't even have the language for the theater. I think there was glitz and excitement. Oh, you know what I like a lot, there was a huge cast of Asian Americans, and they all had a different American accent. So there were critics who were just, you know, they were saying all the actors should be speaking in a Chinese American Cantonese accent. And I was thinking that we can't do that nowadays. How can we train all these people? I really loved it that we were getting Vietnamese, Korean, Hawaiian, Japanese—all these different kinds of American accents. It's what Wittman tried to do in *Tripmaster Monkey*.

LST: I was wondering, has there been an attempt to stage *Tripmaster Monkey?*

MHK: Someone has written a film script, and we tried for years to get someone to make a movie and put up the money, but nobody ever seemed interested.

LST: Well, Hollywood has a very simplistic, almost recipelike way of categorizing films. And there's no easy way for them to, you know, it's not *Diehard Meets Ghost,* or something like this. It almost seems as though only an independent would be able to conceive of that kind of a production, because it's just too far afield in terms of what Hollywood's doing.

MHK: *Woman Warrior* and *China Men* are also optioned for movies. We just haven't been able to, I mean, it is still in our dreams that they will be filmed someday. At one point an Iranian independent came in, and they wanted to make a movie if we would use like the Iranian mountain people or desert people or something for actors, it just didn't work out.

LST: I can't quite see it, interesting thought. I first read *Woman Warrior* in the mid eighties, and what I took from that reading was I loved the sense of freedom to express anger. Here was a woman who is speaking, who is angry and didn't seem to suffer tremendous residual guilt. Even though when I teach the text to my students that's exactly what frightens them, the note of anger. And a lot of them say that they are scared of the book, and I don't have them say that about other books.

MHK: Oh, how interesting. It must be the anger and that must come from people asking, how did your mother feel when she read it? And I think that must come from the anger, too. But they see the anger as maybe just toward the mother, but I see it as so large.

LST: Oh yes, I think that actually one of the dearest parts of the book is the relationship that you have with your mother and obviously the depth of that relationship and the kind of commitment. Maybe it was just that there aren't a lot of books that women write where they express that.

MHK: Yes, usually the anger dissipates by the end or gets resolved.

LST: Or bad things happen to women who express anger. An angry woman is one to be dismissed or there's a problem with them.

MHK: But if you can't put it into a book, where can you put it? You know?

LST: I don't know, I think that you just keep it within and it gnaws at you.

MHK: I really encourage all my students to use all of that, all the feelings. It's just raw fuel for the art; it is like a gift that you can put into words. And there you have a beautiful garden, otherwise one is a psychopath.

LST: That's true, or they become a very repressed, unhappy person.

MHK: Oh, if you repress it. I must say that hadn't occurred to me.

LST: And maybe that's why I loved your response to the critics because the critics were having, in addition to the what-genre-it-is difficulty, problems with, "What do we do with this angry person?"

MHK: Oh yes. Yes, I guess, yeah.

LST: And, "Well, maybe this person, well, they're Chinese."

MHK: Yeah, yeah. Oh, that takes care of it. That's what Chinese people are like, that.

LST: Exactly, so we don't have to deal with that issue.

MHK: Oh yes. That's right, it can't just be, you know, genre. That's sort of an intellectual way of dealing with something. So there's emotion and the anger and emotion are so strong that it bursts through genres and boundaries, and it is barely contained because the text isn't that coherent, I don't think, I mean the organization. So, yeah, I can see how thinking about how it would be organized is also thinking about how to contain it.

LST: A lot of the essays talk very specifically about how the text is organized because they are clearly trying to find patterns and structure and a sense of, I guess, unity, and it's almost like trying to create order out of the chaos, and that makes critics and readers uncomfortable.

MHK: That is what I'm doing.

LST: Right, that's the point, isn't it?

MHK: That's what they're doing, too. What the critics are also doing.

LST: When I was reading through some of the criticism, at a certain point I felt as though they were becoming very removed from what you were writing. There is a kind of academic discourse that exists that at times seems to have its own life.

MHK: Yeah, they're talking about Derrida and Lacan and all this stuff, and then where am I in all this?

LST: It is as if the text begins to disappear. There were some statements that people made that I just wanted to ask you to get your sense of them. Now, this is about *Tripmaster Monkey* and this particular critic says, "It is a fake book, in the postmodernist sense, in that it is not a source of original thought, but rather itself a repetition and catalogue of other textual, experiential, and cultural constructs."

MHK: Oh dear, I just think that this person's so off because it is original thought. To take movies that one's seen, a book that one has read, experiences that one has had and try to integrate them and try to understand them on one's own terms, in one's own words. It takes original thinking to deal with surrealist writing, the beat writers that come right before, with Rilke. It takes original thinking in order to ask oneself, what do these books that I am reading, what do they have to do with my life? To answer that takes a tremendous amount of original thinking, and besides, there's all kinds of other stuff that's happening besides what Wittman reads. My idea of the fake book, that's a term that comes from jazz. I don't know whether this person quite gets it, that it's a jazz term, in that it's a book of tunes that the jazz musicians improvise off of. They are semi-illegal, because you know they're breaking all kinds of copyright laws, but that book's not original, a fake book doesn't have original stuff, but I was hoping that the reader could use *Tripmaster Monkey* as a fake book in the same way musicians use a fake book. When they read *Tripmaster Monkey*, I give lots of suggestions, "Well now, here's a trip you might take, here's a part of a story, you finish it."

LST: It seemed very interactive to me.

MHK: Yeah, well, that's what I'm doing to get the reader to continue thinking of the trip.

LST: When I read *Tripmaster Monkey*, I read it as a Californian and what I knew of California at that time, and the term tripmaster and all these kinds of things, all have a particular resonance for me. So I read it as your expectation for the reader to continue the riff.

MHK: Oh, exactly. As I end up saying, "Oh, I want to trip you out." You continue the riff, you go on with the trip, you finish this story. I think lines of stories that I never finish and I said, "O.K., you continue." I was trying to replicate in text what happens in talk story and in music where you tell your version of the story. I've told this far, I've told my version, now you go on with it.

LST: I was struck by that particular critic's statement.

MHK: Gosh, I know they got a lot out of that statement. I was also making a joke about trying to put ambiguity into a title because, you know, normally they first put the title, then they put a novel on the cover, so I just thought I'd put "A Fake Book," it's called a fake book. And then now it says *Tripmaster Monkey*, a fake book, a novel.

LST: Again, in the published criticism there are all different takes on critics trying to understand the fake book part of it.

MHK: There were some people who got that about the jazz.

LST: There is a very good essay, Debra Shostak's essay, where her focus is the fake book.

MHK: There was a review I feel very good about. It was in a music magazine, a jazz magazine. They reviewed *Tripmaster Monkey* in a music magazine. I just felt so good. I thought, "Oh good, they got it."

LST: That almost seems to be the most appropriate place in some ways.

MHK: Yeah, they looked at the music, the language. It was really nice.

LST: Here's another critic's observation: "Kingston recreates the Chinese American autobiography in her free mixing of genres. Chinese were literally forced to rewrite their own histories for a fake history in order to enter America and be erased from history."

MHK: This person really conflated a lot of history, you know, things like Cultural Revolution diaries, then there's a different kind of autobiography that one told the immigration service, a part of American history. This is an interesting quote because Frank Chin has written against my work by saying that there have been so many Chinese American women's autobiographies and he's saying that it's not a traditional form. There never was an autobiographical Chinese form, he says.

LST: Traditionally, there was not, which is how he is tending to view things.

MHK: But traditionally there were. Because people wrote poetry in which they wrote about themselves. There were monks who wrote spiritual pieces, writing about their own spiritual lives, and that was done in the first person. There seems to be disagreement about whether or not there were ever any autobiographies in China, and therefore somehow this has to do with whether or not I. . . .

LST: I don't make the leap either. It is kind of reductionist in the way that he tends to view things, again it's very much, "Is this strictly according to forms that have existed?" And if there's a deviation, it seems to imply that this is not legitimate.

MHK: Yes. There are a lot of Asian American autobiographies. To say they are not legitimate or there's something wrong with them, that has to do with ranking the genres. That somehow autobiography is a lower form, that one doesn't have to be an artist, that all you have to do is just live an interesting life and take notes. So to call something an autobiography politically is an attack on the work because that is the bottom. The top, I guess, is poetry, and the novel and then nonfiction is lower than that, and autobiography is the lowest.

LST: Biography is pretty low, too.

MHK: Biography is pretty low.

LST: Because then you haven't even led an interesting life, you're writing about someone else's.

MHK: And you don't have to pay attention to the beauty of language, and all you do is just write it down. Journalism, maybe that's the lowest. You know you can take any of those forms and write something beautiful.

LST: I don't think that people realize how much biography or autobiography are fiction.

MHK: Yes, that's right. And also think about it like this, someone has led a wonderful, exciting, adventurous life and writes about it beautifully. That makes it really hard. You have to find time in this exciting life, to sit down and write it down.

LST: And that's something women always have so much of.

MHK: Oh yeah, we have lots of free time.

LST: I wanted to ask you about the famous hyphen now, and again this is quoting a critic: "Kingston has long written against this practice of masking exclusionary politics with the rhetoric of inclusion, calling (as Wittman does in *Tripmaster Monkey*) for Americans of Chinese ancestry to call themselves unhyphenated 'Chinese Americans' and so to reject the exoticizing implication that, for the racially Asian, both sides of the hybrid ethnic/

national equation have equal weight." I think that's a pretty accurate statement.

MHK: Yeah, yeah. I think so.

LST: What I'm curious to ask you about, in terms of the hyphen, juxtaposed against today's politics, particularly in California in view of recent propositions, what do you think of what is happening in California and how it's affecting immigrants?

MHK: I think California handles those questions very hard. In the newspapers I can see they seem to be going back and forth. I see them take out the hyphen in some articles, and then the next one that comes along they leave it in. It looks like their style sheet is not firmly in place, and also back and forth between Asian American, and then they'll leave out the American. Or they'll say, "Asian laundering Democratic party funds" on the front page, and then you read the article and they are actually writing about Asian Americans, but they leave American out. And they do this all the time. When I was writing this I thought, "Oh my, this is such a small thing and I'm really gonna date myself because any moment now everybody's gonna understand this and change." Every day I pick up the paper and they are writing about a Chinese or Asian and it is really about Americans. Or they'll talk about the Asian vote, and then you realize they are talking about the California vote.

LST: Yeah, the American vote.

MHK: Yeah, oh, it's still a problem.

LST: California has always been such an interesting state in terms of various groups that entered the state, the kinds of struggles that have gone on, the class struggles. There is an abundance of riches in the state, and also now particularly over the past eight years with the recession, there was a lot of finger-pointing going on. I don't think it's any surprise that now we're getting things like propositions 187 and 209, and it really gave me a sense of the middle section in *China Men* with "the Laws." Here we're seeing the laws that are being created.

MHK: Yeah, the laws. Setting up this kind of reality and reflecting it. It's so shortsighted, I mean, I looked at it so personally. If children of illegal immigrants don't get to go to school, then I wouldn't have gotten to go to school.

LST: It seems to me there is an obvious racial agenda here.

MHK: How can we separate a Latino who belongs here from a Latino who is from another country? In my recent writing I've been calling the people "Asian-looking" or "Japanese-looking" or "Latino-looking." There's a hyphen in there, but instead of calling them something else, I just . . . how can you identify people? It's so hard identifying people.

LST: I'll admit in advance I like this particular quotation because I saw it as applying to some of the reviews that you've received: "[Kingston] is given a choice, in effect, between an exclusionary inclusion (being admitted, but only as a marked commodity), and an inclusionary exclusion (being admitted only if deemed 'worthy' by virtue of having suppressed her particularity and made herself indistinguishable from the 'mainstream')."

MHK: Inclusion and exclusion and exclusion and inclusion. All right.

LST: On the one hand you're in the canon, but you're a particular aspect of the canon, you're a new aspect of the canon. Or, yes you are included, but then you have repressed everything that makes you the writer you are or the particular subject that you want to focus on.

MHK: I just think that is really not a very good strategy to write towards the market, and that would be the same thing, writing to be included in a canon or even to pick up assignments. That means that someone else is telling you what to write. They set up the goal. I encourage students to write whatever they want, whatever comes from inside, and then you send it out and you change the market. Because that's what I want to do, you know, to be included in the canon means the canon has to change. I think even the concept of a canon, it has to get bigger and bigger.

LST: I don't know what will happen to it, but I remember when I was a doctoral student, one of my classmates asked the professor, "What do we need to know in order to know American literature?" And he said, "Everything." At the time I didn't really understand the reply, but now I think that was a very good answer. I think she was asking it in terms of, well, do I read Whittier? Which one of these American writers should I read? And his response was you need to understand history, culture, you need to know all these various texts. And so eventually maybe the question of a canon just falls apart.

MHK: You know, at the beginning when the discussion first took place, it was like, "Well, if you're going to put in Toni Morrison, then you have to throw out the *Odyssey*." It was like one for one.

LST: And now some people think it's terrible because you can get through your undergraduate education . . .

MHK: . . . and you don't have to read Shakespeare. There's this college where you do two out of three: Shakespeare, Chaucer, or Milton.

LST: I know you were just in Vietnam, and I was curious—was this for pleasure?

MHK: It was pleasurable, but it's a continuation of the work that I'm doing. I'm writing this book, it's called *The Fifth Book of Peace*. I heard that there were three lost books of peace in China. The books of war are everywhere, but the books of peace are lost. So I was trying to find them and write a new one for our time. And now, oh the book that I was doing was burned in the fire here, so that was the fourth book of peace.

LST: Yes, I heard about that.

MHK: So this one is called *Fifth Book of Peace.* And during the time of writing this book of peace I gave writing workshops to war veterans because I was trying to learn about war and learn about peace. And so for three years, actually longer than that if I count other workshops, maybe six years, I've given veterans a series of retreats and workshops that last all day. They're working on their writing and I'm working on my writing, and so I've been learning a whole lot about war and peace. And some of the techniques I use to teach them are Buddhist meditations, Buddhist pacifist techniques. Sometimes there's more war consciousness than peace consciousness. At one point I took a group of the Vietnam veterans to a Buddhist commune run by monks, and a lot of Vietnamese people live there, and so the veterans learned to be with them. And then we also have peace activists in the groups, and we've had confrontations between peace activists and war activists. Oh, and we also met veterans from North and South Vietnam. I went to Vietnam, met with writers and veterans. I'm getting what I need for this book.

LST: It sounds like a wonderful project. Now, do you read what the veterans write?

MHK: Oh yes. I'm trying to gather the veterans' words and making an anthology of their writings that were in the workshops. Actually, this is an extension from the last chapter of *China Men,* the brother who went to Vietnam, it's the continuation of that.

LST: There's also a sense of Wittman and his attitude toward the war.

MHK: He's gonna be in the book, too. So just look for a large section in there of nonfiction. Then there's gonna be this whole section where Wittman and Taña appear. I don't know how critics will categorize it. It's very different from the other books in that—fiction and nonfiction not mixed either, it's like a sandwich. That's the way I see it. There's a nonfiction section at the beginning and at the end, and the middle part is Wittman and Taña. They're putting together a peace sanctuary.

LST: Is Wittman still writing?

MHK: He's putting together a play.

LST: I'm glad to know that. He's very talented in that area.

MHK: And then he and Taña have a kid, and so they have to deal with how are they going to be an older, responsible generation and take their marriage further and their parenting, how would that work?

LST: It's a new world when that happens. This is something that I just observed in the men that I have known, but I always found that there was something markedly different in people who had been to the war, than those who had not. My husband was in the war.

MHK: Did you know him from before?

LST: No. But he was very young and grew up in the Adirondacks and very unworldly and he went and enlisted because it was the right thing to do. He went into the war and was assigned to a spy ship in the middle of the Atlantic and later went to photography school and wound up at the White House photographing Nixon. That happened right when he began to become a peace activist.

MHK: They are very different, and they try to understand their own difference. There was a series of writings where they talked about the Vietnam vet—a breed apart. They could see their separation from others in all of its different ways, is it good to be a breed apart? I mean, that isolates you from other human beings, and on the other hand, why are they different, can they put their finger on it? One way to look at it is pathologically, which is PTSD [posttraumatic stress disorder]. All of them deal with that. One observation I have is that to me they look physically different. They look like they've been parboiled, you know. Their skin looks more sensitive than other people's skin. And another thing I notice is they seem so young, in a way really young, because they're very boyish, you know, they're like adolescents. Quite often I have this motherly role and I think, oh, is it because they missed their youth? That adolescent time, so when they came back, you know they dress and act adolescent.

LST: Well, they were still so young when they came back.

MHK: Then they came back and it was like they were trying to catch up with fashion, so they grow their beard and they grow their hair long. Some of them are middle-aged, they still have long hair. Most of them are single and so some of them are still struggling with dating.

LST: And the men that I've known, they have always had difficulty with relationships.

MHK: Oh, it's very hard. They'll start relationships and then something happens and it comes apart. I find them tremendously brave when I see them try again. They are all wonderful writers. You know, I advertised a writing workshop, of course they selected themselves as writers. Maybe they're good writers because they have so much material that they had been holding, so it just pours out. It is hard to get them to rewrite because it is already so good. And helping them deal with a Vietnam vet, a breed apart—there's a Buddhist tenet that one be ordinary. Just be the ordinary human being. Ordinary in the sense of daily, all the time, be ordinary. I think Buddhist methods work well with people who are extraordinary.

LST: What was your reaction to Ginsberg's death?

MHK: Oh, my goodness. I was really surprised. I just somehow always expect everybody to live as long as my parents. There's a poem that Ferlinghetti wrote, and I read it to my class. It's a coincidence; I was teaching *Armies of the Night* and we had come to the part where they levitate the Pentagon, and I had asked Allen Ginsberg a long time ago, I said, how come it didn't work? And he said it was because we were using *om; om,* which goes around in a circle like this, but if we had said *ahh* it would have worked. That's a wonderful story, to a poet sound, every sound, makes a tremendous difference. Allen Ginsberg was on our [1984] trip to China, that was so special. [Kingston traveled to China with Ginsberg, Toni Morrison, Francine DuPlessix Gray, Leslie Marmon Silko, William Least Heat Moon, Gary Snyder, William Gass, Harrison E. Salisbury, and Robert Rees.] He was thrilled whenever he found a root. He bowed to a dinosaur bone. It was just wonderful to be on the road in China with him.

LST: It frightens me when I see people go. I worry about their legacy and hope that what they've done remains recognized. Some of the articles that I've read said, "He was a poet." And that was such a small part of who he was.

MHK: He was enormous. He went everywhere, he knew everybody. I don't feel scared in that I know that just last year he sold the archives to Stanford for a million dollars. Oh, what a wonderful triumph that he got money. And also he was so careful, he saved every scrap of paper, you know. And also he was seeing huge audiences, they filled Wheeler Auditorium with the kids here. I don't think he's going to be lost. He led such a big life, he was so wonderful. And a political life and a religious life. He had actually two religions, he was able to practice Judaism and Buddhism and strengthen both of them. And that whole life as a homosexual, it was all so big. He had a chance to talk to people before he lost consciousness, and I read one article where he wrote half a dozen poems on his deathbed. I think he probably had a chance to do all those Tibetan chants. I hope that happened. On the day he died, I just felt that his presence was everywhere, and I think it's going through those *bardos* and he's probably choosing which lake he's going to jump into and how he is going to reincarnate.

OVERVIEW

◆

Maxine Hong Kingston's Fake Books

Debra Shostak

"That's it, my present to you," said Wittman. "Got no money. Got no home. Got story."

> —Maxine Hong Kingston, *Tripmaster Monkey: His Fake Book*

Maxine Hong Kingston has noted that she relishes the discrepancies that emerge when her brothers and sisters share with her their memories of events from their family's history: "sometimes there's disagreement, like when one brother said 'That wasn't opium the men were smoking,' and my other brother said 'Oh yes, it was. That *was* opium.' And I like that difference in seeing because it could have been either way; one remembered it one way and one the other. That gives me two stories for one event" (Interview 14). Clearly, her interest lies less in history per se than in events as they are remembered; that is, the past provides pleasure and meaning not insofar as it is reconstructed authoritatively (as if such reconstruction were possible), but rather to the degree that memories provide a record of human participation in recreating the past. That accounts of the past are multiple and contradictory is a testament to human invention instead of a failure of record keeping.

Kingston reminds us that "history" includes the variable possibilities of memory, and each of her books is an attempt to weave an understanding of the historical experience of being Chinese-American. Scraps of memory—Kingston's own memories, as well as those of her family—provide the warp, while story, lore, and fantasy supply the weft. *The Woman Warrior* (1977), *China Men* (1980), and *Tripmaster Monkey: His Fake Book* (1989) all complicate our understanding of what constitutes memory, how memory can document the past, and how the past itself is plural. Kingston's narratives accomplish this feat by their metafictional self-references; she foregrounds the act of story-telling as the means by which culture is remembered and transmitted. She is

From *Memory, Narrative, and Identity: New Essays in Ethnic American Literatures,* edited by Amritjit Singh, Joseph T. Skerrett Jr., and Robert E. Hogan. Boston: Northeastern University Press, 1994: 233–60. Copyright 1994 by Northeastern University Press. Reprinted by permission of Northeastern University Press.

by no means alone in her assault on positivist assumptions about historiography. In exploring how humans use narrative to make sense of the past, for example, the historian Louis O. Mink works to unseat the "commonsense" distinction between history and fiction (129). Hayden White presses the point further, arguing that historical narratives are "verbal fictions, the contents of which are as much invented as found and the forms of which have more in common with their counterparts in literature than they have with those in the sciences" (42); he insists, however, that the formal character of historical narratives "in no way detracts from the status as knowledge that we ascribe to historiography" (61). The point here is that narrative, whatever its purposes and materials, by definition both creates—rather than reflects—story and draws on formal conventions. It provides a way of knowing the real world, building knowledge according to the familiar patterns of story. Like other approaches to knowledge, narrative finds a primary source in memory. Memory can serve as a kind of narrating subject, making coherent wholes out of meaningless fragments, and White's conclusions are key in explaining how the selective and inventive functions of memory construct knowledge by reconstructing versions of the past.

The powers of memory are inextricable from those of the imagination in their workings and effects. Both are inventive, both work from pieces of material reality, and both strive for coherence. As Mary Warnock has observed, "in recalling something, we are employing imagination; . . . in imagining something, exploring it imaginatively, we use memory" (76). Memory's ability to engender knowledge is particularly significant in the development of a multiethnic historical record. For self or community to be identified as multiethnic, it must derive from at least two places, locales that are either literally (spatially) or figuratively (culturally) distinct, and often at great distance from one another. The self or group then resides at significant remove from at least one of the home places, real or symbolic. Because identity originates in one's knowledge of personal and group history—that is, in accounts of events involving known actors in particularized places—the multiethnic person defines him- or herself in part by what he or she is absent from. In general, memory is *about* absence. It concerns itself with the pastness of time past and with filling gaps in the known continuum of experience. The imaginative capacity of memory to recover and reinvent images and ideas of absent places bridges the locales, supplying a crucial sense of self.[1] Where knowledge of the past may be obscured by geographical, temporal, and social conditions, as in the historical understandings of a people dispossessed of a sense of place, memory most poignantly takes on the fundamental character described by Natalie Zemon Davis and Randolph Starn: it is "a substitute, surrogate, or consolation for something that is missing," an "index of loss" (3, 4). As Kingston shows in each of her books, memory becomes an obvious source for the past both when the past remains undocumented in conventional ways and when the events of the past have been played out thousands of miles distant from those who would recover and retell them. Such has been the historiographical predicament of what Kingston terms the "brief and dying culture" of Chinese America (*Tripmaster* 6). This culture lasted approximately a century, from the waves of Chinese immigration during the 1850s and 1860s to the evidence of assimilation over the last few decades, found by Ronald Takaki among such clues as the " 'Yappies'—'young Asian professionals'—[who] drive BMWs, wear designer clothes, and congregate at continental restaurants" (79, 4). Especially for Chinese-Americans like Kingston, living at the latter end of the "dying" culture's century, the vacuum of historical identity created by immigration and assimilation can be, at least in part, filled by the imaginative exercise of memory.

Significantly, Kingston envisions memory not only as the product of individual consciousness, but also as a communal phenomenon, most noticeable in the oral tradition of storytelling, in which stories recount the lives and events, real or apocryphal, that support a culture's understanding of itself.[2] Public texts, either orally transmitted or fixed in written documents, in what Dominick LaCapra calls "textualized remainders" (128), serve as the material of both private and cultural memory. Kingston gives access to these textualized remainders—which may be myths, legends, histories, films, novels, poems, or plays—by quoting them directly, by alluding to them, and by retelling them. Kingston's writings draw attention to the very documents that might be used in writing history, the texts of a culture, and at once both undermine and validate their authority as documentary evidence. The nature of the evidence is responsible for this effect: because many of the "documents" have been transmitted orally rather than written, they are plural and, frequently, contradictory.

The plurality of the historical record, conceived in this manner, might seem at first glance to limit its value as historical knowledge. Not only are the textualized remainders in large part verbal fictions, but they also almost by definition compete among themselves for authoritative status. Kingston, however, has the tradition of Chinese letters behind her implied critique of positivist historiography. The classic novels of Chinese dynastic history (compiled between the fourteenth and the eighteenth centuries, and upon several of which Kingston draws heavily in *Tripmaster Monkey*) were culled from the elaborate and lengthy plots of storytellers, who were known to tell a single story over the course of months or a year during many storytelling sessions at the local teahouse (Hsia 9). A novelist—the literate compiler of oral materials—might have a wealth of versions, variations, and embellishments at the disposal of his fictive imagination. At the same time, the novels were based on historical events, and the storytellers whose stories the novelists whittled into shape had always, according to C. T. Hsia, "honored the convention of treating fiction as fact" (16). Like the storytellers and their audiences, writers and readers drew no distinction between the fictive and the "real" to limit the authenticity of the novelistic accounts as historical, and this is borne out in the dynastic novels' reception, since they were generally "written and read as popular history" (16). Within the culture to which the stories were addressed, then, their authority as sources of historical knowledge was not in question, and this despite both their accommodation to the novelist's aesthetic and imaginative play and their inclusion of fantastic and supernatural episodes.

In a sense, Kingston, her sources, and I are all collapsing one of the important distinctions between oral and written culture—that between the fluidity and diversity of oral transmissions and the fixity of the written word, which appears to carry the weight of authority in its very stasis. The classic Chinese novels that stabilized the dynastic stories obliterated or elided the differences among those stories, seeming to offer to their readership the "facts" of the past. Likewise, Kingston's fashioning of fragmented memories and textualized remainders gives the illusion of the whole cloth of experience, but when she exposes the source of historical knowledge as narration—as the *process* of narrating and comprehending narrative—she makes the oral/written distinction, as well as its implied difference in authority, consistently evasive.[3] If history is known through stories, what does it matter whether the stories are told or read? In any event, whatever illusion of definitiveness Kingston's recorded narration maintains in her readership is soon punctured, since even where the sources are written documents, the memories they constitute made comparatively static, their meanings are nonetheless transformed by their recitation in a culture—and, often, a language—alien to their place of origin.

Transformation, of course, is an essential principle of oral culture. Each storyteller puts his or her personal stamp on the story, and each telling is different. Memory and invention are the supreme authorities, and no version carries greater truth value than another. In fact, as Barbara Herrnstein Smith has argued, narrative versions remind us that

> For any particular narrative, there is no single *basically* basic story subsisting beneath it but, rather, an unlimited number of other narratives that can be *constructed in response* to it or *perceived as related* to it. . . .
> . . . For any given narrative, there are always *multiple* basic stories that can be constructed in response to it because basic-ness is always arrived at by the exercise of some set of operations, in accord with some set of principles, that reflect some set of interests, all of which are, by nature, variable and thus multiple. (217, Smith's emphasis)

That there is no "basic" story suggests that those who participate in a culture are free to reinvent stories in accord with their—and their culture's—principles and interests, without losing power or truth value as the stories are transformed.

This is notably useful in a multiethnic setting, like that of Kingston's Chinese-American culture, where the source materials are widely disparate in language and custom; their revision allows for an emerging body of "texts," both oral and written, that is truly multicultural. In other words, Kingston's use of both Chinese and American cultural references, in quotations, allusions, and embedded legends, begins the work of documenting a unique Chinese-American culture. These public texts, reimagined in terms of Chinese-American experience, both emerge from the memories of that culture and its members and become its common memory. Were Kingston not to reinvent her source materials, her narratives would be marred by an either/or fallacy—each textualized remainder would be either Chinese (in translation), or American (in English),[4] but not convincingly integrated so as to provide historical identity to Chinese-American experience. Recreation, rather than simple repetition or translation, is essential. As Joanne Frye notes, in exploring Kingston's use of legends in *The Woman Warrior,* "The stories . . . become interpretive strategies for her own lived experience as a female and are never severed from that experience. Each story . . . interacts profoundly with the foundation narrative of her own immediate experience: the autobiography of fact, of daily lived reality" (298). In like manner, the public texts Kingston incorporates to tell her culture's story are no longer discrete or independent; they, too, become enmeshed with the daily and more broadly historical lives of Chinese-Americans.

Kingston recognizes how liberating narrative can be, both for the story-teller and for the culture about whom (and/or to whom) the story is told, because one can shape the products of memory—and so their meaning—through selection, elaboration, and context. She put the issue succinctly, from another direction: "Somehow I think there's something wrong with oral his-tories. People are treating them like *sacred* material when what they are is *raw* material" ("This is the Story" 6, Kingston's emphasis). The process Kingston advocates revises memory itself, and transformation keeps meanings vital in cultures, which are always themselves evolving. As she remarked in a 1987 address, "Mythology dies if you don't change it" ("Moving Images"). In a sense, what her work suggests is a way to recapture in writing the fluidity of oral transmission, which she sees as functioning actively in the world. King-ston told Arturo Islas that the oral tradition "has the impact of command, of directly influencing action. . . . Writing is static. The story will remain as printed for the next two hundred years and it's not going to change. That really bothers me, because what would be wonderful would be for the words to change on the page every time, but they can't. The way I tried to solve this problem was to keep ambiguity in the writing all the time" (Interview 18). Memory for Kingston is both bearer and transformer of culture, and it is pre-cisely at the point of ambiguity, where it seems possible that the words are changing on the page to reflect contradictory memories, that transformation begins. The transformation is of conventionally Chinese or Western cultural material into specifically Chinese-American material, in order to construct a Chinese-American past.

It is important to consider precisely what material Kingston chooses for her sources, because she links popular and "high" cultures in her attempt to devise a multiethnic past. Included among the public texts she quotes or alludes to are Chinese legends and ballads, which emerge from a long tradition of oral transmission and which bridge the gap in paradoxical ways. While several of the Chinese legends she draws on are classic codifications of popular oral stories, the form in which they are available to Kingston—as novels—may be seen as a reaction against the oral tradition (Hsia 11).[5] Despite their attempts to give the seal of authority to selected narrative versions, however, the novels were at first disdained for their vernacular style by the contemporaneous scholarly elite trained to esteem poetry, philosophy, essays, and commentaries on the classics of the Chou dynasty (ca. 1027–256 B.C.) and to despise colloquial stories (Scott 18). Nevertheless, as Arthur Waley has observed, the novels "were read by everybody who could read, although nobody probably would admit having read them. And schoolboys were severely punished for having read and enjoyed them" (Wu 3). These novels became so widely known that, as Kingston reports in *Tripmaster Monkey,* they were performed as plays among Chinese immigrants in nineteenth-century America. That is, the novelistic form that endeavored to make the historical record literate never fully succeeded in wresting the material from the hands of public performers and storytellers, and this parallel tradition of letters and oral recitation is part of what seems to fascinate Kingston about her Chinese cultural legacy. The idea of narrative to which Kingston first drew attention in the "talk-stories" of *The Woman Warrior* precisely captures this parallel. As a child she heard legends and familial stories, which her book fixes and attempts to understand, by remembering (and re-membering) them and making them coherent within an interpretive scheme. At the same time, she recaptures the very changeability of their nature as oral artifacts, presenting her uncertainty about their details as well as their uneasy relationship to historical "fact."

In addition to retelling the talk-stories about China, Kingston massively incorporates Western materials that likewise emerge from both popular and educated culture. This is particularly true in *Tripmaster Monkey.* In Kingston's last book and only novel, one finds the most extravagant array of quotations, allusions, and embedded stories—in fact, one might argue that the whole point of the novel is to weave a Chinese-American fabric out of snippets of apparently unrelated cultural memories.[6] In the novel, Robert Service's poetry rubs shoulders with excerpts from Whitman and Rilke; the meditations of the protagonist shift from *Hamlet* to *West Side Story.* Clearly, for Kingston, the effort to understand a multiethnic historical identity makes any cultural influences fair game, but there is another explanation as well, most visible in *Tripmaster Monkey,* but applying convincingly to both *China Men* and *The Woman Warrior.* The clue can be found in a guiding metaphor of the novel, mentioned only in *Tripmaster Monkey*'s subtitle: *His Fake Book.*

The fake book is the text used by pop and jazz musicians to jog the memory; it contains simple melodies and chordal accompaniments for standard tunes and is used as the basis for improvisation. The idea of a fake book is Kingston's translation not just of the language but of the cultural artifact of *hua-pen,* the prompt books used by professional Chinese storytellers in the serial recitals of their epics (Scott 17; Ma and Lau xxii).[7] *Hua-pen* would typically include the major episodes of a traditional story, but storytellers were known for adding new episodes in their recitations (Scott 68). The contents of the prompt books would have been available to the compilers of the dynastic novels, who, like the professional storytellers, would edit, elaborate, and add to the major episodes. The improvisational nature of both telling and writing down the classic stories is clear, and it is this characteristic that Kingston translates into the idiom of American popular culture when she refers to the "fake book." In a sense, each of her books can be seen as a fake book, gathering both central and peripheral texts—the melodies and accompaniments, as it were—from Chinese, American, and Chinese-American culture, from her past as well as her family's, to inspire the creative memory. In remembering, narrating, and recreating these sources, Kingston works like a musician in performance. She avails herself of any useful materials at hand, incorporating figures from both elite and common culture. She improvises upon familiar tunes and rhythms to make them new—and to make them express her understanding of herself and her multiethnic culture.

That understanding seems to change across the three narratives, in part because Kingston grapples in different ways with the meaning of having a hyphenated cultural identity. The first book, *The Woman Warrior,* seems both to question and celebrate the hyphen, to place emphasis equally on either side of it. Kingston plumbs the memories of her childhood in the United States, including the talk-stories she heard and the fantasies she entertained, but it is a childhood haunted by China, by a place that is other to her own experience except as it is narrated to her. In this sense, she is trying to construct, through her own narration of remembered stories, half of what she feels as a plural identity. But she later begins to repudiate the doubleness suggested by the hyphen, partly as a response to the misreadings of her first book ("Cultural Mis-readings" 60). In *China Men,* she demonstrates the historical shift from one singular identity (the Chinese father in the first main chapter) to another singular identity (the American brother in the final main chapter), a shift that indicates that her family's experience has passed through hyphenated identity but has attempted to leave it behind. She writes: "I want to discern what it is that makes people go West and turn into Americans. I want to compare China, a country I made up, with what country is really out there" (*China Men* 87). Making distinctions between her cultures of origin remains important; she endeavors to observe and classify the particulars of cultural identity conceived in geographical terms. *Tripmaster Monkey* defiantly reasserts the shift in the preceding book, emphasizing the result of the process of cultural transformation through assimilation.[8] But Kingston is careful to define assimilation neither as appropriation nor annihilation; the assimilation process changes the local—American—culture in contact with the Chinese as much as the Chinese culture is changed in contact with the American. She satirizes hyphenation and pleads for a reorientation of cultural identity: "We need to take the hyphen out—'Chinese American.' 'American,' the noun, and 'Chinese,' the adjective" (327).

Because of her developing notion of cultural identity, and despite the notable fierceness of *The Woman Warrior,* Kingston's project in that book is in some ways less insistent, more qualified and uncertain, than it is in *Tripmaster Monkey.* While the autobiographical inquiry of *The Woman Warrior* is directed largely toward exploring the meaning of being Chinese-American (the hyphen still intact), the means of the inquiry is for Kingston to recover the Chinese past from which she feels excluded. Her motivation is to "try to understand what things in [her] are Chinese," and to do this, she needs to distinguish "What is Chinese tradition and what is the movies" (*Warrior* 5–6)— that is, Western representations of Chinese culture. What she knows of this past she learns only through her mother's habit of "talking-story," by nature unreliable, as she accuses her mother toward the end of the book: "You lie with stories. You won't tell me a story and then say, 'This is a true story,' or, 'This is just a story.' . . . I can't tell what's real and what you make up" (202). The irony is that Kingston's relationship to her mother resembles the reader's relationship to Kingston's narrator; the narrator also flouts the distinction between reality and fantasy, fiction and nonfiction, in her efforts to rethink her culturally assigned role.[9] What she has learned from her mother about storytelling is, of course, what enables her to create a version of Chinese-American cultural history by revising and multiplying the stories she remembers, at the risk of contradiction—and, perhaps, *because* of contradiction.

Three prominent examples of Kingston's method of storytelling in *The Woman Warrior* are instructive. In the first, which draws on a cautionary tale her mother tells about Kingston's aunt, the "No Name Woman" of the opening chapter, Kingston makes visible her process of revising raw material to suit her interests. She transforms her mother's memory into several wildly divergent stories; once she reaches a final interpretation, it becomes her own memory of her aunt. Where Kingston's mother has told her only the "facts" of her aunt's illegitimate pregnancy, punishment by the villagers, and death in the family well, Kingston tries to imagine her aunt's secret life, obscured by the "facts" that have been arranged to warn Kingston about the necessity of obedience, chastity, and devotion to the family. In her effort to make her aunt's life touch her own, Kingston conjures her variously as a victim (7), a wild woman (8), a martyr (11), and, finally, a spite suicide (16), the configuration that seems most satisfying to her sense of justice.

The development of this narration serves as a model for the way Kingston later improvises on public texts. The most striking example appears in the story of the woman warrior, Fa Mu Lan, based on an anonymous ballad from northern China in the sixth century (Waley 113). In the original ballad,

Fa Mu Lan epitomizes filial piety, humility, and loyalty to her community: she serves in the emperor's army in place of her father, fights as a skilled soldier to defeat the enemy, and returns to her village to resume her domestic duties. The "facts" of Kingston's version are the same, but the thrust and details of the story—its meaning—are vastly different, in keeping with the defining questions of Kingston's narrative. She herself commented that the "White Tigers" chapter in which the story appears "is not a Chinese myth but one transformed by America, a sort of kung fu movie parody" ("Cultural Misreadings" 57). Like the 1970s TV show *Kung Fu,* Kingston's version of Fa Mu Lan subverts Chinese values and customs even as it introduces them to her Western audience—most obviously, in incorporating a focus on individual attainment and independence. Here, the girl spends many years in training, isolated from her family, in order to be the savior of her people; she learns superhuman powers of self-control; she leads vast armies into battle, rather than simply following as a foot soldier; and she secretly has a family, in defiance of the assumption that the heroic and the domestic cannot mix. In addition, Kingston freely interpolates details from another well-known Chinese figure, Yue Fei, a patriot on whose back was carved a mandate for revenge (*China Men* 53). In adopting the male experience to testify to her woman warrior's power and devotion, she is clearly untroubled by any need to maintain the integrity of the central text of Fa Mu Lan. Throughout, she allows the meanings of her added material to exist in seemingly harmonious contradiction to the meaning of the original ballad. Most important, she appropriates the revenge fantasy of Fa Mu Lan for herself, transforming the community's legend into a first-person account. The narration records, as it were, Kingston's memory of her own past, even as it comes to stand for her understanding of her position as a Chinese-American who is not so much *between* two worlds is *in* both of them.

That peculiar cultural positioning is represented concretely in the final example of a reimagined public text included in Kingston's autobiographical narrative. The story of the second-century poetess, Ts'ai Yen, who was abducted by the Southern Hsiung-nu (the Huns) and made the commander's wife, is well known in China, especially from her cycle of poems, *Hu chia shih pa p'ai* (Eighteen songs of a barbarian reed pipe), and from subsequent cycles by Liu Shang and Wang An-shih.[10] Ts'ai Yen stands for the exile, the unwilling immigrant, who must learn to survive in the midst of a culture—and, importantly, a language—not her own. In Kingston's sources, Ts'ai Yen grieves; she seems a desolate victim of her captors, passive, yearning, and even self-pitying. The nomad landscape seems harsh, barren, and unforgiving, and she barely speaks of the people among whom she is living. As David Leiwei Li has observed, this aggrieved tone is missing from Kingston's account of the tale (510–11). In its place is power and even exhilaration: Ts'ai Yen fights like a warrior woman, "cut[ting] down anyone in her path during the madness of close combat" (*Woman Warrior* 208), and she communicates through song with the people whose language she cannot speak. This is a significant improvisation on Kingston's part. In Liu Shang's sixth poem, Ts'ai Yen laments that "All day and all year I keep my mouth closed. / 'Yes' and 'no' and accepting and giving things away all depend on finger gestures; / For expressing our feelings, speech has become less useful than the hand" (*Eighteen Songs* [32]). Kingston picks up on the captive's linguistic isolation, but she alters the experience to speak to her own history. In *The Woman Warrior,* Ts'ai Yen's sons, who speak no Chinese, laugh at her and cruelly imitate her "with senseless singsong words" (208), suggesting the cultural distance between first- and second-generation Chinese-Americans, like Kingston and her parents, who seem often to fail to understand one another. The Ts'ai Yen of the poetic cycles never seems to connect with her captors and is no more at peace when she returns to the Han people than when she was in captivity; the eighteenth and final verse of *Hu chia shih pa p'ai* concludes on a despairing note: "Just as the sky and the earth are separated from each other, my sons are in the west while I am in the east. / Poor me, my unhappiness can fill the whole sky. / Although the universe is large, it is probably not big enough to hold my sorrow" (*Hu chia* [20]). Kingston turns the tale toward a hopeful cultural resolution, however, when the words of Ts'ai Yen's song communicate her feelings across the language barrier to the barbarians, and when, upon narrating her return to the Han lands, Kingston asserts that her song "translated well" (209). In other words, Ts'ai Yen comes to stand for the poet who, like Kingston, reshapes her memories of otherness into a meaningful narrative that can be taken as historical truth in her home culture.[11]

Kingston's second book, *China Men,* takes up similar questions in a different way. She becomes a bit player in the history of the men in her family, told across several generations. This family "history," compiled of memories recited to her and events she has witnessed or researched, and fleshed out by the fictive imagination into a full account, represents for Kingston the larger history of Chinese immigration and acculturation to the United States. As in *The Woman Warrior,* to recapture this past she makes recourse to public texts from both Western and Chinese cultural history. Juxtaposed in interchapters to the family's story, these texts gain new resonances that bear specifically on Chinese-American experiences of immigration and acculturation.[12]

A case in point is the legend of Tang Ao, which serves as a prologue to the book. Tang Ao, journeying to find the Gold Mountain—the Chinese metaphor for North America—is captured instead in the Land of Women. There he is feminized, his ears pierced, his feet bound, his face plucked, powdered, and painted (*China Men* 3–4). Kingston's source for the tale is *Flowers in the Mirror (Chin hua yuan),* written in the early nineteenth century by Li Ju-chen. Li's novel is a satiric, very funny, and often fantastic story of the journey of Tang Ao, a scholar of the lowest rank, who seeks, through charitable acts, to "become an immortal by 'cultivating Tao' " (Tai-yi Lin 5, 7). Like Swift's Gulliver, Tang Ao and the family members who accompany him find themselves in all manner of places whose mores allow Li to comment upon contemporary Chinese society. One such place is the Land of Women to which Kingston alludes. But there are significant differences between the source and its reinvention in *China Men*. In Li's novel, it is Tang Ao's brother-in-law, Merchant Lin, who suffers the pain and humiliation of the traditional Chinese woman, and not Tang Ao himself, who manages to rescue Lin through a ruse. Perhaps Kingston alters this for the sake of economy, but a more compelling effect of her conflation of characters—her reinvention of the remembered tale—is to change its tone. Whereas Li's division of the story into the two characters makes for slapstick romance, in which Tang Ao by dumb luck and some cleverness can compensate for the foolish gullibility of his brother-in-law, Kingston's version emphasizes the isolation, pain, and humiliation of the captive man. When Li writes about the customs of the Land of Women, where gender roles are wholly reversed, he does so in order to expose comically what he sees as the absurd cruelty of conventional Chinese practices relating to femininity. Kingston uses the details of Li's story—especially those concerned with the feminizing of Merchant Lin—and adds some of her own, such as the threat to sew Tang Ao's mouth shut (4), to very different purpose. The conventional icons of Chinese femininity—silencing, crippling, grooming—stand for Kingston less as a critique of Chinese conceptions of womanhood (although that is implied) and more as metaphors for the experience of Chinese males emigrating to America, where they were often effectively emasculated by Caucasian-American culture. Like his fellow workers, for instance, Kingston's great grandfather was prohibited from speaking by the overseer of the Hawaiian sugar plantation on which he labored (*China Men* 99–100, 102). The story of Tang Ao, remembered and transformed, becomes a way of rendering symbolically the analogous experience of the Chinese male in America.

Later, Kingston summarizes the epic elegy *Li Sao* (Lament on Encountering Sorrow) by Ch'u Yuan, China's earliest known poet (256), as a way to create a context of interpretation for what follows—the story of Kingston's brother who was sent to Vietnam. Ch'u Yuan is exiled because he advises his king against war; he wanders many years and finally drowns himself in despair because "he could not find one uncorrupted human being" (258). Kingston's allusion to the *Li Sao* makes sense only in ironic juxtaposition to her brother's experience. A pacifist like Ch'u Yuan, the brother is first exiled from the Chinese-American culture of his birth when he enlists in the Navy in order to avoid being drafted into another branch of the services. During basic training, he loses his appetite (286), signifying his will to live, as he learns how to participate in military activity, the symbol, to him, of human corruptibility. The irony that he is being trained as an American to kill people who are in profound ways like himself does not escape Kingston, but rather becomes an emblem of confused cultural identity. Disillusioned when he finally reaches Hong Kong, her brother finds that his life makes no more sense than it did before—that is, unlike the expectations in his "childish dream" (294), being in China does not clarify for him either his Americanness or his Chineseness. He returns from the war quietly despairing that "the things people did seemed to have no value" (304). The notion of corruptibility suggested by Ch'u Yuan's story comes for Kingston to represent the problem of the multicultural identity, which by definition implies a "corruption" of the cultural identities that stand to either side of the hyphen. Kingston documents the resulting experience of exile from each culture.

In another vein, Kingston transforms a public text in the reverse direction—from Western culture back toward Chinese culture. She represents an interchapter, "The Adventures of Lo Bun Sun," as a summary of "a book from China about a sailor named Lo Bun Sun." As the story develops, however, it becomes increasingly clear that "Lo Bun Sun" is a parody of the way Anglo-Americans mock the English pronunciation of Chinese-American immigrants ("l's" for "r's," and so forth), and it also suggests self-parody; at the same time, Kingston satirizes the Anglicizing of Chinese culture. Lo Bun Sun is Robinson, as in Robinson Crusoe, and it is Defoe's novel that Kingston summarizes, translated into Chinese terms. Like the legend of Tang Ao, as well as the material of several other interchapters and interpolated stories—"The Ghostmate," for example, or "The Wild Man of the Green Swamp"—the story of Lo Bun Sun metaphorically documents the history of Chinese-American cultural exile, where the immigrants experienced their transition to American culture as castaways who must use their resources to survive in a hostile environment. Kingston's memory of this as "a book from China" (225), expressed ambiguously (is this a book that happened to come in Chinese translation, or one that originated in China?), nevertheless suggests the way a transformed version may be taken for memory—that is, can testify to the past.[13]

Numerous other examples of reimagined textualized remainders appear in both of Kingston's earlier books, but I would like to explore the novel *Tripmaster Monkey: His Fake Book* in greater depth because it provides such a wildly playful range of examples in which oral and written stories are transformed into cultural memory. In this book, too, Kingston makes most explicit the way in which she sees memory at work in the process of transformation, providing a sense of historical identity to the dispossessed. The process is epitomized when the protagonist, Wittman Ah Sing, and his new wife, Taña, visit the rooms of his grandmother, PoPo. There they see a "memory village" (191), a tiny but detailed model of a Chinese village, complete with houses, pigs, a well, fields, and thirty-three lichee trees (192). The memory village is a relic of immigration; new immigrants would study it so that when they had to tell U.S. immigration officials about their place of origin, the stories of all the immigrants would agree. The point, as Wittman notes, is that the village as it appears in the model never existed: "It is not a model *of* anything, do you understand? It's a memory village" (192, Kingston's emphasis). That is, the memory village is a fabrication, a story created and retold for purposes of self-protection, in order to give the immigrants the appearance of an authoritative historical identity. The irony, as Kingston suggests, is that the immigrants came to believe the stories they told, incorporating them into their memories and understandings of themselves, so that Wittman is able to tell Taña that PoPo fetched water from this well and that twenty of the lichee trees belonged to his great-great-uncle (192). The fictive narrative has been transformed into historical truth.

But there is no bitterness to Kingston's irony here; rather, she meets the transformative power of memory with awe and affection. The principle of transformation, in fact, is crucial to Kingston's conception of Wittman. Wittman often appears in the guise of the titular Monkey, a beloved figure from the sixteenth-century epic novel by Wu Ch'eng-en, *The Journey to the West (Hsi yu chi)*.[14] Monkey is the King of the Monkeys, who possesses magical powers and is spiritually advanced; he protects a seventh-century monk, known as Tripitaka, who is journeying to India in order to bring Buddhist sutras back to China. The novel is a comic allegory about the Buddhist notion of *maya* (illusion) and human attachment to the world of the senses (Hsia 148), and Monkey is the character most savvy about human fallibility. A trickster and shape-shifter, Monkey is known for his seventy-two transformations (Wu 241), and Kingston translates this capacity into Wittman's ingenuity when he repeatedly reinvents himself and the artifacts of his culture.

Wittman Ah Sing is a self-proclaimed bardic singer. He declares that he "want[s] so bad to be the first bad-jazz China Man bluesman of America" (*Tripmaster* 27), and his fake book seems to include the whole range of Western and Chinese culture. At quick count, there are more than two hundred references in the novel to icons of Eastern and Western culture, especially modern American culture, both elite and popular. Poets, playwrights, and novelists find transhistorical and transcultural mention alongside actors, actresses, musicians, and political figures; Mao Tse Tung and Marilyn Monroe appear together on one page (198), James Boswell and Tonto on another (120). *Tripmaster Monkey* alludes to dozens of novels, plays, films, even TV shows, many of which had virtual cult followings in the late sixties and early seventies, the time in which the novel is set. Kingston quotes freely from other public texts, especially poems; poems of Walt Whitman, for example, make appearances both in chapter titles (e.g., "Trippers and Askers," which derives from the fourth section of "Song of Myself") and in excerpts.

Walt Whitman, in fact, provides a clue to Kingston's method here. Wittman Ah Sing was named by his father after the American poet: the "Ah Sing" echoes Whitman's mission to celebrate his country and himself; and the misspelled "Wittman" represents both the connection to and distance from American culture of this character whom, Kingston has implied, she sees as a new Everyman ("The Coming Book" 184). That is, Wittman stands for the transformation of American culture in contact with Chinese-American culture. He is an American Everyman, not only a Chinese-American Everyman. His significance to Kingston may in part explain her choice of setting for the novel: the San Francisco Bay area in the 1960s. Kingston creates in her reference to this time and place an additional level of historiographic inquiry, since she reimagines in multiethnic terms—thereby claiming for multiethnic experience—a part of the past that has become iconic for a certain generation of Americans. She alters our memories of the center of the counterculture at the same time that she makes use of some of the counterculture's most storied features. In public memory, of course, the sixties were a time of revolution, a time of altering consciousness in social and personal spheres through "mind-expanding" drugs and political action. The aim of the counterculture was both to rewrite history and reinvent the future, in part by incorporating the fabulous into the everyday. Kingston's Wittman becomes a representative of this movement, participating in the drug culture at Lance Kamiyama's party and creating an improbable community in the improbably short time it takes him to stage his epic drama. The result of his activities is to revise our memories of the countercultural movement so that it is no longer Caucasian or even black and white, but has a distinctively multiethnic cast. Wittman's barrage of allusions and quotations is the raw material of cultural memory that he needs to create his epic vision of Chinese-American historical experience. His vision is, ultimately, of the unhyphenated *American* experience that Kingston wishes to offer as our common history when she has Wittman revise the title of Wu's novel: "There is no East here. West is meeting West. . . . This is The Journey *In* the West" (308, Kingston's emphasis). Wittman translates both Chinese and Western texts into his own culture; his ambition is to be the "reader of the tribe" (247), and he aspires for someone to "dig his allusions" (13). Like Monkey, he incarnates the principle of transformation, playing complicated riffs on old stories for the sake of his culture's knowledge of itself.

Wittman is a raging, exuberant talker and storyteller whom even the narrator cannot seem to shut up (282). As a storyteller, he is metaphorically the novel's "tripmaster," the person who talks others through their drug trips, enriching their hallucinations and keeping them from harm, and his reading is part of what qualifies him for the role. When the narrator remarks, "It must be that people who read go on more macrocosmic and microcosmic trips" (88), she suggests that it is one's contact with public texts that gives one the power to imagine even without artificial stimulation and the grounding to make the trip safe for everyone. Wittman's function as tripmaster is most obvious in the novel's several set-pieces, in which Kingston transforms her sources—the classic Chinese novels—in order to create the epic Chinese-American theater that is Wittman's dream. Each retelling becomes a mixture of Chinese and Western motifs. For example, in Wittman's version of the fourteenth-century compilation *The Romance of the Three Kingdoms (San-kuo-chih yen-i)*, probably by Lo Kuan-chung,[15] he describes a palace that "is defended against the elephant army by knights on black stallions, *Trigger* palominos, and stout Mongolian ponies" (170, emphasis added). The Roy Rogers allusion both startles with its incongruity and tames for the reader embedded in American culture the potential exoticism of the translated story. Later, when Wittman acts out a scene from the novel *The Water Verge (Shui hu chuan),*[16] a story of 108 Chinese outlaws, he turns it into a combination of Southwestern tall tale, with references to Three-Finger Jack and Sacramento (260–61), and Marx Brothers' slapstick routine: he steals the Groucho Marx sight-gag, saying "Walk this way" and then following with "a banana-peel run, slip-sliding around the room" (258). In each case Wittman's memory of the tale is informed by his contact with American popular culture, and what he illuminates in his narration are the unexpected resemblances between disparate cultural materials—resemblances and sympathies that make the blending of elements into a Chinese-American cultural memory seem possible.

Kingston's most extensive reinvention of a source appears as Wittman begins to stage his epic play, running across several nights. In narrating Wittman's play, Kingston at times quotes verbatim from *The Romance of the Three Kingdoms,* and she condenses much of the climactic part of its plot, but in addition to conflating and reordering the episodes, she narrates some subtle but telling variations and embellishments. Whereas Lo Kuan-chung's novel emphasizes the nobility of one of its heroes, Gwan Goong,[17] Kingston chooses to underscore his supernatural reappearances after his death and his "powers over illusions" (177). In Chinese mythology, Gwan Goong is the god of war and literature (Scott 37), and as such, he has presided over each of Kingston's books—riding to battle before her self-projection in the "White Tigers" fantasy of *The Woman Warrior* (38) and represented in a picture in her family's dining room in *China Men* (126). In *Tripmaster Monkey,* Gwan Goong serves as the model for Wittman's dramatic role and his muse, as he becomes the director and master of ceremonies for the cultural improvisation of his theatrical epic. *The Romance of the Three Kingdoms,* set in the second and third centuries, concerns a hundred years of political strife and war over the Chinese empire. As such, its story metaphorically represents for Wittman—and Kingston—the ethnic "battleground" of America and the hundred years of struggle over the turf of cultural identity.

A few examples of Wittman's Monkey-like narrative transformations of his source should suffice. In Kingston's source, when Gwan has been captured by Sun Ch'uan and is about to be put to death, his response to Sun's offer that he surrender in order to save his life is heroically contemptuous; he calls Sun "My blue-eyed boy! My red-whiskered rodent!" (Lo 240). The rest of the short scene concerns politics and military strategy: Sun, respecting Gwan, wants to encourage him to defect, but his officers counsel execution (240–42). Kingston quotes Gwan's line but elaborates the scene to another effect. Wittman narrates that Sun Ch'uan offers "brotherhood, familyhood, a marriage for your daughter with my son." When Gwan scorns the offer, Sun calls him a "barbarian" for continuing the war (*Tripmaster* 275). Kingston has translated the exchange so that it signifies an offer of assimilation, not political power; Gwan Goong's refusal of the symbolic marriage represents for Kingston a larger refusal to assimilate according to the terms set by the dominant culture. In this sense, she represents both a historical observation about Chinese resistance to assimilation into American culture and an ideological point about the reasons for this resistance. Later, she interpolates an episode in which Gwan's line—"My blue-eyed boy! My red-whiskered rodent!" (284)—is repeated. Here, Gwan is an apparition haunting Sun, and the line is what alerts us (and Sun) to the identity of the alien voice emerging from the body of one of Sun's men. When Gwan's visage takes shape across the man's face, "His eyebrows and the creases beside his mouth are vertical black lines; his eyes and face are blood red—War incorporated" (284). Kingston, then, stresses the god Gwan's reign over warfare, reinventing Gwan's presence as the spirit of vengeance in order to bespeak anger against the dominant power; this anger foreshadows that which Wittman expresses at length in the novel's concluding chapter, when he recites a list of stereotypes and a partial history of discrimination against Chinese-Americans. A similar transformation of the remembered text appears near the end of this passage. In the source, Liu Pei, one of Gwan Goong's two sworn brothers, is ill, and the ghosts of Gwan and Chang Fei, the third brother, appear to him. Gwan tells him that "the time is not far off when we shall be reunited" (Lo 277), which Liu interprets as foretelling his death. Kingston retains the line as "The time is not far off when we shall be together again," but in her version, Liu Pei responds that "We will the three of us all go home" and the narrator—who may be either Wittman or Kingston's narrative voice—apostrophizes, "O home-returning powers, where might home be? How to find it and dwell there?" (284). Clearly, she is reinterpreting the story as one of cultural exile.

Kingston reinvents not just the plots, but also the conventions of her source materials. The Chinese stories that originated in prompt books were notable for their use of the vernacular (Ma and Lau xxii); Kingston's diction, which attempts to capture the richness of the American idiom, emerges from a range of linguistic styles and class origins, here flippant, hip, or snappy, there elevated. A randomly chosen example, from Wittman's farewell to his job, juxtaposes the line "A green razzberry to you, World" to Melville's famous lines, "Ah Bartleby. Ah Humanity" (65). Likewise, Kingston avails herself of some of the formal characteristics and motifs of her sources. Her use of self-reflexive linking devices between chapters imitates the conventions of a novel like *Flowers in the Mirror,* whose chapters generally end with the formulation, "If the reader would like to know . . . please read/turn to the next chapter" (e.g., Lin 23, 31, 35, and so forth). The convention is a throwback to the oral tradition, in which storytellers would encourage their audience to reappear for the next night's narration. In early chapters, Kingston copies the sources directly, concluding the second chapter, for example, this way: "*Our monkey man will live—he parties, he plays—though unemployed. To see* how he does it, go on to the next chapter" (65). But by the end of the novel, she is altering the tag-like form in accordance with its cultural context. Chapter 7 ends with the lines, "To entertain and educate the solitaries that make up a community, the play will be a combination revue-lecture. You're invited" (288). Here she takes on the confiding tone of the carnival barker, and the casualness is appropriate to a twentieth-century American audience raised on television commercials. Too, the excess and busy-ness of *Tripmaster Monkey,* which has elicited adverse—or at least weary—responses among some reviewers,[18] resembles the rhythms of traditional Chinese stories; C. T. Hsia, for example, has described the "interminable campaigns" and "fuss and bustle" of *The Water Verge* (85). But here as well Kingston translates her sources into the terms of her subject matter, because the extravagance of her imagination in the narrative is in keeping with the fuss and bustle of the culture about which she writes—the time of Day-glo colors, acid rock, happenings, and "free love." In each case, Kingston transforms source narratives and narrative conventions to erase the boundaries implied by her two cultural traditions, so as to create an indivisibly multicultural narrative.

Clearly, then, the form of her narrative is dictated by Kingston's need to represent the experience of ethnic hyphenation in such a way that she can affirm it as *American* experience. The difficulties of such affirmation are suggested when Wittman insists "We allthesame Americans" (282); his locution simultaneously makes an important claim to cultural identity and undermines it by showing the symptomatic linguistic alienation of some Chinese-Americans. Because of these complex relations to "American" identity, the marriage that Kingston has Gwan Goong refuse becomes a potent symbol for her. Wittman marries white Taña, not Chinese-American Nanci Lee; going one better on the "integrated marriage" (150) of his friend Lance, Wittman learns to make the marriage work by looking beyond the chaos of domestic life toward the satisfactions that can come from unromantic union. This is precisely the pragmatism Kingston finds necessary within multicultural relations. The conjugal metaphor is at play in numerous ways in the novel, ranging from linguistic to sexual unions. The very title of the novel weds the Chinese Monkey to the American hippie tripmaster. Wittman's last defiant act at his sales job is to set up a Barbie doll to be "raped" by a mechanical monkey (64–65); here, the union metaphor is inverted, as Kingston, inspired by both her protean prototype and her recreated image of Gwan Goong, takes vengeance against the exploitation of Chinese-American culture by American consumer culture—that is, against the kind of stereotyping that causes whites to associate Chinese-Americans with Buddha-shaped bottles of Jade East cologne (27). The marriage metaphor is, however, righted again when Wittman and Taña make love for the first time and share a hallucination, a kind of waking dream that they narrate together (157–58). Significantly, the proof of their cultural union, of their shared consciousness, is their common story.

Kingston's understanding of storytelling as an act in which teller and hearer participate mutually explains why multicultural references proliferate in the novel. Wittman's chosen venue, the theater, is representative of the way Kingston envisions narrating as a unifying social act. Wittman has a dual recognition that "The ethnos is degenerating" (255) and the "theater has died" (141)—meaning the century of Chinese-American theater, whose many acting companies performed the Chinese classics. Desiring to bring it back as "deep-roots American theater" (141), Wittman determines, in the spirit of the old Judy Garland/Mickey Rooney movies, to put on a play. The play, which garners a wide and enthusiastic audience, climaxes the novel and develops as an extravagant pastiche of cultural references. In addition to rehearsing central events from *The Romance of the Three Kingdoms,* it includes a minstrel show starring the Siamese twins Chang and Eng, whose physical joining satirizes the problem of hyphenated identity; it recapitulates the history of Chinese-American immigrants in the guise of a John Wayne western; and its finale is a fireworks display that causes actors and audience to mingle, "breaking rules of reality-and-illusion" (303). This concluding scene proves that the play has served one radical function of the theater, to unify a community ritually. And it has unified the community of the novel by evolving a common set of memories, drawn from other, fragmented cultural materials, to interpret the community's experience.

Kingston underscores the need for community in a number of ways, each centered on the possibilities of storytelling. Her narrator, for example, often makes herself visible as both observer and participant in the narrated action, and the result is that the boundaries between narrator and object of narration become vague. When she describes the local scene at Grant Avenue, she writes that "they/we call it Du Pont Gai" (26). Later, a question of Wittman's suggests that he is "remembering when *we* were kids and poor" (101, emphasis added). The narrator's use of the first-person plural is only the most obvious example of the way Kingston undermines "us/them" thinking, otherwise implicit in the conventional third-person narration that seems to dominate the novel. By breaking the convention, Kingston works toward a reimagining of the narrative situation in communal terms that hark back to her oral sources. What she attempts in devising her narrative voice is to accomplish the union signified when, in the parable of cultural exile Lance tells as his life story, he repeats the redemptive line "Our stories are your stories" (125).

The infiltration of the narrative voice into the community constructed in the narrative—a process imitated by Wittman himself as he narrates his stories and play excerpts—suggests one of the more interesting effects of Kingston's conception of storytelling in this novel. That effect, which happens to accord with some postmodern notions of subjectivity, is that the unitary, essentialist self disappears into the web of discourses about the self. Thomas Docherty has described postmodern subjectivity in apt terms for understanding Kingston's narration: "the speaking subject is never a single individual; in discourse, the subject is constituted discontinuously at every discrete moment not only by what it says, but also by the languages or discourses and silence which surround it: this is as much as to say that the subject can never be the singular 'I'—if subjectivity exists at all, it can only do so in the form of communal subjectivity, 'we' " (269).[19] When Wittman acknowledges that he has been "inventing selves" (19) through talking, he admits to a kind of fluid subjectivity, a dissolution of the self in narrative. Fittingly, of course, this view of subjectivity resembles in its flexibility the variations of the oral tradition. As we have seen in considering narrative versions, no single representation of the self—no single story about it—can stand as the authoritative version. It is in this sense that another possible meaning of the novel's subtitle comes into play: in a postmodern disclaimer of the book's authority, Kingston can dismiss it as a *fake* book, like the "fake" selves or stories she and her protagonist spin out.

The novel refuses to rest at this interpretation, however. Rather, it engages in the double or contradictory movement that Linda Hutcheon identifies as characteristic of postmodern fiction. The fake book (or self) nevertheless has presence, a being in time. Hutcheon writes: "postmodernism establishes, differentiates, and then disperses stable narrative voices (and bodies) that use memory to try to make sense of the past. It both installs and then subverts traditional concepts of subjectivity" (118). That is, *Tripmaster Monkey* asserts the selfhood of its central figure—and Wittman is wont to assert himself vociferously—by narrating the history of that self, at the same time that his very narration, by its plurality of stories, makes such an assertion impossible.

But even this explanation is insufficient to account for the trajectory of the novel. Kingston's significant departure is to show the dissolution of self in the narrative act for other, more social purposes. When Wittman is "inventing selves," he is inventing them not just for himself, but for the audience to whom (and for whom) he speaks. His "we" is both the self as many selves and the self as continuous with its social environment. His audience assembles by the accidents of time and place to form his community; as the narrator reports in summarizing Wittman's philosophy of life: "Do the right thing by whoever crosses your path. Those coincidental people are your people" (223). Whereas Wittman resists the assumption of a ready-made and externally defined community of Chinese-Americans ("I am not going to the prom with the only Chinese girl in the class" [59]), he welcomes the multiethnic community that forms around his storytelling. Yet even though he retains his noisy individuality, Wittman still is dispersed as a presence across the community created by his narrative, so that he frequently becomes indistinguishable from the novel's narrative voice. When, for example, Wittman is dismayed by a screening of *West Side Story,* a two-line paragraph appears, reading, "Where are you, Bugs Bunny? We need you, Mr. Wabbit in Wed"

(72). Is this Wittman's comment, or the narrator's? In this manner, Kingston suggests the possibility of a transpersonal or communal self. It is a self created by the narrative process. Such a self, conceived inextricably as part of a larger social body, has its own past, but it also participates directly in—and can recite—the past of the group. It speaks, then, a multivocal discourse that, not surprisingly, is reminiscent of folk culture, of the oral mode of storytelling that is so much a part of Kingston's conception of narrative. The self can be figured as the speaker of the tale and the bearer of memory, but they are a tale and memory that belong first and foremost to the community.

What Kingston has done is analogous to what her character Charley does earlier in the novel: he recites the plot of a film, *The Saragossa Manuscript*, in such a way that "he got [his audience] to be inhabiting the same movie" (103). Even though Wittman is unable thereafter to locate the film, to prove that it existed as something other than Charley's fantasy or his own hallucination, he recognizes the power of Charley's retelling to create memory: "Some of those who heard the movie told at the fireside will think they'd seen it. All of them will remember a promise of something good among cannonballs and skulls" (103–4). The apparently unrecoverable *Saragossa Manuscript* epitomizes the importance of the oral tradition; its visual reality lost to history, it becomes a purely verbal text, existing only in memory and its retellings. Kingston teases us with the very title of the film, which suggests a written and provisional text (a manuscript) rather than a visual text—and thereby points to another way to make the words seem "to change on the page every time."

Like the actual film of *The Saragossa Manuscript,* which Vincent Canby described as a "spirited and often completely incomprehensible mélange of tall story, miller's tale, surreal dream and philosophical double-talk" (Canby 247), and which Kingston summarizes as a film about stories within stories as a way of telling history, *Tripmaster Monkey* is a lavish, wildly assembled novel about the making of cultural memory. The richness of reference in this book, as in the earlier ones, suggests the almost limitless possibilities of Monkey's seventy-two transformations. The array of tunes in Kingston's fake books appears large enough to fill a library—it encompasses the whole range of texts from Chinese and Western culture. Indeed, Kingston seems to point in each multifoliate text to a very particular understanding of memory: to remember is to translate and to translate is to improvise. Such translation is how we know ourselves as cultural beings.

Notes

1.   See Kingston's comment that memory is "insignificant, except when it haunts you and when it is a foundation for the rest of the personality" ("Eccentric Memories" 178).

Mary Warnock has written wisely about the relationship between memory and personal identity. She argues that "any truly recalling memory must . . . contain the idea of self. Whether through images or through direct knowledge, to count as a memory a cognitive experience, or thought, must contain the conviction that I myself was the person involved in the remembered scene. The image, if there is one, must be labelled not only 'this belongs to the past' but also 'it belongs to *my* past' " (58–59). In this sense, identity is dependent upon memory. The notion can be extended to include memories of those who are connected to one—one's family or cultural group—so that their involvement in a remembered scene, when narrated to one, also belongs to one's past.

2. Linda Ching Sledge makes an important point in regard to Kingston's particular version of cultural transmission when she notes that Kingston relies on the Chinese tradition of "talk-story" (*gong gu tsai*) throughout her books: "Talk-story is by my definition a conservative, communal folk art by and for the common people. . . . Because it served to redefine an embattled immigrant culture by providing its members immediate, ceremonial access to ancient lore, talk-story retained the structures of Chinese oral wisdom (parables, proverbs, formulaic description, heroic biography, casuistical dialogue) long after other old-country traditions had died" (143). In general, Sledge's recognition that Kingston has a "notion of the ethnic literary artist as one in a long line of performers shaping a recalcitrant history into talk-story form" (146) provides a significant precedent for arguing that memory and narration can construct a story of the past that bears truth value for its culture.

3. Kingston expresses her deconstruction of this distinction—and especially of the hierarchical value normally assigned to literate culture—when she tells Linda Ching Sledge, "The way I see it, there has been continuous talk-story for over 4,000 years and it spans China and America. Once in a long while during these millenia, somebody writes things down; writing 'freezes' things for a bit, like a rock, but the talk-story goes on around and from this rock" (Kingston to Sledge, 23 July 1981, qtd. in Sledge 147).

4. Although, obviously, Kingston is writing in English, the linguistic pair Chinese/English is not imbalanced or misleading in the same way that I am suggesting untransformed texts might be. This is because English *is* the language of Chinese America—that is, of those people who see themselves as Chinese-Americans rather than as Chinese living in the United States. (In this sense, clearly, there are many "Chinese Americas.") Not only is English the language available to Kingston, but it is also the only language that can faithfully render Chinese-American experience.

5. Hsia argues that, while the professional storytellers tended to interpret history and legend "in accordance with the concept of moral retribution . . . reward[ing] the virtuous and punish[ing] the wicked," the compilers of the historical novels were "inclined to follow the official historians and to share their Confucian view of history as a cyclic alternative between order and disorder, as a record of the careers of great men engaged in a perpetual struggle against the periodically rampant forces of anarchy and sensuality" (11).

6. Like the previous two texts, *Tripmaster Monkey* is not easily classifiable by genre, in large part because of its incorporation of other materials. Patricia Lin argues that "any attempts at reading Kingston require a revision on the part of the reader's assumptions about literary genres, authorial voice, and the question of veracity—particularly as her works pertain to 'truthful' or 'accurate' representations of Chinese Americans" (333) and that the "failure to recognize *Tripmaster Monkey* as something both more and less than a novel deprives the work of a place among the representative voices of the postmodern era" (334). Lin makes the point about genre in order to argue for the book's postmodernity. Because, however, the book is structured around the actions of fully invented characters—who, unlike those in *The Woman Warrior* and *China Men,* are suggested to be projections neither of Kingston herself nor of her family—and because the point of the novel is largely to underscore the way that fictive narrative creates meaningful cultural history, I will refer to the book as a novel.

7.   Ma and Lau point out that, while the scholar Lu Hsun interpreted *hua-pen* as prompt books, specialists no longer accept that interpretation, seeing the term *hua-pen* simply as another term for "story" (xxii). Nevertheless, the idea of the prompt book lies firmly within the information about Chinese cultural history available to Kingston and, given her use of public texts, seems an apt analogy.

8.   In important ways, Kingston conceives of this shift linguistically: "when I wrote *The Woman Warrior* and *China Men* . . . I was trying to find an American language that would translate the speech of the people who are living their lives with the Chinese language. They carry on their adventures and their emotional life and everything in Chinese. I had to find a way to translate all that into a graceful American language. Which is my language. But . . . I ha[dn't] had a chance to play with this language that I speak, this modern American language—which I love. . . . So I was trying to write a book with American rhythms. This is what *Tripmaster Monkey* is" ("*MELUS* Interview" 71).

9.   For an excellent discussion of Kingston's refusal to distinguish "fact" from "fiction," see Frye 294–95.

10.   Liu Shang wrote his cycle in the eighth century (these poems are translated in *Eighteen Songs of a Nomad Flute*), and Wang An-shih composed yet another cycle in the eleventh century (*Eighteen Songs* [1]). Kingston may be drawing on any or all of the cycles. Significantly, while Ts'ai Yen's and Liu Shang's cycles differ in a number of details, the tone and meaning of the narratives comprising the two cycles remain the same: Ts'ai Yen mourns bitterly over her abduction and distance from her home, she despairs, and yet when the Han messenger arrives twelve years later to ransom her and bring her back to China, she feels great pain to leave behind the two sons she bore to the Hsiung-nu chief.

I wish to thank Vivien Chan for her invaluable help in translating Ts'ai Yen's *Hu chia shih pa p'ai* for me. The translation cited is hers.

11.   For a parallel argument about Kingston's use of this legend in developing a sense of female identity, see Joanne Frye, who writes that Kingston "claim[s] for herself the power of Ts'ai Yen, the power of language both to shape and to convey reality: the power of narrative to bridge cultural barriers and to reinfuse the female identity with the strength of an affirmed selfhood" (300).

12.   Kingston has discussed the different ways she incorporates the mythic texts into the structure of her first two books as a response to the differences between men's and women's experiences in the United States: "In *The Woman Warrior,* when the girls and women draw on mythology for their strengths, the myth becomes part of the women's lives and the structure of the stories. In the men's stories . . . they are separate narratives. . . . [T]hose men went to a place where they didn't know whether their mythology was giving them any strength or not. They were getting very broken off from their background. . . . So, the myth story and the present story become separated" ("Eccentric Memories" 179–80).

13.   Kingston's ambiguous language nicely reflects her own uncertain knowledge: "I didn't know until I got to school that *Robinson Crusoe* was an English novel. Because it had gone into Chinese as spoken story. So my parents spoke the story *Robinson Crusoe*. . . . I got to school, and I thought, oh, so this is what this stuff is" ("*MELUS* Interview" 70). Her text reproduces for the reader the epistemological confusion concerning origins inherent in the multiethnic experience.

14.   Thirty of the one hundred original chapters of *Hsi yu chi* have been translated by Arthur Waley under the title *Monkey.*

15.   About half of the original 120 chapters are translated by Moss Roberts in *Three Kingdoms* (1976), and Roberts has recently published a more complete translation: *Three Kingdoms: A Historical Novel* (Berkeley: U of California P-Foreign Language, 1993).

16.   *Shui hu,* compiled in the fourteenth century, is attributed variously to Lo Kuanchung, to Shih Nai-an, or to them jointly (Hsia 77). J. H. Jackson translated the novel under the title *Water Margin,* attributing it solely to Shih Nai-an.

17.   I adopt Kingston's transliteration of the Chinese name for the god as it appears in *Tripmaster Monkey*. She has changed this from book to book: in *The Woman Warrior*, the figure appears as Kuan Kung and in *China Men* as Guan Goong. Roberts translates his name as Kuan Yu (*Three Kingdoms*), the historical personage from whom the god derives. Elsewhere, I adopt the transliteration of Chinese names as they appear in the various translations I have consulted, even though they may be inconsistent with one another.

18.   See, for example, Le Anne Schreiber's comment that "too often [Wittman] is just a windbag" (9); Nicci Gerrard's assertion that "Chinatown speech and its stereotypes collide and allusions accelerate until *Tripmaster Monkey* loses the downward drag of plot" (28); or the remark of Anne Tyler, who is otherwise favorable: "at other times the effect is exhausting— much as if that 23-year-old had taken up residence in our living room, staying way too long . . . and wearing us out with his exuberance" (46).

19.   See Malini Johar Schueller's argument that ethnicity is linguistically constructed— that is, a matter of discursivity (73–74). Schueller is attempting to gainsay essentialist defini- tions of ethnicity, and her argument about the relations between cultural discourse and iden- tity provides important theoretical support for thinking about Wittman's—and Kingston's— capacity to create cultural memory out of textualized remainders.

Works Cited

Canby, Vincent. Rev. of *The Saragossa Manuscript*. *New York Times Film Reviews, 1971–1972*. New York: New York Times and Arno, 1973. 247.

Davis, Natalie Zemon, and Randolph Starn. Introduction. *Memory and Counter-Memory*. Special issue of *Representations* 26 (Spring 1989): 1–6.

Docherty, Thomas. *Reading (Absent) Character: Towards a Theory of Characterization in Fiction*. Oxford: Clarendon, 1983.

Eighteen Songs of a Nomad Flute: The Story of Lady Wen-chi. Intro. and trans. Robert A. Rorex and Wen Fong. New York: Metropolitan Museum of Art, 1974. N. pag.

Frye, Joanne S. "*The Woman Warrior:* Claiming Narrative Power, Recreating Female Selfhood." *Faith of a (Woman) Writer*. Ed. Alice Kessler-Harris and William McBrien. New York: Greenwood, 1988. 293–301.

Gerrard, Nicci. "Wittman Ah Sing." Rev. of *Tripmaster Monkey*, by Maxine Hong Kingston. *New Statesman and Society* 2 (25 Aug. 1989): 28.

Hsia, C. T. *The Classic Chinese Novel: A Critical Introduction*. New York: Columbia UP, 1968.

Hu chia shih pa p'ai. Ed. Nanjing Museum. N.p.: Shanghai People's Art [1961]. N. pag.

Hutcheon, Linda. *A Poetics of Postmodernism: History, Theory, Fiction*. New York: Routledge, 1988.

Kingston, Maxine Hong. *China Men*. New York: Knopf, 1980.

———. "The Coming Book." *The Writer on Her Work*. Ed. Janet Sternburg. New York: Nor- ton, 1980. 181–85.

———. "Cultural Mis-readings by American Reviewers." *Asian and Western Writers in Dia- logue: New Cultural Identities*. Ed. Guy Amirthanayagan. London: Macmillan, 1982. 55–65.

———. "Eccentric Memories: A Conversation with Maxine Hong Kingston." With Paula Rabinowitz. *Michigan Quarterly Review* 26.1 (Winter 1987): 177–87.

———. Interview. *Women Writers of the West Coast: Speaking of Their Lives and Careers*. Ed. Mari- lyn Yalom. Interview by Arturo Islas. Santa Barbara: Capra, 1983. 11–19.

———. "A *MELUS* Interview: Maxine Hong Kingston." With Marilyn Chin. *MELUS* 16.4 (Winter 1989–90): 57–74.

———. "Moving Images: From Shao-lin to Woman Warrior." Keynote address. U of Wiscon- sin, Madison. 2 Apr. 1987.

————. "This Is the Story I Heard: A Conversation with Maxine Hong Kingston and Earll Kingston." With Phyllis Hoge Thompson. *Biography* 6.1 (Winter 1983): 1–12.

————. *Tripmaster Monkey: His Fake Book.* New York: Knopf, 1989.

————. *The Woman Warrior: Memoirs of a Girlhood among Ghosts.* New York: Knopf, 1977.

LaCapra, Dominick. *History and Criticism.* Ithaca: Cornell UP, 1985.

Li, David Leiwei. "The Naming of a Chinese American 'I': Cross-Cultural Significations in *The Woman Warrior.*" *Criticism* 30.4 (Fall 1988): 497–515.

Lin, Patricia. "Clashing Constructs of Reality: Reading Maxine Hong Kingston's *Tripmaster Monkey: His Fake Book* as Indigenous Ethnography." *Reading the Literatures of Asian America.* Ed. Shirley Geok-lin Lim and Amy Ling. Philadelphia: Temple UP, 1992. 333–48.

Lin, Tai-yi, trans. and ed. *Flowers in the Mirror.* By Li Ju-chen. Berkeley: U of California P, 1965.

Lo Kuan-chung. *Three Kingdoms.* Trans. and ed. Moss Roberts. New York: Pantheon, 1976.

Ma, Y. W., and Joseph S. M. Lau. *Traditional Chinese Stories: Themes and Variations.* New York: Columbia UP, 1978.

Mink, Louis O. "Narrative Form as a Cognitive Instrument." *The Writing of History: Literary Form and Historical Understanding.* Ed. Robert H. Canary and Henry Kozicki. Madison: U of Wisconsin P, 1978. 129–49.

Schreiber, Le Anne. "The Big, Big Show of Wittman Ah Sing." Rev. of *Tripmaster Monkey,* by Maxine Hong Kingston. *New York Times Book Review* 23 Apr. 1989: 9.

Schueller, Malini Johar. "Theorizing Ethnicity and Subjectivity: Maxine Hong Kingston's *Tripmaster Monkey* and Amy Tan's *The Joy Luck Club.*" *Genders* 15 (Winter 1992): 72–85.

Scott, Dorothea Hayward. *Chinese Popular Literature and the Child.* Chicago: American Library Association, 1980.

Shih, Nai-an. *Water Margin.* 2 vols. Trans. J. H. Jackson. Hong Kong: Commercial, 1976.

Sledge, Linda Ching. "Oral Tradition in Kingston's *China Men.*" *Redefining American Literary History.* Ed. A. LaVonne Brown Ruoff and Jerry W. Ward, Jr. New York: MLA, 1990. 142–54.

Smith, Barbara Herrnstein. "Narrative Versions, Narrative Theories." *On Narrative.* Ed. W. J. T. Mitchell. Chicago: U of Chicago P, 1981. 209–32.

Takaki, Ronald. *Strangers from a Different Shore: A History of Asian Americans.* Boston: Little Brown, 1989.

Tyler, Anne. "Manic Monologue." Rev. of *Tripmaster Monkey,* by Maxine Hong Kingston. *New Republic* 200 (17 Apr. 1989): 44–46.

Waley, Arthur, trans. *Chinese Poems.* London: Allen, 1946.

Warnock, Mary. *Memory.* London: Faber, 1987.

White, Hayden. "The Historical Text as Literary Artifact." *The Writing of History: Literary Form and Historical Understanding.* Ed. Robert H. Canary and Henry Kozicki. Madison: U of Wisconsin P, 1978. 41–62.

Wu Ch'eng-en. *Monkey.* Trans. and ed. Arthur Waley. New York: John Day, 1943.

REVIEWS OF
THE WOMAN WARRIOR
◆

In Defiance of 2 Worlds

John Leonard

Those rumbles you hear on the horizon are the big guns of autumn lining up, the howitzers of Vonnegut and Updike and Cheever and Mailer, the books that will be making loud noises for the next several months. But listen: this week a remarkable book has been quietly published; it is one of the best I've read in years.

"The Woman Warrior" is itself anything but quiet. It is fierce intelligence, all sinew, prowling among the emotions. As a portrait of village life in pre-Mao China, it is about as sentimental as Celine. As an account of growing up female and Chinese-American in California, in a laundry of course, it is antinostalgic: It burns the fat right out of the mind. As a dream—of the "female avenger"—it is dizzying, elemental, a poem turned into a sword.

For Maxine Hong Kingston, who was born in Stockton, Calif., there are two sets of ghosts. One set is Chinese legends, traditions, folklore, and always the unwanted girl-child. The other set is Western, American, barbarian, the machine-myths of the Occident. Somewhere in between, like the poet Ts'ai Yen, she is a hostage. And it isn't clear whether there is a place for her to return to, with her songs "from the savage lands."

"The Warrior Woman" traffics back and forth between sets of ghosts, re-imagining the past with such dark beauty, such precision and anger and sadness, that you feel you have saddled the Tao dragon and see all through the fiery eye of God. Then, suddenly, you are dumped into the mundane, into scenes so carefully observed, so balanced on a knife-edge of hope and humiliation, that you don't know whether to laugh or cry. Other writers come to mind—Garcia Marquez, who also knows how to dress myth up in living flesh: or, thinking about warrior women, Monique Witting, if she had a sense of humor and before she lapsed into balderdash.

But this shuttling, on an electric line of prose, between fantasy and specificity, is wonderfully original. I can't remember when a young writer walked up to and into every important scene in a book and dealt with it outright, as Mrs. Kingston does, without any evasions whatsoever. Or an old writer, for that matter: they have their avoidance tricks. It wearies a writer always having to be in the best form, compromising the least with difficult material, unruly characters. It doesn't weary Mrs. Kingston. And Brave Orchid, the mother to end all mothers in this book, is more real to me than most of the people I see every day.

Who is Maxine Hong Kingston? Nobody at Knopf seems to know. They have never laid eyes on her. She lives in Honolulu, nicely situated between Occident and Orient, with a husband and small son. She teaches English and creative writing. There is no one more qualified to teach English and creative writing.

Ghosts

DIANE JOHNSON

Autobiography, by far the more durable tradition, has never been honored for art the way fiction has, presumably because it lacks the requisite property of "invention." But it might be argued that to impose significant form on the chaotic materials of life lived, instead of fashioning them from the more restricted, more determined, more orthodox contents of the imagination, or from the more restrictive conventions of fictional genres, requires a superior faculty of invention, or at least the grace and clearheadedness of an inventor. The artist writing his memoir is in double jeopardy; first he must lead the risky life worth reading, must come through it and face in retrospect the awful disparity between what it meant and what he had intended. Then he must make a fiction of it, a work that has many or most of the formal properties of fiction.

Autobiography, that is, requires some strategy of self-dramatization. It normally contains, as in fiction, a crisis and denouement, and it appears, very generally, that the form of this crisis in autobiography by men has tended to be different from that of women, and that fully fictionalized dramatizations tend to be different still. Men, for instance in the great nineteenth-century autobiographies (Mill, Carlyle, Newman, and countless others), recount disillusion and depression, followed by recovery and action. In fiction this is, curiously, often dramatized as crime, as in much of Dickens.

In writing, as in mourning, it sometimes appears that women have reserved or been assigned the duty of expressing human resentment, leaving men to fashion the consolations. Perhaps this is division of labor, rather than native querulousness; but it has meant that wisdom and "adjustment" are often qualities of the masculine tone, and women since Margery Kempe have tended to write in tones of protest and madness. The crisis is of silence or withdrawal, and is dramatized as "being silenced."

There are exceptions, of course, but three recent memoirs, by N. Scott Momaday, Maxine Hong Kingston, and Carobeth Laird, reflect these sexual distinctions and also suggest that the distinction between what is autobio-

From *The New York Review of Books,* 3 Feb. 1977: 19–20, 29. Reprinted with permission from *The New York Review of Books.* Copyright © 1977 Nyrev, Inc.

graphically true and fiction has become somewhat arbitrary; fiction and memoir have come to resemble each other more and more. Novelists make real historical figures speak to fictional characters. Memorialists dramatize the thoughts and speeches of their forefathers, as in a novel about them. The access of the autobiographer to dramatic techniques has allowed him to handle root meanings, the mysterious crises of spirit, even the intangibles of heritage more essentially, that is more truly, than he once could.

Ancestors in autobiographies seem really to belong there, unlike the fashionable gramps and grannies whose rather boring recurrence in contemporary fiction probably arises from the same nostalgic impulse. How much more immediate the sometimes baleful influence of real ancestors than the academic caperings of those prehistorical ancestors whose tribal arrangements and religious rituals we are asked so often lately to believe have determined our "reading readiness," our attitudes toward violence, to motherhood, and so on.

Momaday is an American Indian man, and Kingston a Chinese-American woman. Both explore the way in which their ethnic traditions have made them as they are. The differences in tone between the two memoirs, the one nostalgic and approving, the other vital and angry, reflect, no doubt, cultural differences, but also perhaps sexual differences.

How manly is this reverent sense of the past bequeathing to the present the special intention that the present shall include oneself. But what of malevolent ancestors who harry the living and blight the life of the young American with their old ways of terror? Maxine Hong Kingston's memoir of a Chinese-American girlhood presents another side, perhaps the female side, of growing up in a tradition, perhaps any tradition. Women perform for any society the service of maladjustment that Kingston here brilliantly performs for the society of Chinese immigrants in California. She, like Momaday (and unlike most Chinese-Americans), fulfills an American pattern by moving away from an ethnic tradition the distance required to memorialize and cherish it; but she is unlike Momaday because her ancestors have hurt and haunted her.

The little girl grows up in Stockton's Chinatown surrounded by the ghostly similar Americans and other foreigners, and by the many ghosts her family has brought with them from China. There is the ghost of an aunt who drowned herself in a well after the people of her village savaged the house, protesting her illegitimate pregnancy. Afterward the family killed her name, so little Maxine, who hears the story from her mother Brave Orchid, does not know the name of that ghost. Then there is the sitting ghost who sat on Brave Orchid's stomach all one night; and the ghosts of all the murdered women and little female babies left out to die back in China.

In Maxine's imagination she is herself a ghost, a swordswoman, a female avenger of these cruel murders. She has been given hints of female power, and also explicit messages of female powerlessness, from her mother, who in China had been a doctor and now toiled in the family laundry where they wore masks and burned candles to avoid "the germs that fumed out of the ghosts' clothes." "She said I would grow up a wife and a slave, but she taught me the story of the warrior woman, Fa Mu Lan. I would have to grow up a warrior woman."

The warrior woman of Maxine's imagination avenges with her sword the injustices that a real little California girl can only throw tantrums about. When other Chinese said, "Feeding girls is feeding cowbirds," she would scream and cry.

"What's the matter with her?"

"I don't know. Bad, I guess. You know how girls are. 'There's no profit in raising girls. Better to raise geese than girls.' " In China, she has heard, girls were often sold by their families. The Chinese word for the female "I" is "slave."

"What do you want to be when you grow up, little girl?" "A lumberjack in Oregon"—that is, American and a man. She was glad to be a bad little girl: "Isn't a bad girl almost a boy?"

> I read in an anthropology book that Chinese say, "Girls are necessary too"; I have never heard the Chinese I know make this concession. Perhaps it was a saying in another village. I refuse to shy my way anymore through our Chinatown, which tasks me with the old sayings and the stories.

Messages which for Western girls have been confusingly obscured by the Victorian pretense of woman worship are in the Chinese tradition elevated to epigram: "When fishing for treasures in the flood, be careful not to pull in girls."

Like many other women, Kingston does not wish to reject female nature so much as the female condition, and at that she would reserve the female biological destiny: "marriage and childbirth strengthen the swordswoman, who is not a maid like Joan of Arc." But she is not without a sense of its difficulty:

> Do the women's work; then do more work, which will become ours too. No husband of mine will say, "I could have been a drummer, but I had to think about the wife and kids. You know how it is." Nobody supports me; . . . I am not loved enough to be supported. That I am not a burden has to compensate for the sad envy when I look at women loved enough to be supported. Even now China wraps double binds around my feet.

But of course these are the bindings on every woman's feet. In the vivid particularity of her experience, and with the resources of a considerable art, Kingston reaches to the universal qualities of female condition and female anger that the bland generalities of social science and the merely factual history cannot describe.

Women may reject the culture that rejects them, but such brave and rare disassociations are not without serious cost. Kingston is dealing here with the fears and rebellions that recur in much women's writing, often displaced in other ways, and dramatized or actually experienced as suicide, catatonia, hysteria, anorexia—maladies common to many female protagonists, both fictional and alive, from Brontë heroines to Sylvia Plath. Kingston recounts such a gesture of protest in her own life, a period of refusal to play culture's game.

In a strange scene, she tortures another little girl in the bathroom after school, a passive little Chinese girl who never speaks. Maxine pulls her hair, twists her nose and ears, pinches her cheeks, derides, berates her. The other child weeps but will not speak even so, goading Maxine to greater desperation and fear:

> You don't see I'm trying to help you out, do you? Do you want to be like this, dumb (do you know what dumb means?), your whole life? Don't you ever want to be a cheerleader? Or a pompon girl? What are you going to do for a living? Yeah, you're going to have to work because you can't be a housewife. Somebody has to marry you before you can be a housewife. And you, you are a plant. Do you know that? That's all you are if you don't talk. . . .

But the other child never speaks, and in her silence is triumphant. This scene has many fictional analogues, for instance Susan Yankowitz's recent novel *Silent Witness,* where the woman protagonist is a mute, accused of a crime, and is raped by the other women in prison. In life, the protests she cannot make the other girl utter are Maxine's own, and consume her; she must spend "the next eighteen months sick in bed with a mysterious illness. There was no pain and no symptoms, though the middle line on my left palm broke in two." She herself recognizes the tradition of this illness, its relation to women in general: "I lived like the Victorian recluses I read about." One thinks of Catherine Earnshaw in *Wuthering Heights,* consuming herself in her willful decline until death. But Maxine thinks her malady is particularly Chinese, too. In all the Chinese households she knows, women fall into implacable protesting silences; every family has its "crazy woman," and she is afraid she is hers.

The Chinese-Americans are a notably unassimilated culture. It is not unusual in San Francisco to find fourth- or fifth-generation American-born Chinese who speak no English. Generations have not eased their mistrust of American culture, and they will not tell Americans certain things about theirs. Once Maxine's teachers, concerned because her school paintings are entirely covered in black paint, call her parents in, but there can be no communication, only in part because the parents speak no English. The parents would say nothing anyway, because in China, "the parents and teachers of criminals were executed." All the Chinese children in the class laugh at one of their number who does not know his father's name, pretending to think, as the teacher did, that he was stupid, but knowing, really, that a Chinese child does not know his father's name. They pitilessly abandon anyone who attracts the special attention of the ghosts. Their own parents have given them fake names to say.

There is much Americans would not know. There, in Stockton in the 1940s, the mother was cooking them raccoons, snakes, garden snails, turtles, hawks, city pigeons, wild ducks and geese, catfish, a skunk, flowers from the garden, weeds. Chinese people began coming to California before the gold rush, but still the names, the food, the shape of the parapets, defying the earthquake rules, remain Chinese.

But since the revolution in China, many of these people are being forced to relinquish a dream of someday returning there. Torn between the reality of the known America and the mysteries of the new China, many make their peace with the idea of staying. To Kingston this was welcome because it would reduce the likelihood of being sold.

> While the adults wept over the letters about the neighbors gone berserk turning Communist . . . I was secretly glad. As long as the aunts kept disappearing and the uncles dying after unspeakable tortures, my parents would prolong their Gold Mountain [California] stay. We could start spending our fare money on a car and chairs, a stereo.

They do. With the loss of the old, the new becomes more possible. Her generation turns with less reluctance toward America, let the ancestors scold as they were used to do. Third Grand-Uncle is in the habit of denouncing all the girls in the family:

> "Maggots! Where are my grandsons? . . . Eat, maggots. . . . Look at the maggots chew."
> "He does that at every meal," the girls [his granddaughters] told us in English.
> "Yeah," we said. "Our old man hates us too. What assholes."

* * * *

The Mysterious West
[and Diane Johnson's Reply]

JEFFERY PAUL CHAN AND DIANE JOHNSON

To the Editors:

How clever of Diane Johnson ("Ghosts," *NYR,* February 3) to stumble on a second-generation Chinese-American writing English well in the unassimilated Chinese-American enclave where even "fourth- or fifth-generation American-born Chinese" speak no English, much less write. Johnson sheds about as much critical light on Kingston's *Woman Warrior* as a Warner Oland revival flickering in the eyeball of a dead white missionary. Well, nearly dead, these moribund missionaries sustain the egotistical hallucination that their moral universe is after all universal. "Kingston reaches to the universal qualities of female condition and female anger that the bland generalities of social science and the merely factual history cannot describe." It's Pearl Buck shaping converts in the oriental orphanage of her imagination. Never mind history, Johnson has uncovered a feminist. Thus she can conveniently ignore what are key historical themes in Kingston's book, themes that help shape that mongrel sensibility Johnson admires and incidentally touch on the major currents of Chinese-American literary development since Sui Sin Far published short stories about the Chinese-American communities in Seattle, San Francisco, and Los Angeles at the turn of the century. But I can't expect Ms. Johnson to know much about Chinese-American literature since she knows nothing about Chinese-American society. But the utter stupidity, the button-popping arrogance of her own bland generalities leave me depressed at the state of university teaching faculties here in California. Ms. Johnson teaches at the University of California at Davis, a facility currently dismantling its Asian American Studies Program. I would hope she enrolls for a class. There's still time. If she did, she might begin to understand what are statewide legendary facts of California and Chinese-American life.

The Chinese-Americans are a notably unassimilated culture. It is not unusual in San Francisco to find fourth- or fifth-generation American-born Chinese

From *The New York Review of Books,* 28 Apr. 1977: 41. Reprinted with permission from *The New York Review of Books.* Copyright © 1977 Nyrev, Inc.

who speak no English. Generations have not eased their mistrust of American culture, and they will not tell Americans certain things about theirs.

In California, it is the law that children attend school. My second-generation parents attended public school. They spoke English to their classmates, to their teachers. My grandparents, like most Chinese-Americans in California, worked at jobs most Chinese-Americans were allowed to take in restaurants, laundries, barbershops, grocery stores requiring fairly aggressive verbal contact with English-speaking whites. It is more the case that Chinese-Americans in the second and third generation speak no Chinese. Common sense would inform Ms. Johnson that fourth- and fifth-generation American-born Chinese speak English.

Common sense would also inform Ms. Johnson that any society of immigrants separated from their home culture by two world wars, two social revolutions, plagues and famine only fear the threat of mass deportation. Mass deportation was a distinct possibility in the minds of my parents' generation whose peers might reach back another three generations when mass deportation was a possibility. The Chinese in California effected illegal entries into the United States, maintained illegal property holdings; Chinese-Americans in California were unable to represent themselves in courts of law; a Chinese-American woman marrying a Chinese citizen lost her citizenship. What is it that Ms. Johnson would like to know about American culture? What would she like to know about Chinese-American culture? There are no secrets here, these are historical facts. There is an explicit sociology in the development of Chinese-American writings, and they can be gleaned from a cursory examination of public records, a matter of public law. A Chinese-American who mistrusts the society of whites has come to a just and proper conclusion about the nature of reality. A Chinese-American who feels uneasy about segregated schooling, real estate covenants protecting all-white neighborhoods, employers who hire Chinese-American women to fill two categories under affirmative action mandates, is assimilated and knowledgeable of American culture. Notably assimilated.

The fact that Kingston's publisher (Knopf) published *Woman Warrior* as "memoirs," as biography rather than fiction (which it obviously is) may have encouraged Ms. Johnson's racist generalizations. A white reading public will rave over ethnic biography while ignoring a Chinese-American's literary art. (It puts me in mind of the reviews granted Frank Chin's *Chickencoop Chinaman,* a play produced by the American Place Theater in 1973. Nearly unanimous: "I never heard a Chinese talk English like that.") Now why that is I am sure I do not know. But it makes me suspicious. Engenders the feeling that perhaps Chinese-Americans have no authority over the language and culture that expresses our sensibility best—at the same time, assuring my assimilation.

That *The New York Review* would publish a review by a writer who knows nothing of Chinese-American society, not unlike a white publishing house distributing an obvious fiction for fact, is a complexity only assimilation can solve. Kingston, for example, mistranslates the word "ghosts." Chinese-Americans call whites *bok gwai,* white devils, as in demons, not ghosts. Ghosts of the dead are not *gwai,* though they could be. *Gwai* are inherently unfriendly. When Chinese-Americans call a white person *bok gwai,* it is an insult. If that person is liked, the term *lo fan* is applied. A *lo fan* is a foreigner. Kingston uses the word ghost in the popular white Christian sense of the word, not Chinese-American. The difference between *lo fan* and *bok gwai* is as obvious to any Chinese-American as the difference between "mister" and "asshole." Of course, it would be difficult to subtitle "memoirs of a girlhood among assholes."

Too, Kingston may mislead naïve white readers when she suggests that our generations go nameless in America. In fact, no Chinese-American parent would allow their children to believe any relative had no name. The thought is ridiculous. The Chinese-American custom of being an illegal entry, a paper descendant of Hom when you are really a Wong, was simple and common-place. A son or daughter simply claimed an "American" name and a "Chinese" name, taking advantage of the white Christian missionary invention of the double name system to break down the hold of Chinese language and culture on converts. If Kingston did not know her father's name as a child, her experience is unique. She has created a wonderful, an artful fiction drawn from a sensibility shaped by a white culture predisposed to fanciful caricatures of a Shangri-la four thousand years wise, but feudally binding.

I suspect a number of Chinese-Americans today may regard things Chinese as Kingston and Johnson suggest, a difference in the quality of assimilation without history. Such stereotypes are, however, chinoiserie, a furniture style adapted for the silver screen.

Jeffery Paul Chan

Chairperson
Asian American Studies Program
San Francisco State University
San Francisco, California

Diane Johnson *replies:*

I'm not sure whether Mr. Jeffery Chan's chief complaint is directed to me or to Mrs. Kingston, for slyly writing a memoir, a form which he can neither dismiss as fiction nor quarrel with as fact. Mostly he just seems to wish that she had written differently, as when he criticizes her translation of "*gwai*" as "ghosts" (which is certainly given in the Chinese-English dictionary as one of the meanings of "*gwai,*"), because he would have preferred "white devils." Mrs. Kingston is certainly entitled to decide which meanings she intends.

It is true that I, like most other admirers of *The Woman Warrior*, am a general reader, not a specialist in Asian studies, and that is one reason I was particularly interested to find out what it was like to have grown up a Chinese-American girl—an experience I cannot have had, and neither can Mr. Chan. He deplores her "mongrel" sensibility but admits that "a number of Chinese-Americans today may regard things Chinese as Kingston and Johnson suggest," that is, that her view of things has validity for many others, if not for him. He could write his own memoir, of course—but would he believe that non-Chinese people could understand it? My own remarks, in any case, were not about Chinese-American culture but about themes in autobiographies by women. I quite understand that Mr. Chan would have preferred another perspective, but that is as it happens.

As to the matter of assimilation, Mr. Chan seems to imagine that I intended to denigrate where I was simply noting what I have never before heard disputed: that Chinese-Americans have retained considerable cultural solidarity, and, in particular, have remained a cohesive language group. That is the reason election ballots in California are provided in Chinese as well as in English and Spanish. By his account, Mr. Chan's own family has come to this country recently enough to profit from, or suffer from—I am not sure of his point—accelerated processes of acculturation, but the descendants of the original nineteenth-century immigrants include people now in their eighties who, whether they can speak English or not, evidently prefer not to or refuse to, as doctors, hospitals, community workers, even the phone company all attest.

"Ghosts" of Girlhood Lift Obscure Book to Peak of Acclaim

NAN ROBERTSON

"From afar I can believe my family loves me fundamentally. They only say 'When fishing for treasures in the flood, be careful not to pull in girls,' because that is what one says about daughters. But I watched such words come out of my own mother's and father's mouths. . . . And I had to get out of hating range."-From "The Woman Warrior."

Maxine Ting Ting Hong Kingston, now 36, lives in Honolulu with her husband and 13-year-old son, 2,500 miles away from the stifling Chinese laundry and the little Victorian house in Stockton, Calif., where she grew up.

She is far from the ghosts that haunted her childhood: the ghosts of ancestors and taboo and tradition her parents brought from China; the pale Caucasian ghosts all around in the inexplicable land called America.

Maxine Hong Kingston's first book, a memoir-fantasy that mingles fact and dreams, is called "The Woman Warrior: Memoirs of a Girlhood Among Ghosts." It crept on the scene last fall, with almost no advance ballyhoo and a small printing, and left reviewers stunned and admiring. "Brilliant," "thrilling," "a poem turned into a sword," they said. It has become a best seller and has just won the National Book Critics Circle award as the best nonfiction book of 1976, upsetting the expected winner, Irving Howe's "World of Our Fathers."

"Who is Maxine Kingston?" a critic asked when her book came out. "Nobody at Knopf seems to know. They have never laid eyes on her." Last month they did.

Mrs. Kingston journeyed from Honolulu for the awards ceremony and to see her family, parents and five younger brothers and sisters, scattered from California to South Carolina.

From The *New York Times*. New York: New York Times Company, 12 Feb. 1977: 26. Copyright © 1977 by the New York Times Company. Reprinted by permission of the New York Times Company.

Tiny, Like Charlotte Brontë

She came out of a snowstorm into her publisher's offices for an interview, a tiny thing with masses of black hair already threaded with white, muffled in scarf and cap and oversized coat. She is 4 feet 9 inches tall. "Charlotte Brontë was 4 feet 9", she said, drawing herself up proudly and with a grin.

The book is dedicated to her father and mother, who cannot read English.

"It is part of a product of over a quarter of a century of writing," Mrs. Kingston said, "I began writing when I was 9. The day was very clear to me. I was in fourth grade and all of a sudden this poem started coming out of me. On and on I went, oblivious to everything, and when it was over I had written 30 verses. It is a bad habit that doesn't go away."

It was also her escape, as were the fantasies that transformed her into Fa Mu Lan of her mother's "talk-stories"—the woman warrior who fought gloriously in battle and became a legend to the Chinese people centuries ago.

Mrs. Kingston's mother, Brave Orchid, leaps from the pages—infuriating, indomitable, full of admonitory tales. A doctor and midwife in China, she followed her husband years later to the United States in 1939, bearing six children after the age of 45. Her lot was drudgery in the laundry: "You have no idea how much I have fallen coming to America," she told her daughter.

A Sullen, Unruly Child

Brave Orchid was often cruel to Maxine, a girl-child in an immigrant village culture, and worse, sullen, troubled and unruly. When her parents or neighbors would say, "Feeding girls is feeding cowbirds" she would thrash on the floor and scream so hard she could not stop. At her American school, she did not speak up in class for three years, and once bullied a smaller girl, who did not talk at all, shrieking "Talk! Talk!" at the bruised and sobbing child, as if a single word would free them both.

And yet the family was there, strong and rich in history and an imaginative language. Maxine "wanted to get away—to see what else there was. I had a great sense of curiosity. I would make friends with odd-looking kids with red hair. The Negroes—I wanted to get inside their houses. I would follow them home after school. I wanted to explore everything—everything," she said.

Talk of Poetry

Her working method when she was doing the book was to "talk-story" to herself, as her mother had done. "Sometimes I told sections to myself in Chinese and then would do it in English on the typewriter to get the rhythm and power. Americans are knocked out by Mao's poetic images, like 'running dog' or 'paper tiger.' We all talk like that, in colorful poetic images."

She said of Brave Orchid: "My mother is the creative one—the one with the visions and the stories to tell. I'm the technician. She's the great inspiration. I never realized it until I finished the book."

One of the book's climaxes comes when Maxine is in high school and lashes out at her mother in a brutal, liberating tirade in which she establishes her own, tremulous identity. "I'm going away. . . . Do you know what the Teacher Ghosts say about me? They say I'm smart. . . . I won't let you turn me into a slave or a wife. . . . At college I'll have the people I like for friends."

She went off to Berkeley and immediately experienced "terrible culture shock. I went to class and was sick for two weeks after I got there. I didn't understand what anything was," she said. "I got terrible grades at first. Even my writing didn't save me."

The reason, she said, was that for the first time she did not have her big, vital, "exhilarating" family close around her, no matter what bad times there had been.

By her second year she had adapted and found college life exciting. Later she met and fell in love with Earl Kingston, a student who had spent a two-year Pacific hitch in the Navy. They became involved in the peace movement. At Berkeley and thereafter, "we marched and we went to meetings. It was the most political time of our lives. I saw Vietnam as a war against Asians," she said. But the movement languished and sickened, and many of her friends turned to drugs.

LOVE HAWAIIAN ATMOSPHERE

In 1967, they decided to get away from the mainland with their son Joseph, then 3 years old. They moved to Hawaii, but, they found, "you don't escape America anywhere."

Nor did they get away from the war. There were convoys of trucks with soldiers, "shooting at target practice up in those beautiful mountains, doing their war games;" war material being shipped to Vietnam, bodies being shipped home.

"Life is a lot easier now that the Vietnamese war is over," Mrs. Kingston said. She and her husband have always loved the "airy, light feeling" of Hawaii. She now teaches English and creative writing at the Mid-Pacific Institute in Honolulu. Earl Kingston is an actor in a touring company that puts on festivals and shows in parks and schools.

The author has had little published before "The Woman Warrior": a poem printed in a "little anthology," and an essay in the "English Journal" put out by the National Council of Teachers of English. When her book was finished, she mailed off the manuscript to a list of New York literary agents. The third one, John Shaffner, agreed by mail to handle it.

Mrs. Kingston has told her mother that she, too, "talks-story" in her book. Brave Orchid—who, at the age of 80, was queuing up with men to demand a day's work in the tomato fields—already has an idea for her daughter's next book. What is it?

"She says I ought to write about discrimination in hiring."

RESPONSE TO REVIEWS OF
THE WOMAN WARRIOR

◆

Cultural Mis-readings by American Reviewers

Maxine Hong Kingston

When reading most of the reviews and critical analyses of *The Woman War-rior*, I have two reactions: I want to pat those critics on their backs, and I also giggle helplessly, shaking my head. (Helpless giggles turn less frequently into sobs as one gets older.) The critics did give my book the National Book Critics Circle Award; and they reviewed it in most of the major magazines and newspapers, thus publicising it enough to sell. Furthermore, they rarely gave it an unfavourable review. I pat them on the back for recognising good writing—but, unfortunately, I suspect most of them of perceiving its quality in an unconscious sort of way; they praise the wrong things.

Now, of course, I expected *The Woman Warrior* to be read from the women's lib angle and the Third World angle, the *Roots* angle; but it is up to the writer to transcend trendy categories. What I did not foresee was the critics measuring the book and me against the stereotype of the exotic, inscrutable, mysterious oriental. About two-thirds of the reviews did this. In some cases, I must admit, it was only a line or a marring word that made my stomach turn, the rest of the review being fairly sensible. You might say I am being too thin-skinned; but a year ago I had really believed that the days of gross stereotyping were over, that the 1960s, the Civil Rights movement, and the end of the war in Vietnam had enlightened America, if not in deeds at least in manners. Pridefully enough, I believed that I had written with such power that the reality and humanity of my characters would bust through any stereotypes of them. Simple-mindedly, I wore a sweat-shirt for the dust-jacket photo, to deny the exotic. I had not calculated how blinding stereotyping is, how stupefying. The critics who said how the book was good because it was, or was not, like the oriental fantasy in their heads might as well have said how weak it was, since it in fact did not break through that fantasy.

Here are some examples of exotic-inscrutable-mysterious-oriental reviewing:

Margaret Manning in *The Boston Globe*: "Mythic forces flood the book. Echoes of the Old Testament, fairy tales, the *Golden Bough* are here, but they have their own strange and brooding atmosphere inscrutably foreign, oriental."

From *Asian and Western Writers in Dialogue: New Cultural Identities*, edited by Guy Amirthanayagam. Copyright 1982 by Macmillan Ltd. Reprinted with the permission of Macmillan Ltd.

Barbara Burdick in the *Peninsula Herald:* "No other people have remained so mysterious to Westerners as the inscrutable Chinese. Even the word China brings to mind ancient rituals, exotic teas, superstitions, silks and fire-breathing dragons."

Helen Davenport of the Chattanooga *News–Free Press:* "At her most obscure, though, as when telling about her dream of becoming a fabled 'woman warrior' the author becomes as inscrutable as the East always seems to the West. In fact, this book seems to reinforce the feeling that 'East is East and West is West and never the twain shall meet,' or at any rate it will probably take more than one generation away from China."

Alan McMahan in the Fort Wayne *Journal–Gazette:* "The term 'inscrutable' still applies to the rank and file of Chinese living in their native land." (I do not understand. Does he mean Chinese Americans? What native land? Does he mean America? My native land is America.)

Joan Henriksen in a clipping without the newspaper's name: "Chinese-Americans always 'looked'—at least to this WASP observer—as if they exactly fit the stereotypes I heard as I was growing up. They were 'inscrutable.' They were serene, withdrawn, neat, clean and hard-workers. *The Woman Warrior,* because of this stereotyping, is a double delight to read." She goes on to say how nicely the book diverges from the stereotype.

How dare they call their ignorance our inscrutability!

The most upsetting example of this school of reviewing is Michael T. Malloy's unfavourable review in *The National Observer:* "The background is exotic, but the book is in the mainstream of American feminist literature." He disliked the book *because* it is part of the mainstream. He is saying, then, that I am not to step out of the "exotic" role, not to enter the mainstream. One of the most deadly weapons of stereotyping is the double bind, damned-if-you-do-and-damned-if-you-don't.

I have a horrible feeling that it is not self-evident to many Caucasian Americans why these reviews are offensive. I find it sad and slow that I have to *explain*. Again. If I use my limited time and words to explain, I will never get off the ground. I will never get to fly.

To say we are inscrutable, mysterious, exotic denies us our common humanness, because it says that we are so different from a regular human being that we are by our nature intrinsically unknowable. Thus the stereotyper aggressively defends ignorance. *Nor* do we want to be called *not* inscrutable, exotic, mysterious. These are false ways of looking at us. We do not want to be measured by a false standard at all.

To call a people exotic freezes us into the position of being always alien—politically a most sensitive point with us because of the long history in America of the Chinese Exclusion Acts, the deportations, the law denying us citizenship when we have been part of America since its beginning. By giving the "oriental" (always Eastern, never *here*) inhuman, unexplainable qualities, the racist abrogates human qualities, and, carrying all this to extremes, finds it easier to lynch the Chinaman, bomb Japan, napalm Vietnam. "How amazing," they may as well be saying, "that she writes like a human being. How un-oriental." "I cannot understand her. It has to be her innate mystery." Blacks and women are making much better progress. I did not read any reviews of *Roots* that judged whether or not Alex Haley's characters ate watermelon or had rhythm. And there were only two cases I encountered of sexist stereotyping: one from my home-town paper, *The Stockton Record:* "Mrs. Kingston is a 36-year-old housewife and mother who teaches creative writing and English." The above was a news story on *The Woman Warrior* winning the National Book Critics Circle Award, so the paper might have described me as a writer. The other was *Bookshelf,* a journal of Asian Studies: "The highly acclaimed first book by a Chinese-American school-teacher."

How stubbornly Americans hang on to the oriental fantasy can be seen in their picking "The White Tigers" chapter as their favourite. Readers tell me it ought to have been the climax. But I put it at the beginning to show that the childish myth is past, not the climax we reach for. Also, "The White Tigers" is not a Chinese myth but one transformed by America, a sort of kung fu movie parody.

Another bothersome characteristic of the reviews is the ignorance of the fact that I am an American. I am an American writer, who, like other American writers, wants to write the great American novel. *The Woman Warrior* is an American book. Yet many reviewers do not see the American-ness of it, nor the fact of my own American-ness.

Bernice Williams Foley in the *Columbus Dispatch:*

> Her autobiographical story (in my opinion) is atypical of the relationship between Chinese parents and their American Chinese children whom I have known in New York City and Cincinnati. Moreover as a "foreign barbarian of low culture" living in China, I always sensed in the Chinese, whether they were our business friends or our servants, a feeling that the ancient cultural heritage of their Middle Kingdom—the Center of the Universe—was superior to ours . . . She rebels against the strict pattern of life inherited from old China and based on Confucius' moral teachings, which preserves the strength of the family's heritage, and which are the basis of Chinese ethics and virtues.

The headline for this article was "Rebellious Chinese Girl Rejects Ancient Heritage." Foley goes on to say that she does not find the book "likeable." Of course not. What she would like is the stereotype, the obedient-Confucian-Chinese-servant-businessman. (What is a "business friend" anyway?)

Kate Herriges in an ecstatically complimentary review in *The Boston Phoenix:* "Subtle, delicate yet sturdy, it [*The Woman Warrior*] is ineffably Chinese." No. No. No. Don't you hear the American slang? Don't you see the American settings? Don't you see the way the Chinese myths have been transmuted by America? No wonder the young Asian American writers are so relentlessly hip and slangy. (How I *do* like Jane Howard's phrase in her

Mademoiselle review: "Irrevocably Californian." I hope the thirty per cent of reviewers who wrote sensible pieces accept my apologies for not praising them sufficiently here.)

The Saturday News and Leader of Springfield, Missouri: "Maxine Ting Ting Hong Kingston is a Chinese woman, even though the place of her birth was Stockton, California." This does not make sense. *Because* I was born in Stockton, California, I *am* an American woman. I am also a Chinese American woman, but I am not a Chinese woman, never having travelled east of Hawaii, unless she means an "ethnic Chinese woman," in which case she should say so.

Rose Levine Isaacson, in the *Clarion–Ledger* of Jackson, Mississippi: ". . . the revelation of what it was like for a Chinese girl growing up." She tells of Chinese laundries she has seen as a child. Though I enjoy her childhood recollections, I cringe with embarrassment when she says, "We knew they lived in back of the laundry. . . ." That was one thing I always hated—that they *knew* we lived there when we owned a house.

Margaret E. Wiggs in the Fort Wayne *News Sentinel:* "The timid little Chinese girl in San Francisco . . . Clever girl, this little Chinese warrior." Ms. Wiggs does not know that as a kid I read "Blackhawk" comics, and was puzzled, then disgusted, that Chop Chop was the only Blackhawk who did not get to wear a uniform, was not handsome, not six feet tall, had buck teeth and a pigtail during World War II, wore a cleaver instead of a pistol in his belt, and never got to kiss the beautiful ladies. Blackhawk was always saying, "Very clever, these little Chinese."

I know headline writers are under time and space deadlines, but many of them did manage to leave the "American" in "Chinese American." Here are some exceptions: Malloy's article in *The National Observer:* "On Growing Up Chinese, Female and Bitter." *The Sunday Peninsula Herald:* "Memoir Penetrates Myths Around Chinese Culture." *The Baltimore Sun:* "Growing Up Female and Chinese." *The Cleveland Plain Dealer:* "A California-Chinese Girlhood." (I wouldn't mind "Chinese-Californian.") Harold C. Hill's article in a clipping without the newspaper's name: "Growing Up Chinese in America."

That we be called by our correct name is as important to Chinese Americans as it is to native Americans, Blacks and any American minority that needs to define itself on its own terms. We should have been smart like the Americans of Japanese Ancestry, whose name explicitly spells out their American citizenship. (Semantics, however, did not save the AJAs from the camps.) Chinese-American history has been a battle for recognition as Americans; we have fought hard for the right to legal American citizenship. Chinese are those people who look like us in Hong Kong, the People's Republic and Taiwan. Apparently many Caucasians in America do not know that a person born in the USA is automatically American, no matter how he or she may look. Now we do call ourselves Chinese, and we call ourselves Chinamen, but when we say, "I'm Chinese," it is in the context of differentiating ourselves from Japanese, for example. When we say we are Chinese, it is short for Chinese-

American or ethnic Chinese; the "American" is implicit. I had hoped that this was the usage of the reviews, but instead there is a carelessness, an unawareness.

As for "Chinaman," I think we had better keep that word for use amongst ourselves, though people here in Hawaii do use it with no denigrating overtones as in the popular name for Mokolii, "Chinaman's Hat." And lately, I have been thinking that we ought to leave out the hyphen in "Chinese-American," because the hyphen gives the word on either side equal weight, as if linking two nouns. It looks as if a Chinese-American has double citizenship, which is impossible in today's world. Without the hyphen, "Chinese" is an adjective and "American" a noun; a Chinese American is a type of American. (This idea about the hyphen is my own, and I have not talked to anyone else who has thought of it; therefore, it is a fine point, "typical" of no one but myself.)

I hope that the above explanation makes clear why I and other Chinese Americans felt a clunk of imperfection when reading Peter S. Beagle's and Jane Kramer's otherwise fine pieces in *Harper's Bookletter* and *The New York Times Book Review* respectively. Both gathered from the dust-jacket, and perhaps from my name, that I had "married an American." Chinese Americans read that and groaned, "Oh, no!" immediately offended. I guess Caucasian Americans need to be told why. After all, I *am* married to an American. But to say so in summing up my life implies these kinds of things: that I married someone different from myself, that I somehow became *more* American through marriage, and that marriage is the way to assimilation. The phrase is also too general. We suspect that they might mean, "She married a Caucasian." Too many people use those two words interchangeably, "American" and "Caucasian." In some ways, it is all right to say that I am "Chinese" or my husband is "American" if they did not stop there but go on to show what has been left out.

Another problem in the reviews is New York provincialism, which *The New Yorker* teased in one of their covers, which showed nothing west of the Rockies except Los Angeles and San Francisco. New Yorkers seem to think that all Chinese Americans in California live in San Francisco. Even my publisher did not manage to correct the dust-jacket copy completely, and part of it says I am writing about Stockton, and part says San Francisco. The book itself says that the Chinese Americans in the San Joaquin Valley town, which is its setting, are probably very different from the city slickers in San Francisco. I describe a long drive *away from* San Francisco to the smaller valley town, which I do not name; I describe Steinbeck country. Yet, *New West,* which published an excerpt, prefaced it by twice calling it a San Francisco story—ironically, it was the very chapter about the San Joaquin valley. How geographically confused their readers must have been. *New West* is a California magazine; so the theory about New York provincialism applies to more places than New York.

The New Yorker. "A Picture of nineteen-forties and fifties Chinese-American life in San Francisco. . . ."

The Fort Wayne News Sentinel: "The timid little Chinese girl in San Francisco. . . ."

The Boston Globe: ". . . the "foreigner-ghosts" of San Francisco. . . ."

Newsweek: "The most interesting story in *The Woman Warrior* tells how Brave Orchid brought her sister, Moon Orchid, from China to San Francisco."

Sometimes you just have to laugh because there really is no malice, and they are trying their best. *Viva* magazine published the "No Name Woman" chapter with a full-page colour illustration of Japanese maidens at the window; they wear kimonos, lacquered hair-dos, and through the window is lovely, snow-capped Mt Fuji. Surprise, Asian brothers and sisters! We may as well think of ourselves as Asian Americans because we are all alike anyway. I did not feel angry until I pointed out the Japanese picture to some Caucasians who said, "It doesn't matter." (And yet, if an Asian American movement that includes Chinese, Japanese, Filipinos is possible, then solidarity with Caucasian Americans is possible. I for one was raised with vivid stories about Japanese killing ten million Chinese, including my relatives, and was terrified of Japanese, especially AJAs, the only ones I had met.)

It appears that when the critics looked at my book, they heard a jingle in their heads, "East is east and west is west. . . ." Yes, there were lazy literary critics who actually used that stupid Kipling British-colonial cliché to get a handle on my writing:

"East Meets West," said *Newsweek's* headline. (*Time* was more subtle with "A Book of Changes.")

The Philadelphia Bulletin: "The Twain Did Meet Among the Ghosts."

The Sacramento Bee: "East and West Collide Inside a Human Mind."

The San Francisco Examiner: "East Meets West in a Large New Talent."

The Chattanooga *News-Free Press:* "In fact, this book seems to reinforce the feeling that 'East is East and West is West and never the twain shall meet,' or at any rate, it will probably take more than one generation away from China."

I do not want the critics to decide whether the twain shall or shall not meet. I want them to be sensitive enough to know that they are not to judge Chinese American writing through the viewpoint of nineteenth-century British-colonial writing.

Interviewers, including those from Taiwan and Hong Kong, as well as reviewers have been concerned about how "typical" of other Chinese Americans I am. Michael T. Malloy in the *National Observer* says, "I'd like to report that *The Woman Warrior* seemed as singular to my Chinese Canadian wife as it did Irish American me." (Malloy is the critic who attacked the book for being "mainstream feminist.") And I have already quoted Bernice Williams Foley of *The Columbus Dispatch:* "Her autobiographical story (in my opinion) is atypical of the relationship between Chinese parents and their American-Chinese children whom I have known in New York City and Cincinnati." Here is a paragraph from a review in the San Francisco Association of Chinese Teachers newsletter (I think they mean Chinese American teachers):

> It must be pointed out that this book is a very personal statement, and is a subjective exposition of one person's reactions to her family background. It would be dangerous to infer that this "unfamiliar world" represents or typifies that of most Chinese Americans. *The Woman Warrior* is not an easy book to grasp, both in terms of style or content. Especially for students unfamiliar with the Chinese background, it could give an overly negative impression of the Chinese American experience.

(This review gave the book a seventh grade reading level by using a mathematical formula of counting syllables and sentences per one hundred-word passage.) These critics are asking the wrong question. Instead of asking, "Is this work typical of Chinese Americans?" why not ask, "Is this work typical of human beings?" Then see whether the question makes sense, what kinds of answers they come up with.

I have never before read a critic who took a look at a Jewish American spouse and said, "There's something wrong with that Saul Bellow and Norman Mailer. They aren't at all like the one I'm married to." Critics do not ask whether Vonnegut is typical of German Americans; they do not ask whether J. P. Donleavy is typical of Irish Americans. You would never know by reading the reviews of Francine du Plessix Gray's *Lovers and Tyrants* that it is by and about an immigrant from France. Books written by Americans of European ancestry are reviewed as American novels.

Now I agree with these critics—the book *is* "personal" and "subjective" and "singular." It may even be one-of-a-kind, unique, exceptional. I am not a sociologist who measures truth by the percentage of times behaviour takes place. Those critics who do not explore why and how this book is different but merely point out its difference as a flaw have a very disturbing idea about the role of the writer. Why must I "represent" anyone besides myself? Why should I be denied an individual artistic vision? And I do not think I wrote a "negative" book, as the Chinese American reviewer said; but suppose I had? Suppose I had been so wonderfully talented that I wrote a tragedy? Are we Chinese Americans to deny ourselves tragedy? If we give up tragedy in order to make a good impression on Caucasians, we have lost a battle. Oh, well, I'm certain that some day when a great body of Chinese American writing becomes published and known, then readers will no longer have to put such a burden on each book that comes out. Readers can see the variety of ways for Chinese Americans to be.

(For the record, most of my mail is from Chinese American women, who tell me how similar their childhoods were to the one in the book, or they say their lives are not like that at all, but they understand the feelings; then they tell me some stories about themselves. Also, I was invited to Canada to speak on the role of the Chinese Canadian woman, and there was a half-page ad for the lecture in the Chinese language newspaper.)

The artistically interesting problem which the reviewers are really posing is: How much exposition is needed? There are so many levels of knowledge and ignorance in the audience. "It's especially hard for a non-Chinese," says Malloy, "and that's a troubling aspect of this book." A Chinese Canadian man writes in a letter, "How dare you make us sound like savages with that disgusting monkey feast story!" (Since publishing the book, I have heard from many monkey feast witnesses and participants.) Diane Johnson in *The New York Review of Books* says that there are fourth and fifth generation Chinese Americans who can't speak English. (It is more often the case that they can't speak Chinese. A fourth or fifth generation Chinese American and Caucasian American are not too different except in looks and history.) There is a reviewer who says that it is amazing what I could do with my IQ of zero. (How clumsy the joke would be if I explained how IQ tests aren't valid because they are culturally biased against a non-English-speaking child.) There are Chinese American readers who feel slighted because I did not include enough history. (In my own review of Laurence Yep's *Child of the Owl* in the *Washington Post,* I praised him for his bravery in letting images stand with no exposition.) My own sister says, "You wrote the book for us—our family. It's how we are in our everyday life. I have no idea what white people would make of it." Both my sisters say they laughed aloud. *Harper's* says the book is marred by "gratuitous ethnic humor," and *Publisher's Weekly* says the humour is "quirky." So who is the book for?

When I write most deeply, fly the highest, reach the furthest, I write like a diarist—that is, my audience is myself. I dare to write anything because I can burn my papers at any moment. I do not begin with the thought of an audience peering over my shoulder, nor do I find my being understood a common occurrence anyway—a miracle when it happens. My fantasy is that this self-indulgence will be good enough for the great American novel. Pragmatically, though, since my audience would have to be all America, I work on intelligibility and accessibility in a second draft. However, I do not slow down to give boring exposition, which is information that is available in encyclopedias, history books, sociology, anthropology, mythology. (After all, I am not writing history or sociology but a "memoir" like Proust, as Christine Cook in the *Hawaii Observer* and Diane Johnson in *The New York Review of Books* are clever enough to see. I am, as Diane Johnson says, "slyly writing a memoir, a form which . . . can neither [be] dismiss[ed] as fiction nor quarrel[ed] with as fact." "But the structure is a grouping of memoirs," says Christine Cook. "It is by definition a series of stories or anecdotes to illuminate the times rather than be autobiographical.") I rarely repeat anything that can be found in other books. Some readers will just have to do some background reading. Maybe my writing can provide work for English majors. Readers ought not to expect reading always to be as effortless as watching television.

I want my audience to include everyone. I had planned that if I could not find an American publisher, I would send the manuscript to Britain, Hong Kong, Canada, Taiwan—anywhere—and if it did not then find a publisher, I would keep it safe for posthumous publication. So I do believe in the timelessness and universality of individual vision. It would not just be a family book or an American book or a woman's book but a world book, and, at the same moment, my book.

The audience of *The Woman Warrior* is also very specific. For example, I address Chinese Americans twice, once at the beginning of the book and once at the end. I ask some questions about what life is like for you, and, happily, you answer. Chinese Americans have written that I explain customs they had not understood. I even write for my old English professors of the new criticism school in Berkeley, by incorporating what they taught about the structure of the novel. I refer to Virginia Woolf, Elizabeth Barrett Browning, Shakespeare; but those who are not English majors and don't play literary games will still find in those same sentences the other, main, important meanings. There are puns for Chinese speakers only, and I do not point them out for non-Chinese speakers. There are some visual puns best appreciated by those who write Chinese. I've written jokes in that book so private, only I can get them; I hope I sneaked them in unobtrusively so nobody feels left out. I hope my writing has many layers, as human beings have layers.

ESSAYS ON
THE WOMAN WARRIOR
◆

The Woman Warrior
versus The Chinaman Pacific:
Must a Chinese American Critic
Choose between Feminism and Heroism?

KING-KOK CHEUNG

The title of the anthology notwithstanding, I will primarily be speaking not about topics that divide feminists but about conflicting politics of gender, as reflected in the literary arena, between Chinese American women and men.[1] There are several reasons for my choice. First, I share the frustrations of many women of color that while we wish to engage in a dialogue with "mainstream" scholars, most of our potential readers are still unfamiliar with the historical and cultural contexts of various ethnic "minorities." Furthermore, whenever I encounter words such as "conflicts," "common differences," or "divisive issues" in feminist studies, the authors more often than not are addressing the divergences either between French and Anglo-American theorists or, more recently, between white and nonwhite women. Both tendencies have the effect of re-centering white feminism. In some instances, women of color are invited to participate chiefly because they take issue with white feminists and not because what they have to say is of inherent interest to the audience. Finally, I believe that in order to understand conflicts among diverse groups of women, we must look at the relations between women and men, especially where the problems of race and gender are closely intertwined.

It is impossible, for example, to tackle the gender issues in the Chinese American cultural terrain without delving into the historically enforced "feminization" of Chinese American men, without confronting the dialectics of racial stereotypes and nationalist reactions or, above all, without wrestling with diehard notions of masculinity and femininity in both Asian and Western cultures. It is partly because these issues touch many sensitive nerves that the writings of Maxine Hong Kingston have generated such heated debates among Chinese American intellectuals. As a way into these intricate issues, I

From *Conflicts in Feminism*, edited by Marianne Hirsch and Evelyn Fox Keller. New York, Routledge, 1990: 234–51. Copyright © 1990 by Routledge. Reprinted by permission of Routledge.

will structure my discussion around Kingston's work and the responses it has elicited from her Chinese American male critics, especially those who have themselves been influential in redefining both literary history and Asian American manhood.

Attempts at cultural reconstruction, whether in terms of "manhood" and "womanhood," or of "mainstream" versus "minority" heritage, are often inseparable from a wish for self-empowerment. Yet many writers and critics who have challenged the monolithic authority of white male literary historians remain in thrall to the norms and arguments of the dominant patriarchal culture, unwittingly upholding the criteria of those whom they assail. As a female immigrant of Cantonese descent, with the attendant sympathies and biases, I will survey and analyze what I construe to be the "feminist" and "heroic" impulses which have invigorated Chinese American literature but at the same time divided its authors and critics.

I

Sexual politics in Chinese America reflect complex cultural and historical legacies. The paramount importance of patrilineage in traditional Chinese culture predisposes many Chinese Americans of the older generations to favor male over female offspring (a preference even more overt than that which still underlies much of white America). At the same time Chinese American men, too, have been confronted with a history of inequality and of painful "emasculation." The fact that ninety percent of early Chinese immigrants were male, combined with anti-miscegenation laws and laws prohibiting Chinese laborers' wives from entering the U.S., forced these immigrants to congregate in the bachelor communities of various Chinatowns, unable to father a subsequent generation. While many built railroads, mined gold, and cultivated plantations, their strenuous activities and contributions in these areas were often overlooked by white historians. Chinamen were better known to the American public as restaurant cooks, laundry workers, and waiters, jobs traditionally considered "women's work."[2]

The same forms of social and economic oppression of Chinese American women and men, in conjunction with a longstanding Orientalist tradition that casts the Asian in the role of the silent and passive Other,[3] have in turn provided material for degrading sexual representations of the Chinese in American popular culture. Elaine H. Kim notes, for instance, that the stereotype of Asian women as submissive and dainty sex objects has given rise to an "enormous demand for X-rated films featuring Asian women and the emphasis on bondage in pornographic materials about Asian women," and that "the popular image of alluring and exotic 'dream girls of the mysterious East' has created a demand for 'Oriental' bath house workers in American cities as well as a booming business in mail order marriages."[4] No less insidious are the inscriptions of Chinese men in popular culture. Frank Chin, a well-known writer and one of the most outspoken revisionists of Asian American history, describes how the American silver screen casts doubts on Chinese American virility:

> The movies were teachers. In no uncertain terms they taught America that we were lovable for being a race of sissies . . . living to accommodate the white-men. Unlike the white stereotype of the evil black stud, Indian rapist, Mexican macho, the evil of the evil Dr. Fu Manchu was not sexual, but homosexual. . . . Dr. Fu, a man wearing a long dress, batting his eyelashes, surrounded by muscular black servants in loin clothes, and with his bad habit of caressingly touching white men on the leg, wrist, and face with his long fingernails is not so much a threat as he is a frivolous offense to white manhood. [Charlie] Chan's gestures are the same, except that he doesn't touch, and instead of being graceful like Fu in flowing robes, he is awkward in a baggy suit and clumsy. His sexuality is the source of a joke running through all of the forty-seven Chan films. The large family of the bovine detective isn't the product of sex, but animal husbandry. . . . *He never gets into violent things* [my emphasis].[5]

According to Chin and Jeffery Paul Chan, also a writer, "Each racial stereotype comes in two models, the acceptable model and the unacceptable model. . . . The unacceptable model is unacceptable because he cannot be controlled by whites. The acceptable model is acceptable because he is tractable. There is racist hate and racist love."[6] Chin and Chan believe that while the "masculine" stereotypes of blacks, Indians, and Mexicans are generated by "racist hate," "racist love" has been lavished on Chinese Americans, targets of "effeminate" stereotypes:

> The Chinese, in the parlance of the Bible, were raw material for the "flock," pathological sheep for the shepherd. The adjectives applied to the Chinese ring with scriptural imagery. We are meek, timid, passive, docile, industrious. We have the patience of Job. We are humble. A race without sinful manhood, born to mortify our flesh. . . . The difference between [other minority groups] and the Chinese was that the Christians, taking Chinese hospitality for timidity and docility, weren't afraid of us as they were of other races. They loved us, protected us. Love conquered.[7]

If "racist love" denies "manhood" to Asian men, it endows Asian women with an excess of "womanhood." Elaine Kim argues that because "the characterization of Asian men is a reflection of a white male perspective that defines the white man's virility, it is possible for Asian men to be viewed as asexual and the Asian woman as only sexual, imbued with an innate understanding of how to please and serve." The putative gender difference among Asian Americans—exaggerated out of all proportion in the popular imagination—has, according to Kim, created "resentment and tensions" between the sexes within the ethnic community.[8]

Although both the Asian American and the feminist movements of the late sixties have attempted to counter extant stereotypes, the conflicts between Asian American men and women have been all the more pronounced in the wake of the two movements. In the last two decades many Chinese American men—especially such writers and editors as Chin and Chan—have begun to correct the distorted images of Asian males projected by the dominant culture. Astute, eloquent, and incisive as they are in debunking racist myths, they are often blind to the biases resulting from their own acceptance of the patriarchal construct of masculinity. In Chin's discussion of Fu Manchu and Charlie Chan and in the perceptive contrast he draws between the stock images of Asian men and those of other men of color, one can detect not only homophobia but perhaps also a sexist preference for stereotypes that imply predatory violence against women to "effeminate" ones. Granted that the position taken by Chin may be little more than a polemicist stance designed to combat white patronage, it is disturbing that he should lend credence to the conventional association of physical aggression with manly valor. The hold of patriarchal conventions becomes even more evident in the following passage:

> The white stereotype of the Asian is unique in that it is the only racial stereotype completely devoid of manhood. Our nobility is that of an efficient housewife. At our worst we are contemptible because we are womanly, effeminate, devoid of all the traditionally masculine qualities of originality, daring, physical courage, creativity. We're neither straight talkin' or straight shootin'. The mere fact that four of the five American-born Chinese-American writers are women reinforces this aspect of the stereotype.[9]

In taking whites to task for demeaning Asians, these writers seem nevertheless to be buttressing patriarchy by invoking gender stereotypes, by disparaging domestic efficiency as "feminine," and by slotting desirable traits such as originality, daring, physical courage, and creativity under the rubric of masculinity.[10]

The impetus to reassert manhood also underlies the ongoing attempt by Chin, Chan, Lawson Inada, and Shawn Wong to reconstruct Asian American literary history. In their groundbreaking work *Aiiieeeee! An Anthology of Asian-American Writers,* these writers and co-editors deplored "the lack of a recognized style of Asian-American manhood." In a forthcoming sequel entitled *The Big Aiiieeeee! An Anthology of Asian American Writers,* they attempt to revive an Asian heroic tradition, celebrating Chinese and Japanese classics such as *The Art of War, Water Margin, Romance of the Three Kingdoms, Journey to the West,* and *Chushingura,* and honoring the renowned heroes and outlaws featured therein.[11]

The editors seem to be working in an opposite direction from that of an increasing number of feminists. While these Asian American spokesmen are recuperating a heroic tradition of their own, many women writers and scholars, building on existentialist and modernist insights, are reassessing the entire Western code of heroism. While feminists question such traditional values as competitive individualism and martial valor, the editors seize on selected maxims, purportedly derived from Chinese epics and war manuals, such as "I am the law," "life is war," "personal integrity and honor is the highest value," and affirm the "ethic of private revenge."[12]

The *Aiiieeeee!* editors and feminist critics also differ on the question of genre. According to Chin, the literary genre that is most antithetical to the heroic tradition is autobiography, which he categorically denounces as a form of Christian confession:

> the fighter writer uses literary forms as weapons of war, not the expression of ego alone, and does not {waste} time with dandyish expressions of feeling and psychological attitudinizing. . . . A Chinese Christian is like a Nazi Jew. Confession and autobiography celebrate the process of conversion from an object of contempt to an object of acceptance. You love the personal experience of it, the oozings of viscous putrescence and luminous radiant guilt. . . . It's the quality of submission, not assertion that counts, in the confession and the autobiography. The autobiography combines the thrills and guilt of masturbation and the porno movie.[13]

Feminist critics, many of whom are skeptical of either/or dichotomies (in this instance fighting vs. feeling) and are impatient with normative definitions of genre (not that Chin's criteria are normative), believe that women have always appropriated autobiography as a vehicle for *asserting,* however tentatively, their subjectivity. Celeste Schenck writes:

> the poetics of women's autobiography issues from its concern with constituting a female subject—a precarious operation, which . . . requires working on two fronts at once, *both* occupying a kind of center, assuming a subjectivity long denied, *and* maintaining the vigilant, disruptive stance that speaking from the postmodern margin provides—the autobiographical genre may be paradigmatic of all women's writing.[14]

Given these divergent views, the stage is set for a confrontation between "heroism" and "feminism" in Chinese American letters.

II

The advent of feminism, far from checking Asian American chauvinism, has in a sense fueled gender antagonism, at least in the literary realm. Nowhere is this antagonism reflected more clearly than in the controversy that has erupted over Maxine Hong Kingston's *The Woman Warrior.* Classified as auto-biography, the work describes the protagonist's struggle for self-definition amid Cantonese sayings such as "Girls are maggots in the rice," "It is more profitable to raise geese than daughters," "Feeding girls is feeding cowbirds" (51, 54). While the book has received popular acclaim, especially among fem-inist critics, it has been censured by several Chinese American critics—mostly male but also some female—who tax Kingston for misrepresenting Chinese and Chinese American culture, and for passing fiction for autobiography. Chin (whose revulsion against autobiography we already know) wrote a satir-ical parody of *The Woman Warrior;* he casts aspersions on its historical status and places Kingston in the same company as the authors of Fu Manchu and Charlie Chan for confirming "the white fantasy that everything sick and sick-ening about the white self-image is really Chinese."[15] Jeffery Paul Chan casti-gates Knopf for publishing the book as "biography rather than fiction (which it obviously is)" and insinuates that a white female reviewer praises the book indiscriminately because it expresses "female anger."[16] Benjamin Tong openly calls it a "fashionably feminist work written with white acceptance in mind."[17] As Sau-ling Wong points out, "According to Kingston's critics, the most pernicious of the stereotypes which might be supported by *The Woman Warrior* is that of Chinese American men as sexist," and yet some Chinese American women "think highly of *The Woman Warrior* because it confirms their personal experiences with sexism."[18] In sum, Kingston is accused of fal-sifying culture and of reinforcing stereotype in the name of feminism.

At first glance the claim that Kingston should not have taken the liberty to infuse autobiography with fiction may seem to be merely a generic, gender-neutral criticism, but as Susan Stanford Friedman has pointed out, genre is all too often gendered.[19] Feminist scholars of autobiography have suggested that women writers often shy away from "objective" autobiography and prefer to use the form to reflect a private world, a subjective vision, and the life of the imagination. *The Woman Warrior,* though it departs from most "public" self-representations by men, is quite in line with such an autobiographical tradi-tion. Yet for a "minority" author to exercise such artistic freedom is perilous business because white critics and reviewers persist in seeing creative expres-sions by her as no more than cultural history.[20] Members from the ethnic community are in turn upset if they feel that they have been "misrepre-sented" by one of their own. Thus where Kingston insists on shuttling between the world of facts and the world of fantasy, on giving multiple ver-sions of "truth" as subjectively perceived, her Chinese American detractors demand generic purity and historical accuracy. Perhaps precisely because this author is female, writing amid discouraging realities, she can only forge a viable and expansive identity by refashioning patriarchal myths and invoking imaginative possibilities.[21] Kingston's autobiographical act, far from be-tokening submission, as Chin believes, turns the self into a "heroine" and is in a sense an act of "revenge" (a word represented in Chinese by two ideographs which Kingston loosely translates as "report a crime") against both the Chinese and the white cultures that undermine her self-esteem. Discrediting her for taking poetic licence is reminiscent of those white reviewers who reduce works of art by ethnic authors to sociohistorical documentary.

The second charge concerning stereotype is more overtly gender-based. It is hardly coincidental that the most unrelenting critics (whose grievance is not only against Kingston but also against feminists in general) have also been the most ardent champions of Chinese American "manhood." Their response is understandable. Asian American men have suffered deeply from racial oppression. When Asian American women seek to expose anti-female prejudices in their own ethnic community, the men are likely to feel betrayed.[22] Yet it is also undeniable that sexism still lingers as part of the Asian legacy in Chinese America and that many American-born daughters still feel its sting. Chinese American women may be at once sympathetic and angry toward the men in their ethnic community: sensitive to the marginality of these men but resentful of their male privilege.

III

Kingston herself seems to be in the grips of these conflicting emotions. The opening legend of *China Men* captures through myth some of the baffling intersections of gender and ethnicity in Chinese America and reveals the author's own double allegiance. The legend is borrowed and adapted from an eighteenth-century Chinese novel entitled *Flowers in the Mirror*, itself a fascinating work and probably one of the first "feminist" novels written by a man.[23] The male protagonist of this novel is Tang Ao, who in Kingston's version is captured in the Land of Women, where he is forced to have his feet bound, his ears pierced, his facial hair plucked, his cheeks and lips painted red—in short, to be transformed into an Oriental courtesan.

Since Kingston explicitly points out at the end of her legend that the Land of Women was in North America, critics familiar with Chinese American history will readily see that the ignominy suffered by Tang Ao in a foreign land symbolizes the emasculation of Chinamen by the dominant culture. Men of Chinese descent have encountered racial violence in the U.S., both in the past and even recently.[24] Kingston's myth is indeed intimating that the physical torment in their peculiar case is often tied to an affront to their manhood.

But in making women the captors of Tang Ao and in deliberately reversing masculine and feminine roles, Kingston also foregrounds constructions of gender. I cannot but see this legend as double-edged, pointing not only to the mortification of Chinese men in the new world but also to the subjugation of women both in old China and in America. Although the tortures suffered by Tang Ao seem palpably cruel, many Chinese women had for centuries been obliged to undergo similar mutilation. By having a man go through these ordeals instead, Kingston, following the author of *Flowers in the Mirror,* disrupts the familiar and commonplace acceptance of Chinese women as sexual objects. Her myth deplores on the one hand the racist debasement of Chinese American men and on the other hand the sexist objectification of Chinese women. Although *China Men* mostly commemorates the founding fathers of Chinese America, this companion volume to *The Woman Warrior* is also suffused with "feminist anger." The opening myth suggests that the author objects as strenuously to the patriarchal practices of her ancestral culture as to the racist treatment of her forefathers in their adopted country.

Kingston reveals not only the similarities between Chinamen's and Chinese women's suffering but also the correlation between these men's umbrage at racism and their misogynist behavior. In one episode, the narrator's immigrant father, a laundryman who seldom opens his mouth except to utter obscenities about women, is cheated by a gypsy and harassed by a white policeman:

> When the gypsy baggage and the police pig left, we were careful not to be bad or noisy so that you [father] would not turn on us. We knew that it was to feed us you had to endure demons and physical labor. You screamed wordless male screams that jolted the house upright . . . Worse than the swearing and the nightly screams were your silences when you punished us by not talking. You rendered us invisible, gone. (8)

Even as the daughter deplores the father's "male screams" and brooding silences, she attributes his bad temper to his sense of frustration and emasculation in a white society. As in analogous situations of Cholly Breedlove in Toni Morrison's *The Bluest Eye* and Grange Copeland in Alice Walker's *The Third Life of Grange Copeland,* what seems to be male tyranny must be viewed within the context of racial inequality. Men of color who have been abused in a white society are likely to attempt to restore their sense of masculinity by venting their anger at those who are even more powerless—the women and children in their families.

Kingston's attempt to write about the opposite sex in *China Men* is perhaps a tacit call for mutual empathy between Chinese American men and women. In an interview, the author likens herself to Tang Ao: just as Tang Ao enters the Land of Women and is made to feel what it means to be of the other gender, so Kingston, in writing *China Men,* enters the realm of men and, in her own words, becomes "the kind of woman who loves men and who can tell their stories." Perhaps, to extend the analogy further, she is trying to prompt her male readers to participate in and empathize with the experiences of women.[25] Where Tang Ao is made to feel what his female contemporaries felt, Chinese American men are urged to see parallels between their plight and that of Chinese American women. If Asian men have been emasculated in America, as the aforementioned male critics have themselves argued, they can best attest to the oppression of women who have long been denied male privilege.

IV

An ongoing effort to revamp Chinese American literary history will surely be more compelling if it is informed by mutual empathy between men and women. To return to an earlier point, I am of two minds about the ambitious attempt of the *Aiiieeeee!* editors to restore and espouse an Asian American heroic tradition. Born and raised in Hong Kong, I grew up reading many of the Chinese heroic epics—along with works of less heroic modes—and can appreciate the rigorous effort of the editors to introduce them to Asian American and non-Asian readers alike.[26] But the literary values they assign to the heroic canon also function as ideology. Having spoken out against the emasculation of Asian Americans in their introduction to *Aiiieeeee!*, they seem determined to show further that Chinese and Japanese Americans have a heroic—which is to say militant—heritage. Their propagation of the epic tradition appears inseparable from their earlier attempt to eradicate effeminate stereotypes and to emblazon Asian American manhood.[27] In this light, the special appeal held by the war heroes for the editors becomes rather obvious. Take, for example, Kwan Kung, in *Romance of the Three Kingdoms:* loud, passionate, and vengeful, this "heroic embodiment of martial self-sufficiency" is antithetical in every way to the image of the quiet, passive, and subservient Oriental houseboy. Perhaps the editors hope that the icon of this imposing Chinese hero will dispel myths about Chinese American tractability.

While acquaintance with some of the Chinese folk heroes may induce the American public to acknowledge that Chinese culture too has its Robin Hood and John Wayne, I remain uneasy about the masculist orientation of the heroic tradition, especially as expounded by the editors who see loyalty, revenge, and individual honor as the overriding ethos which should be inculcated in (if not already absorbed by) Chinese Americans. If white media have chosen to highlight and applaud the submissive and nonthreatening characteristics of Asians, the Asian American editors are equally tendentious in underscoring the militant strain of their Asian literary heritage.[28] The refutation of effeminate stereotypes through the glorification of machismo merely perpetuates patriarchal terms and assumptions.

Is it not possible for Chinese American men to recover a cultural space without denigrating or erasing "the feminine"? Chin contends that "use of the heroic tradition in Chinese literature as the source of Chinese American moral, ethical and esthetic universals is not literary rhetoric and smartass cute tricks, not wishful thinking, not theory, not demagoguery and prescription, but simple history."[29] However, even history, which is also a form of social construct, is not exempt from critical scrutiny. The Asian heroic tradition, like its Western counterpart, must be re-evaluated so that both its strengths and limits can surface. The intellectual excitement and the emotional appeal of the tradition is indisputable: the strategic brilliance of characters such as Chou Yu and Chuko Liang in *Romance of the Three Kingdoms* rivals that of Odysseus, and the fraternal bond between the three sworn brothers—Liu Pei, Chang Fei, and Kuan Yu (Kwan Kung)—is no less moving than that between Achilles and Patrocles. But just as I no longer believe that Homer speaks for humanity (or even all mankind), I hesitate to subscribe wholeheartedly to the *Aiiieeeee!* editors' claim that the Asian heroic canon (composed entirely of work written by men though it contains a handful of heroines) encompasses "Asian universals."

Nor do I concur with the editors that a truculent mentality pervades the Chinese heroic tradition, which generally places a higher premium on benevolence than on force and stresses the primacy of kinship and friendship over personal power. By way of illustration I will turn to the prototype for Kingston's "woman warrior"—Fa Mu Lan (also known as Hua Mulan and Fa Muk Lan). According to the original "Ballad of Mulan" (which most Chinese children, including myself, had to learn by heart) the heroine in joining the army is prompted neither by revenge nor by personal honor but by filial piety. She enlists under male disguise to take the place of her aged father. Instead of celebrating the glory of war, the poem describes the bleakness of the battlefield and the loneliness of the daughter (who sorely misses her parents). The use of understatement in such lines as "the general was killed after hundreds of combats" and "the warriors returned in ten years" (my translation) connotes the cost and duration of battles. The "Ballad of Mulan," though it commits the filial and courageous daughter to public memory, also contains a pacifist subtext—much in the way that the *Iliad* conceals an anti-war message beneath its martial trappings. A re-examination of the Asian heroic tradition may actually reveal that it is richer and more sophisticated than the *Aiiieeeee!* editors, bent on finding belligerent models, would allow.[30]

Kingston's adaptation of the legend in *The Woman Warrior* is equally multivalent. Fa Mu Lan as re-created in the protagonist's fantasy does excel in martial arts, but her power is derived as much from the words carved on her back as from her military skills. And the transformed heroine still proves problematic as a model since she can only exercise her power when in male armor. As I have argued elsewhere, her military distinction, insofar as it valorizes the ability to be ruthless and violent—"to fight like a man"—affirms rather than subverts patriarchal mores.[31] In fact, Kingston discloses in an interview that the publisher is the one who entitled the book "The Woman Warrior" while she herself (who is a pacifist) resists complete identification with the war heroine:

> I don't really like warriors. I wish I had not had a metaphor of a warrior, a person who uses weapons and goes to war. I guess I always have in my style a doubt about wars as a way of solving things.[32]

Aside from the fantasy connected with Fa Mu Lan the book has little to do with actual fighting. The real battle that runs through the work is one against silence and invisibility. Forbidden by her mother to tell a secret, unable to read aloud in English while first attending American school, and later fired for protesting against racism, the protagonist eventually speaks with a vengeance through writing—through a heroic act of self-expression. At the end of the book her tutelary genius has changed from Fa Mu Lan to Ts'ai Yen—from warrior to poet.

Kingston's commitment to pacifism—through re-visioning and re-contextualizing ancient "heroic" material—is even more evident in her most recent book, *Tripmaster Monkey*. As though anticipating the editors of *The Big Aiiieeeee!,* the author alludes recurrently to the Chinese heroic tradition, but always with a feminist twist. The protagonist of this novel, Wittman Ah Sing, is a playwright who loves *Romance of the Three Kingdoms* (one of the aforementioned epics espoused by Chin). Kingston's novel culminates with Wittman directing a marathon show which he has written based on the *Romance*. At the end of the show he has a rather surprising illumination:

> He had made up his mind: he will not go to Viet Nam or to any war. He had staged the War of the Three Kingdoms as heroically as he could, which made him start to understand: The three brothers and Cho Cho were masters of the war: they had worked out strategies and justifications for war so brilliantly that their policies and their tactics are used today, even by governments with nuclear-powered weapons. And they *lost*. The clanging and banging fooled us, but now we know—they lost. Studying the mightiest war epic of all time, Wittman changed—beeen!—into a pacifist. Dear American monkey, don't be afraid. Here, let us tweak your ear, and kiss your other ear.[33]

The seemingly easy transformation of Wittman—who is curiously evocative of Chin in speech and manner—is achieved through the pacifist author's sleight of hand. Nevertheless, the novel does show that it is possible to celebrate the ingenious strategies of the ancient warriors without embracing, wholesale, the heroic code that motivates their behavior and without endorsing violence as a positive expression of masculinity.[34]

Unfortunately, the ability to perform violent acts implied in the concepts of warrior and epic hero is still all too often mistaken for manly courage; and men who have been historically subjugated are all the more tempted to adopt a militant stance to manifest their masculinity. In the notorious Moynihan report on the black family, "military service for Negroes" was recommended as a means to potency:

> Given the strains of the disorganized and matrifocal family life in which so many Negro youth come of age, the Armed Forces are a dramatic and desperately needed change: a world away from women, a world run by strong men of unquestioned authority.[35]

Moynihan believed that placing black men in an "utterly masculine world" will strengthen them. The black men in the sixties who worshipped figures that exploited and brutalized women likewise conflated might and masculinity. Toni Cade, who cautions against "equating black liberation with black men gaining access to male privilege," offers an alternative to patriarchal prescriptions for manhood:

> Perhaps we need to let go of all notions of manhood and femininity and concentrate on Blackhood. . . . It perhaps takes less heart to pick up the gun than to face the task of creating a new identity, a self, perhaps an androgynous self. . . .[36]

If Chinese American men use the Asian heroic dispensation to promote male aggression, they may risk remaking themselves in the image of their oppressors—albeit under the guise of Asian panoply. Precisely because the racist treatment of Asians has taken the peculiar form of sexism—insofar as the indignities suffered by men of Chinese descent are analogous to those traditionally suffered by women—we must refrain from seeking antifeminist solutions to racism. To do otherwise reinforces not only patriarchy but also white supremacy.

Well worth heeding is Althusser's caveat that when a dominant ideology is integrated as common sense into the consciousness of the dominated, the dominant class will continue to prevail.[37] Instead of tailoring ourselves to white ideals, Asian Americans may insist on alternative habits and ways of seeing. Instead of drumming up support for Asian American "manhood," we may consider demystifying popular stereotypes while reappropriating what Stanford Lyman calls the "kernels of truth" in them that are indeed part of our ethnic heritage. For instance, we need not accept the Western association of Asian self-restraint with passivity and femininity. I, for one, believe that the respectful demeanor of many an Asian and Asian American indicates, among other things, a willingness to listen to others and to resolve conflict rationally or tactfully.[38] Such a collaborative disposition—be it Asian or non-Asian, feminine or masculine—is surely no less valid and viable than one that is vociferous and confrontational.

V

Although I have thus far concentrated on the gender issues in the Chinese American cultural domina, they do have provocative implications for feminist theory and criticism. As Elizabeth Spelman points out, "It is not easy to think about gender, race, and class in ways that don't obscure or underplay their effects on one another."[39] Still, the task is to develop paradigms that can admit these crosscurrents and that can reach out to women of color and perhaps also to men.

Women who value familial and ethnic solidarity may find it especially difficult to rally to the feminist cause without feeling divided or without being accused of betrayal, especially when the men in their ethnic groups also face social iniquities. Kingston, for instance, has tried throughout her work to mediate between affirming her ethnic heritage and undermining patriarchy. But she feels that identification with Asian men at times inhibits an equally strong feminist impulse. Such split loyalties apparently prompted her to publish *The Woman Warrior* and *China Men* separately, though they were conceived and written together as an "interlocking story." Lest the men's stories "undercut the feminist viewpoint," she separated the female and the male stories into two books. She says, "I care about men . . . as much as I care about women. . . . Given the present state of affairs, perhaps men's and women's experiences have to be dealt with separately for now, until more auspicious times are with us."[40]

Yet such separation has its dangers, particularly if it means that men and women will continue to work in opposing directions, as reflected in the divergences between the proponents of the Asian heroic tradition and Asian American feminists. Feminist ideas have made little inroad in the writing of the *Aiiieeeee!* editors, who continue to operate within patriarchal grids. White feminists, on the other hand, are often oblivious to the fact that there are other groups besides women who have been "feminized" and puzzled when women of color do not readily rally to their camp.

The recent shift from feminist studies to gender studies suggests that the time has come to look at women and men together. I hope that the shift will also entice both men and women to do the looking and, by so doing, strengthen the alliance between gender studies and ethnic studies. Lest feminist criticism remain in the wilderness, white scholars must reckon with race and class as integral experiences for both men and women, and acknowledge that not only female voices but the voices of many men of color have been historically silenced or dismissed. Expanding the feminist frame of reference will allow certain existing theories to be interrogated or reformulated.[41] Asian American men need to be wary of certain pitfalls in using what Fou-

cault calls "reverse discourse," in demanding legitimacy "in the same vocabulary, using the same categories by which [they were] disqualified."[42] The ones
who can be recruited into the field of gender studies may someday see feminists as allies rather than adversaries, and proceed to dismantle not just white
but also male supremacy. Women of color should not have to undergo a self-
division resulting from having to choose between female and ethnic identities. Chinese American women writers may find a way to negotiate the tangle
of sexual and racial politics in all its intricacies, not just out of a desire for
"revenge" but also out of a sense of "loyalty." If we ask them to write with a
vigilant eye against possible misappropriation by white readers or against
possible offense to "Asian American manhood," however, we will end up
implicitly sustaining racial and sexual hierarchies. All of us need to be conscious of our "complicity with the gender ideologies" of patriarchy, whatever
its origins, and to work toward notions of gender and ethnicity that are non-
hierarchical, nonbinary, and nonprescriptive; that can embrace tensions rather
than perpetuate divisions.[43] To reclaim cultural traditions without getting
bogged down in the mire of traditional constraints, to attack stereotypes
without falling prey to their binary opposites, to chart new topographies for
manliness and womanliness, will surely demand genuine heroism.

Notes

1. Research for this essay is funded in part by an Academic Senate grant and a grant
from the Institute of American Cultures and the Asian American Studies Center, UCLA. I wish
to thank the many whose help, criticism, and encouragement have sustained me through the
mentally embattled period of writing this essay: Kim Crenshaw, Donald Goellnicht, Marianne
Hirsch, Evelyn Fox Keller, Elaine Kim, Elizabeth Kim, Ken Lincoln, Gerard Maré, Rosalind
Melis, Jeff Spielberg, Sau-ling Wong, Richard Yarborough, and Stan Yogi.
    A version of this article was delivered at the 1989 MLA Convention in Washington,
DC. My title alludes not only to Maxine Hong Kingston's *The Woman Warrior* and *China Men*
but also Frank Chin's *The Chickencoop Chinaman* and *The Chinaman Pacific & Frisco R. R. Co.* The
term "Chinamen" has acquired divers connotations through time: "In the early days of Chinese
American history, men called themselves 'Chinamen' just as other newcomers called themselves 'Englishmen' or 'Frenchmen': the term distinguished them from the 'Chinese' who
remained citizens of China, and also showed that they were not recognized as Americans.
Later, of course, it became an insult. Young Chinese Americans today are reclaiming the word
because of its political and historical precision, and are demanding that it be said with dignity
and not for name-calling" (Kingston, "San Francisco's Chinatown: A View from the Other Side
of Arnold Genthe's Camera," *American Heritage* [Dec. 1978]: 37). In my article the term refers
exclusively to men.
    2. The devaluation of daughters is a theme explored in *The Woman Warrior* (1976;
New York: Vintage, 1977); as this book suggests, this aspect of patriarchy is upheld no less by
women than by men. The "emasculation" of Chinese American men is addressed in *China Men*
(1980; New York: Ballantine, 1981), in which Kingston attempts to reclaim the founders of
Chinese America. Subsequent page references to these two books will appear in the text.
Detailed accounts of early Chinese immigrant history can be found in Victor G. Nee and Brett

De Bary Nee, *Longtime Californ': A Documentary Study of an American Chinatown* (1973; New York: Pantheon, 1981); and Ronald Takaki, *Strangers from a Different Shore: A History of Asian Americans* (Boston: Little Brown, 1989), 79–131.

3. See Edward Said, *Orientalism* (New York: Vintage, 1979). Although Said focuses on French and British representations of the Middle East, many of his insights also apply to American perceptions of the Far East.

4. "Asian American Writers: A Bibliographical Review," *American Studies International* 22.2 (Oct. 1984): 64.

5. "Confessions of the Chinatown Cowboy," *Bulletin of Concerned Asian Scholars* 4.3 (1972): 66.

6. "Racist Love," *Seeing through Shuck,* ed. Richard Kostelanetz (New York: Ballantine, 1972), 65, 79. Although the cinematic image of Bruce Lee as a Kung-fu master might have somewhat countered the feminine representations of Chinese American men, his role in the only one Hollywood film in which he appeared before he died was, in Elaine Kim's words, "less a human being than a fighting machine" ("Asian Americans and American popular Culture," *Dictionary of Asian American History,* ed. Hyung-Chan Kim [New York: Greenwood Press, 1986], 107).

7. "Racist Love," 69.

8. "Asian American Writers: A Bibliographical Review," 64.

9. "Racist Love," 68. The five writers under discussion are Pardee Lowe, Jade Snow Wong, Virginia Lee, Betty Lee Sung, and Diana Chang.

10. Similar objections to the passage have been raised by Merle Woo in "Letter to Ma," *This Bridge Called my Back: Writings by Radical Women of Color,* ed. Cherrie Moraga and Gloria Anzaldúa (1981; New York: Kitchen Table, 1983), 145; and Elaine Kim in *Asian American Literature: An Introduction to the Writings and Their Social Context* (Philadelphia: Temple UP, 1982), 189. Richard Yarborough delineates a somewhat parallel conundrum about manhood faced by African American writers in the nineteenth century and which, I believe, persists to some extent to this day; see "Race, Violence, and Manhood: The Masculine Ideal in Frederick Douglass's 'Heroic Slave,' " forthcoming in *Frederick Douglass: New Literary and Historical Essays,* ed. Eric J. Sundquist (Cambridge, MA: Cambridge UP). There is, however, an important difference between the dilemma faced by the African American men and that faced by Asian American men. While writers such as William Wells Brown and Frederick Douglass tried to reconcile the white inscription of the militant and sensual Negro and the white ideal of heroic manhood, several Chinese American male writers are trying to disprove the white stereotype of the passive and effeminate Asian by invoking its binary opposite.

11. *Aiiieeeee! An Anthology of Asian-American Writers* (1974; Washington: Howard UP, 1983), xxxviii; *The Big Aiiieeeee! An Anthology of Asian American Writers* (New York: New American Library, forthcoming). All the Asian classics cited are available in English translations: Sun Tzu, *The Art of War,* trans. Samuel B. Griffith (London: Oxford UP, 1963); Shi Nai'an and Luo Guanzhong, *Outlaws of the Marsh* [*The Water Margin*], trans. Sidney Shapiro (jointly published by Beijing: Foreign Language P and Bloomington: Indiana UP, 1981); Luo Guan-Zhong, *Romance of the Three Kingdoms,* trans. C. H. Brewitt-Taylor (Singapore: Graham Brash, 1986), 2 vols.; Wu Ch'eng-en, *Journey to the West,* trans. Anthony Yu (Chicago: U of Chicago P, 1980), 4 vols.; Takeda Izumo, Miyoshi Shoraku, and Namiki Senryu, *Chushingura (The Treasury of Loyal Retainers).* trans. Donald Keene (New York: Columbia UP, 1971). I would like to thank Frank Chin for allowing me to see an early draft of *The Big Aiiieeeee!.* For a foretaste of his exposition of the Chinese heroic tradition, see "This is Not an Autobiography," *Genre* 18 (1985): 109–30.

12. The feminist works that come to mind include Paula Gunn Allen, *The Sacred Hoop: Recovering the Feminine in American Indian Traditions* (Boston: Beacon: 1986); Nina Auerbach, *Communities of Women: An Idea in Fiction* (Cambridge: Harvard UP, 1978); Zillah R. Eisenstein, *The Radical Future of Liberal Feminism* (New York: Longman, 1981); Carol Gilligan, *In a Differ-*

ent Voice: Psychological Theory and Women's Development (Cambridge: Harvard UP, 1982); Christa Wolf, *Cassandra: A Novel and Four Essays,* trans. Jan van Heurck (New York: Farrar, 1984). The Chinese maxims appear in the introduction to *The Big Aiiieeeee!* (draft) and are quoted with the editors' permission. The same maxims are cited in Frank Chin, "This Is Not an Autobiography."

13. Chin, "This Is Not An Autobiography," 112, 122, 130.

14. "All of a Piece: Women's Poetry and Autobiography," *Life/Lines: Theorizing Women's Autobiography,* ed. Bella Brodzki and Celeste Schenck (Ithaca: Cornell UP, 1988), 286. See also Estelle Jelinek, ed., *Women's Autobiography: Essays in Criticism* (Bloomington: Indiana UP, 1980); Donna Stanton, *The Female Autograph* (New York: New York Literary Forum, 1984); Sidonie Smith, *Poetics of Women's Autobiography: Marginality and the Fictions of Self-Representation* (Bloomington: Indiana UP, 1987).

15. "The Most Popular Book in China," *Quilt 4,* ed. Ishmael Reed and Al Young (Berkeley: Quilt, 1984), 12. The essay is republished as the "Afterword" in *The Chinaman Pacific & Frisco R. R. Co.* The literary duel between Chin, a self-styled "Chinatown Cowboy," and Kingston, an undisguised feminist, closely parallels the paper war between Ishmael Reed and Alice Walker.

16. "The Mysterious West," *New York Review of Books,* 28 April 1977: 41.

17. "Critic of Admirer Sees Dumb Racist," *San Francisco Journal,* 11 May 1977: 20.

18. "Autobiography as Guided Chinatown Tour?," *American Lives: Essays in Multicultural American Autobiography,* ed. James Robert Payne (Knoxville: U of Tennessee P, forthcoming). See also Deborah Woo, "The Ethnic Writer and the Burden of 'Dual Authenticity': The Dilemma of Maxine Hong Kingston," forthcoming in *Amerasia Journal.* Reviews by Chinese American women who identify strongly with Kingston's protagonist include Nellie Wong, "The Woman Warrior," *Bridge* (Winter 1978): 46–48; and Suzi Wong, review of *The Woman Warrior, Amerasia Journal* 4.1 (1977): 165–67.

19. "Gender and Genre Anxiety: Elizabeth Barrett Browning and H. D. as Epic Poets," *Tulsa Studies in Women's Literature* 5.2 (Fall 1986): 203–28.

20. Furthermore, a work highlighting sexism within an ethnic community is generally more palatable to the reading public than a work that condemns racism. *The Woman Warrior* addresses both forms of oppression, but critics have focused almost exclusively on its feminist themes.

21. Susanne Juhasz argues that because women have traditionally lived a "kind of private life, that of the imagination, which has special significance due to the outright conflict between societal possibility and imaginative possibility, [Kingston] makes autobiography from fiction, from fantasy, from forms that have conventionally belonged to the novel" ("Towards a Theory of Form in Feminist Autobiography," *International Journal of Women's Studies* 2.1 [1979]: 62).

22. Cf. similar critical responses in the African American community provoked by Alice Walker's *The Color Purple* and Toni Morrison's *Beloved.*

Although I limit my discussion to sexual politics in Chinese America, Asian American women are just as vulnerable to white sexism, as the denigrating stereotypes discussed by Kim earlier suggest.

23. Li Ju-Chen, *Flowers in the Mirror,* trans. and ed. Lin Tai-Yi (London: Peter Owen, 1965).

24. A recent case has been made into a powerful public television documentary: "Who Killed Vincent Chin?" (directed by Renee Tajima and Christine Choy, 1989). Chin, who punched a white auto-worker in Detroit in response to his racial slurs, was subsequently battered to death by the worker and his stepson with a baseball bat.

25. The interview was conducted by Kay Bonetti for the American Audio Prose Library (Columbia, MO, 1986).

Jonathan Culler has discussed the various implications, for both sexes, of "Reading as a Woman" (*On Deconstruction: Theory and Criticism after Structuralism* [Ithaca: Cornell UP, 1982], 43–64); see also *Men in Feminism,* ed. Alice Jardine and Paul Smith (New York: Methuen, 1987).

26.   The other modes are found in works as diverse as T'ao Ch'ien's poems (pastoral), Ch'u Yuan's *Li sao* (elegiac), selected writing by Lao Tzu and Chuang Tzu (metaphysical), and P'u Sung-ling's *Liao-Chai Chih I* (Gothic). (My thanks to Shu-mei Shih and Adam Schorr for helping me with part of the romanization.) One must bear in mind, however, that Asian and Western generic terms often fail to correspond. For example, what the *Aiiieeeee!* editors call "epics" are loosely classified as "novels" in Chinese literature.

27.   Epic heroes, according C. M. Bowra, are "the champions of man's ambitions" seeking to "win as far as possible a self-sufficient manhood" (*Heroic Poetry* [London: Macmillan, 1952], 14). Their Chinese counterparts are no exception.

28.   Benjamin R. Tong argues that the uneducated Cantonese peasants who comprised the majority of early Chinese immigrants were not docile but venturesome and rebellious, that putative Chinese traits such as meekness and obedience to authority were in fact "reactivated" in America in response to white racism ("The Ghetto of the Mind," *Amerasia Journal* 1.3 [1971]: 1–31). Chin, who basically agrees with Tong, also attributes the submissive and "unheroic" traits of Chinese Americans to Christianity ("This Is Not An Autobiography"). While Tong and Chin are right in distinguishing the Cantonese folk culture of the early immigrants from the classical tradition of the literati, they underestimate the extent to which mainstream Chinese thought infiltrated Cantonese folk imagination, wherein the heroic ethos coexists with Buddhist beliefs and Confucian teachings (which do counsel self-restraint and obedience to parental and state authority). To attribute the "submissive" traits of Chinese Americans entirely to white racism or to Christianity is to discount the complexity and the rich contradictions of the Cantonese culture and the resourceful flexibility and adaptability of the early immigrants.

29.   "This Is Not an Autobiography," 127.

30.   Conflicting attitudes toward Homeric war heroes are discussed in Katherine Callen King, *Achilles: Paradigms of the War Hero from Homer to the Middle Ages* (Berkeley: U of California P, 1987). Pacifist or at least anti-killing sentiments can be found in the very works deemed "heroic" by Chin and the editors. *Romance of the Three Kingdoms* not only dramatizes the senseless deaths and the ravages of war but also betrays a wishful longing for peace and unity, impossible under the division of "three kingdoms." Even *The Art of War* sets benevolence above violence and discourages actual fighting and killing: "To subdue the enemy without fighting is the acme of skill" (77).

31.   " 'Don't Tell': Imposed Silences in *The Color Purple* and *The Woman Warrior,*" *PMLA* (March 1988): 166. I must add, however, that paradoxes about manhood inform Chinese as well as American cultures. The "contradictions inherent in the bourgeois male ideal" is pointed out by Yarborough: "the use of physical force is, at some levels, antithetical to the middle-class privileging of self-restraint and reason: yet an important component of conventional concepts of male courage is the willingness to use force" ("Race, Violence, and Manhood: The Masculine Ideal in Frederick Douglass's 'Heroic Slave' "). Similarly, two opposing ideals of manhood coexist in Chinese culture, that of a civil scholar who would never stoop to violence and that of a fearless warrior who would not brook insult or injustice. Popular Cantonese maxims such as "a superior man would only move his mouth but not his hands" (i.e. would never resort to physical combat) and "he who does not take revenge is not a superior man" exemplify the contradictions.

32.   Interview conducted by Kay Bonetti.

33.   *Tripmaster Monkey: His Fake Book* (New York: Knopf, 1989), 348.

34.   I am aware that a forceful response to oppression is sometimes necessary, that it is much easier for those who have never encountered physical blows and gunshots to maintain

faith in nonviolent resistance. My own faith was somewhat shaken while watching the tragedy of Tiananmen on television; on the other hand, the image of the lone Chinese man standing in front of army tanks reinforced my belief that there is another form of heroism that far excels brute force.

35.   Lee Rainwater and William L. Yancey, *The Moynihan Report and the Politics of Controversy* (Cambridge: M.I.T. Press, 1967), 88 (p. 42) in the original report by Daniel Patrick Moynihan).

36.   "On the Issue of Roles," *The Black Woman: An Anthology,* ed. Toni Cade (York, ON: Mentor-NAL, 1970), 103; see also Bell Hooks, *Ain't I a Woman: Black Women and Feminism* (Boston: South End Press, 1981), 87–117.

37.   *Lenin and Philosophy and Other Essays* (New York: Monthly Review Press, 1971), 174–83.

38.   Of course, Asians are not all alike, and most generalizations are ultimately misleading. Elaine Kim pointed out to me that "It's popularly thought that Japanese strive for peaceful resolution of conflict and achievement of consensus while Koreans—for material as much as metaphysical reasons—seem at times to encourage combativeness in one another" (personal correspondence, quoted with permission). Differences within each national group are no less pronounced.

39.   *Inessential Woman: Problems of Exclusion in Feminist Thought* (Boston: Beacon, 1988), 115. I omitted class from my discussion only because it is not at the center of the literary debate.

40.   Elaine Kim, *Asian American Literature: An Introduction to the Writings and Their Social Context* (Philadelphia: Temple UP, 1982), 209.

41.   Donald Goellnicht, for instance, has argued that a girl from a racial minority "experiences not a single, but a double subject split: first, when she becomes aware of the gendered position constructed for her by the symbolic language of patriarchy; and second, when she recognizes that discursively and socially constructed positions of racial difference also obtain . . . [that] the 'fathers' of her racial and cultural group are silenced and degraded by the Laws of the Ruling Fathers" ("Father Land and/or Mother Tongue: The Divided Female Subject in *The Woman Warrior* and *Obasan,*" paper delivered at the MLA Convention, 1988).

42.   *The History of Sexuality,* vol. 1, trans. Robert Hurley (New York: Vintage, 1980), 101.

43.   Teresa de Lauretis, *Technologies of Gender: Essays on Theory, Film, and Fiction* (Bloomington: Indiana UP, 1987), 11.

The Subject of Memoirs:
The Woman Warrior's Technology
of Ideographic Selfhood

LEE QUINBY

In his 1982 essay "The Subject and Power," Michel Foucault argues that the modern era places individuals in a "kind of political 'double-bind,'" which is the simultaneous individualization and totalization of modern power structures." He further suggests that "maybe the target nowadays is not to discover what we are but to refuse what we are," adding that, since this is the case, "we have to promote new forms of subjectivity through the refusal of this kind of individuality which has been imposed on us for several centuries."[1] I do not know whether Foucault was familiar with Maxine Hong Kingston's *The Woman Warrior,* published six years earlier. But Kingston, it seems, in the words she uses to describe her childhood dream of becoming a warrior woman, had anticipated that "the call would come."[2] In *The Woman Warrior* she promotes "new forms of subjectivity" by refusing the totalizing individuality of the modern era.

Kingston's refusal rejects the fields of representation that have promoted that subjectivity. The subtitle of *The Woman Warrior* specifies its genre: *Memoirs of a Girlhood among Ghosts.* Kingston has emphasized the importance of this subtitle in an essay called "Cultural Mis-readings by American Reviewers," in which she reemphasizes her work's genre by stating that she is "not writing history or sociology but a 'memoir' like Proust." She writes approvingly of two reviewers who recognize this point, stating that she is, "as Diane Johnson says, 'slyly writing a memoir, a form which . . . can neither [be] dismiss[ed] as fiction nor quarrel[ed] with as fact,' " and confirming Christine Cook's comment that "the structure is a grouping of memoirs. . . . It is by definition a series of stories or anecdotes to illuminate the times rather than be autobiographical."[3]

Despite these efforts at clarification, critics have continued to ignore or resist the implications of Kingston's work as memoirs. The insightful and eloquent discussions of Paul John Eakin and Sidonie Smith acknowledge that Kingston's work challenges distinctions between fact and fiction, but they still treat the work as an autobiography rather than as memoirs. Although their respective discussions convert the *autos* or self of autobiography into a "self" understood as self-invention (Eakin) or self-representation (Smith), their readings of the work *as an autobiography*—even a postmodern one— delimit its full-scale assault on modern power structures.[4] My contention is that autobiography is a field of self-representation that has historically promoted the normalizing and disciplinary form of subjectivity that, as Foucault points out, we should "target." In what follows, I examine the ways in which the five memoirs that constitute *The Woman Warrior* subject modern power formations to the scrutiny of one who has been subjected by them.[5] I want to illuminate the ways in which *The Woman Warrior* constructs a new form of subjectivity, what I call an *ideographic selfhood*. This new subjectivity refuses the particular forms of selfhood, knowledge, and artistry that the systems of power of the modern era (including the discourses of autobiography) have made dominant.

Reading *The Woman Warrior* as memoirs rather than as autobiography has more at stake than redressing aesthetic assumptions regarding genre. It serves to direct attention to the particular formation of subjectivity constructed by these different discourses and the technologies of power within which they operate as self-constituting practices. Modern memoirs as a genre emerged more than two centuries prior to modern autobiography; the *Oxford English Dictionary* (OED) lists the date of the first appearance of the singular *memoir* as 1567 and of the plural *memoirs* as 1659. *Autobiography* makes its first appearance in 1809. But as James M. Cox has argued, the term *autobiography* is now "so dominant that it is used retroactively to include as well as to entitle books from the present all the way back into the ancient world."[6] This expansion of autobiography is a form of discursive colonization that, both as an authorial choice of genre and as a critical designation, produces and is produced by the normalizing subjectivity that has come to dominate the post-Enlightenment West.

The ways of constituting an "I" within these respective discursive formations demonstrate some of the key differences between them, differences that have been instrumental in establishing autobiography as a privileged aesthetic and ethical discourse of the modern era and in maintaining a marginalized status for memoirs. Whereas autobiography promotes an "I" that shares with confessional discourse an assumed interiority and an ethical mandate to examine that interiority, memoirs promote an "I" that is explicitly constituted in the reports of the utterances and proceedings of others. The "I" or subjectivity produced in memoirs is externalized and, in the Bakhtinian sense, overtly dialogical.[7] Unlike the subjectivity of autobiography, which is presumed to be unitary and continuous over time, memoirs (particularly in their collective form) construct a subjectivity that is multiple and discontinuous. The ways that an "I" is inscribed in the discourse of memoirs therefore operate in resistance to the modern era's dominant construction of individualized selfhood, which follows the dictum to, above all else, know thy interior self. In relation to autobiography, then, memoirs function as countermemory.

In situating autobiography historically as a self-normalizing practice of the modern era, it is important to recognize the ways in which autobiographies by marginalized people have often challenged the conventions and power relations of traditional autobiography, as recent feminist scholarship such as Sidonie Smith's work and the essays in such collections as *The Private Self* and *Life/Lines* demonstrate.[8] If I risk making too harsh a case against autobiography, it is certainly not to dismiss those challenges. But it is to insist that we scrutinize the extent to which such writings promote, despite their challenges, the subjectivity—the totalized individuality—of the modern era.[9] It is also to point out that applying the label "autobiographical" to all types of life writings—even when their titles announce them as memoirs, testimonials, confessions, or the like—tends to reduce and narrow our reading of the text.[10] On the other side of the issue, my argument risks overvalorizing memoirs. Memoirs as a discourse could, of course, be used to promote reprehensible political programs, but my point is that—in the modern era, at any rate—it would provide a less effective means of doing so, given its marginalized status in relation to autobiography or other more dominant genres and given its dialogical format, which destabilizes unified selfhood. What I wish to show are the ways in which Kingston's use of memoirs negotiates a confrontation with disciplinary power relations, a confrontation that can be suggestive for feminist theorizing as well as for literary criticism.

As an ensemble of several discourses, the genre of memoirs rejects the discursive unity that constructs subjectivity as simultaneously individualized and totalized, for, as the *OED* indicates, *memoirs* names a type of writing that is a composite of several generic discourses. The *OED* defines *memoir* as a "note, memorandum; record" and the collective plural *memoirs* as "a record of events, not purporting to be a complete history, but treating of such matters as come within the personal knowledge of the writer, or are obtained from certain particular sources of information"; and "a person's written account of records in his [*sic*] own life, of the persons whom he has known, and the transactions or movements in which he has been concerned; an autobiographical record"; also, "a biography, or biographical notice"; "an essay or dissertation on a learned subject on which the writer has made particular observations. Hence *pl.* the record of the proceedings or transactions of a learned society"; and, finally, "a memento, memorial." *The Woman Warrior* is precisely such a composite.

The etymology of *memoirs* is also particularly resonant for characterizing *The Woman Warrior.* Again from the *OED:* "F. *memoire* masc., a specialized use, with alteration of gender, of *memoire*, fem., MEMORY. The change of gender is commonly accounted for by the supposition that the use of the word in this sense is elliptical for *écrit pour mémoire*; Sp. Pg. and It. have *memoira* fem. in all senses." English usage retains a quasi-French pronunciation but has anglicized the spelling, making the word, according to the *OED*, "somewhat anomalous." Thus the word itself may be understood as a metonymy of Kingston's particular discursive position. As a Chinese-American, her linguistic heritage is informed by two different language systems. As a woman, she is a "somewhat anomalous" memoirist, using a grammatically feminine term that has been colonized by a masculine form. The word *memoirs* in Kingston's subtitle is in this sense a signifier of subjugated femininity subversively erupting against linguistic and literary exclusion.

Even as Kingston draws on the term *memoirs* as a generic description, the word *ghosts* in her subtitle indicates that memoirs are not an exclusively empirical record of events and individuals. This use of ghosts places her in lineage with Virginia Woolf, who, as Shari Benstock points out, also associates memoir writing with the inclusion of material on "invisible presences." In *Moments of Being*, which includes five pieces Benstock calls "fragments of a memoir," Woolf describes the importance of these "invisible presences": "This influence, by which I mean the consciousness of other groups impinging upon ourselves; public opinion; what other people say and think; all those magnets which attract us this way to be like that, or repel us the other and make us different from that; has never been analyzed in any of those Lives which I so much enjoy reading, or very superficially." Benstock explains that Woolf's mother is one of these "invisible presences," not because she is absent from the memoir, but rather because she is so much present, "too central, too close, to be observed." Woolf argues, "If we cannot analyze these invisible presences, we know very little of *the subject of the memoir*."[11]

In *The Woman Warrior* ghosts have their own specificity as "invisible presences." Kingston represents her girlhood as triply displaced because of America's deeply embedded Sinophobia, her parents' ambivalence about America and the poverty they face, and the misogynistic attitudes she finds in both her American and Chinese heritages. The idea of ghosts thus suggests the profound confusion she felt as a child amid the concealed but felt hatreds of both China and America. She is haunted by the stories of China that her mother told her, stories of women's oppression and female infanticide. She discloses that she also lived in fear of those who performed the regular but often unseen services of quotidian life in America, which was, she says, "full of machines and ghosts—Taxi Ghosts, Bus Ghosts, Police Ghosts, Fire Ghosts, Meter Reader Ghosts, Tree Trimming Ghosts, Five-and-Dime Ghosts" (pp. 96–97)—members of American society who came regularly but without friendship, who filled the world with frightening noises and kept her family under surveillance. Both kinds of ghosts haunt her even into adulthood. But in adulthood the writing of her memoirs serves as a ritual of exorcism that "drives the fear away" (p. 205). As Woolf points out, memoirs confront what other forms of life writing too often ignore—the pervasive "invisible presences" that are the most profound determinants of subjectivity.

The form of subjectivity explored in *The Woman Warrior* may be located at the nexus of two patriarchal technologies of power, the deployment of alliance and the deployment of sexuality, which operate in interlocking ways in the American nuclear family. Foucault argues that the deployment of alliance— the "mechanisms of constraint" that operate through "a system of marriage, of fixation and development of kinship ties, of transmission of names and possessions"—predominated in the West prior to the eighteenth century.[12] With the decline of monarchical rule and the emergence of modern nation-states, a second technology of power—the deployment of sexuality—came to be superimposed on this system. Rather than operating through constraint and the law, this technology functions by "proliferating, innovating, annexing, creating, and penetrating bodies in an increasingly detailed way, and in controlling populations in an increasingly comprehensive way."[13] In *The Woman Warrior* the deployment of alliance is associated with Kingston's Chinese heritage and the deployment of sexuality with hegemonic American culture.

Although, as Foucault demonstrates, the deployment of sexuality took shape from the practices of alliance, particularly the confession and penance, it now operates through and within the domains of medicine, education, police surveillance, and psychiatry. In regard to women in particular, one of the primary axes of the deployment of sexuality is the process of "hysterization of women, which involved a thorough medicalization of their bodies and their sex . . . carried out in the name of the responsibility they owed to the health of their children, the solidity of the family institution, and the safeguarding of society." The bourgeois family is the "interchange of sexuality and alliance."[14]

Kingston situates the events of *The Woman Warrior* within her family's interchange of these two systems of power.[15] Through her depiction of her relationship to her mother, she portrays the dramatic intensity given to mother-daughter relations within these interlocking power structures, for within the family the mother is a site of intersection between the systems of alliance and sexuality, and so too the daughter is constituted as a future mother. In keeping with the dynamics of alliance, the mother's body perpetuates the father's lineage, oversees the exchange of daughters in marriage, and maintains kinship ties. In keeping with the dynamics of sexuality, the mother's body is the site of integration (for herself and her children) into the medical sphere, and her fecundity is integral to the social body through the reproduction and moral education of children.[16]

Within the nuclear family, then, it is the mother's obligation to turn her daughter into a mother. To the extent that she succeeds, she aligns her daughter with herself at the point of intersection between the deployment of alliance and the deployment of sexuality. *The Woman Warrior* is a discourse of resistance to the subjectification of the daughter within this family dynamic. Such resistance is fraught with difficulties. Paramount among them is that, in trying to push away from the constraints of alliance's patriarchal law, daughters are pulled toward the enticements of sexuality's medicalizations. And in regard to mother-daughter bonds, a daughter's resistance carries with it a danger of completely severing her ties with her mother.

This dilemma is a paradigm of female subjectivity as it has been constituted in the modern era in the West. It is also a dilemma that plagues feminist theorizing. On the one hand, insofar as feminist discourse rejects patriarchal constraint by valorizing what Foucault has called "a hermeneutics of desire," it enters the domain of the deployment of sexuality; such a hermeneutics constructs subjects for whom the "truth of their being" is to be found in desire (including but not limited to sexual acts).[17] On the other hand, insofar as feminist discourse rejects the proliferating mechanisms within the deployment of sexuality by valorizing womanhood, matriarchal kinship, and feminine essence, it reverts to the system of alliance. *The Woman Warrior* is a particularly important work in this regard, for it combats both deployments of power by saying no to the repressions of patriarchal constraint without saying yes to the enticements of the sexualized body. At the same time, it forges mother-daughter bonds in which the daughter is not required to become yet another "dutiful daughter" in preparation for patriarchally circumscribed motherhood.[18]

Throughout *The Woman Warrior,* language, both oral and written, is one of the "invisible presences" that constitute the subject of memoirs.[19] The memoirs recount extensively Kingston's own difficulties with language, focusing on them as a feature of the conflict of cultural impulses within Chinese-American culture generally and her Chinese-American family specifically. As Sidonie Smith has pointed out, Kingston suggests that her difficulty with language "originates in the memory of her mother's literally cutting the voice out of her" when her mother cut her daughter's frenum.[20] In Kingston's words: "She pushed my tongue up and sliced the frenum. Or maybe she snipped it with a pair of nail scissors. I don't remember her doing it, only her telling me about it, but all during childhood I felt sorry for the baby whose mother waited with scissors or knife in hand for it to cry—and then, when its mouth was wide open like a baby bird's, cut" (pp. 163–64). The cut frenum serves as a figure for the dilemma of the conflicting subjectivities produced by the systems of alliance and sexuality, for the frenum is a membrane that both restrains and supports the tongue. "The Chinese," Kingston reports, "say 'a ready tongue is an evil' " (p. 164). Yet her mother tells her that she cut her frenum in order to *give* her a ready tongue, telling her that her "tongue would be able to move in any language," that she would be "able to speak languages that are completely different from one another" (p. 164). By the end of the text, this capacity is shown to be necessary in an interdependent world.

Whatever her mother's motives, the predicament that Kingston discloses as the result of the cutting is that of being caught between alliance's imposition of muteness on women and sexuality's pathology of hysterical babbling. Finding herself suspended in the spaces between her family's use of Chinese and her birth society's use of English, Kingston recounts that she fell into semi-muteness and experienced physical pain when required to speak aloud. After an episode of cruelty to another young girl, in many ways her double but one who had been less resistant to the imposed passivity of Chinese-American femininity, she herself experienced an eighteen-month-long "mysterious illness" in which she, like "the Victorian recluses," remained indoors, a virtual invalid. Upon returning to school, she had "to figure out again how to talk" (p. 182). But to talk is to risk becoming garrulously incoherent. Kingston cites examples of several women who are called insane, including her mother's sister, and fears that she too might lapse into mental illness. "Insane people," she observes, seemed to be "the ones who couldn't explain themselves" (p. 186). Her own self-explanations are so often blurred by the mix of two incommensurate languages that as a child she feels unable not only to explain herself but even to understand the explanations of others. She finds consolation in talking to the "adventurous people inside [her] head" but fears that such a practice is yet another sign of abnormality.[21]

From the perspective of adulthood, the point of view from which the memoirs are composed, Kingston indicates that these problems derived not so much from within her as from the refusal of others to listen to the experiences of those they deem Other and their readiness to designate that otherness as abnormal. "A Song for a Barbarian Reed Pipe," the last of the five intertwining accounts that make up *The Woman Warrior,* relates a humiliating incident that crystallizes the sense of confused self she had as a child. Asked by her first-grade teacher to read a lesson aloud to the rest of the class, she falters over the word "I." "I could not understand 'I,' " she recalls. The teacher, enmeshed in the disciplinary pedagogical regime of the modern era, exiles her to a site of public shame—"the low corner under the stairs . . . where the noisy boys usually sat" (pp. 166–67).

The irony, of course, is that the child has stumbled onto a profundity about which the teacher is unaware: the first person pronoun "I" is not at all simple; nor is it as unified as the "I" of autobiography implies. To clarify this point, Kingston invites readers to see through her eyes as a Chinese-American child for whom writing had hitherto been ideographic. "The Chinese 'I' has seven strokes, intricacies. How could the American 'I,' assuredly wearing a hat like the Chinese, have only three strokes, the middle so straight?" (p. 166). The child's question challenges the sense of self associated in Kingston's memoirs with nonideographic writing, a self that promises autonomy, certainty, and unequivocal moral righteousness. The memoirs record that the phallic American "I" systematically denies its multiplicity and interconnectedness, masquerading as self-contained, independent subjectivity and imposing its will on others, often in the name of justice. The self/other dichotomy concealed within the American "I" stationed immigrant families in slums, then paved over the slums with parking lots; relegated immigrants to menial, low-paying labor; sneered at Chinese voices; used logic, science, and mathematics against "superstitious" modes of knowing; and branded children unable to read English with a "zero IQ" (pp. 48, 183).[22] Such an "I," she warns, is not merely a harmful illusion, it is a form of imperialism.

Yet the alternative Chinese "I" is not without its own traps, for Kingston also points out that there is a "Chinese word for the female *I*—which is 'slave,' " adding with a note of bitterness that the Chinese "break the women with their own tongues!" (p. 47). Thus the ideographic conjunction of slave and female "I" makes visible the added problem for selfhood confronting Kingston—her gender redoubles the second-class status imposed on Chinese-Americans. So pronounced is the legacy of female inferiority that it unsettles the love her family gives her. Even after she has left home as an adult, conflicting experiences of familial love and female disdain haunt her. "From afar I can believe my family loves me fundamentally," she writes. "They only say, 'When fishing for treasures in the flood, be careful not to pull in girls,' because that is what one says about daughters." But such rationalization fails to satisfy in the face of nagging memories: "I had watched such words come out of my mother's and father's mouths; I looked at their ink drawing of poor people snagging their neighbors' flotage with long flood hooks and pushing the girl babies on down the river. And I had to get out of hating range" (p. 52).

Kingston's "I" does not remain caught between the American "I"'s facade of autonomy (belied, in any case, for women by the demands of what Kingston calls "American-feminine" behavior) and the Chinese "I"'s designation of women as inferior. Rather, even at the level of writing as graphic inscription, *The Woman Warrior* challenges the operations of power that have historically and culturally been invested in the Chinese ideograph and the American alphabet.[23] Kingston's resistance to these graphic signifiers of power/knowledge rejects the notion that one can discover (invent or find) a language that "transcends" existing power formations. Instead, *The Woman Warrior* problematizes inherited intertwinings of writing, meaning, artistry, and experience and constructs a technology of the self that resists the subjectivities promoted by patriarchal ideographic and alphabetic language.[24] In other words, Kingston uses each tradition to intervene against the other. From this intervention, she constructs a subjectivity through a form of writing that forces the American script of her text to reveal its intricacies in the way Chinese ideographs do.

The ideographic "I" of Kingston's memoirs valorizes individual freedom while at the same time defining selfhood as an ensemble subjectivity. In terms of narrative time, the ideographic "I" of *The Woman Warrior* intersects the distanced time of a retrospective point of view with a displayed time of processive narration.[25] This use of time past and time present thus disrupts Western conventions of historical and sociological discourse that promote the notion of objective reporting of events. Instead, Kingston's memoirs display the intersection of knowing subject and known object. The subjectivity that emerges from this conjunction is interdependent and interrelational, a self that acknowledges separation and difference from others even while cultivating intimacy and interconnection. It is a subjectivity that recognizes the selfhood of the other and acknowledges its own alterity.[26] In short, Kingston's interventions in her inherited subjectivity constitute a new technology of ideographic selfhood.

As Foucault has argued and as Kingston's critique of the Chinese and American "I"s demonstrates, writing is a significant exercise of selfhood. Kingston's memoirs challenge the ways that the deployment of alliance and the deployment of sexuality function to, in Foucault's words, turn "real lives into writing." *The Woman Warrior* rejects alliance's "procedure of heroization" that has traditionally chronicled the lives of powerful men, those who have power over others, by relating instead stories about women who have been subordinated by such men. The memoirs also refuse the deployment of sexuality's "procedure of objectification and subjection" that disciplines and normalizes individuals in modern society.[27] Those practices of writing construct a subjectivity that either monumentalizes individuals in the system of alliance or normalizes them in the system of sexuality. Although different from one another, both of these forms of subjectivity deny or conceal the incoherencies, confusions, contradictions, and gaps constituting any selfhood. In opposition to claims for a unified and coherent subjectivity, Kingston's memoirs accentuate the conflicts and confusions of identity that constitute her discursive "I." The evocation of an ideographic selfhood acknowledges a complex, discontinuous, multilayered subjectivity.

Kingston's technology of ideographic selfhood and its corresponding aesthetics and ethics entail putting into written discourse stories from the Chinese oral tradition, many of them told to her by her mother. Each story adds a stroke to her ideographic selfhood, and each stroke is a form of resistance to the deployments of power that would either constrain women's sexuality or hystericize it. Structurally, the five titled accounts that make up *The Woman Warrior* clarify the operations of these power formations and Kingston's oppositions to each. The first two enact, in the telling of the stories of No Name Woman and Fa Mu Lan, respectively, limited attempts to counter the deployments of alliance and of sexuality. The third and fourth reveal, through representing the lives of Kingston's mother and aunt, respectively, the detrimental effects of alliance and sexuality. And the final piece combines stories about the poetess Ts'ai Yen and Kingston's grandmother, who "loved the theater," to represent a subjectivity that emerges in resistance to both systems of power.

The first chapter of the memoirs, "No Name Woman," retells a story told to Kingston by her mother on the occasion of the daughter's onset of menses. It rehearses the plight of her father's sister, whose pregnancy by a man not her husband brands her a transgressor of village morality. No Name Woman refuses to identify the father of her child, thus giving her designation a double meaning—she has no name because she refuses to reveal his name. "She kept the man's name to herself throughout her labor and dying," Kingston writes. "She did not accuse him that he be punished with her. To save her inseminator's name she gave silent birth" (p. 11). The villagers live by the deployment of alliance's code of patriarchal justice, which entitles them to slaughter the family's animals, smear blood on the walls and doors, and yell curses at the pregnant woman. Facing a life of such ostracism for herself and her family, the aunt kills herself and her newborn baby by plunging into a well. This is a "spite suicide," Kingston notes, for it ruined the family's water supply; but drowning the baby with her is an act of love: "Mothers who love their children take them along" (p. 15).

Over the years her aunt's drowned, "weeping" body with "wet hair hanging and skin bloated," seemed always to wait "silently by the water to pull down a substitute" (p. 16). In keeping with alliance's system of power, her mother had told her this story of family shame as a warning against women's transgressive sexuality, with a strict injunction never to tell of No Name Woman's existence, adultery, and suicide. Kingston not only tells her readers about her aunt, she embellishes her version of the story with an empathy and her aunt with a sexuality that her mother would not tolerate, perpetuating as she does the villagers' sense of justice and the aunt's immorality. Twenty years after hearing about No Name Woman, Kingston refuses to continue her silent complicity in the code of moral vengeance and strictures on women that had exacted her aunt's death. In her public disclosure she too transgresses the code of alliance and thus allies herself with her aunt. As Sidonie Smith has argued, Kingston's "story thus functions as a sign, like her aunt's enlarging belly, publicizing the potentially disruptive force of female textuality and the matrilineal descent of the texts."[28]

Kingston's revelation of the story of No Name Woman serves as her memoirs' first act of self-empowerment through writing and a rejection of village morality. As such, it demarcates the nexus of alliance and sexuality within the family, a place where transgression within the system of alliance readily converts into the confessional mode of the system of sexuality.[29] *The Woman Warrior* allows us to see the ways in which feminist efforts to liberate women from the repressions of the patriarchal juridical code run the risk of entrenching women more deeply within the deployment of sexuality's proliferating dynamics of power. More important, Kingston's work manages to resist this pull by employing what Foucault has called a "movement of de-sexualization," which displaces the apparatuses of morality, normality, and artistry operating within the deployment of sexuality; such de-sexualization looks for "new forms of community, co-existence, pleasure."[30] "White Tigers," the second piece in the memoirs, may be understood as a point of departure for diffusing the power dynamics that would otherwise pull her sexual/textual transgression into the confessional dynamic inherent to the deployment of sexuality with which autobiography is complicit.

It should be stressed that "White Tigers" is a beginning point of resistance, for the blending of self-sacrifice and justice enacted at this stage is a child's fantasy of heroics, a fantasy that powerfully but *playfully* brings together the legend of Fa Mu Lan—derived from a chant her mother had taught her about a woman warrior who had avenged her village—and heroes from American movies.[31] As a child, Kingston had become infatuated with this woman warrior, a woman who, in contrast to the American and Chinese women she knew, received honor for her deeds both in battle, from which women are traditionally excluded, and in patriarchal motherhood, through which women have been subordinated. Imagination thus provides an outlet against the double devaluation she has experienced as a Chinese-American girl, and in her theater of the mind she herself becomes this woman warrior who undergoes strenuous years of discipline and training so that she may take her place as both soldier and mother. Ultimately, however, like No Name Woman, whose sexual transgression is limited in its challenge to the system of alliance, Kingston's fantasies of being a female avenger deflect, without fully challenging, the process of sexualization to which an adolescent female is subjected in the United States.

Ideographs inaugurate the fantasy world of "White Tigers" and mark points of development of an ideographic selfhood. Initially, nature's ideographs summon the child to the challenge of greater humanity. "The call would come," she writes, "from a bird that flew over our roof. In the brush drawings it looks like the ideograph for 'human,' two black wings" (p. 20). When the call comes, the girl of seven leaves home to join an old man and old woman who train her to become a warrior, a training that includes exercises resembling body writing. "I learned to move my fingers, hands, feet, head, and entire body in circles. I walked putting heel down first, toes pointing outward thirty to forty degrees, making the ideograph 'eight,' making the ideograph 'human.' . . . I could copy owls and bats, the words for 'bat' and 'blessing' homonyms" (p. 23). After years of preparation, she returns home to bid her parents farewell before leaving for battle. Again, the theme of inscription is repeated as her parents mark her body with their love and desire for revenge. By carving into her back their "oaths and names," they transform her body into a testament of family honor. "My father first brushed the words in ink," she records. "Then he began cutting; . . . My mother caught the blood and wiped the cuts with a cold towel soaked in wine. It hurt terribly—the cuts sharp; the air burning; the alcohol cold, then hot—pain so various. . . . If an enemy should flay me, the light would shine through my skin like lace" (pp. 34–35). In battle, the woman warrior avenges her family and village, regaining their lands; she marries her childhood friend, bears a child, and upon victory returns to her village to live out her days in honor.

The fantasy portion of "White Tigers," with its heroic deeds and "happily ever after" ending, is juxtaposed in its concluding section against feelings of frustration, impotence, and confusion in bringing about gender, racial, and class equality. Marching and studying at Berkeley in the 1960s does not turn Kingston into the boy her parents would have preferred. Confronting an employer with his racism, she is dismissed from her job. In describing the death of an uncle in China who was killed by the Communists for stealing food for his family rather than giving it to the "commune kitchen to be shared," she admits that it is "confusing that my family was not the poor to be championed" (p. 51). And she laments her inability to avenge her family: "I'd have to storm across China to take back our farm from the Communists; I'd have to rage across the United States to take back the laundry in New York and the one in California. Nobody in history has conquered and united both North America and Asia" (p. 51).

Although the heroics of Fa Mu Lan are naive in terms of political practice, the story of the female avenger constitutes a bold stroke in Kingston's ideographic selfhood. The avenger's feats of courage are an inverse expression of the powerlessness imposed on Kingston as a Chinese-American female, but an expression that ultimately empowers her as an author and allows her to become a different kind of warrior, one who makes public the wrongs done against her people. Comparing herself to the woman warrior of her fantasy, as the title of the memoirs also does, she observes that what "we have in common are the words at our backs. The ideographs for *revenge* are 'report a crime' and 'report to five families.' The reporting is the vengeance—not the beheading, the gutting, but the words. And I have so many words—'chink' words and 'gook' words too—that they do not fit on my skin" (p. 53). As a writer-warrior, then, Kingston's image of words *in excess* of her body suggests that writing itself must veer away from monumentalizing and normalizing regimes of power and serve instead to corporealize a subjectivity that can take revenge on forces of domination. This excess of words disrupts racist and sexist categories of containment through which the dominant and dominating regimes of power are constructed.

Much of the drama of *The Woman Warrior* derives from Kingston's representation of her mother as a force of domination.[32] Rather than denying or suppressing the deeply embedded ambivalence her mother arouses in her, Kingston unrelentingly evokes the powerful presence of her mother, arduously and often painfully exploring her difficulties in identifying with and yet separating from her. Her record of differentiation from her mother involves confrontation with the two systems of power that intersect within the family. This ethical-political process of separation is a precarious one, for it threatens repudiation of the mother or abandonment by her, the two opposing responses that Kingston depicts as terrifying to her as a child. Yet emulating her mother would perpetuate two modes of oppression: the subordination of women under the Law of the Father within the deployment of alliance, and the proliferating hysterization of women within the deployment of sexuality. Writing the memoirs provides a means for altering this dynamic by separating herself from her mother without severing their ties.

Kingston does this by weaving together two intertwined discursive threads integral to her technology of ideographic selfhood: healing and artistry. In order to create a new pattern, she must first unravel the preexisting designs of alliance's shamanism and maternal orality as well as that of the medicalization of sexuality and paternal literacy. Throughout *The Woman Warrior,* particularly in "Shaman," the third chapter, devoted to her mother, Brave Orchid, Kingston describes her mother's practices of midwifery and healing. Brave Orchid's shamanistic practices seem to the child a form of magic in comparison to the science and logic learned by the American-educated daughter as "American-normal." Although Kingston admires her mother and the other women of the To Keung School of Midwifery as "outside women," and "new women, scientists who changed the rituals," she deems her mother's practices to be superstitious and frightful. Such is the case, for example, with the "big brown hand with pointed claws stewing in alcohol and herbs" stored in a jar from which Brave Orchid would draw "tobacco, leeks, and grasses" to apply to her children's wounds (p. 91). Such is also the case with the power over life and death that her midwife mother possessed in China. Furthermore, her mother's diploma is disparaged by American health agencies, and as a result Brave Orchid must labor long hours as a laundry worker and tomato picker instead of in the profession for which she was trained. "This is terrible ghost-country," she reports her mother as saying, "where a human being works her life away" (p. 104).

Although Kingston sympathizes with her mother's professional exclusion in America, she nonetheless indicates that she holds many of the American attitudes that devalue her mother's methods of shamanistic healing. These conflicting feelings are intensified when her mother's treatments prove ineffectual and possibly harmful to the mental health of her sister Moon Orchid, whose story of deterioration is the subject of the fourth account, "At the Western Palace." Brave Orchid's ministrations might well have worked in the sisters' Chinese village decades before, where alliance's system of knowledge and morality prevailed. But in America they lead Moon Orchid to be declared insane by Western medical authorities, and she is placed in a California state mental asylum. Acceptance of her mother's beliefs, Kingston implies, might impose this judgment on her as well. She determines to differentiate herself from her mother through adherence to Western science and logic.

Yet this determination has another side, revealed in the description of Moon Orchid's response to the mental asylum. There she finds happiness in the company of other women, all of whom "speak the same language" (p. 160). The combined dread of and longing for insanity that Kingston expresses throughout *The Woman Warrior* results from the deployment of sexuality's process of hysterization of women. For to be a "proper" (procreative) woman within this technology of power means to be medicalized, means becoming either the "American-normal" Good Mother or the abnormal hysterical woman. In describing her own eighteen-month illness, when she lived "like the Victorian recluses," she reveals the thrill of invalidation that is so central to the invalidism of hystericized womanhood: "It was the best year and a half of my life. Nothing happened" (p. 182). Such yearning for nothingness is a consequence of overidentification with patriarchally inscribed motherhood: a paradoxical desire to return to prelinguistic infancy and remain forever a dependent daughter in order to evade the subjectivity that becoming a mother entails in the nexus of alliance and sexuality. This yearning may be understood as a form of resistance to women's subordination in a misogynistic society, but it is a resistance that turns back on itself, destroying not misogyny but the woman who suffers it.

Instead of entering this sphere of hysterization, Kingston creates a self-healing aesthetics. This requires differentiation from her mother's artistry, for, as with Brave Orchid's medicine, her form of art functions primarily within the system of alliance. Throughout her childhood, her mother's talk-stories had filled her imagination with "pictures to dream," some of them reveries of hope, as with the legend of Fa Mu Lan, and others leaving nightmarish images, as with the story of No Name Woman and the monkey story, in which eaters feast on the brain of a still-living monkey. Even though Brave Orchid is an artist, then, she is one who remains exclusively within the oral tradition and whose stories are often accompanied by the admonition not to tell anyone else. Kingston's written memoirs are a sign of separation from her mother's oral tradition and women's enforced silences, but they are also a sign of tribute to her mother: to the vividness of her stories and to her readiness to confront some of life's most terrifying moments.

Enthralled by her mother's courage and yet aware of her vulnerability in both China and America, and caught within her mother's complicated and often hostile attitude toward females, Kingston situates her childhood in the interstices of her two cultures, a place where she is in danger of plunging into either "feminine" muteness or hysteria. Acquiring a new voice is a feature of her new subjectivity. When she first gains a voice, however, she finds it through an overzealous repudiation of her mother. One day as they work together in the family laundry, she blurts out angrily, "I won't let you turn me into a slave or wife. . . . They say I'm smart now. Things follow in lines at school. They take stories and teach us to turn them into essays. . . . And I don't want to listen to any more of your stories; they have no logic. They scramble me up. You lie with stories" (pp. 201–2). Although the memoirs suggest that such vehemence was crucial for Kingston's construction of a new subjectivity, she follows this passage with a note of regret: "Be careful what you say. It comes true. It comes true. I had to leave home in order to see the world logically, logic the new way of seeing. I learned to think that mysteries are for explanation" (p. 204). Acquisition of the deployment of sexuality's empirical knowledge displaces the system of alliance's shamanistic knowledge.

But the acquisition of Western logic as constitutive of Kingston's new subjectivity does not entirely supplant Brave Orchid's way of knowing, and the memoirs are neither talk-stories nor logical essays but something of each and a challenge to both. In *The Woman Warrior* Kingston brings together her mother's talk-stories and conventions of Western logic in order to tell (her) truth without reducing its complexities. She divulges about No Name Woman what Brave Orchid has declared must never be revealed beyond the family. And she gives tribute to her mother as artist and healer even as she separates herself from her mother. In these ways, the memoirs show how through writing one can symbolically revisit one's mother, not as a child but as an adult who gives birth to herself as artist with the aid of her mother's midwifery.

Despite the troubled relationship between Kingston and her mother, and the difficulties that arise between them because of their clashing views of morality, healing, and artistry, that relationship nonetheless ultimately provides the momentum for Kingston's new—but never complete, never closed—subjectivity. Kingston's memoirs refuse alignment with phallic conceptualizations of art that ignore the mother's role as a teacher of language, define the mother tongue as crude in relation to the fatherly text, or see artistry as a symbolic playing out of the oedipal conflict between father and son. *The Woman Warrior* gives tribute to Brave Orchid's talk-stories and shamanism even as it marks Kingston's turn toward a written art that reveals and heals the wounds of patriarchal motherhood and daughterhood.[33]

The story of Ts'ai Yen, which concludes the memoirs with a tribute to the power of a woman who transformed sounds of captivity into piercingly beautiful music, enacts this turn. Kingston writes that this is a "story my mother told me, not when I was young, but recently, when I told her I also am a story-talker. The beginning is hers, the ending, mine" (p. 206). Her mother's story is about her own mother, Kingston's grandmother, who so loved the theater that she moved the entire family, as well as some of the household furnishings, to the theater when the actors came to her village. Although this is done in order to ensure the household's safety from bandits while the family is away enjoying the performance, as the story goes, the bandits attack the theater. They scatter the family and very nearly kidnap Lovely Orchid, Kingston's youngest aunt. By the end of the ordeal, however, "the entire family was home safe, proof to my grandmother that our family was immune to harm as long as they went to plays." She adds, "They went to many plays after that" (p. 207).

The family's frequent attendance at the theater is both a logical non sequitur and a meaning-producing narrative thread between her mother's story and Kingston's. "I like to think that at some of those performances, they heard the songs of Ts'ai Yen," writes Kingston (p. 207). This telling phrase, "I like to think," encapsulates the poetics and politics of Kingston's memoirs. As Trinh Minh-ha has observed, Kingston's writing, which is "neither fiction nor non-fiction, constantly invites the reader either to drift naturally from the realm of imagination to that of actuality or to live them both without ever being able to draw a clear line between them yet never losing sight of their differentiation."[34] Just as the village theater serves in her mother's story as the space of both fear and fortune, of cause and effect, so too the phrase "I like to think" serves in her memoirs as the field of the represented and the unrepresented, the recalled and the constructed. And the ending of the tale demonstrates that what is representable—and what is not—is subject to change.

The tale of Ts'ai Yen, a poet born in A.D. 175, is that of a young woman captured at the age of twenty by a barbarian tribe. By day over the twelve years of her captivity, she could hear only the "death sounds" of war; but night after night, the desert air would be filled with the sharp, high notes of her captors' reed flutes. Fascinated by their disturbing music, she finally taught herself to sing "a song so high and clear, it matched the flutes," a song in her own language, in words her captors could not understand, but filled with a "sadness and anger" that they could not fail to comprehend. When she was later ransomed and returned home, she brought her songs with her. One of these songs is "Eighteen Stanzas for a Barbarian Reed Pipe," a song the Chinese now "sing to their own instruments" (pp. 206–9).

Perhaps, like Ts'ai Yen's song, Kingston's memoirs sustained her in a hostile land. But unlike Ts'ai Yen, who eventually returned home, the hostile land from which Kingston writes *is* her homeland. The endemic ethnic, gender, and class hatreds that the memoirs document give rise to a sense of displacement and corresponding yearning for place akin to the ambivalence evoked by her mother. As with her relationship to her mother, Kingston poses a rethinking of women's place in regard not only to the family but also to territoriality.[35] This issue arises during a visit to her parents' home when she is an adult. Upon witnessing her mother's distress over having had to relinquish the last of their land in China, she responds: "We belong to the planet now, Mama. Does it make sense to you that if we're no longer attached to one piece of land, we belong to the planet? Wherever we happen to be standing, why, that spot belongs to us as much as any other spot" (p. 107). This is a remark that consoles, even as it refuses a mythologized evocation of an originary homeland.

Kingston's proposal of belonging to the planet also contrasts with the ways Edward Said, Tzvetan Todorov, and Julia Kristeva have proposed the metaphor of perpetual exile as an ethical guide. Both Said and Todorov have quoted Erich Auerbach (who was quoting Hugh of St. Victor, from the twelfth century): "The man who finds his country sweet is only a raw beginner; the man for whom each country is as his own is already strong; but the man for whom the whole world is as a foreign country is perfect."[36] And Kristeva has argued that exile "is an irreligious act that cuts all ties," a severing necessary for *"thought."*[37] *The Woman Warrior* suggests that even such a stance is too much a denial of the ties between individuals and their planet. To hold that one belongs to the planet, and to claim as one's own the spot wherever one stands, presents a signifying space that resists nation-state mythologies without mythologizing exile.

"Chinese-Americans, when you try to understand what things in you are Chinese, how do you separate what is peculiar to childhood, to poverty, insanities, one family, your mother who marked your growing with stories, from what is Chinese? What is Chinese tradition and what is the movies?" asked Kingston in the opening pages of *The Woman Warrior* (pp. 5–6). Over the course of her memoirs she indicates that she cannot, in fact, separate what is peculiar to her own life and family from what is Chinese, or even from the American version of what is Chinese. Indeed, the memoirs insist that experience is neither separable nor unmediated, but is instead always a knot of significations. One can, however, perhaps especially through the genre of memoirs, give new meanings to the twists and ties of knotted experiences, new meanings that challenge those prescribed by and inscribed in hegemonic technologies of power and selfhood.

A metaphor of knotmaking opens the final memoir of *The Woman Warrior.* Kingston contrasts her form of storytelling with her brother's, which is notable for its barrenness: it is not "twisted into designs" like hers. She points to the dangers of such knotmaking but insists on its importance. "Long ago in China," she writes, "knotmakers tied strings into buttons and frogs, and rope into bell pulls. There was one knot so complicated that it blinded the knotmaker. Finally an emperor outlawed this cruel knot, and the nobles could not order it anymore." "If I had lived in China," she adds, "I would have been an outlaw knotmaker" (p. 163). In this vignette, as in her discussion of the American and Chinese "I" 's, Kingston uses a practice from the Chinese tradition to intervene in American traditions. Storytelling as knotmaking alludes to the ancient Chinese practice called *chien sheng,* or knotted cord, which was used as a method for keeping records and communicating information.[38] By knotting together her life experiences, even when it means trying a "cruel knot" of blinding truth, Kingston becomes an "outlaw knotmaker," a not-maker or negator of patriarchal law and normalizing power.[39]

Just as the ideograph's several intersecting strokes display its polysemy, so too the knot as discursive form suggests the possibility of untying old meanings and retying new ones. Through such untying and retying, Kingston seeks to "figure out how the invisible world the emigrants built around our childhoods fit in solid America" (p. 5). In this figuring out—which is a figuring of—what is peculiar to her, Kingston thinks the limits of her subjectivity. As Foucault has observed, "The critique of what we are is at one and the same time the historical analysis of the limits that are imposed on us and an experiment with the possibility of going beyond them."[40] As *The Woman Warrior* demonstrates, ideographic self-stylization is a practice of going beyond imposed limits.

Notes

I would like to thank Tom Hayes, Sidonie Smith, and Julia Watson for their suggestions in revising this essay.

1. Michel Foucault, "The Subject and Power," in *Art After Modernism: Rethinking Representation,* ed. Brian Wallis (New York: New Museum of Contemporary Art, 1984), 424.

2. Maxine Hong Kingston, *The Woman Warrior: Memoirs of a Girlhood among Ghosts* (New York: Alfred A. Knopf, 1977), 20. All further citations of this book will include page numbers in parentheses in the text.

3. Maxine Hong Kingston, "Cultural Mis-readings by American Reviewers," in *Asian and Western Writers in Dialogue,* ed. Guy Amirthanayagam (London: Macmillan, 1982), 64.

4. Despite my disagreement with Eakin and Smith regarding the genre of *The Woman Warrior,* I find their readings of the work compelling and am in agreement with them in their treatment of a number of textual details. See John Paul Eakin, *Fiction in Autobiography: Studies in the Art of Self-Invention* (Princeton, N.J.: Princeton University Press, 1985); Sidonie Smith, *A Poetics of Women's Autobiography: Marginality and the Fictions of Self-Representation* (Bloomington: Indiana University Press, 1987). Also see Patricia Lin Blinde, "The Icicle in the Desert: Perspective and Form in the Works of Two Chinese-American Women Writers," *MELUS* 6 (1979): 51–71; Suzanne Juhasz, "Towards a Theory of Form in Feminist Autobiography: Kate Millett's *Fear of Flying* and *Sita;* Maxine Hong Kingston's *The Woman Warrior,"* *International Journal of Women's Studies* 2 (1979): 62–75; Jan Zlotnik Schmidt, "The Other: A Study of Persona in Several Contemporary Women's Autobiographies," *CEA Critic* 43 (1981): 24–31, for discussions of the search for self and autobiographical form.

5. Elizabeth Bruss discusses the disappearance of autobiography in our time as a result of changes in our cultural formation. Such changes, which include a shift from writing to film and video, constitute changes in "our notions of authorship, the difference between narrating (on the one hand) and perceiving or 'focalizing' (on the other), the conventions of representational realism." "Eye for I: Making and Unmaking of Autobiography in Film," in *Autobiography: Essays Theoretical and Critical,* ed. James Olney (Princeton, N.J.: Princeton University Press, 1980), 299.

6. James M. Cox, "Recovering Literature's Lost Ground through Autobiography," in *Autobiography: Essays Theoretical and Critical,* ed. James Olney (Princeton, N.J.: Princeton University Press, 1980), 124. Cox makes this point in regard to Thomas Jefferson's memoir, which he reads as part of Jefferson's efforts as an American revolutionary "to destabilize everything fixed before him" (p. 145).

7. It would be in keeping with Bakhtin's arguments to see memoirs as novelistic in their accentuation of dialogue. This is not to say that a memoir is a novel, but, rather, that novelization is a process by which genres move toward "liberation from all that serves as a brake on their unique development, from all that would change them along with the novel into some sort of stylization of forms that have outlived themselves." M. M. Bakhtin, "Epic and Novel,"

in *The Dialogic Imagination,* ed. Michael Holquist, trans. Caryl Emerson and Michael Holquist (Austin: University of Texas Press, 1981), 39.

8. In an analysis of Simone de Beauvoir's memoirs, Kathleen Woodward comments on Estelle Jelinek's characterization of female "life stories" as "more often discontinuous and fragmentary, written in a straightforward, objective manner, yet nonetheless emphasizing the personal rather than the public" by saying that she (Woodward) would "reserve Jelinek's characterization of the female life story for the *memoir,*" See Kathleen Woodward, "Simone de Beauvoir: Aging and Its Discontents," in *The Private Self: Theory and Practice of Women's Autobiographical Writings,* ed. Shari Benstock (Chapel Hill: University of North Carolina Press, 1988), 99. I generally concur with this point, but would place less stress on the memoir's emphasis of the personal over the public. Kingston's memoirs blur traditional distinctions between the personal and the public.

9. For an example of such analysis, see Biddy Martin's exploration of the complexities of lesbian autobiography in light of a variety of questions involving generic normalization versus the challenge of lesbian politics. "Lesbian Identity and Autobiographical Difference(s)," in *Life/Lines: Theorizing Women's Autobiography,* ed. Bella Brodzki and Celeste Schenck (Ithaca, N.Y.: Cornell University Press, 1988), 77–103.

10. Doris Sommer underscores this point in her analysis of testimonials by Latin American women, pointing out that accepting these works as autobiographical tends to divert attention away from the significance of the testimonials' collective self. " 'Not Just a Personal Story': Women's *Testimonios* and the Plural Self," in *Life/Lines: Theorizing Women's Autobiography,* ed. Bella Brodzki and Celeste Schenck (Ithaca, N.Y.: Cornell University Press, 1988), 107–30.

11. Woolf, quoted in Shari Benstock, "Authorizing the Autobiographical," in *The Private Self: Theory and Practice of Women's Autobiographical Writings,* ed. Shari Benstock (Chapel Hill: University of North Carolina Press, 1988), 26–27; emphasis mine.

12. Michel Foucault, *The History of Sexuality,* vol. 1, trans. Robert Hurley (New York: Vintage, 1980), 106. For a feminist corrective to Foucault's lack of focus on the patriarchal dimensions of the deployment of sexuality, see the essays in Irene Diamond and Lee Quinby, eds., *Feminism and Foucault: Reflections on Resistance* (Boston: Northeastern University Press, 1988).

13. Foucault, *History of Sexuality,* 107.

14. Ibid., 146–47, 108.

15. Kingston's *China Men* also relates family difficulties in America but focuses in that work on the men of her family. Regarding the changing family power dynamics between Chinese men and women upon coming to America, see Linda Ching Sledge's argument that because of the "deleterious effects of male emigration," the "mother from China is forced by the father's increasing passivity to take on 'masculine' traits of aggressiveness and authority." "Maxine Kingston's *China Men:* The Family Historian as Epic Poet," *MELUS* 7 (1980), 10–11.

16. Foucault, *History of Sexuality,* 104–6.

17. Michel Foucault, *The Use of Pleasure,* trans. Robert Hurley (New York: Pantheon, 1985), 5.

18. Kingston's use of the word *memoirs* in her subtitle also places her work alongside Simone de Beauvoir's account of resistance to bourgeois daughterhood in *Memoirs of a Dutiful Daughter,* trans. James Kirkup (Cleveland: World, 1959).

19. For an insightful comparative discussion of the issue of language and silence, see King-Kok Cheung, " 'Don't Tell': Imposed Silences in *The Color Purple* and *The Woman Warrior,*" *PMLA* 103 (1988): 162–74.

20. Smith, *Poetics of Women's Autobiography,* 168.

21. As Foucault argues, the deployment of sexuality operates through oppositional categories of normality versus abnormality. The desire to attain "normality" is thus a generative function of power in contrast to alliance's juridical and prohibitive mode. *History of Sexuality,* 42–43.

22.   Kingston reports a variation on this particular form of pedagogical domination by citing a *Teachers Newsletter* review that "gave the book a seventh grade reading level by using a mathematical formula of counting syllables and sentences per one hundred-word passage." "Cultural Mis-readings," 62.

23.   Woon-Ping Chin Holaday has compared Ezra Pound and Kingston in regard to their respective involvement with China and the use of the ideograph to represent that relationship. Holaday notes that in Pound's writings China tends to be "an ideal abstraction" drawn from written sources, whereas Kingston's "Chinese-American world is a tangible, changeable reality drawn from a living culture" and oral sources. "From Ezra Pound to Maxine Hong Kingston: Expressions of Chinese Thought in American Literature," *MELUS* 5 (1978): 15–24.

24.   "Technology of the self" is Foucault's term for the specific techniques that "permit individuals to effect by their own means or with the help of others a certain number of operations on their own bodies and souls, thoughts, conduct, and way of being, so as to transform themselves in order to attain a certain state of happiness, purity, wisdom, perfection, or immortality." "Technologies of the Self," in *Technologies of the Self: A Seminar with Michel Foucault,* ed. Luther H. Martin, Huck Gutman, and Patrick H. Hutton (Amherst: University of Massachusetts Press, 1988), 18. My analysis seeks to show that the technology of ideographic selfhood put forward in *The Woman Warrior* operates in opposition to the technologies of self produced through the formations of power that are hegemonic in the modern era.

25.   Norman Bryson argues for this distinction in painting by associating the distanced time technique with the tradition of Western painting and the displayed, processive time technique with the visible brush strokes of Chinese painting. See *Vision and Painting: The Logic of the Gaze* (New Haven, Conn.: Yale University Press, 1983), 89–92.

26.   Carol Gilligan's analysis of gender differences in conceptualizations of selfhood and morality helps illuminate Kingston's depiction of an interrelational self insofar as it resembles the model of interdependence that Gilligan associates with women at a mature stage of moral development. Gilligan's theories, however, do not attend to cultural and ethnic differences in moral development. *The Woman Warrior* problematizes that blind spot in Gilligan's model. See *In a Different Voice* (Cambridge, Mass.: Harvard University Press, 1982).

27.   Michel Foucault, *Discipline and Punish,* trans. Alan Sheridan (New York: Vintage, 1979), 192.

28.   Smith, *Poetics of Women's Autobiography,* 156.

29.   Foucault observes, "For us, it is in the confession that truth and sex are joined, through the obligatory and exhaustive expression of an individual secret." And also: "The obligation to confess is now relayed through so many different points, is so deeply ingrained in us, that we no longer perceive it as the effect of a power that constrains us; on the contrary, it seems to us that truth, lodged in our most secret nature, 'demands' only to surface; that if it fails to do so, this is because a constraint holds it in place, the violence of a power weighs it down, and it can finally be articulated only at the price of a kind of liberation." *History of Sexuality,* 60–61.

30.   Michel Foucault, "The Confession of the Flesh," in *Power/Knowledge,* ed. Colin Gordon, trans. Colin Gordon et al. (New York: Pantheon, 1980), 219–20.

31.   Kingston calls the "White Tigers" fantasy a "sort of kung fu movie parody" in her critical review of American reviews of her work. "Cultural Mis-readings," 57. I had a similar Saturday serial fantasy in my own girlhood, styled on a wild-west Zorro-like character. Clad boldly in black, and riding a black horse, I would valiantly fight off desperadoes (always men) who preyed upon defenseless men, women, and children.

32.   Although they have been both astutely critiqued and further developed, the pioneering discussions about mother-daughter ambivalence by Chodorow, Dinnerstein, and Flax have been helpful here. See Nancy Chodorow, *The Reproduction of Mothering* (Los Angeles: University of California Press, 1978); Dorothy Dinnerstein, *The Mermaid and the Minotaur* (New

York: Harper & Row, 1976); Jane Flax, "The Conflict between Nurturance and Autonomy in Mother-Daughter Relationships and within Feminism," *Feminist Studies* 4 (1978): 171–89.

33. Also see Leslie Rabine's important reading of "Kingston's work as a unique kind of feminine writing that in its own way fractures the logic of opposition into a play of difference . . . [which] clarifies relations between social and symbolic gender." "No Lost Paradise: Social Gender and Symbolic Gender in the Writings of Maxine Hong Kingston," *Signs* 12 (1987): 474. And see Celeste Schenck's discussion of the story of Ts'ai Yen as representing a "return to the exiled mother as the source of poetry and the difference between mother and daughter which allows this female subject to find her own writing voice." "All of a Piece: Women's Poetry and Autobiography," in *Life/Lines: Theorizing Women's Autobiography*, ed. Bella Brodzki and Celeste Schenck (Ithaca, N.Y.: Cornell University Press, 1988), 303.

34. Trinh T. Minh-ha, *Woman, Native, Other: Writing Postcoloniality and Femininity* (Bloomington: Indiana University Press, 1989), 135.

35. Kingston thus broaches from a different register many of the questions raised by Julia Kristeva. Kristeva sees a new generation of women whose "attitude" toward issues raised by feminism "could be summarized as an *interiorization of the founding separation of the socio-symbolic contract,* as an introduction of its cutting edge into the very interior of every identity whether subjective, sexual, ideological, or so forth." "Women's Time," in *The Kristeva Reader,* ed. Toril Moi (New York: Columbia University Press, 1986), 210.

36. Tzvetan Todorov, *The Conquest of America,* trans. Richard Howard (New York: Harper Colophon, 1984), 250.

37. Julia Kristeva, "A New Type of Intellectual: The Dissident," in *The Kristeva Reader,* ed. Toril Moi (New York: Columbia University Press), 298–99.

38. Paul Carus, *Chinese Astrology* (La Salle: Open Court Press, 1974), 2–3. This edition is an abridgment of the 1907 text.

39. Also see Nancy K. Miller's discussion of "quipos," a system of knotting used in the Inca empire, which she interprets as a "signature" of feminist writing. *Subject to Change: Reading Feminist Writing* (New York: Columbia University Press, 1988), 137–42.

40. Foucault, "What Is Enlightenment?" in *The Foucault Reader,* ed. Paul Rabinow (New York: Pantheon, 1984), 50.

Autobiography as Guided Chinatown Tour? Maxine Hong Kingston's *The Woman Warrior* and the Chinese-American Autobiographical Controversy

SAU-LING CYNTHIA WONG

Maxine Hong Kingston's autobiography, *The Woman Warrior*, may be the best-known contemporary work of Asian-American literature. Winner of the National Book Critics Circle Award for the best book of nonfiction published in 1976, *The Woman Warrior* remains healthily in print and on the reading lists of numerous college courses; excerpts from it are routinely featured in anthologies with a multicultural slant. It is safe to say that many readers who otherwise do not concern themselves with Asian-American literature have read Kingston's book.

In spite—or maybe, as we shall see, because—of its general popularity, however, *The Woman Warrior* has by no means been received with unqualified enthusiasm by Kingston's fellow Chinese Americans. A number of Chinese-American critics have repeatedly denounced *The Woman Warrior*, questioning its autobiographic status, its authenticity, its representativeness, and thereby Kingston's personal integrity. Though often couched in the emotionally charged, at times openly accusatory, language characteristic of what the Chinese call "pen wars," the critical issues raised in this debate are not merely of passing interest. Rather, they lie at the heart of any theoretical discussion of ethnic American autobiography in particular and ethnic American literature in general. It would therefore be instructive to set out the terms of the controversy and explore their theoretical ramifications, with a view to understanding the nature of Kingston's narrative enterprise in *The Woman Warrior*.

The most fundamental objection to *The Woman Warrior* concerns its generic status: its being billed as autobiography rather than fiction, when so much of the book departs from the popular definition of autobiography as an unadorned factual account of a person's own life. Responding to a favorable

From *Multicultural Autobiography: American Lives,* edited by James Robert Payne. Knoxville: University of Tennessee Press, 1992: 248–79. Copyright 1992 by University of Tennessee Press. Reprinted by permission of University of Tennessee Press.

review of the book by Diane Johnson in the *New York Review of Books,* Jeffery Chan notes how "a white reading public will rave over ethnic biography while ignoring a Chinese American's literary art" and attacks Knopf, "a white publishing house," for "distributing an obvious fiction for fact" (6). The thrust of Chan's message is that the autobiographical label is a marketing ploy in which the author, to her discredit, has acquiesced. Chan's stricture is echoed by Benjamin Tong, who finds *The Woman Warrior* "obviously contrived," a work of "fiction passing for autobiography" ("Critic of Admirer" 6). By way of contrast, while the unusual generic status of *The Woman Warrior* is also widely noted by non-Chinese-American critics, it is seldom cited as either a weakness or a matter of personal, as opposed to artistic, purpose.[1]

How far is Kingston personally responsible for the nonfiction label on the covers of *The Woman Warrior?* According to her, very little:

> The only correspondence I had with the publisher concerning the classification of my books was that he said that Non-fiction would be the most accurate category; Non-fiction is such a catch-all that even "poetry is considered non-fiction."

And poetry is something in whose company she would be "flattered" to see her books.[2] The entire matter might have rested here—but for some theoretical issues raised by the controversy which command an interest beyond the topical.

Although Kingston's detractors do not use the term, at the heart of the controversy is the question of fictionalization: to what extent "fictional" features are admissible in a work that purports to be an autobiography. The Chinese-American critics of *The Woman Warrior* focus their attention on the social effects of admitting fictionalization into an autobiographical work. Their concern, variously worded, is summed up most concisely, if baldly, by Katheryn Fong:

> I read your references to mythical and feudal China as fiction. . . . Your fantasy stories are embellished versions of your mother's embellished versions of stories. As fiction, these stories are creatively written with graphic imagery and emotion. The problem is that non-Chinese are reading your fiction as true accounts of Chinese and Chinese American history. (67)

Thus stated, the *Woman Warrior* "problem" is seen to rest ultimately on the readers, not the author; the basis for denouncing *The Woman Warrior* is pragmatic, response-contingent, and reader-specific. Why, then, has Kingston been implicated at all in the misreadings of her audience? It is possible to reject the very question as irrelevant, in that authors have little control over how their published works will be read. On the other hand, when critics like Chan, Tong, or Fong hold Kingston responsible for her readers' failings, they do so from a set of assumptions about ethnic literature that are grounded in a keen awareness of the sociopolitical context of minority literary creation. Such an awareness is precisely what is missing in many white reviewers' remarks on *The Woman Warrior;* moreover, the autobiographical genre, with its promise (perceived or real) of "truthfulness," by nature encourages preoccupation with a work's sociopolitical context. Thus the charge of unwarranted fictionalization must be addressed.

The Woman Warrior can be considered fictionalized in a number of ways. On the most obvious formal level, it violates the popular perception of autobiography as an ordered shaping of life events anchored in the so-called external world. It aims at creating what James Olney calls "a realm of order where events bear to one another a relationship of significance rather than of chronology" ("Some Versions" 247). According to an early student of the genre, autobiographies must contain, "in some measure, the germ of a description of the manners of their times" (Pascal 8–9). Although recent scholars have found the referential grounding of autobiography much more problematic and its defining essence much more elusive (e.g., Olney, "Autobiography and the Cultural Moment" 3; Bruss 2; Eakin 5), the term *autobiography* usually does evoke, at least among general readers, a chronologically sequenced account with verifiable references to places, people, and events. As one critic puts it, in more abstruse language: "Texts bound by the real insist upon an epistemological status different from works of the imagination in which the real is more nearly hypothetical" (Krupat 25). But what if the "real" that an autobiography is bound by is the "imagination" of the protagonist?[3] This is the thorny problem of generic differentiation posed by *The Woman Warrior.*

By an outwardly oriented definition of autobiography, *The Woman Warrior* is at best only nominally autobiographical: to borrow a phrase from Pascal, it is a work "so engrossed with the inner life that the outer world becomes blurred" (Pascal 9), told by a narrator who, as a child, regularly sees "free movies" on "blank walls" and "[t]alks to people that aren't real inside [her] mind" (221). The prose slips from the subjunctive to the declarative with but the slightest warning: the No Name Woman story begins with *perhaps*'s and *could have been*'s (7) but soon dispenses with these reminders of conjecture. Likewise, while the Fa Mu Lan segment in "White Tigers" is initially marked as an enumeration of the possible and desirable—"The call *would* come from a bird. . . . The bird *would* cross the sun. . . . I *would* be a little girl of seven. . . ." (24–25; my italics)—the bulk of the narration is in the simple past tense, as if recounting completed events in the actual world. Two divergent accounts are given of Brave Orchid's encounter with the Sitting Ghost (81–84, 85–86), neither of which could have been definitive since the event (or alleged event) predates the birth of the daughter/narrator. "At the Western Palace," presented as a deceptively conventional, self-contained short story, is revealed in the next chapter to be a third-hand fiction (189–90). In short, the referential grounding of *The Woman Warrior* is tenuous and presented in a potentially misleading manner. A few public places and events in the "outer" world are recognizable from what we know about author Kingston's life; all else is recollection, speculation, reflection, meditation, imagination. Verifiability is virtually out of the question in a work so self-reflexive. Presumably, then, readers who do not pay sufficient attention to the narrative intricacies of *The Woman Warrior,* especially white readers with biased expectations, will mistake fiction for fact.

The critics of *The Woman Warrior* also detect fictionalization—in the sense of "making things up"—in the way Kingston has chosen to translate certain Chinese terms. A central example is the word *ghost,* based on Cantonese *kuei* or *gwai,* a key term in the book appearing in the subtitle as well as several important episodes.[4] Kingston renders *kuei* as *ghost.* Chan and Tong ("Critic of Admirer" 6), while conceding that the character can indeed mean "*ghost*" (as in "spirit of the dead"), insist that it be translated as *demon* (or *devil* or *asshole*). They object to the connotations of insubstantiality or neutrality in Kingston's translation, finding it unsanctioned by community usage and lacking in the hostility toward whites indispensable to true works of Chinese-American literature.[5]

Tong further elevates the rendition of *kuei* as *ghost* into a "purposeful" act of pandering to white tastes and adds another example of "mistranslation" ("Critic of Admirer" 6): referring to "frogs" as "heavenly chickens" (77), which should have been "field chickens" in Cantonese. (*Tien,* "sky" or "heaven," and *tien,* "field" or "meadow," differ only in tone, which is phonemic in Chinese dialects.) Tong suggests that Kingston must have knowingly selected the wrong term, the one with the "familiar exotic touristy flavor" relished by "whites checking out Chinese America" ("Critic of Admirer" 6).

A more serious charge of fictionalization concerns the way Kingston handles not just single Chinese terms but Chinese folklore and legends. The story of Fa Mu Lan,[6] the woman warrior invoked as the young protagonist's patron saint, is recognizable only in bare outline to a reader conversant with traditional Chinese culture. The section on the girl's period of training in the mountains draws extensively on popular martial arts "novels" or "romances" (*wuxia xiaoshuo*) as well as from traditional fantasy lore on *shenxian* ("immortals").[7] As for the way Kingston makes use of the traditional Fa Mu Lan story, at least the version fixed in the popular "Mulan Shi" or "Ballad of Mulan,"[8] deviations from it in *The Woman Warrior* are so numerous that only a few major ones can be noted here. The tattooing of the woman warrior is based on the well-known tale of Yue Fei, whose mother carved four characters (not entire passages) onto his back, exhorting him to be loyal to his country. Also, the spirit-marriage to the waiting childhood sweetheart, a wish-fulfilling inversion of the No Name Woman's fate (7), is utterly unlikely in ancient China, considering the lowly place of women. The traditional Fa Mu Lan is never described as having been pregnant and giving birth to a child while in male disguise. The episode of the wicked baron is fabricated. The Fa Mu Lan of "Mulan Shi" is a defender of the establishment, her spirit patriarchal as well as patriotic, a far cry from a peasant rebel in the vein of the heroes of *Outlaws of the Marsh*.[9]

Because of these and other liberties Kingston has taken with her raw material, *The Woman Warrior* has been criticized by a number of Chinese Americans varying in their knowledge of traditional Chinese culture. Chinese-born scholar Joseph S. M. Lau dismisses the book as a kind of mishmash, a retelling of old tales that would not impress those having access to the originals (Lau 65–66). Writer Frank Chin, who is fifth-generation, attacks Kingston for her "distortions" of traditional Chinese culture. In a parody of *The Woman Warrior* filled with inversions and travesties, Chin creates a piece entitled "The Unmanly Warrior," about a little French girl growing up in Canton and drawing inspiration from "her imagined French ancestor Joan of Arc."

> [Her] picture of Joan of Arc . . . was so inaccurate as to demonstrate that the woman has gone mad, the French people of Frenchtown on the edge of the port city said. The French girl is writing not history, but art, the Chinese who loved the book said, and continued: She is writing a work of imagination authenticated by her personal experience. ("Most Popular Book" 7)

Clearly, the personal authority of an autobiographer is not easy to challenge. Perhaps sensing this, some of Kingston's critics concede it but blend the charge of fictionalization with that of atypicality. Again, the projected reactions of the white audience are kept constantly in sight. Speaking of the protagonist's account of not knowing her father's name, Chan calls this experience "unique" and expresses fears that Kingston "may mislead naive white readers" by not giving any background on the system of naming unique to Chinese Americans. Fong complains: "Your story is a *very personal* description of growing up in Chinese America. It is *one* story from one Chinese American woman of one out of seven generations of Chinese Americans" (67; italics in original). Like Chan, she feels that a narrative as personal as Kingston's must be made safe for white consumption by means of a sobering dose of Chinese-American history; the historical information to be incorporated should emphasize the "causes" behind the "pains, secrets, and bitterness" portrayed in *The Woman Warrior* (67).[10] Fong lists various excerpts that she finds especially dangerous and glosses each with a summary of experiences considered canonical to an ideologically correct version of Chinese-American history. Without such a corrective, she suggests, Kingston will reinforce the white readers' stereotype of Chinese Americans as eternally unassimilable aliens, "silent, mysterious, and devious" (67). Tong feels that Kingston's upbringing in the one-street Chinatown of Stockton, an agricultural town in California's Central Valley (instead of in a bigger, geographically more distinct and presumably more "typical" Chinatown) disqualifies her from attaining "historical and cultural insight" about Chinese America ("Chinatown Popular Culture" 233).

According to Kingston's critics, the most pernicious of the stereotypes that might be supported by *The Woman Warrior* is that of Chinese-American men as sexist. Some Chinese-American women readers think highly of *The Woman Warrior* because it confirms their personal experiences with sexism (e.g., Suzi Wong, Nellie Wong). Others find Kingston's account of growing up amidst shouts of "Maggot!" overstated, yet can cite little to support the charge besides *their* own personal authority.[11] Contrasting *The Woman Warrior*'s commercial success with the relatively scant attention received by books like Louis Chu's *Eat a Bowl of Tea* and Laurence Yep's *Dragonwings,* both of which present less negative father images, Fong implies that Kingston's autobiography earns its reputation by "over-exaggerat[ing]" the ills of Chinese-American male chauvinism (68). She is willing to grant that a more understanding response from white readers might have given Kingston more creative license but finds the existing body of Chinese-American literature small enough to justify a more stringent demand on the Chinese-American writer, especially the woman writer.

If Chinese-American women disagree about the accuracy of Kingston's portrayal of patriarchal culture, it is hardly surprising to find male Chinese-American critics condemning it in harsh terms. Chan attributes the popularity of *The Woman Warrior* to its depiction of "female anger," which bolsters white feminists' "hallucination" of a universal female condition; and Tong calls the book a "fashionably feminist work written with white acceptance in mind" ("Critic of Admirer" 6). If Chinese-American literature is, according to the editors of *Aiiieeeee!,* distinguished by emasculation (Chin et al. xxx–xxxi), then Chinese-American writers cannot afford to wash the culture's dirty linen in public. Frank Chin declares that personal pain—merely a matter of "expression of ego" and "psychological attitudinizing"—must be subordinated to political purpose ("This Is Not an Autobiography" 112).

For Chin, the very form of autobiography is suspect because of its association with the Christian tradition of confession. Although *The Woman Warrior* does not deal with Christianity, Chin places it in a tradition of Christianized Chinese-American autobiographies from Yung Wing's *My Life in China, and America* through Pardee Lowe's *Father and Glorious Descendant* to Jade Snow Wong's *Fifth Chinese Daughter.* His rationale is that all autobiography, like religious confessions and conversion testimonials, demonstrates "admission of guilt, submission of my self for judgment," for "approval by outsiders." "[A] Chinaman can't write an autobiography without selling out." In fact, claims Chin, the autobiography is not even a native Chinese form, and Chinese-American writers have no business adopting it. Unfortunately, however, "[t]he Christian Chinese American autobiography is the only Chinese American literary tradition" ("This Is Not an Autobiography" 122–24).

Some of the generalizations made by Kingston's critics, such as the exclusively Western and Christian origin of autobiography, may be called into question by existing scholarship. According to one student of the genre, a complex autobiographical tradition does exist in Chinese literature, its origins traceable to the first century A.D., in the Han Dynasty (Larson; esp. chap. 1). Moreover, the confessional mode attributed by Chin solely to a guilt-obsessed Christianity can also be found in traditional Chinese writing (Wu). This does not invalidate Georges Gusdorf's important insight on the cultural specificity of the modern Western autobiography: the point is not to claim that the modern Western autobiography as we know it was practiced in ancient China (it was not) but merely to point out the oversimplification in many of the statements that have been made about *The Woman Warrior*. When Chin links the genre with Christian self-accusation, he overlooks the possibility that the late medieval *breakdown* of Christian dogma might have been responsible for the emergence of autobiography as an autonomous literary tradition (Gusdorf 34). Furthermore, emphasis on the confessional element represents only one school of autobiographical scholarship, the Anglo-American; there are others (Eakin 202). Even if autobiography were an entirely Western phenomenon, according to Chin's own pronouncements on the unique, nonderivative nature of Asian-American literature (especially on its separateness from Asian literature), Chinese-American writers have a right to appropriate a genre not indigenous to the Chinese in China but indigenous to the Chinese in America. As Chin and his *Aiiieeeee!* co-editors put it in their prefatory manifesto on Chinese and Japanese-American literature, an "American-born Asian, writing from the world as Asian-American," should not be expected to "reverberate to gongs struck hundreds of years ago" (Chin et al. xxiv).

Other more or less self-contained disputes on isolated assertions by Kingston's critics could be explored. On the whole, however, one may say that the entire Chinese-American autobiographical debate touches on articles of ideology so jealously held that the existence of a variety of opinions, scholarly or otherwise, may itself be seen as a problem rather than as a possible source of solutions. Given the peremptory tone in which much of the criticism of *The Woman Warrior* has been conducted, it is important that the tacit assumptions of the critics be articulated.

The theoretical underpinnings of the hostile criticism may be summarized as a series of interlocking propositions, some concerning the nature of autobiography as a genre (regardless of the author's background), others generalizable to autobiography by all American ethnic writers, still others peculiar to Chinese-American autobiography.

First of all, autobiography is seen to be self-evidently distinguishable from fiction. If the two genres blur at all at the edges, the interaction merely takes the form of fiction providing "techniques" to render the mundane material of autobiography more attractive; the epistemological status of the narrated material is not affected. In the same way that language is considered a sort of sugarcoating on dry nuggets of fact, the autobiographer's subjectivity is seen as having little or no constitutive power; rather, it is a Newtonian body moving about in a world of discrete, verifiable—and hence incontrovertible—facts, its power being limited to the choice between faithfully recording or willfully distorting this external reality. In principle, therefore, autobiography is biography which just happens to be written by one's self. It claims no special privilege, poses no special problems.[12] Finally, the *graphe* part of *autobiography,* the act of writing, the transformation of life into text, is seen by Kingston's critics as a mechanical conveyance of facts from the auto-biographer's mind to the reader's via a medium in the physical world, the process pleasant or not depending on the author's literary talents. In the case of the *Woman Warrior* debate, correspondence between word and thing is deemed so perfect that a Chinese term, *kuei,* is supposed to be translatable by only one English equivalent, with all other overtones outlawed. The arbiter here is to be the individual critic backed by the authority of "the Chinese American community" (as if Kingston herself were not a member of this community).

Recognition of a preexisting external reality, however, imposes a special obligation on the ethnic American autobiographer: to provide a positive por-trayal of the ethnic community through one's self-portrayal. At the very least, the autobiographer's work should be innocent of material that might be seized upon by unsympathetic outsiders to illustrate prevalent stereotypes of the ethnic group; the author should stress the diversity of experience within the group and the uniqueness and self-definition of the individual. Ideally, an ethnic autobiography should also be a history in microcosm of the commu-nity, especially of its sufferings, struggles, and triumphs over racism. In other words, an ethnic autobiographer should be an exemplar and spokesperson whose life will inspire the writer's own people as well as enlighten the igno-rant about social truths.

The collective history of the ethnic community—one does not speak of *a* history in this theoretical framework—provides the ultimate reference point for the ethnic autobiographer. Here is where the Newtonian analogy begins to break down, for the self proves, after all, to be subjective in the everyday sense of "biased" or "unreliable." Handicapped by its interiority, it cannot be the equal of other "bodies" which can be summed up as a bundle of externally ascertainable properties. The self is epistemologically underprivileged, not privileged; to discover the validity of its private truths, it must appeal to the arbitration of the community (however defined). The history of the collectiv-ity is ballast for the ethnic autobiographer's subjectivity; it is a yardstick against which the author can measure how representative or how idiosyn-cratic his or her life is, how worthy of preservation in writing. Should individ-ual experience fail to be homologous to collective history, personal authority must yield to ideological imperatives, and the details of the narrative must be manipulated to present an improved picture. According to this logic, the eth-nic woman autobiographer victimized by sexism must be ready to suppress potentially damaging (to the men, that is) material; to do less is to jeopardize the united front and prostitute one's integrity for the sake of white approval.

Bios is of little worth unless it is "representative"—averaged out to become sociologically informative as well as edifying.

A series of mutually incompatible demands on ethnic autobiography follows from the tenets outlined above. Initially, ethnic autobiography is thought useful because its focus on the uniqueness of the individual establishes a minority's right to self-definition; a sufficient number of autobiographies will disabuse white readers of their oversimplified preconceptions. Autobiography's allegedly pure factuality is also prized for its educational value: unlike fiction, it can be counted on to "tell it like it is" and resist charges of artistic license made by doubting readers. Nonetheless, autobiography cannot, by definition, be more than *one* person's life story; thus it cannot be fully trusted. What if the single individual's life happens to confirm or even endorse white perceptions instead of challenging them? Hence the insistence that ethnic autobiography be "representative." The requirement would have been easily fulfilled if the autobiographer happened—that vexatious word again!—to have already been "representative," in the sense of conforming to a view of the group agreed upon by the members making that determination. Short of that, the "representativeness" will have to be formed out of recalcitrant material, through an editorial process true to the spirit but not necessarily the letter of the "ethnic experience."

The minute this is done, however, the attempt to make absolute the generic distinctions between autobiography and fiction ends up dissolving the boundaries altogether: autobiography loses its putative authority in fact and turns into fiction. Language loses its innocuous transmitting function and assumes the unruly power of transmutation. The individual loses his or her uniqueness and becomes a sociological category. From the effort to counter homogenization by offering depictions of diversity, a new uniformity emerges: one set of stereotypes is replaced by another. In the final analysis, the main reason the critics attack *The Woman Warrior* is not that it is insufficiently factual but that it is insufficiently fictional: that the author did not tamper more freely with her own life story. And ironically—given the critics' claimed championship of self-definition and literary autonomy—the kind of fiction they would like Kingston to have written is closely dictated by the responses of white readers.

Only when safeguards against misreadings are supplied may the autobiographical label once more be affixed with confidence, the benefits of the genre now purged of the inconvenient admixture of potential harm. The ignorance of white readers seems to be taken for granted as immutable by Kingston's critics. The possibility that the less unregenerate readers may learn to read the allusions in *The Woman Warrior,* just as generations of minority readers have learned to read the Eurocentric canon, is never once raised; nor is the possibility that a Chinese-American writer may by right expect, and by duty promote, such learning in his or her audience.

These issues naturally have their counterparts in other ethnic American literatures. The differing versions of Frederick Douglass's early life found in his autobiographies provide a classic example of how a black autobiographer might feel compelled to edit "factual" details in the interest of anticipated social effect (e.g., Gates 98–124). It is worth noting that, while critic Henry Louis Gates, Jr., justifies the "crafting or making [of a 'fictive self'] by design," citing the urgent need to establish the black man's right to speak for himself, he also finds a certain flatness of aesthetic effect when Douglass begins to substitute "one ideal essence for another." "Almost never does Douglass allow us to see him as a human individual in all of his complexity" (103, 119, 109).

Though the dilemma is shared by other ethnic American autobiographies, the conflicting claims of typicality and uniqueness take a particularly acute form in Chinese-American autobiography: at stake is not only the existence of the minority writer's voice but the possible perversion of that voice to satisfy the white reader's appetite for exoticism. Indeed, it is only within the context of the Chinese-American autobiographical tradition that both the vehemence of Kingston's critics and the novelty of the narrative undertaking in *The Woman Warrior* can be understood.

To borrow a phrase applied to early African-American writers, Chinese-American writers "entered into the house of literature through the door of autobiography" (Olney, "Autobiography and the Cultural Moment" 15). Autobiographies predominate in Chinese-American writing in English.[13] Some autobiographies are by Chinese-born writers who grew up in China (Lee, Yung, Kuo, Su-ling Wong, Wei); others are by writers born and brought up in the United States (Lowe, Jade Snow Wong, Goo, Kingston). An autobiography from the former group typically focuses on the protagonist's early experiences in China, often ending very abruptly upon his or her arrival in the United States. The author tends to believe the life depicted as representing Chinese life of a certain period or social milieu, and of interest to the Western reader chiefly for this reason rather than for its uniqueness; such a conviction may easily degenerate into the accommodating mentality of a friendly guide to an exotic culture.[14] The autobiographies in the second group, those by American-born writers, are primarily set in the United States.[15] Given the distressing tendency of white readers to confuse Chinese Americans with Chinese in China, and to attribute a kind of ahistorical, almost genetic, Chinese essence to all persons of Chinese ancestry regardless of their upbringing, the pressure on American-born writers to likewise "represent Chinese culture" is strong. Removed from Chinese culture in China by their ancestors' emigration, American-born autobiographers may still capitalize on white curiosity by conducting the literary equivalent of a guided Chinatown tour: by providing explanations on the manners and mores of the Chinese-American community from the vantage point of a "native." This stance has indeed been adopted by some, and, in a sort of involuntary intertextuality, even those works that do not share it will most likely be read as anthropological guide-books. The curse is potent enough to extend at times to nonautobiographical literature; for a book like *The Woman Warrior,* then, it would be all but impossible to prevent some readers from taking the autobiographical label as a license to overgeneralize.

A few examples will characterize the stance of the cultural guide found among both Chinese-born and American-born autobiographers. In Lee Yan Phou's *When I Was a Boy in China,* personal narrative slows at every turn to make room for background material; seven of the twelve chapter titles—"The House and Household," "Chinese Cookery," "Games and Pastimes," "Schools and School Life," "Religions," "Chinese Holidays," "Stories and Story-Tellers"—could have come out of a general survey of Chinese society. The individual's life serves the function of conveying anthropological information; the freight, in fact, frequently outweighs the vehicle. Lee directly addresses white American readers as "you" throughout the book and consciously assumes the persona of a tour guide: "The servants were . . . sent out to market to buy the materials for breakfast. Let us follow them"; "Now, let me take you into the school where I struggled with the Chinese written language for three years" (27, 57). In Helena Kuo's tellingly titled *I've Come a Long Way,* the tour guide role seems to have become second nature to the author. Like Lee, Kuo addresses her audience as "you" and constantly takes into account their likely reactions. Her descriptions of place are filtered through the eyes of her white readers (e.g., 27); the similes she favors are pure *chinoiserie* (e.g., 23). In the midst of a narrative about her journalistic career, Kuo solicitously inserts a mini-disquisition on traditional Chinese painting, to ensure that her charges will not be lost in the future when she is no longer around (171).[16]

It is perhaps no accident that a good number of the autobiographies by Chinese-born writers are rather abruptly cut off soon after the author's arrival in the United States, in apparent contrast to the structure of immigrant autobiography described in William Boelhower's typology (*Immigrant Autobiography* 25–52). Unlike the European works cited by Boelhower, these do not chronicle the author's experience of encountering and coming to terms with American culture. While only further study can elucidate this observed difference, one might venture a guess on its cause: the Chinese authors may have sensed how far American interest in their life writings is based on the image of otherness, on exotic scenery and alien cultural practices. As the autobiographers become Americanized, the fascination they hold for the reader would fade; hence the sketchy coverage of their experience in the United States.[17]

Some American-born Chinese autobiographers also seem to have adopted the narrative stance of a cultural guide, though the presence of the audience is more implicit in their works than in Lee's or Kuo's. *Father and*

Glorious Descendant, by Pardee Lowe (a contemporary and friend of Kuo's), abounds in descriptions of Chinatown customs and rituals, such as *tong* banquets, Chinese New Year festivities, celebration of the father's "Great Birthday," preparation of unusual (by Western standards) foods, and funeral practices. The name of the Lowes' ancestral village in China, Sahn Kay Gawk, is periodically rendered by the quaint circumlocution "The-Corner-of-the-Mountain-Where-the-Water-Falls," although that etymological information has been given on the first page of the book. Two chapters are devoted to a series of letters between Father and his cousin, written in a comically florid, heavily literal prose purporting to be a translation of classical Chinese (249–58). Lowe's handling of the English language betrays a habitual awareness of the white audience's need to be surprised and amused by the mystifying ways of the Chinese. Jade Snow Wong's autobiography, *Fifth Chinese Daughter,* shares with Lowe's an emphasis on Chinatown customs and rituals; with Lee's and Kuo's, a tendency to intersperse the narrative of her life with discursive segments of information on Chinese culture. A description of a dinner party for her American friends includes a step-by-step record of how egg foo young and tomato beef are cooked; an account of a visit to a Chinatown herbalist for her cough is interrupted by a clarification of the Chinese medical theory of humors (160–62, 224).[18]

Although there is much else in Lowe's and Wong's books besides these gestures of consideration for the sensibilities of white readers, it is undeniable that both of these authors, like their Chinese-born counterparts, are conscious of their role as cultural interpreters who can obtain a measure of recognition from whites for the insider's insight they can offer. The title of a chapter in Wong's book, "Rediscovering Chinatown," aptly epitomizes one way American-born Chinese may make peace with their cultural background in the face of intense assimilative pressures: to return to one's ethnic heritage with selective enthusiasm, reassessing once-familiar (and once-despised) sights and sounds according to their acceptability to white tastes.

As a form characterized by simultaneous subjectivity and objectivity, simultaneous expression and documentation (e.g., Stone 10–11; Sands 57), autobiography easily creates in its readers expectations of "privileged access" (Olney, "Autobiography and the Cultural Moment" 13) to the experience and vision of an entire people. From an intraethnic point of view, the writing of autobiography may be valued as a means of preserving memories of a vanishing way of life, and hence of celebrating cultural continuity and identity; in an interethnic perspective, however, the element of *display,* whether intentional or not, is unavoidable. Many "outsiders" will thus approach ethnic autobiographies with the misguided conviction that the authors necessarily speak for "their people." The practice of reading autobiography for "cultural authenticity" may be a particularly serious danger for Chinese-American autobiography, given the group's unique situation in United States society. The ancestral land of Chinese Americans, due to its long history, sophisticated civilization, and complex encounters with American imperialism in recent history, casts an inordinately strong spell on the white imagination. Moreover, Chinese Americans, who have been subjected to genocidal immigration policies,[19] are placed in the situation of permanent guests who must earn their keep by adding the spice of variety to American life—by selectively maintaining aspects of traditional Chinese culture and language fascinating to whites. In the terminology of Werner Sollors, if the essence of the American experience is the formation of a society based on "consent" rather than "descent," Chinese Americans have clearly been (and still are) excluded from participation in "consent" by the dominant group's insistence on the primacy of their "descent." The irony is that many readers from within the ethnic group itself have, like the detractors of *The Woman Warrior,* inadvertently contributed to this simplified and often condescending view by likewise positing a direct pipeline of cultural authenticity between the collectivity and the individual. The idea of overdetermination by "descent" is thus left unchallenged. Demanding "representativeness," the Chinese-American critics of Kingston differ from the white literary tourists only in the version of cultural authenticity subscribed to.

This tension between "consent" and "descent" is reminiscent of W. E. B. Du Bois's well-known concept of "double consciousness."[20] The writers are aware of themselves as "insiders" with unique experiences that cannot be fully captured by ethnic categories alone. On the other hand, they cannot but sense the "outsiders' " constant gaze upon their skin color, their physiognomy, their "difference." Their American right of "consent"—here taking the form of the freedom to create literature true to their felt lives—is perpetually called into question or qualified by reader expectations based on "descent." Some Chinese-American autobiographers have, indeed, sought distinction in their exotic "descent," allowing the dominant group's perceptions to define their identity. However, it is important to recognize that Kingston has taken an altogether different path in *The Woman Warrior.* The protagonist has eschewed the facile authority which self-appointment as guide and spokesperson could confer on her. The discursive space occupied by *The Woman Warrior* is between the two poles of the "double consciousness"; the audience the narrator addresses in the second person is composed of fellow Chinese Americans sharing the protagonist's need to establish a new Chinese-American selfhood:

> Chinese-Americans, when you try to understand what things in you are Chinese, how do you separate what is peculiar to childhood, to poverty, insanities, one family, your mother who marked your growing with stories, from what is Chinese? What is Chinese tradition and what is the movies? (6)

Boelhower writes:

> In the mixed genre of autobiography, . . . the question of identity involves matching the narrator's own self-perception with the self that is recognized by

others, so as to establish a continuity between the two (self and world), to give a design of self-in-the-world. ("Brave New World" 12)

If the "others" are the potential "misreaders" among her white audience, Kingston is in truth far less obsessed than her critics with "the self that is recognized by others." There are, of course, other "others" in the protagonist's lonely struggle: her Chinese family, relatives, fellow "villagers," whose perceptions of her do not match her self-perceptions either. "Descent" notwithstanding, connection to them has to be forged, which can take place only after an initial recognition of difference. Neither American nor Chinese culture, as given, offers a resting place; the protagonist of *The Woman Warrior* has to discover that there is "[n]o higher listener. No higher listener but myself" (237). Her project is to reach "an avowal of values and a recognition of the self by the self—a choice carried out at the level of essential being—not a revelation of a reality given in advance but a corollary of an active intelligence" (Gusdorf 44). This project is so bold, so unfamiliar, that even her fellow Chinese Americans sometimes mistake it for the accommodationism of earlier autobiographers. For resemblances can indeed be found between *The Woman Warrior* and its predecessors—like Lee, Kingston retells Chinese tales heard in childhood; like Kuo, she makes general remarks on Chinese culture; like Lowe, she speaks of unusual Chinese foods; like Wong, she recounts experiences of sexist oppression. The crucial question is whether these resemblances are merely superficial or whether they bespeak a basic commonality in autobiographical stance. Only a careless reader, I submit, would be able to conclude that Kingston's stance in *The Woman Warrior* is that of the trustworthy cultural guide.

For the "native" in this case, having been born and raised in "ghost country" without benefit of explicit parental instruction in cultural practices, is barely more enlightened than an "outsider" would be: "From the configuration of food my mother set out, we kids had to infer the holidays" (215). Quite unlike the generalizations about Chinese culture in *I've Come a Long Way* or *Father and Glorious Descendant,* which are meant to be encapsulations of superior knowledge, those in *The Woman Warrior* bespeak a tentative groping toward understanding. From fragmentary and haphazard evidence, the protagonist has to piece together a coherent picture of the culture she is enjoined to preserve against American influence. The effort is so frustrating that she exclaims in exasperation: "I don't see how they kept up a continuous culture for five thousand years. Maybe they didn't; maybe everyone makes it up as they go along" (216). But the point, of course, is that the Chinese who remain in Chinese-dominant communities would have no trouble at all transmitting culture through osmosis. It is the protagonist's American-born generation who must "make it up as they go along." The emigrant parents' expectation of a "continuous culture" is, if entirely human, ahistorical and therefore doomed. (So, one might add, is the critics' similar demand for cultural authenticity. Purity is best preserved by death; history adulterates.)

Given *The Warrior Woman*'s situation in the broader cultural timescape of Chinese America, then, the so-called distortions of traditional Chinese culture found in the text are simply indications of how far removed from it the protagonist has become. As Deborah Woo rightly observes, "where culture is problematic as a source of identity, cultural ignorance itself is part of what is authentic about the experience" (186). Thus the substitution of "heavenly chicken" for "field chicken" is not exoticization but an example of how a young Chinese child in an English-dominant society may misunderstand a tonal language. The protagonist's cosmological speculations on the omnipresent number six (91), involving a misinterpretation of *dai luk* (which in Cantonese pronunciation can be "the big six," a nonexistent collocation, or "the big continent/the mainland"), betray her "craving for coherence" in the face of a bewildering mass of unexplained cultural data (Hsu 434). It is not an actual Chinese fortune-teller who confuses the homophones, which might have justified the charge of willful distortion on Kingston's part; the phrase "the Big Six" is framed by the young girl's meditation on her mother's life, the fortune-teller a fictive one whom she imagines her mother consulting.

It is, in fact, essential to recognize that the entire *Woman Warrior* is a sort of meditation on what it means to be Chinese American. To this end, the protagonist appropriates whatever is at hand, testing one generalization after another until a satisfactory degree of applicability to her own life is found. As she says of the differing versions of the No Name Woman's story: "Unless I see her life branching into mine, she gives me no ancestral help" (10). The aphoristic statements about Chinese ways interspersed in the narrative— "Women in the old China did not choose" (7); "Chinese communication was loud, public" (13); "Among the very poor and the wealthy, brothers married their adopted sisters, like doves" (14)—are not offered for the benefit of readers hungry for tidbits of anthropological information. Rather, they are threads in a larger tapestry of inferences, some sturdy, some thin, which the protagonist weaves for her own use. Rejecting the theory that the aunt is a "wild woman" (9) or a passive rape victim, the narrator decides on a version relevant to her life in an immigrant family: a story of assertion of "private life" (14) against the harsh demands of group survival.

Even with material that attempts with its air of certainty, the protagonist finds it necessary to tailor-make meanings from altered details. Thus she spurns the simplistic lesson of the traditional Fa Mu Lan tale, creating instead a potentially subversive woman warrior to whom even traditions yield. While the heroine of "Mulan Shi" sees herself merely as a second-best substitute for an aged father (there being no elder son to take his place), the little girl in "White Tigers" is a *chosen* one, destined to be called away by "immortals." Martial artists typically pass on their skills to sons or male disciples; the old couple in the mountains, in contrast, devote years exclusively to her training.

For the traditional Mulan, the campaigns are but a detour; at the end of the poem, the erstwhile general puts on makeup, ready to resume her interrupted feminine life. Kingston's Fa Mu Lan chooses wifehood and motherhood in the midst of battle. Her fellow villagers know of her identity before her triumphant return from battle (43); their relinquishment of their precious sons to her army is thus an affirmation of faith in her female power. Of course, the very necessity of male disguise means that the narrator's fantasized challenge to patriarchy can never be complete; in the last analysis, she would like to be remembered for "perfect filiality" (54). Yet even Fa Mu Lan's return to her parents' house has an element of active choice. All in all, working within the constraints of internalized values, the protagonist has done her best to make of unpromising material an inspiring, if not entirely radical, tale.

The treatment of the T'sai Yen story (241–43) follows much the same pattern of sifting out details to arrive at a relevant meaning. Kingston's retelling omits a crucial scene in the original "Eighteen Stanzas for a Barbarian Reed Pipe":[21] T'sai Yen's painful leave-taking from her half-barbarian sons. Though by now attached to her captor and heartsick at the prospect of never seeing her children again, T'sai Yen nevertheless chooses Han lands as her real home, negating the twelve years spent in the steppes as a mere unfortunate interlude. Herself a half-barbarian to her China-obsessed parents ("Whenever my parents said 'home,' they suspended America" [116]), the narrator might have found such a detail too close for comfort, and too contrary in spirit to her own undertaking of forming a Chinese-American self. Thus we find a shift of emphasis: the last pages of *The Woman Warrior* celebrate not return from the remote peripheries to a waiting home but the creation of a new center through art. Singing a song that transcends cultural boundaries, T'sai Yen can now leave "her tent to sit by the winter campfires, ringed by barbarians" (243).

As with the "Eighteen Stanzas," the moral that the protagonist draws from the assorted Chinese ghost stories diverges from the one intended by the source. No automatic authority on Chinese culture simply by virtue of "descent," the protagonist must resort to public, written texts in her quest for meanings not forthcoming in her mother's private oral tradition. (Contrary to one critic's judgment that the Mandarin transliteration of some names in *The Woman Warrior* betrays how Kingston passes library research for her Cantonese mother's bedtime stories,[22] Kingston does not attempt to cover her trails, as any self-respecting cultural guide would. She provides dates with the Mandarin names and identifies the source, "the research against ghost fear published by the Chinese Academy of Science" (Zhongguo Kexueyuan Wenxueyanjiusuo 104). The lesson she constructs to make sense of her experiences in a frugal immigrant family—"Big eaters win" (105)—bears little relation to the political allegory of the Communist-compiled anthology. But what matters is not the fit (for which Procrustean beds are notorious). The most useful lesson the protagonist can learn from her research is that a passive staking of her life on some preestablished reality, like looking up *Ho Chi Kuei* (237–38) in a dictionary filled with decontextualized definitions, will always prove fruitless.

The narrator's methodology of self-redemption is thus remarkably consistent. Over and over, we find her forgoing the security of ready-made cultural meanings, opting instead to painstakingly mold a new set suited to her condition as a Chinese-American woman. The many questions about "facts" plaguing the narrator—Were there an Oldest Daughter and Oldest Son who died in China (120)? Did Brave Orchid cut her frenum (190)? Did the hulk exist or was he made up (239)?—function much like a series of Zen *koan,* frustrating because impossible to answer by appeal to an external authority (mother, in this case). In the end, realization of their very impossibility frees her to explore the fecund uncertainties of her Chinese-American existence.

The readers who fault *The Woman Warrior* for not being more responsible toward "facts" would do well to meditate on their own *koan.* To read departures from traditional material found in *The Woman Warrior* as Kingston's cynical manipulations of naïve white readers, as her critics have done, is not only to fly in the face of textual evidence but to belittle the difficulty and urgency of the imaginative enterprise so necessary to the American-born generation: to make sense of Chinese and American culture from its own viewpoint (however hybrid and laughable to "outsiders"), to articulate its own reality, and to strengthen its precarious purchase on the task of self-fashioning. The Fa Mu Lan story itself, which many of Kingston's critics take to be a fixed and sacred given, actually exists in a multitude of Chinese texts differing from each other in purpose as well as detail.[23]

Kingston's critics have been measuring *The Woman Warrior* "against some extra-textual order of fact," not realizing that this order is "based in its turn on other texts (dignified as documents)" (Eakin 23): an ideologically uplifting version of Chinese-American history revising earlier racist texts, a version of the Fa Mu Lan legend sufficiently hoary to be considered "historical." The critics' concern is understandable in view of widespread ignorance about the sociopolitical context of Chinese-American literary creation, the inherent duality of the autobiographical genre (which encourages reading for "cultural authenticity"), the existence of autobiographies by both Chinese- and American-born writers promising privileged glimpses into the group's secret life and the apparent similarities between them and Kingston's work. These issues are, indeed, vital ones generalizable to other ethnic American autobiographies, even to all ethnic American literatures. Nevertheless, intent on liberating Chinese-American writers from one set of constraints, Kingston's detractors have imposed another, in the meantime failing to take note of the most fundamental freedom of all that *The Woman Warrior* has wrested from a priori generic categories and cultural prescriptions: the freedom to create in literature a sui generis Chinese-American reality.

I am grateful to King-Kok Cheung, Samuel Cheung, Maxine Hong Kingston, Kathy Lo, Stephen Sumida, Shelley Wong, Deborah Woo, and Yiheng Zhao for their assistance in the writing of this essay, and to James Payne for his many valuable suggestions on revision. I am solely responsible for its content.

Notes

1.   For example, both Juhasz and Rabine relate the unconventional narrative structure of *The Woman Warrior* to the feminist act of creating identity, although their interpretations differ.

2.   Personal communication to the author from Kingston, 21 May 1988; quoted with her permission.

3.   On the "real" and the "imaginary," Kingston writes: "My idea [in *The Woman Warrior* and *China Men*] was to invent a new form for telling my stories and thoughts. I needed a form in which I could have real, true human beings who have very imaginative minds tell their lives and dreams. My real characters have artful minds, the minds of fiction writers and storytellers." Personal communication to the author, 21 May 1988; quoted with Kingston's permission.

4.   For example, Brave Orchid's encounter with the "Sitting Ghost"; the Chinese stories of big eaters who devour ghosts and other monsters (104–6); the protagonist's girlhood interactions with many types of "ghosts" (113–16); and Moon Orchid's reunion with her husband, both now having entered the "land of ghosts" (178).

5.   For a reading of the multilayered significance of the term *ghost,* see Sato, who demonstrates how Kingston's rendering of *kuei* focuses many aspects of Chinese-American life and is hardly a "white-washed" usage.

6.   This version of the name appears to be a composite of Cantonese and Mandarin transliterations, *Fa Muk Lan* and *Hua Mu Lan*—another "impurity"?

7.   The prolonged training in still "stances" and feats of balance (like sleeping on a rope), the copying of animal movements, and the gaining of control over normally involuntary bodily functions are standard fare in *wuxia xiaoshuo.* The "calling" of a chosen one for spiritual discipline, the hermit's retreat on misty mountains, the magic water gourd, and the cultivation of immortality are images from *shenxian* stories, which have passed fully into the Chinese popular mind. These and other features from folk traditions found in *The Woman Warrior* would be familiar to children growing up in a Chinese community.

8.   A translation of "The Ballad of Mulan" may be found in Liu and Lo 77–80 (cited in Chua).

9.   *Outlaws of the Marsh,* a classic in Chinese literature, is based on oral tales depicting peasant heroes who form "righteous armies" to defy the corrupt imperial government. The earliest extant written version dates from the sixteenth century. The English title of Shapiro's recent translation, rather than the older *Water Margin,* is used here.

10.   Note that in her next book, *China Men,* Kingston has included a list of discriminatory legislation against Chinese Americans. "The reviews of my first book made it clear that people didn't know the history—or that they thought I didn't. While I was writing about *China Men,* I just couldn't take that tension any more" (Pfaff 26; cited in Kim xvii).

11.   Fong cites her relationship with a "warm, generous and loving father" (68–69) to support her complaint against *The Woman Warrior.*

12.   The critics of *The Woman Warrior* supply almost a textbook example of the assumptions about autobiography, common prior to the recent shifting of critical focus from *bios* to *autos,* described by Olney, "Autobiography and the Cultural Moment" 20.

13. Chinese-American literature has a large Chinese-language component, the exclusive domain of immigrant writers, which is only beginning to be studied and translated. This component falls outside the scope of this essay, but one should note that it contains very few autobiographies.

A partial list (in chronological order) of works explicitly presented as autobiography, of varying literary interest and popularity, include Lee Yan Phou's *When I Was a Boy in China* (1887), Yung Wing's *My Life in China and America* (1909), Helena Kuo's *I've Come a Long Way* (1942), Pardee Lowe's *Father and Glorious Descendant* (1943), Jade Snow Wong's *Fifth Chinese Daughter* (1945), Su-ling Wong (pseud.) and Earl Herbert Cressy's *Daughter of Confucius: A Personal History* (1952), Jade Snow Wong's *No Chinese Stranger* (1975), Thomas York-Tong Goo's *Before the Gods* (1976), Maxine Hong Kingston's *The Woman Warrior* (1976), and Katherine Wei and Terry Quinn's *Second Daughter: Growing Up in China, 1930–1949* (1984).

14. See Kim's discussion of "ambassadors of goodwill" in her chapter on early Asian immigrant writers (24–29).

15. Goo, who undergoes assimilation into Chinese culture in China, is an exception to this pattern.

16. A passage in Korean American Younghill Kang's fictionalized autobiography, *East Goes West* (1937), provides an interesting gloss on the practice of "cultural guiding," which is apparently generalizable from Chinese to other Asian-American autobiographies. Kim, an older Korean exile, advises the protagonist Chungpa Han to retain his classical Oriental learning: "You have to eat. And to eat, you must enter into the economic life of Americans. . . . In making a living, Oriental scholarship may help you more than your American education. . . . [I]n such a field, you would have the advantage. There would be less competition. . . . *You must be now like a Western man approaching Asia.* . . . As a transplanted scholar, this is the only road I could point to, for your happy surviving" (277–78; my italics). Despite his rhetoric of cultural catholicity, what Kim is suggesting is really a kind of self-Orientalization.

17. This possibility is further explored in my "Immigrant Autobiography: Some Questions of Definition and Approach."

18. Recipes are again included in the sequel to *Fifth Chinese Daughter, No Chinese Stranger* (e.g., 187–88). In the latter, Wong and her husband lead tours to the Far East, thus making cultural interpretation their trade.

19. The Chinese Exclusion Act, passed in 1882 to keep out Chinese laborers, as well as subsequent anti-Chinese measures (including antimiscegenation laws and laws prohibiting laborers' wives from entering), created a "bachelor society" unable to reproduce itself. The situation did not begin to change until the Exclusion Act was repealed in 1943.

20. This concept has been related by more than one scholar (e.g., Rubin 75; Rampersad 13) to the duality of autobiography.

21. Rorex and Fong provide a complete translation of the poem as well as color illustrations from a traditional scroll. Kingston's use of the T'sai Yen material is discussed in greater detail in my forthcoming "Kingston's Handling of Traditional Chinese Sources."

22. Statement delivered by Marlon Hom at the roundtable discussion, "Asian American Literature: State of the Art and Criticism," Fifth National Conference of the Association for Asian American Studies, 26 Mar. 1988, Washington State University, Pullman.

23. According to Zhao 77–79, since the Tang dynasty (618–907) there have been many versions of the Fa Mu Lan story, some poetic, others operatic or novelistic. One Qing dynasty (1644–1911) version features a sister; another adds a cowardly cousin. During the Anti-Japanese War (1937–45), the Fa Mu Lan story was frequently staged as plays, with the moral modified to emphasize nationalism (even though the "original" heroine was not Han but a member of a northern tribe.) I have seen a film version from the 1960s sung in *huangmeidiao*, a variety of popular Chinese opera, available in videotape rental outlets serving Chinese-American communities. This version includes statements on the equality of the sexes reflecting modern, Westernized ideas.

Works Cited

Boelhower, William. "The Brave New World of Immigrant Autobiography." *MELUS* 9, no. 2 (1982): 5–23.

———. *Immigrant Autobiography in the United States.* Verona: Essedue, 1982.

Bruss, Elizabeth. *Autobiographical Acts: The Changing Situation of a Literary Genre.* Baltimore: Johns Hopkins UP, 1976.

Chan, Jeffery Paul. "Jeff Chan, Chairman of SF State Asian American Studies, Attacks Review." *San Francisco Journal,* 4 May 1977, 6.

Chang, Diana. *Frontiers of Love.* New York: Random, 1956.

Chin, Frank. "The Most Popular Book in China." *Quilt* 4 (1984): 6–12.

———. "This Is Not an Autobiography." *Genre* 18, no. 2 (1985): 109–30.

Chin, Frank, Jeffery Paul Chan, Lawson Fusao Inada, and Shawn Wong, eds. *Aiiieeeee! An Anthology of Asian-American Writers.* 1974. Rpt. Washington, DC: Howard UP, 1983.

Chu, Louis. *Eat a Bowl of Tea.* Seattle: U of Washington P, 1961.

Chua, Cheng Lok. "Golden Mountain: Chinese Versions of the American Dream in Lin Yutang, Louis Chu, and Maxine Hong Kingston." *Ethnic Groups* 4 (1982): 57.

Chuang Hua (pseud.). *Crossings.* New York: Dial, 1968.

Eakin, John Paul. *Fictions in Autobiography: Studies in the Art of Self-Invention.* Princeton: Princeton UP, 1985.

Fong, Katheryn M. "To Maxine Hong Kingston: A Letter." *Bulletin for Concerned Asian Scholars* 9, no. 4 (1977): 67–69.

Gates, Henry Louis, Jr. *Figures in Black: Words, Signs, and the "Racial" Self.* New York: Oxford UP, 1987.

Goo, Thomas York-Tong. *Before the Gods.* New York: Helios, 1976.

Gusdorf, Georges. "Conditions and Limits of Autobiography." Trans. James Olney. In Olney, *Autobiography* 28–48.

Hsu, Vivian. "Maxine Hong Kingston as Psycho-Autobiographer and Ethnographer." *International Journal of Women's Studies* 6, no. 5 (1983): 429–42.

Johnson, Diane. "Ghosts." Rev. of *The Woman Warrior,* by Maxine Hong Kingston. *New York Review of Books,* 3 Feb. 1977, 19+.

Juhasz, Suzanne. "Maxine Hong Kingston: Narrative Technique and Female Identity." In Rainwater and Scheik 173–89.

Kang, Younghill. *East Goes West: The Making of an Oriental Yankee.* Chicago: Follett, 1937.

Kim, Elaine H. *Asian American Literature: An Introduction to the Writings and Their Social Context.* Philadelphia: Temple UP, 1982.

Kingston, Maxine Hong. *China Men.* New York: Knopf, 1980.

———. *The Woman Warrior: Memoirs of a Girlhood among Ghosts.* 1976. New York: Random, 1977.

Krupat, Arnold. "The Indian Autobiography: Origins, Type, and Function." *American Literature* 53, no. 1 (1981): 22–42.

Kuo, Helena. *I've Come a Long Way.* New York: Appleton, 1942.

Larson, Wendy Ann. "Autobiographies of Chinese Writers in the Early Twentieth Century." Diss. U of California, Berkeley, 1984.

Lau, Joseph S. M. [Liu Shaoming]. "Tangrenjie de xiaoshuo shijie" ["The Fictional World of Chinatown"]. *Ming Pao Monthly* 173 (1980): 65–66.

Lee, Yan Phou. *When I Was a Boy in China.* Boston: Lothrop, 1887.

Lim, Genny, ed. *The Chinese American Experience: Papers from the Second National Conference on Chinese American Studies (1980).* San Francisco: Chinese Historical Society of America and Chinese Culture Foundation, 1980.

Liu, Wu-Chi, and Irving Yucheng Lo, trans. *Sunflower Splendor: Three Thousand Years of Chinese Poetry.* Bloomington: Indiana UP, 1975.

Lowe, Pardee. *Father and Glorious Descendant.* Boston: Little, 1943.

Olney, James. "Autobiography and the Cultural Moment: A Thematic, Historical, and Bibliographical Introduction." In Olney, *Autobiography* 3–27.

———, ed. *Autobiography: Essays Theoretical and Critical.* Princeton: Princeton UP, 1980.

———. "Some Versions of Memory/Some Versions of Bios: The Ontology of Autobiography." In Olney, *Autobiography* 236–67.

Pascal, Roy. *Design and Truth in Autobiography.* Cambridge: Harvard UP, 1960.

Pfaff, Timothy. "Talk with Mrs. Kingston." *New York Times Book Review,* 18 June 1980.

Rabine, Leslie W. "No Lost Paradise: Social Gender and Symbolic Gender in the Writings of Maxine Hong Kingston." *Signs: Journal of Women in Culture and Society* 12, no. 3 (1987): 471–92.

Rainwater, Catherine, and William J. Scheik, eds. *Contemporary American Women Writers: Narrative Strategies.* Lexington: UP of Kentucky, 1985.

Rampersad, Arnold. "Biography, Autobiography, and Afro-American Culture." *Yale Review* 73, no. 1 (1983): 1–16.

Rorex, Robert A., and Wen Fong. *Eighteen Songs of a Nomad Flute: The Story of Lady Wen-Chi.* New York: Metropolitan Museum of Art, 1974.

Rubin, Steven J. "Ethnic Autobiography: A Comparative Approach." *Journal of Ethnic Studies* 9, no. 1 (1981): 75–79.

Sands, Kathleen Mullen. "American Indian Autobiography." In *Studies in American Indian Literature: Essays and Course Designs,* ed. Paula Gunn Allen. New York: MLA, 1983. 55–65.

Sato, Gayle K. Fujita. "Ghosts as Chinese-American Constructs in Maxine Hong Kingston's *The Woman Warrior.*" In *Haunting the House of Fiction: Feminist Perspectives on Ghost Stories by American Women,* ed. Lynette Carpenter and Wendy K. Kolmar. Knoxville: U of Tennessee P, 1991. 193–214.

Shapiro, Sidney, trans. *Outlaws of the Marsh.* Beijing: Foreign Language Press, 1980.

Sollors, Werner. *Beyond Ethnicity: Consent and Descent in American Culture.* New York: Oxford UP, 1986.

Stone, Albert. "Autobiography in American Culture: Looking Back at the Seventies." *American Studies International* 19, no. 3–4 (1981): 3–14.

Tong, Benjamin R. "Chinatown Popular Culture: Notes toward a Critical Psychological Anthropology." In Lim 233–41.

———. "Critic of Admirer Sees Dumb Racist." *San Francisco Journal,* 11 May 1977, 6.

Wei, Katherine, and Terry Quinn. *Second Daughter: Growing Up in China, 1930–1949.* New York: Holt, 1984.

Wong, Jade Snow. *Fifth Chinese Daughter.* 1945. Rev. ed. New York: Harper, 1950.

———. *No Chinese Stranger.* New York: Harper, 1975.

Wong, Nellie. Review of *The Woman Warrior. Bridge* 6, no. 4 (1978–79): 46–48.

Wong, Sau-ling C. "Immigrant Autobiography: Some Questions of Definition and Approach." In *American Autobiography: Retrospect and Prospect,* ed. Paul John Eakin. Madison: U of Wisconsin P, 1991. 142–70.

———. "Kingston's Handling of Traditional Chinese Sources." *Approaches to Teaching Kingston's The Woman Warrior,* ed. Shirley Geok-lin Lim. New York: MLA, 1991.

Wong, Shawn. *Homebase.* New York: I. Reed, 1979.

Wong, Su-ling (pseud.), and Earl Herbert Cressy. *Daughter of Confucius: A Personal History.* New York: Farrar, 1952.

Wong, Suzi. Review of *The Woman Warrior. Amerasia Journal* 4, no. 1 (1977): 165–67.

Woo, Deborah. "Maxine Hong Kingston: The Ethnic Writer and the Burden of Dual Authenticity." *Amerasia Journal* 16, no. 1 (1990): 173–200.

Wu, Pei-Yi. "Self-Examination and Confession of Sins in Traditional China." *Harvard Journal of Asiatic Studies* 39, no. 1 (1979): 5–38.

Yep, Laurence. *Dragonwings.* New York: Harper, 1975.

Yung, Wing. *My Life in China and America*. New York: Holt, 1909.

Zhao, Jingshen. *Minzu wenxue xiaoshi* [*A Brief History of National Literature*]. N.p.: Shijie Shuju, 1940.

Zhongguo Kexueyuan Wenxueyanjiusuo [Chinese Academy of Science, Institute of Literary Studies]. *Bupagui de gushi* [*Stories of Those Who Are Not Afraid of Ghosts*]. Hong Kong: San Lian, 1961.

Maxine Hong Kingston and the Dialogic Dilemma of Asian American Writers

AMY LING

In June 1993, at Cornell University during the tenth national conference of the Association for Asian American Studies, Robert Ku, a lecturer at Hunter College, delivered a provocative paper in which he lamented that Asian American writers themselves in writing of the cultural specificities of their own cultural backgrounds are forced into the language of anthropological ethnography and thereby partake of the hierarchical binaries of Same and Other, Normal and Exotic, Advanced and Backward, Superior and Inferior. As "native informants," they naturally fall within the second half of these categories. To demonstrate the similarity of the language used in anthropology, psychology, and literature, Ku read five brief unidentified passages, two by noted social scientists and three by noted Asian American writers. He later identified the authors of these passages as Bronislaw Malinowski, Carlos Bulosan, Younghill Kang, Maxine Hong Kingston, and Sigmund Freud.

What these passages had in common, it seemed to me, was not so much their language as their subject matter. Each passage described an event or ritual, either a marriage or punishment for a violation of a prohibition, that described customs specific to a culture outside of the dominant Anglo-European culture, such as the peasant wedding in the Philippines in the first chapter of *America Is in the Heart,* in which the bride is discovered not to be a virgin and therefore stoned by the villagers, and the similarity brutal treatment of the No Name Woman in Kingston's opening chapter of *The Woman Warrior.* Ku was disturbed and distressed by the "uneasy relationship between literature, ethnography, [and] psychoanalysis"[1] which Asian American writers, by their very position within a dominant society, cannot escape. He was puzzled and paralyzed because he wants to write his own story, presumably a Korean American *Bildungsroman,* but cannot figure out how to do so without sounding like an ethnographic "insider informant."

From *Having Our Way: Women Rewriting Tradition in Twentieth-Century America,* edited by Harriet Pollack. London: Associated University Presses, 1995: 151–66. Copyright 1995 by Associated University Presses. Reprinted by permission of Associated University Presses.

Moved by this predicament, I tried to console him by remarking that his role and that of all minority writers in this society, if we wish to be understood by a majority audience, cannot help but be that of cultural explainers until such time as everyone is informed on the myriad cultures that make up the United States. Given the size of the task and the inertia or chauvinism of most people, this universal enlightenment is not likely to happen in the near future. We have no choice, except of course, if we choose to speak only to others exactly like ourselves. If Ku wishes to address exclusively a Korean American audience, then, he can feel relieved of what he considers an onerous duty. But he will also be relieved of a great many readers. Moreover, I thought, in my self-righteous missionary mode, as teachers, it is our mission and our privilege to educate.

I suggested also that it is not so much the specificities of what is being conveyed as the tone and manner in which they are conveyed that sets apart the outsider standing aloof and above from the insider standing beside. The outsider creates the sense of otherness; the insider relates the norm.

At the same time, of course, we are all doubly conscious, in the Du Boisian sense, constantly aware of how we are being perceived while we are in the act of perceiving. Readers from outside the Asian American perspective, readers who may be reluctant in the first place, such as students taking a course in Asian American literature because they must satisfy an ethnic studies requirement for graduation, will complain that the material is so foreign and strange that they cannot possibly relate to it. (One would think they'd been asked to read stories written by baboons.) When confronted with several such responses this semester, I finally replied, "What about relating to this material as a human being?" (My sense of mission and privilege as an educator was growing faint.) The other response I found totally exasperating was the "Is-this-characteristic-of-Asian-Americans?" response. For example: "The narration in this text is fragmented. Is this a characteristic of Asian Americans?" Or "These novels devote a lot of time and space to food and family—are these characteristically Asian American concerns?" Where does such lack of comprehension come from? Is it so impossible for such students to think of Asian Americans as part of the human species? Teaching Asian American literature to white students in the midwest can be at times comparable to handling nitroglycerine; the material, the students, and I are all, for different reasons, volatile.

Kingston herself has published an essay about the cultural misreadings by two-thirds of the reviewers of *The Woman Warrior*, who measured "the book and me against the stereotype of the exotic, inscrutable, mysterious oriental":

I thought the reality and humanity of my characters would bust through any stereotypes of them. Simple-mindedly, I wore a sweatshirt for the dust-jacket photo, to deny the exotic. I had not calculated how blinding stereotyping is, how stupefying. The critics who said how the book was good because it was, or was not, like the oriental fantasy in their heads might as well have said how weak it was, since it in fact did not break through the fantasy. . . . "How amazing," they may as well be saying. "That she writes like a human being. How unoriental."[2]

It is not just reviewers from other cultures that "misread" an author's intent. Readers from within that very culture feel particularly free to use their own authors for target practice. Perhaps the author has objected to a cultural practice close to the heart of the reader, but such an objection is an author's right. It is bold and courageous, for example, for Kingston to counteract the erasure of her transgressive paternal aunt by writing about her, as it is bold and courageous of Alice Walker to depict the act and the consequences of clitorectomy. It is good and right of Bulosan to sympathize with the bride who did not pass the virginity test and to call her stoning a "cruel" and "backward" custom.

But these bold and courageous stands are also provocative acts which place the multicultural writer in a visible and vulnerable position, susceptible to attack from all sides. All too often the most vociferous slings and arrows are flung from those within the minority culture itself, with such barbs as these: this writer is a traitor to the community and to the cause; she's not telling the story right or she's telling the wrong one; he's hanging out dirty laundry for other people's eyes; she's falling into stereotypes and catering to base appetites for the exotic and the barbaric. Amy Tan, David Henry Hwang, and particularly Maxine Hong Kingston—the best-known Asian American writers—have all been attacked along these lines by Asian American critics.

Sau-ling Wong, a scholar born and reared in Hong Kong, takes American-born Amy Tan to task for mistranslating the Chinese words *tang jieh* as "sugar sister" instead of "older female cousin on the father's side," but Tan's mistake in homonyms may also be seen as poetic license and, further, as affirmation of what it is to be Chinese American. Tan's error in the Chinese language confirms the distance between Chinese and Chinese American, a distinction most Asian Americans are vocal and insistent about maintaining. William Chang has complained that there are no positive images of Asian males for him to identify with in Hwang's *M. Butterfly*. Since the only Asian male in the play is a transvestite, he berates Hwang for not presenting the Asian male in a favorable light. But I haven't heard any French men complaining that they are being portrayed as idiots who after twenty years do not know the sex of their own lovers. The problem is clear: despite the recent efflorescence in Asian American literature, we still do not have enough writers to allow each one the right to write according to his or her own lights.

But most vociferous and persistent among Asian American critics is Frank Chin, who stands out for being uncompromisingly hostile. He has publicly called Kingston a "yellow agent of stereotype" who "falsifies Chinese history" and thereby "vilifies Chinese manhood."[3] When I protested during my only conversation with Frank Chin last fall that Amy Tan and Maxine Hong Kingston were not racists, as he has been asserting, but feminists, his retort—at full volume—was "feminists are racists!" In the "Afterword" to his collection of short stories, *The Chinaman Pacific & Frisco R. R. Co.* (1988), Chin writes a scathing parody of Kingston's *The Woman Warrior,* which he calls "The Unmanly Warrior." As a countermove to Chinese American feminism, and to the effeminization of Chinese American men, Chin offers the Chinese heroic tradition found in *Romance of the Three Kingdoms,* certain of whose heroes he incorporates into his latest novel, *Donald Duk.* But as critic King-Kok Cheung has rightly pointed out: "The refutation of effeminate stereotypes through the glorification of machismo merely perpetuates patriarchal terms and assumptions," and she asks plaintively, "Is it not possible for Chinese American men to recover a cultural space without denigrating or erasing 'the feminine' "?[4]

As a means of putting Chin in his place, though she publicly denies that this was her intent, Kingston has captured Chin's voice and character in her protagonist, Wittman Ah Sing, in her novel *Tripmaster Monkey.* However, instead of placing Chin in the tradition of Gwang Gung, the god of literature and war, one of the one hundred and eight heroes of *Romance of the Three Kingdoms,* which Chin claims for himself, Kingston finds his counterpart in the mischievous and irrepressible Monkey King, a trickster figure from the picaresque Chinese folk novel *Journey to the West.* (Shawn Wong, novelist and colleague of Chin's, told me that he was amazed at how accurately Maxine had caught Frank's voice; he phoned Frank to say, "She must have been a fly on the wall when you were talking!")[5] Kingston, however, claims that the narrative voice in this novel belongs to Gwan Yin, the goddess of mercy, and it is her power that disarms the militant Wittman, transforming him into a pacifist, and her voice that has the last word, "Dear American monkey, don't be afraid. Here, let us tweak your ear, and kiss your other ear."[6] Her tone is slightly mocking and yet loving, like that of an indulgent mother with a naughty but beloved son.

Other Chinese and Chinese American readers have complained that Kingston has mixed up Cantonese and Mandarin romanizations of Chinese words, that she has combined the legends of Fa Mulan and Yueh Fei—*he's* the general who had words carved into his back—that she shouldn't have written about the monkey brain feast, that she mustn't emphasize footbinding and misogynist Chinese sayings because these are only a small part of Chinese culture and tradition. But these complaints seem petty and in no way diminish the considerable achievement of *The Woman Warrior,* which in my opinion stands as the supreme Chinese American feminist text. To read this text as the voice of insider informant, or exotic orientalism, or community historian is to miss the forest for some mosses under certain trees. It is to deny the text its complexity and richness as the embodiment of a multiplicity of perspectives, of reflexivity, dialogism, and heteroglossia. Let us now focus on these aspects of this text.

In the indeterminacy of its narrative style, we find what anthropologists like Barbara Myerhoff are calling reflexivity, the visible sign in the text of the writer's awareness of the act of writing, the writer in dialogue with herself. In "No Name Woman," for example, Kingston tells the aunt's story many times, first giving her mother's brief version, the bare-bone facts, then imagining all the possible narratives behind these bare bones, freely employing the word "perhaps" and the conditional present perfect tense ("A bun could have been contrived") to indicate the tentativeness of these versions. Later, in the story of Moon Orchid's meeting with her long-lost husband, Kingston gives us a detailed version of the encounter in her chapter "At the Western Palace" and in the next chapter undercuts the entire narration by stating, "What my brother actually said was . . ." and correcting herself and becoming even more specific: "In fact, it wasn't me my brother told about going to Los Angeles; one of my sisters told me what he'd told her." In other words, narratives are all created and creative acts; "reality" is created through words, and words are ripe with possibility. In providing her reader with so many possible narratives, Kingston demonstrates her awareness of the act of writing as a reflection of multiple and multiplying images. Where the "truth" lies is not her concern; her delight is in the richness of possibilities and in her own creativity in imagining them.

In applying Bakhtin to *The Woman Warrior,* one may read the entire text as an extended exploration of the internal dialogism of three words: *Chinese, American,* and *female.* Each term carries a multitude of meanings in dialogue, if not open warfare, with each other. To be specific, what does the word *Chinese* mean from the inside, that is, to the people so designated? What does it mean to the first-generation immigrant, to the second-generation American born, to the fourth or fifth generation? At what point does an immigrant Chinese become an American? What does the term mean from the outside, to the designators, to the stereotypers, to whites who feel that their places have been usurped? What are the word's historical, political, and social ramifications, underpinnings, and overlays? How does it differ from other related terms, such as *Japanese* or *Korean?* Similar questions may be applied to the other two terms: *American* and *female.* The entire book is devoted to an exploration of these words in an attempt at a self-definition that, finally, is never definitive in the sense of complete, conclusive, static. Paradox, flux, a "surplus of humanness," a defiance of fixation and categories characterize *The Woman Warrior,* as they characterize life. *The Woman Warrior* has gone further than any other text in exploring the complexities of these terms. Amy Tan's *Joy Luck Club* continues this exploration, but with somewhat less complexity.

We find dialogism and polyphony most apparent in the fissures or fault lines in the narrative, in the places where Kingston's language shifts abruptly and the disruptive is visible. It is these fissures between and overlappings of linguistic plates which are the most revealing and to which we shall direct our attention. One obvious example occurs in the first chapter. Between describing the lengths that women and girls endured to be Chinese beautiful, Kingston interjects this sentence: "I hope that the man my aunt loved appreciated a smooth brow, that he wasn't just a tits-and-ass man."[7] The abruptness of this male-locker-room or fraternity-house lingo in the midst of rather detailed, even poetic, if painful, descriptions of Chinese female beauty secrets brings the reader up short. In Bakhtin's terms, Kingston here "exhibits" these American male words as a "unique speech thing,"[8] language that is totally alien and unassimilable in the context, and yet it is a voice, one of thousands, in Kingston's head. That Kingston places this particular sentence in this particular setting is not only a linguistic act with stylistic ramifications but a culturally significant statement as well, for form, style, and content, as Bakhtin noted, are all inextricably linked. The context, the sentences surrounding "tits-and-ass man," show the excruciating pain that Chinese women endure in the removal of eyebrow and forehead hairs and facial freckles in order to win favor from the male gaze, but their attention to such Lilliputian detail is wasted in the United States where the Brobdingnagian male gaze is ostensibly only concerned with gross anatomical parts. The linguistic shift, the insertion of this sentence, emphasizes the contrast between the Chinese women's attention to fine detail and the jock expression's reductionism and objectification.

But Kingston's own position between the two is ambiguous. Is she proud of the "needles of pain" which her mother forced her to endure for the Chinese ideal of beauty or relieved that, in America, a woman is free from these "Chinese tortures"? Does she interject the slang expression to parody its reductionist view or does she appropriate this language to counteract the "demure" and silent Chinese girl stereotype that she hates?

I would argue that Kingston does both and that the ambiguity of her tone in this small episode reflects her tone throughout the entire text. Let us look at another example. In the "White Tigers" chapter, when the young girl, let's call her Maxine, first meets the old couple who will be her teachers on the mountain, we find this dialogue:

> "Have you eaten rice today, little girl?" they greeted me. "Yes, I have," I said out of politeness. "Thank you." ("No, I haven't," I would have said in real life, mad at the Chinese for lying so much. "I'm starved. Do you have any cookies? I like chocolate chip cookies.") (*WW,* 21)

The first exchange of question and response is pure Chinese convention, valuing politeness, displaying modesty and consideration of the other, saving face.

It is, in fact, so conventional a question that it has become a salutation rather than a request for information—much as Americans ask "How are you?" but don't really expect an answer other than "Fine, thanks." The parenthetical addition—what she would have said "in real life"—is, of course, the assimilated American response, valuing honesty and directness, frankly looking out for number one, and tinged with humor. Kingston's words denote impatience with the Chinese way; nonetheless, by the very act of presenting the two opposing ways of greeting strangers, she allows readers to judge for themselves the preferable social code. The expressed fondness for chocolate chip cookies seems a playful and somewhat greedy response, which I'm sure Kingston intended. Can it then be that Kingston is advocating Chinese politeness at the same time that she is complaining about it? Is she subverting American directness while seeming to embrace it? Is she, consciously or unconsciously, displaying the linguistic habit that her mother finally revealed, "That's what Chinese say, We like to say the opposite" (*WW,* 203). The answer would seem to be yes to all the above, for as Kingston explains, "I learned to make my mind large, as the universe is large, so that there is room for paradoxes" (*WW,* 29). And in her text, paradoxes abound, and dialogues are continuous.

A third shift in gears, a major one, which certainly every reader of *The Woman Warrior* cannot help but notice, occurs in the "White Tigers" chapter. After twenty-six pages embroidering on the sixty-two-line Chinese narrative poem "Magnolia Lay," after recounting the young girl's rigorous fifteen-year training in physical, spiritual, and mental self-control in lush, mystical, fantastic language, Kingston concludes the story of this paragon of virtue: "From the words on my back, and how they were fulfilled, the villagers would make a legend about my perfect filiality" (*WW,* 45). We are given a brief intermission of a narrow blank space and then the prosaic line, "My American life has been such a disappointment." From the rich, colorful heights of Chinese imaginative wish fulfillment, we are suddenly dropped to the depths of mundane American life. Though elsewhere in the text Kingston complains that Chinese is "the language of impossible stories" (*WW,* 87), in "White Tigers" she clearly indulges herself in embellishing the Chinese story, in making it overwhelmingly beautiful, seductive, and desirable because filled with power and valuation for the usually degraded Chinese girl. The Chinese woman warrior could do it all: excel in the "masculine" sphere of warfare and still return home to take up the "feminine" roles of mother, wife, daughter-in-law.

In fiction, everything is possible. Furthermore, as creator of the fiction, the author has control; she can make the rabbit jump into the fire to provide nourishment; she can have her characters live happily ever after. But "real life" is neither perfect nor controllable. American glories cannot compete with the Chinese glories of Fa Mulan; Maxine's straight A's cannot save her family's laundry, put food on the family table, or eliminate racism. Paradoxically, what Maxine calls "my American life" includes the "binds that China wraps around my feet," which include the misogynist sayings her parents and the other emigrant villagers imported to America: "Feeding girls is feeding cowbirds." "There's no profit in raising girls." "When you raise girls, you're raising children for strangers." "There is a Chinese word for the female I— which is 'slave.' Break the women with their own tongues!" (*WW*, 46–47). Another paradox: the same culture that inspired her with the heroic model of Fa Mulan also oppressed her with hateful sayings that caused her, as a child, to throw tantrums in protest. Words have power. These misogynist sayings of her parents and the racism of her American employers—"Order more of that nigger yellow, willya?" (*WW*, 48)—are the demons that Maxine, the Chinese American woman warrior, must fight. They are what make her American life such a disappointment, for as demons they lack the poetry of swords fighting in midair without hands.

Even in the first portion of "White Tigers" Kingston has not simply retold a Chinese myth, but has given her readers "one transformed by America, a sort of kung fu movie parody" ("CM," 57). The story of Fa Mulan may be a glorious model for a girl to dream about, serving as an antidote to the No Name Woman, but "White Tigers" is also a gross exaggeration, a wish fulfillment which the author indulges in with a smile on her face. The humor and irony are subtle and infrequent, but visible, as in this paragraph:

> So the hut became my home, and I found out that the old woman did not arrange the pine needles by hand. She opened the roof; an autumn wind would come up, and the needles fell in braids—brown strands, green strands, yellow strands. The old woman waved her arms in conducting motions; she blew softly with her mouth. I thought, nature certainly works differently on mountains than in valleys. (*WW*, 23)

In the last sentence, of course, we find the dialogic imagination of Kingston at work. She shifts gears and changes tone, moving from serious-poetic to ironic-parodic, interjecting another perspective on the narrative as she progresses, allowing another voice within her head to comment on the one that has up to now held the floor.

That Kingston's perspective fluctuates between Chinese and American is clearly visible in her shifting choice of personal pronouns; sometimes she identifies with the Chinese, using the first-person plural "we"; at other times, she is distanced, referring to the Chinese as "they." Near the end of chapter one, for example, we find these sentences:

> In an attempt to make the Chinese care for people outside the family, Chairman Mao encourages *us* now to give *our* paper replicas to the spirits of outstanding soldiers and workers, no matter whose ancestors they may be. My aunt remains forever hungry. Goods are not distributed evenly among the dead. (*WW*, 16, emphasis added)

Not only is Kingston here assuming the perspective of her father's extended family in China, but, against her frequent assertions of her Americanness, she here identifies with the Chinese living in the People's Republic: "Chairman Mao encourages *us*." In chapter two, in the voice of the woman warrior general nearing the end of her glorious career, Kingston writes:

> I stood on top of the last hill before Peiping and saw the roads below me flow like living rivers. Between roads the woods and plains moved too; the land was peopled—the Han people, the People of One Hundred Surnames, marching with one heart, *our* tatters flying. The depth and width of Joy were exactly known to me: the Chinese population. (*WW,* 42, emphasis added)

Here again, we find the narrator's expression of pride in the land and unity with the people of China; she is the general and though her army has suffered, their tatters are hers.

At the other end of the spectrum, however, are many passages in which the narrator distances herself from the Chinese, speaking of *them* in the third person: "Chinese people are very weird" (*WW,* 158), Maxine and her brothers and sisters tell each other, rejecting their connection with their mother's incomprehensible sister, Moon Orchid, and asserting their difference. In another significant passage, Maxine clearly situates herself between Chinese and American, attributing an identity to herself through the modulation of voice:

> Normal Chinese women's voices are strong and bossy. We American-Chinese girls had to whisper to make ourselves American-feminine. Apparently we whispered even more softly than the Americans. (*WW,* 172)

Volume here is a trope for confidence and power. In the social hierarchy of Maxine's world, Chinese mothers have the loudest voices, the most power; American girls are next, with voices softer and more feminine. Chinese American girls have the softest voices of all, the least power. From Maxine's perspective, Chinese mothers are tyrannical forces to be struggled against; American girls are the enviable models to emulate; and Chinese American girls, straining to reject one model and to imitate the other, have no confident sense of self, for to whisper is to have no voice, and to have no voice is to be powerless. "Most of us eventually found some voice, however faltering. We invented an American-feminine speaking personality, except for that one girl who could not speak up even in Chinese school" (*WW,* 172). "If you don't talk, you can't have a personality" (*WW,* 180), Maxine screams at this totally silent Chinese girl whom she shockingly and unsuccessfully bullies. Maxine lashes out at this girl in a fury of self-hatred and also of rage against the powerless position of all Chinese American girls. As she punishes the silent girl for not conforming to the American norm, Maxine simultaneously uses her as a scapegoat for her own rage over her necessity to "invent an American-feminine speaking personality." Caught in a double bind, Maxine has been simultaneously silenced by a misogynist Chinese society, including a loud-voiced, domineering mother who may have cut her frenum, and also forced by American social pressures to assume an "invented" personality and voice.

In still another passage, the narrator spurns Chinese ways and seeks refuge in an American identity:

> To make my waking life American-normal, I turn on the lights before anything untoward makes an appearance. I push the deformed into my dreams, which are in Chinese, the language of impossible stories. Before we can leave our parents, they stuff our heads like the suitcases which they jam-pack with home-made underwear. (*WW,* 87)

"Homemade underwear" is itself a multivalent trope, bursting with an internal dialogism encompassing both humiliation at these ill-fitting econ-omy measures and, at the same time, pride in the determined parental love that defies poverty and hardship. On the one hand, one senses that the child leaving home is embarrassed by the homemade underwear packed into her suitcase; on the other hand, she knows that the parents who "jam-packed" and "stuffed" the suitcases were motivated by a surplus of love. As far as the parent is concerned, the beloved child leaving home to brave the world alone cannot be overprotected, cannot have too much to cushion her from the cold she is certain to encounter. One cannot help but be touched by this concern. But who wants awkward, ill-fitting homemade underwear? On still another hand, isn't it good to be loved so well, and who sees one's underwear anyway? The words "jam-packed" and "stuffed" also carry countervailing forces. These are parents who overwhelm with their undesired shows of love. It is no matter that their grown children will not wear this homemade underwear; these parental offerings cannot be refused. (Amy Tan calls parental gifts of food "stern offerings of love.")

Just before this passage, Kingston had been retelling her mother's mon-ster stories: the ape-man that attacked her, the baby born without an anus. In reaction to these frightening tales that haunt her nightmares, she clings to what seems "American-normal"—the illuminated, the rational and logical, plastic, neon, and periodic tables. A few pages later, "I would live on plastic" (*WW,* 92), Kingston says in disgust over the objects her mother has placed on her dinner plate. But here again is a dialogic passage. As plastic does not nourish the body, so periodic tables do not nourish the imagination. Although her mother's stories may have frightened her as a child, these stories, now that she is adult and a writer, are her mother's legacy, for they provide the color, texture, and substance of the daughter's text. Although the daughter/narrator states a preference for the clean, the illuminated, and the plastic, she weaves her actual text from the monstrous, the frightening, the powerful—her mother's stories. The words say one thing; the text does another.

In fact, though the working out of a whole range of meanings around both ethnicity and gender is located in the Chinese/American dichotomy, it is most particularly situated in the mother-daughter relationship. Much of *The Woman Warrior* deals with the oppression of silencing and the liberation of speaking out.[9] And this theme is embodied in the problematic, dialogic mother-daughter relationship which informs the entire book. The mother's voice is so overpowering the daughter cannot speak, even believing that her mother has cut her frenum and, by extension, her vocal cords. Maxine's reaction to this act, imagined or real, is again ambivalent and overtly expressed: "Sometimes I felt very proud that my mother committed such a powerful act upon me. At other times, I was terrified—the first thing my mother did when she saw me was to cut my tongue" (*WW*, 164). Identifying with her mother, she is proud of such strength and power; however, considering herself the recipient of the operation, she is terrified. Is it an act of tyranny and silencing, as she fears, or an act of love, as her mother claims? "I cut it so you would not be tongue-tied. Your tongue would be able to move in any language . . . You'll be able to pronounce anything," her mother explains (*WW*, 164). Later, Kingston writes, "I shut my teeth together, vocal cords cut, they hurt so. I would not speak words to give her pain. All her children gnash their teeth" (*WW*, 101). The daughter is both the pained and angry victim of her mother's powerful act of mutilation, or freeing, as well as the considerate daughter who will not speak words to give her mother pain. (Writing them, however, is another matter, because "the reporting is the vengeance," *WW*, 53).

Describing the trip to Los Angeles to regain Moon Orchid's straying husband, Kingston writes, "Brave Orchid gave her sister last-minute advice for five hundred miles" (*WW*, 143). Note the dialogue within this sentence between the earnestness of the mother—"last minute advice" and the ironic context supplied by the daughter/author "for five hundred miles." Throughout *The Woman Warrior* we find the dialogue between anger/bitterness and love/tenderness as the daughter seeks self-definition apart from the mother. Since the struggle is defined as one of words and voice between one who is a powerful talker with many stories and one who has yet to find her voice, so the resolution of this struggle, and of the book, is a verbal and narrative one in that the final story of Ts'ai Yen is a collaborative effort between mother and daughter: "Here is a story my mother told me, not when I was young, but recently, when I told her I also am a story-talker. The beginning is hers, the ending, mine" (*WW*, 206). It is, however, impossible to tell in this story where the beginning ends and the ending begins, which part of T'sai Yen's story is the mother's, which part the daughter's. Thus, the daughter's journey for her own voice is a struggle in which the "mother-tongue" must be both refused and embraced, both preserved and modified, both acknowledged and gone beyond.

In the critical scene when Maxine finally "confesses" to her mother the two hundred plus items that had been weighing on her conscience "that I had to tell my mother so that she would know the true things about me and to stop the pain in my throat" (WW, 197), when her voice so long repressed finally erupts before the person in whom she had invested all power and authority, she finds "no higher listener. No listener but myself" (WW, 204). This scene is critical because in it Maxine comes into her own voice at the expense of her mother's voice, her mother's authority. She makes an existential discovery—that she must be her own voice, her own listener, her own authority. This discovery is both frightening and liberating, both humiliating and exhilarating. And the voice that she reveals in this book is a composite of many voices: her mother's, her own physical voice, her imaginative voice, the Chinese culture's, American males', and American females' voices. The tonal range is broad, encompassing complaint, confusion, anger, bitterness, pride, resignation, poetry, resolution.

Kingston eventually sees the similarities between herself and her mother, "a dragoness ('my totem, your totem')" (WW, 67). "At last I saw that I too had been in the presence of great power, my mother talking-story" (WW, 19–20). The Chinese customs that had been oppressive and incomprehensible for the child Maxine, the Chinese stories that had frightened and haunted her waking and sleeping, are now seen by the adult Maxine, the writer Kingston, to be a rich source of inspiration, unique materials for her pen, a legacy to show off at the same time one complains about it.

In her last chapter, "A Song for a Barbarian Reed Pipe," Kingston writes of the Chinese rituals her mother followed without bothering to explain, leaving a confused Maxine to hypothesize about the Chinese in the alienated third-person plural:

> "I don't see how they kept up a continuous culture for five thousand years. Maybe they didn't; maybe everyone makes it up as they go along." (WW, 185)

This sentence sums up the dialogic style of Kingston's book; both impulses— the pride of inheritance and a revisionist compulsion—are in dialogue. Her surface tone is complaining and disparaging, but there is an underlying pride in the inclusion of "five thousand years"—this length of time cannot help but be impressive. "Maybe everyone makes it up as they go along" seems to belittle Chinese culture, but for the daughter of a story-talker who is herself a masterful story-talker, as testified to throughout this text, what could be more wonderful than making up stories as one goes along?

In asserting racial and cultural difference, we Asian Americans run the risk of being dismissed as irretrievably and irrevocably "other." We also run the risk of falling into the stereotypes of difference created by the dominant culture. The obverse, however, is that if we assert our similarity to others, our humanness above our cultural specificities, we would seem to be eliminating the reason for multicultural studies in the first place. That Asian Americans are seen as irrevocably "other" was forcibly brought home to me again last fall when our Wisconsin congressman Scott Klug was campaigning on the campus of the University of Wisconsin; he handed fliers to all students except those with Asian faces. His reasoning apparently went something like this: these fliers cost money; Asian students are foreigners who can't vote; therefore, why waste money on foreigners? As Elaine Kim wrote in a recent issue of *A Magazine*, "While we don't generally ask European Americans how come they speak such fluent English, how long they've been here, and when they are going back, these are common questions for Asian Americans."[10] These are what novelist Joy Kogowa has called "ice breaker questions that create an awareness of ice."[11] They are so frequently asked that we've come up with our own answers for them. When I'm complimented on how good my English is, I usually retort, "It should be, I teach it." Maxine Hong Kingston's standard response is kinder and wittier, "Thanks. So's yours."

In *Woman, Native, Other*, Trinh T. Minh-ha expresses the Third World writer's dilemma thus:

> Every path I/i take is edged with thorns. On the one hand, i play into the Savior's hands by concentrating on authenticity, for my attention is numbered by it and diverted from other, important issues; on the other hand, I do feel the necessity to return to my so-called roots, since they are the fount of my strength, the guiding arrow to which i constantly refer before heading for a new direction.[12]

This passage vividly delineates the dialogic dilemma of a person of color: we are identified anthropologically by the outside world according to external physical characteristics and expected by virtue of these characteristics to be "authentic," "the real thing." I note in Minh-ha's expression, "i play into the Savior's hands," that by being singled out for attention from the First World, we are being lifted up and saved from the Third World status into which we were born. Should we be grateful or angry? Are we being rescued or insulted? To be rebellious and subversive, we could, as some of us do, reveal the deceptiveness of exterior signs by asserting our ignorance of that which we are thought to have inside knowledge of and to demonstrate how much we belong to the First World by showing off our ability to employ its "discursive" jargon and by displaying our "inside" knowledge of its canonical texts. On the other hand, are we not then also demonstrating how thoroughly we have been colonized, how disadvantaged and depleted we've grown in being so cut off from our "roots"? Further complication is added when those "roots," as in the case of Chinese American women, are not nurturing but devaluing. As a small example, my father said to me years ago, "Why do you need to go to college, you're only a girl; you'll only get married." What sustenance can we get from such traditions? How can they be "the fount of [our] strength"? These are questions that Maxine Hong Kingston wrestled with in *The Woman Warrior* and she answered them as well as anyone can, I believe, in her line: "I learned to make my mind large, as the universe is large so that it can contain paradoxes."

I conclude with another quote: "I write to show myself showing people who show me my own showing" (*WNO*, 22), writes Trinh Minh-ha to emphasize the multiple reflexivity, the many-mirrored images bouncing back and forth in dialogue with one another when an Asian American speaks and when she writes.

Notes

1. Robert Ji-Song Ku, "Can the Native Informant Write?: The Ethnographic Gaze and Asian American Literature," paper delivered at the Association for Asian American Studies Conference, 3 June 1993.

2. Maxine Hong Kingston, "Cultural Mis-readings by American Reviewers," in *Asian and Western Writers in Dialogue: New Cultural Identities,* ed. Guy Amirthanayagam (New York: Macmillan, 1982), 55–57. Hereafter "CM," cited in the text.

3. Frank Chin, lecture, Oakland, California, 15 September 1989; quoted by Elaine H. Kim in " 'Such Opposite Creatures': Men and Women in Asian American Literature," *Michigan Quarterly* 29 (Winter 1990):76.

4. King-Kok Cheung, "The Woman Warrior versus the Chinaman Pacific: Must a Chinese American Critic Choose between Feminism and Heroism?" in *Conflicts in Feminism,* ed. Marianne Hirsch and Evelyn Fox Keller (New York: Routledge, 1991), 242.

5. Conversation with Shawn Wong, Madison, Wisconsin, October 1991.

6. Maxine Hong Kingston, *Tripmaster Monkey: His Fake Book* (New York: Knopf, 1989), 340.

7. Maxine Hong Kingston, *The Woman Warrior: Memoir of a Girlhood among Ghosts* (New York: Knopf, 1976), 9. Hereafter *WW,* cited in the text.

8. Mikhail M. Bakhtin, *The Dialogic Imagination; Four Essays,* trans. Michael Holquist (Austin: University of Texas Press, 1981), 299. Hereafter *DI,* cited in the text.

9. See King-Kok Cheung, "Don't Tell: Imposed Silences in *The Color Purple,* and *The Woman Warrior,*" *PMLA* 103 (1988):162–74 and her recent book, *Articulate Silences: Hisaye Yamamoto, Maxine Hong Kingston, Joy Kogawa* (Ithaca: Cornell University Press, 1993).

10. Elaine H. Kim, "Business: The Color of Money," *A Magazine* 2 (Spring 1993):30.

11. Joy Kogawa, *Obasan* (1981; reprint, New York: Doubleday, 1992), 271.

12. Trinh T. Minh-ha, *Woman, Native, Other: Writing Postcoloniality and Feminism* (Bloomington: Indiana University Press, 1989), 89. Hereafter *WNO,* cited in the text.

Re-presenting *The Woman Warrior:*
An Essay of Interpretive History

DAVID LEIWEI LI

The year 1976 saw the publication by Alfred A. Knopf of Maxine Hong Kingston's phenomenal *The Woman Warrior: Memoirs of a Girlhood Among Ghosts,* a book that changed forever the face and status of contemporary Asian American literature.[1] Although it could not claim chronological precedence in the post-1965 Asian American corpus—since the group efforts of *Roots, Asian American Authors, Asian American Heritage,* and especially Frank Chin et al.'s *Aiiieeeee!* all predated the discovery of Kingston's individual talent—*The Woman Warrior* was the groundbreaking text that arrested American public imagination.[2] The book pitched the note of critical consensus on formal excellence and postmodern play while striking a resonant chord with the rise of literary feminism as both legitimate and legitimating critical practice. For the first time in history, an Asian American text was embraced as a work of art in the national culture. Its transcendence of racial boundaries on the shared category of gender produced a heterogeneous readership beyond ethnicity and fanned commercial interest in the publication of Asian American texts. Its extensive review and study by critics of legitimate cultural affiliations also enabled the scholarly excavation and preservation of Asian American literary production, especially in academia.

The Woman Warrior's historical entry into public culture has given Asian America such an official literary visibility that it is small wonder that its attribution and appropriation in reception should become controversial. The differences in interpreting the book, in fact, become an instant power contest between the dominant culture and the ethnic community for both the authority and agency of Asian American articulation. "Who is qualified to speak about and for Asian America?" "What is the appropriate language of ethnic artistic representation?" "How should a minority writer publishing with a mainstream press negotiate her double audience, and to whom does she owe allegiance?" These and other related questions that greeted *The Woman Warrior* not only reveal the representational duress that this single text

This essay was written specifically for this volume and is published here for the first time by permission of the author.

has to endure but also inevitably betray the divergent conceptualizations of an emergent Asian American cultural proper. Central to the debate about *The Woman Warrior*'s significance is therefore the definitional struggle of "Asian America," its geopolitical location in and cultural relevance to the construction of the United States.[3]

I

In July 1976, the bound galleys of *The Woman Warrior* reached Frank Chin through Kingston's editor at Alfred A. Knopf, Charles Elliot. Soon afterward, Kingston and Chin had their first and last series of personal correspondence. The epistolary exchange showed their significantly different attitudes about the efficacy of Asian American writing. Chin, though he admired the book's style, thought of *The Woman Warrior* "as another in a long line of Chinkie autobiographies by Pocahontas yellows blowing the same old mixed up East/West soul struggle." Kingston regarded Chin's writing, despite her appreciation of it, as "the angry-young-man-radical-political screaming." Kingston continued:

> [T]he genre *I* am avoiding is the political/polemical harangue [sic], which I dislike because a.) it keeps the writer on the surface of perception; b.) it puts the Asian-Am. writer on the same trip as the racist; we provide the other half of the dialogue, the yin to his yang, as it were, c.) the blacks already wrote that way in the '50's; all we'd do is change black faces to yellow, no furthering of art.[4]

In brief, Kingston did not hold Chin's confrontational politics to be effective, nor did she believe that adversarial art had historically worked for ethnic writers, whether its practitioners were African Americans or Asian Americans.

There are two main differences between Chin and Kingston. The first is the ideological stance of Asian American writing, particularly its positioning toward the dominant American culture, while the second concerns the aesthetic choice of subjective space and symbols. As Kingston vocally disapproves of Chin's ideology of opposition because of its likelihood of reproducing existing racist paradigms, she remains reticent about his apprehension of the "East/West soul struggle" prevalent in earlier Asian American writings. The ideological and the aesthetic differences between the two seem to converge on the conceptualization of Asian American geocultural space, and we may best approach it first by recalling Frank Chin's specific charting in *Aiiieeeee!*.

Although his individual interpretation of historical experience is frequently projected as an unquestionable universal, Chin's *No-No Boy* gesture, to invoke John Okada's text for a different context, at once defies ancestral Asia and white America as the source of an Asian American symbolic and locates a unique Asian American cultural sensibility in the history and body politic of the United States.[5] *Aiiieeeee!*'s repudiation of the dominant cultural "dual personality" thesis that splits the Asian American between the East and the West anticipated Edward Said's formulation of Orientalism four years later, and its aesthetic criteria significantly bounded the Asian American imagination to the geopolitical and historiographical confines of the United States. Chin et al. impel their audience first to refuse the orientalist formula of Asian American subjectivity in such variations as division (e.g., either Asian or American), combination (e.g., both Asian and American), and addition and subtraction (e.g., more Asian less American, 80% American and 20% Asian, etc.); and second, to rethink their actual cultural composition and experience within the historical particulars of time and place, race, and nation.

The no-no maneuver is a preparatory meditation toward the creation and claim of an ethnic national space that resolutely fails to measure up to the dominant Orientalist or Anglo American social geography. By contrast, the author of *The Woman Warrior* "avoid[s]" Chin's approach not by simply saying "yes-yes" (for that will mean giving her "yin to his yang, as it were") to Asia and America, but by first accepting the East/West apartheid and its hold on the popular mind, and then attempting to mediate this age-old dual geography. Kingston's departure from Chin's polemic racial self-inscription, and her breakthrough into mainstream American culture, one may argue, seem to have begun with her deliberate accommodation, adaptation, and appropriation of some familiar orientalist geopolitical imagination.

We can follow this interpretive suggestion by comparing the openings of *The Woman Warrior* and its immediate predecessor, Lawrence Yep's 1975 novel, *Dragonwings:*

"You must not tell anyone," my mother said, "what I am going to tell you. In China your father had a sister who killed herself. She jumped into the family well. We say that your father has all brothers because it is as if she had never been born.[6]

Ever since I can remember, I had wanted to know about the Land of the Golden Mountain, but my mother had never wanted to talk about it. All I knew was that a few months before I was born, my father had left our home in the Middle Kingdom, or *China,* as the white demons call it, and travelled over the sea to work in the demon land. There was plenty of money to be made among the demons, but it was also dangerous. My own grandfather had been lynched about thirty years before by a mob of white demons almost the moment he had set foot on their shores.[7]

Both paragraphs are told from an adolescent's point of view, both episodes have a mother who is unwilling to break the taboo subject, and both stories involve the death of a kins(wo)man. Though Yep's beginning narrative locus is in China, he directs the audience's gaze westward to America, homeward inside their geography proper. America, in the narrator's perspective, is at once a land of plenty and a land of prohibition where immigrants of color had to endure racial violence. As the line between the ethnic subject and the dominant/demonic Other is drawn, so is their antagonistic relationship set within the unfolding narrative space. Such a narrative deployment is prone to create cognitive dissonance among white American readers who may feel somehow implicated in the discursive landscape—after all, the lynch mob is specified as white. Contrary to Yep, Kingston takes a different trajectory. The narrative hand guides the audience eastward to China, venturing into at once an unfamiliar geography and a secretive familial lore that both forbid revelation. China is a repressive space for the Chinese, but the white American reader, an outsider to that land and culture, is invited both to enter the fictional space and to pry into the mysterious death of an Other. The reader is not only granted absolute narrative alibi, for little is being taxed upon his or her receiving/performing consciousness, but also given the power and privilege of imaginative travel and epistemological control. If Yep's America asks readers to confront the devil in themselves, Kingston's China appears to be but an ideal escape route from just such a task, for China, as a spatial and metaphysical alterity, will hold its enigma as long as it serves the Western subject.[8]

Gayatri Chakravorty Spivak's analysis of Derrida's original formulation "Chinese prejudice" proves helpful here. The term describes the mechanics of appropriation that use China as a blueprint, and blueprint only, for western philosophical writing. Chinese prejudice is a particular means of ideological self-justification for a western imperialist project that will sublate Chinese into an easy-to-learn script that will in turn supersede actual Chinese. (Ezra Pound's creative utilization of the Chinese ideograph is only a modern instance, and Kingston's use of the Poundian ideograph in the "White Tiger" chapter is an interesting reappropriation.) It functions purely as a western hallucination that aims to consolidate "an inside, its own subject status" by producing the Chinese Other.[9] In this way, China, whether represented by its language, culture, geography, or any other aspects associated with it, is made independent of its own history while obeying a rigorous necessity in American orientalist discourse as a compensation for an occidental desire.

It is toward this desire and its power of imposition that Sui Sin Far, the nineteenth-century pioneer Asian American female author, directs her satire. Writing in *Leaves from the Mental Portfolio of an Eurasian,* she remarks:

> They [the "funny people who advise me to trade upon my nationality"] tell me that if I wish to succeed in literature in America I should dress in Chinese costume, carry a fan in my hand, wear a pair of scarlet beaded slippers, live in New York, and come of high birth. Instead of making myself familiar with the Chinese Americans around me, I should discourse on my spirit acquaintance

with Chinese ancestors and quote in between the "Good Mornings" and "How
d'ye dos" of editors,
"Confucius, Confucius, how great
  is Confucius,
Before Confucius, there never was
  Confucius,
After Confucius, there never came
  Confucius,"
  etc., etc., etc.,
or something like that, both illuminating and obscuring, don't you know.[10]

An Asian American writer who wishes to make a mark has to perform in both
writing and demeanor the kind of cultural intelligibility required of an oriental. "Chinese costume[s]" and "spirit acquaintance with Chinese ancestors"
and Confucian analects, rather than the knowledge of "the Chinese American" around her, are deemed appropriate aesthetic subjects. Hilarious as Sui
Sin Far's anecdote is, it painfully exemplifies a dilemma that is repeated time
and again, for the discursive need of American Orientalism never fails to
manifest itself in either persuasive temptation (as in the preceding instance)
or powerful coercion (as in denial of publication).[11]

    That Asia is a socially created space in American orientalist discourse
and the discourse of Anglo-Saxon nationalism has a special impact on Asian
American writers. First, Asia has historically occupied the position of the
Other in Western imagination, whether civilizational or colonial, that has to
be subdued or converted. Second, Asia is the superimposed homeland of
Asian Americans whose allegiance to the United States, whether political or
cultural, is perpetually in doubt. Unlike Americans of European descent,
Asian Americans are conflated with Asians whose presence in the States does
not equate with their belonging to it. Third, by the spatial logic of the previous two points, Asia is the proper site of Asian American imagination. For
Asian American writers, finally, Asia no longer represents a physical space, a
geopolitical entity, a cultural resource, an ancestral homebase that can be *dif-
ferentially incorporated* into the immediacy of American experience that they
articulate; it is supposed to epitomize and embody *the* natural experience and
essence of Asian Americans.

    In light of this analysis, Kingston's recourse to China, as opposed to Chin
and Yep's rejection of it, indicates her tentative loop back to a predelineated
discursive site and a set of predetermined geocultural relationships as well. The
choice was timely: China was suddenly of great currency after the 1973 sign-
ing in Shanghai of the communiqué between the United States and the People's Republic of China, a watershed event for the normalization of diplomatic
relations between the two countries. But the public sino-frenzy was only a part
of the upward swing of benevolent Orientalism that occurred in the United
States since the heyday of the 1960s countercultural movements, with their

revival of transcendental yearnings for eastern mysticism. Periodical literature that appeared in the years between the Shanghai communiqué and the publication of *The Woman Warrior* exhibited a marked public curiosity about China.[12] Period fashions, from cotton loafers to kung pao chicken and kung fu movies, also indicated a general receptiveness to Asian products in American markets. All this would not have been possible, however, without the fundamental shift toward "late capital" on the transnational playing field, which not only gave the Asia-Pacific region its unprecedented American significance but also gave rise to the articulation of "Asian America" in the first place.[13] In this context, Kingston's selection of China as the beginning of an Asian American imaginary seemed also to correspond with the nascent development of a transnational diasporic formation to which Frank Chin et al.'s version of ethnic nationalism was essentially antagonistic.[14]

II

As soon as *The Woman Warrior* hit the market, the opposing camps trying to claim it were formed. Sara Blackburn of *Ms.* called the book "a psychic transcript of every woman I know—class, age, race or ethnicity be damned."[15] "In the vivid particularity of her experience, and with the resource of considerable art," wrote Diane Johnson for *The New York Review of Books*, "Kingston reaches to the universal qualities of female condition and female anger that the bland generalities of social science and the merely factual history cannot describe."[16] Such white feminist affirmation of *The Woman Warrior* ignited the book's instant rejection by some Asian American critics. Jeffery Paul Chan named Johnson yet another "Pearl Buck shaping converts in the oriental orphanage of her imagination. Never mind history, Johnson has uncovered a feminist."[17] Benjamin Tong agreed: "Maxine Hong Kingston's *Woman Warrior* is a fashionably feminist work written with white acceptance in mind."[18]

The conflicting reviews probably tell as much about the parties in contention as they do about the text. For the feminist reviewers, the book offers yet another testimonial of female suffering that urges sisterly solidarity. *The Woman Warrior* is good, we are reassured, just because it transcends "class, age, race or ethnicity" and achieves "the universal qualities of female condition."[19] In place of a male omniscience is now a female universal that not only cancels the specificity of ethnic womanhood but also conditions its use value in white feminist terms. While such stamps of approval elevate the status of the book for mainstream readership, they severely limit other possible interpretations. The condescension of cultural colonialism in their rhetoric of acclaim had serious repercussions for the future reception of the text. Both Chan's and Tong's attacks are aimed first at the reviewer; their quarrels with the text were only a *related* response. Due to their priority and position, the initial feminist reviews could have affected the motives of later readers who may have adjusted their responses to the text accordingly. Consequently, the reception of *The Woman Warrior* involves not only the simple writer-reader relationship but also the relationships between different groups of critics whose subject status invariably depends, in this particular instance, on their interpretation.

Let us return to Johnson, Chan, and Tong to see how the textual ground of *The Woman Warrior* has become a battleground between the dominant culture and the ethnic culture. After affiliating *The Woman Warrior* with many western feminist classics, Johnson pauses for a shocking observation:

> The Chinese-Americans are a notably unassimilated culture. It is not unusual in San Francisco to find fourth- or fifth-generation American-born Chinese who speak no English. Generations have not eased their mistrust of American culture, and they will not tell Americans certain things about theirs.[20]

In what Chan calls her "utter stupidity" and "button-popping arrogance," Johnson has blatantly denied the existence of Asian American English and reinforced the Orientalist displacement of Asian American culture onto its ancestral origin. While Johnson could still be under the narrative spell of forbidden tale told, without bothering to check her prejudicial racial slip, the indignant Jeffery Chan, a coeditor of *Aiiieeeee!*, was led to wonder why "[a] white reading public will rave over ethnic biography while ignoring a Chinese American's literary art," with Chin's *The Chickencoop Chinaman* particularly in his mind. This "[e]ngenders the feeling," Chan proceeds sardonically, that "perhaps Chinese-Americans have no authority over the language and culture that expresses our sensibility best."[21] Meanwhile, Tong takes Johnson's equation of "recently immigrated folks from Hong Kong and Taiwan" with all Asian Americans as an attempt to erase their diversity and reduce them to "foreigner Asians except for those few exceptions that prove the rule who write in white for whites."[22]

If Chan is especially sensitive to Johnson's lack of knowledge of Chin and *Aiiieeeee!*, Tong resents both the representative status Johnson awards Kingston's text and the persistent racialization of Asian American foreignness that her review betrays. As these criticisms show, *The Woman Warrior* is caught in an impossible position upon which the crucial conflicts of an emerging Asian American literature are staged. Among these conflicts are not only the mainstream and the marginal critical struggle for the appropriate (re)production of Asian American voices, but also the differences among Asian American writers and intellectuals on who should constitute the mainstay of their culture, whether it is the new immigrants in the post–1965 era who may claim a diasporic sensibility, or the native-born generations whose sensibility is inevitably impacted by a colonial education as well as the structures of exclusion. While the nationalist and transnationalist conflict has become truly intense two decades after its publication, the contestation for the speaking authority of an emerging culture has pivoted on *The Woman Warrior*'s textual validity. In her open letter to Kingston, Katheryn Fong blames the author for her "distortion of the histories of China and Chinese America," her failure to give historical causality to her narrative, and her "overexaggera[tion]" of Asian American female oppression.[23] Poet Nellie Wong, however, offers her personal testimony to back up the accuracy of Kingston's renditions, arguing that the text "supports [her] own explorations of Asian women's relationships to each other."[24] These mixed reviews, with their shared interest in the truth, show not only the ascending representative status of *The Woman Warrior* but also the suggestive power of the book's generic classification.

"Genres," in Fredric Jameson's view, "are essentially literary *institutions,* or social contracts between a writer and a specific public, whose function is to specify the proper use of a particular cultural artifact."[25] Clearly, the reviewers are responding to the generic cue of *The Woman Warrior* as nonfiction. What they do not realize is that genre could be a discursive after-fact. Literary classification is equivalent to the packaging of a final product, which is not always simply determined by the producer or author. The generic social contract could be drafted by an often invisible yet influential agency, the editor. Explaining why *The Woman Warrior* is designated as nonfiction, Charles Elliot, Kingston's editor at Knopf, reportedly said, "Well, first novels are hard to sell. I knew it [*The Woman Warrior*] would stand a stronger chance of selling well as non-fiction autobiography. It could have been called anything else."[26]

Profit motive aside, the editor's exploitation of the generic contract has in effect controlled the way in which the work is likely to be experienced. Generic definition involves therefore not only economic interest but political interest as well. It is to this latter aspect that Frank Chin has been especially sensitive. The history of Asian American works published under the classification of autobiography is to him a history of manipulation and suppression of "yellow art" by "white American publishers." So, after having read the galleys of *The Woman Warrior,* Chin expressed to Kingston his strong reservations not about the book but about its being classified as autobiography. He wrote, "The yellow autobiography is a white racist form, . . . an insult to our writing and characterizes us as freaks, anthropological phenomena kept and pampered in a white zoo and not people whose world is complete and complex." He then advised Kingston to "[g]o for fiction with this book if [you] can and dump the autobiography. . . . As fiction," Chin resumed, "I can like your stuff without necessarily liking or agreeing with the narrator or any of the characters and credit you with subtleties [sic] and knowing lapses I can't give to an autobiographer."[27]

Chin's objection to autobiography in Asian American production hinges not so much on its inherent properties as on the function it is desired to perform for the reading public. Once *The Woman Warrior* is labeled as nonfiction,

it is understood by convention to be a narrative of real events. The consequence is actually twofold. On the one hand, it invites the audience to identify it as an account of real life. On the other hand, it dissuades the possibility
of interpreting it as a symbolic act. Therefore, the generic definition can have
the effect of depriving Asian American expression of its credibility as imaginative art and reducing it into some subliterary status, serving the role of
social scientific data, an encompassing reflection of Asian American totality.[28]

The unease about the authenticity of *The Woman Warrior* shown in the
reviews of Fong and Wong now make sense. Faithfully responding to the
generic signal of the text, the reviewers are literally holding the book as a
mirror to see if "the people" are truly reflected. The distinction between artistic image and existential actuality vanishes, and the problem of representation haunts us again. Representation has both aesthetic and political functions. An artistic object may either "stand for" something and someone, or it
may "act for" something and someone. In fact, the two functions are hardly
distinguishable in the process of a reader's response. The reason that representation is of such paramount importance to Asian Americans, however,
must be explained from the history of their underrepresentation and the history of their involuntary representation. Whereas the former indicates the
general lack of their artistic and cultural presence in American culture, the
latter, paradoxically, refers to the abundance of stereotypes heaped upon them
without their consent. This history of iconic oppression has made the minority community in question particularly vulnerable to the limited exposure it
gets and has ironically increased the representational capacity of the existing
artistic expressions and images. That a piece of ethnic literature is deemed
exemplary and its author designated a community spokesperson provides the
basic context in which works of minority art are received. The advantage of
such a context is that it enhances the affective/persuasive power of an ethnic
text, whose writer suddenly finds herself in a better position to alter in particular the conceptions the majority of nonethnic readers have about an ethnic
entity. Meanwhile, however, simply because it is only through the chosen few
that members of the dominant culture are to learn about an ethnic life, the
representational power of ethnic works as a whole is automatically restricted.
Two immediate consequences thus follow. First, the work of ethnic art has
inevitably shouldered, as historical circumstances so obligate, the burden of
representing the whole humanity of its people in arenas of culture and politics, a task no single work is capable of performing under any condition. Second, ethnic writers are unwillingly caught in the struggle for the hard-to-
obtain position of community representative. It is toward these constraints of
ethnic representation that Kingston's blast at her reviewers is directed:

> Why must I "represent" anyone besides myself? Why should I be denied an
> individual artistic vision? And I do not think I wrote a "negative" book, as the
> Chinese American reviewer said; but suppose I had? Suppose I had been so

wonderfully talented that I wrote a tragedy? Are we Chinese Americans to deny ourselves tragedy? If we give up tragedy in order to make a good impression on Caucasians, we have lost a battle.

"Oh, well," she says—and we almost hear her heaving a heavy sigh but turning optimistic in the end—"I'm certain that some day when a great body of Chinese American writing becomes published and known, then readers will no longer have to put such a burden on each book that comes out. Readers can see the variety of ways for Chinese Americans to be."[29] With this, Kingston proposes a solution to the problem of representation for which all ethnic writers have to strive.

III

Kingston's vision of adequate literary representation for Asian Americans is not something that *is,* but something yet *to be.* The material imperatives surrounding the issue of representation as occasioned by *The Woman Warrior* can once more be witnessed in Chin's "Afterword," which concludes his 1989 collection of short stories, *The Chinaman Pacific & Frisco R.R. Co.* Previously published as an independent piece, its inclusion in the anthology appears, at first look, totally out of place. The afterword is by no means a direct authorial commentary on the stories preceding it. It is probably the only piece in the anthology that was conceived after 1976, the year of *The Woman Warrior*'s publication, and it is unquestionably a parody of Kingston's work. The placing of the afterword therefore suggests several possibilities. *The Woman Warrior* seems to have stunted Chin's creative output for more than a dozen years following its appearance, and it now sets the terms, as Chin himself admits, in which his gallery of works is to be reviewed.

Calling the autobiographer "Mei-jing" and the book "The Unmanly Warrior," Chin points his spearhead right at Kingston. The romanization of Mei-jing in Chinese means either "American dollar" or "MSG," the flavor enhancer in Asian cuisine. This satirical note aside, Chin's fictional reviewer has provided an excellent allegory that evokes not exactly the book but the critical standoff in the interpretive history of *The Woman Warrior:*

> The old French people of Frenchtown on the edge of Canton didn't like the book. They didn't have Smith Mei-jing's grasp of the Chinese language, the Chinese who loved her book said. The people of old Frenchtown said her book falsified history. They are conservative and old-fashioned and don't appreciate good writing, the Chinese who loved the book said . . . The French girl is writing not history, but art, the Chinese who loved the book said, and continued: She is writing a work of imagination authenticated by her personal experience . . . The French people of Frenchtown said, her own experience is an insane,

paranoid distortion of basic knowledge common to all French . . . And the Chinese who loved her book said, her personal experience was authentically French and her unique understanding of both the French and the Chinese views of life brings the Chinese the closest, most human understanding of the French ever produced in the Chinese language . . . Sour grapes, the Chinese who loved her book said, She's not writing history or about history, therefore the accuracy of any of her history is irrelevant to the question of her artistry, authenticity, or psychological reality, her Chinese admirers said.[30]

If "the people of Frenchtown" are critics within the Asian American community, "the Chinese who loved her book" must be establishment critics. If the former detract the text on behalf of "history," the latter defend it for the sake of "art." By speaking for the people of Frenchtown, Chin has arrogated to himself a self-appointed role as a "true" community representative, a role that so empowers him that he is able to accuse Kingston of her representational breach—since the community does not vouch for what she does, her representational material becomes automatically invalid.[31]

The point Chin tries to convey through "The Unmanly Warrior's" story of Joan of Arc is that Kingston has conflated the Chinese legends and deviated from the prototext of Mu Lan. It is Yue Fei (1103–1141 A.D.), for example, a male general of the Sung Dynasty, and not Mu Lan, whose mother tattooed his back to remind him of his loyalty. Kingston's textual transplantation is thereby to Chin a concoction of Chinese misogyny meant to distort Chinese history. In the same vein, both Jeffery Chan and Benjamin Tong charge Kingston with mistranslating the key term of *The Woman Warrior, kuei,* into "ghost," to court white readership.[32] For the sake of comparison, one may again look at Laurence Yep's *Dragonwings,* in which *kuei* is consistently rendered as "demon." This is not to indicate, however, that "ghost" is linguistically impossible; rather, it is a common translation, as Kingston's narrator innocently finds in the dictionary.[33] Even Yep's character Moon Shadow is fully aware of *kuei*'s ambiguities, when he explains in the following:

the Tang [Chinese] word for demon can mean many kinds of supernatural beings. A demon can be the ghost of a dead person, but he can also be a supernatural creature who can use his great powers for good as well as for evil, just like dragons. It is much trickier to deal with a demon of the Middle Kingdom [China] than an *American devil,* because you always know that the *American devil* means you harm.[34]

The issue here is how ethnic linguistic practice is appropriated in the English context and what its manner of appropriation attempts. What is missing in *The Woman Warrior* is the etymological history and the colonial contexts of Asia or Asian America in which the word is uttered. The usage of *kuei* for foreigners became common in the mid-nineteenth century when Western imperial powers invaded the Manchu empire of China with guns and opium. For the first time in history the citizens of the Central Kingdom were decentered, and they strove to retain their centrality by defining their oppressor as the Other, *fan-kuei* or *yang kuei-tzu*, foreign devils of white peril.[35] The usage is so prevalent that even a non–Asian American writer like Tom Wolfe is privy to its import: "*bok gooi* meant not simply *whites*," he notes, "but *white devils*."[36] Such negative connotations associated in the English language with Satanic forces are more or less dropped as Kingston opts for the word "ghost," which accentuates the insubstantiality and neutrality of a specter while diminishing the adversarial context in which *kuei* is cursed under one's breath. In an effort to relieve the white man's historical burden, the world of the memoir is turned phantasmic and its atmosphere phantasmagoric.

Kingston's use of *kuei* has evidenced the regulatory pressure of the dominant culture and has in its own way answered Chin's polemic of history. According to "the Frenchtown" perspective, history is a handful of unchanging facts, and the artist's job is to faithfully transmit such a history, or his or her work falls to the category of falsification. Kingston's attitude seems to suggest otherwise: history by itself will not work unless it is reactivated in language. Since linguistic inscription is always an act of interpretation, the pursuit of historic purity is futile. Here, Frank Lentricchia's contention proves instructive: "To attempt to proceed in purity—to reject the rhetorical strategies of capitalism and Christianity, *as if such strategies were in themselves responsible for human oppression*—to proceed with the illusion of purity," he remarks, "is to situate oneself on the margin of history, as the possessor of a unique truth disengaged from history's flow."[37] The "Frenchtown" view of history seems to have succumbed to just such purist temptations; not only does it imply *the* way of approaching historical reality, but in so doing it also confirms that the faithful reflection of facts is *the* gauge of the ethnic text. This view ostensibly contradicts the belief of Chin and company that Asian American texts ought to be treated as "works of art."[38] On the one hand, it is likely to corroborate the dominant receptive/generic modes of ethnic literature that the *Aiiieeeee!* editors themselves have in the past averted. On the other hand, it can become a self-constraining force that nullifies an ethnic text's necessary power of transformation. Such an ironic entrapment reminds us once again of the difficulty of breaking the vicious cycle of hegemonic denial and ethnic self-denial.

Kingston's mediation of *kuei* shows her grasp of the historical currents that, despite the individual's aversion to them, govern the production of ethnic literature. Tong is certainly right when he links Kingston's textual strategy with the Chinese American tradition of *jaw jieh* ("catching pigs"), "a time-honored practice of bullshitting white people into buying up whatever junk we dig out of basement attics . . . [of] pushing abalone shells, 'beggars chicken,' tour guides, cookbooks and all the rest, both in the name of economic survival *and* revenge."[39] Though Tong will not credit her with such intentionality, Kingston doubtless operates within the tradition of *jaw jieh;* that she comes by through either praxis or intuition. Tong's code of "economic survival and revenge" and Lentricchia's "rhetorical strategies of capitalism and Christianity," both considerations of historical necessity that an author has to face, are calculated into Kingston's plan of *The Woman Warrior.* Nowhere are Houston Baker's comments on Ralph Ellison's "creativity and commerce" more becoming than in this context of our discussion: "If the folk artist is to turn a profit from his monumental creative energies (which are often counteractive, or inversive, *vis-à-vis* Anglo American culture)," he says, "he must, in essence, sufficiently modify his folk forms (and amply advertise himself) to merchandize such forms as commodities on the *artistic* market. The folk artist may even have to don a mask that distorts what he knows is genuine self in order to make his product commensurate with a capitalist market-place."[40] Maxine Hong Kingston, like Ralph Ellison before her, is a master of such strategies.

IV

What is truly a marvel is the way in which the author of *The Woman Warrior* prophetically master codes her work into the masterpiece theater of American literature. In the book's ending, Kingston strategically revises yet another Chinese legend, the capture of the second-century Chinese woman poet Ts'ai Yen by the barbarians, and transforms it into a superb metanarrative of canonical entry. In her autobiographical verse, Ts'ai Yen expresses ever so poignantly her anger and humiliation at being made slave and wife by the invading nomadic tribe. The tone of fury and despondency so pervasive in her poetry is, however, notably absent in Kingston's version.[41] We see instead a baffled Ts'ai Yen living among the understanding noble savages, receiving gifts from the barbarian chieftain when he impregnates her and riding on his horse when he charges into villages and encampments. One day, Kingston tells us, Ts'ai Yen is so struck by the music of barbarian reed pipes filling the desert that she starts to sing:

> out of Ts'ai Yen's tent, which was apart from the others, the barbarian heard a woman's voice singing, as if to her babies, a song so high and clear, it matched the flutes. Ts'ai Yen sang about China and her family there. Her words seemed to be Chinese, but the barbarians understood their sadness and anger. Sometimes they thought they could catch barbarian phrases about forever wandering. Her children did not laugh, but eventually sang along when she left her tent to sit by the winter campfires, ringed by the barbarians.[42]

The poet in exile is no longer alienated. In both sound and image, the passage merges into a mythic vision, "cross[ing] boundaries not delineated in space" and transcending differences in discourse.[43] Not only is her music in tune with that of the barbarians, but her words are perfectly comprehended: the apparent opposition dissolves when the Chinese and the barbarian reach a truce. In a leap toward universal harmony, the poet is integrated into the "ring" that used to marginalize minority groups. In the round aura of the ring is no longer an Other but one of us, the center that holds.

"I do believe in the timelessness and universality of individual vision," Kingston remarks. "It [The Woman Warrior] would not just be a family book or an American book or a woman's book but a world book, and at the same moment, my book." The book would also be one, she adds, "for my old English professors of the new criticism school in Berkeley, by incorporating what they taught about the structure of the novel."[44] Indeed, the traditional humanist vision, the singular autonomy of the text, and the romantic cult of genius all play their parts in the hermeneutic ring of literary canonization. Trained in the school of New Criticism, with all its paradox, irony, and seven types of ambiguity, Kingston appealed to formal excellence to which both the traditional reviewers and the newer textual critics—structuralists and poststructuralists, for example—responded. The Woman Warrior was also able to mobilize the journalistic reviews that decidedly set the canonical process in motion.

John Leonard, then editor of the New York Times Book Review, was reportedly responsible for the first stampede of publicity.[45] His praise and that of others in such major papers and magazines as Time, Newsweek, and The New York Review of Books spurred a tide of journalistic reviews in smaller publications and had a ripple effect on the academic reviews as well. The first printing of 5,000 hardcovers was therefore gone practically overnight. Within months, another 40,000 copies were sold even before the book was tapped for the 1976 National Book Critics Circle Award for nonfiction.[46] Other book awards, including ones from Mademoiselle and Anissfield-Wolf, soon followed, accompanied by rank orderings on the best-seller lists, New York Times Book Review and the Book of the Month Club among them; in 1979 Time rated The Woman Warrior one of the top ten nonfiction works of the decade.[47] It is not insignificant to note that Kingston's institutional recognitions predated those of Alice Walker and Toni Morrison, making her the most prominent female ethnic writer in the seventies and eighties.[48] In almost no time, The Woman Warrior popped up in college reading lists and departmental curricula (it was simultaneously adopted as a text in some twelve departments at the University of California, Berkeley).[49] Before long, it entered prestigious literary anthologies and college readers, was included in literary histories and critical biographies (e.g., Columbia Literary History of the United States and Contemporary Authors), and became the subject of scores of journal articles, scholarly books, and conference papers. The body of criticism on it is still steadily growing, and according to recent Modern Language Association statistics, The Woman Warrior "is the most widely taught book by a living writer in U.S. colleges and universities."[50]

Among the various agencies of authority that helped secure *The Woman Warrior* in the canon and drew the work into the orbit of attention for a population of potential readers, the academic critics have unquestionably been the most powerful. How their normative practices in the scholastic institutions maintain, transmit, and reproduce the meaning and significance of the book, and how Asian American subjects are served by their activities, are therefore most crucial.[51] The type of theoretical savoir faire with which critics of *The Woman Warrior* have elevated the book's artistic status is something no Asian American text has hitherto enjoyed. Attention to the book's "paradoxes of autobiographical enunciation," "fictivity" of "speech act," "bridging of autobiography and fiction," and "the metaphysics of matrilinearism" all enrich *The Woman Warrior*'s formal complexity.[52] But the disregard for autobiography's different suggestion for writers of ethnic minorities has also confirmed the initial anxiety about the book's possible "misreading," prompted by not only its generic misnomer but also its gender depiction and geopolitical location.

At times, such misreading can be not so much the effect of critical cultural illiteracy as an effort to forcibly fit textual analysis into a dominant feminist motif, say, "from silence to voice." "Even as a child," Linda Morante claims, "Kingston realizes the *cultural roots* of her reticence."[53] Since the "cultural roots" she refers to are "Chinese," it begs the question of whether the narrator's silence *is* inherently Chinese. Kingston is not ambiguous about this point: at the Chinese school, she says, "we chanted together, voices rising and falling, loud and soft, some boys shouting, everybody reading together, reciting together and not alone with one voice. . . . The girls were not mute. They screamed and yelled during recess."[54] Elsewhere in the text, the narrator tells us, "I have tried to turn myself American-feminine. Chinese communication was loud, public. Only sick people had to whisper."[55] Is the Chinese culture suppressing voice? Or is it in fact the critic who purposefully ignores the dialogical nature of the narrative, which is, in Kingston's own words, "not alone with one voice"? The vicious patriarchy that presumably silences female expression is nowhere to be heard in the text: the mother is the "champion talker" while the father is almost inaudible.[56]

Morante is right to point out that "the Chinese keep secrets, they conceal their names, they withhold speech," and Brave Orchid "demands the silence that is self-obliteration."[57] But she refuses to acknowledge the cause of this imposed silence, despite the fact that she quotes the following passage:

> "Don't tell," advised my parents. . . . Lie to Americans. Tell them you were born during the San Francisco earthquake. Tell them your birth certificate and your parents were burnt up in the fire. Don't report crimes; tell them we have no crimes and no poverty. Give them a new name every time you get arrested . . .

She could have cited a few more sentences but she did not. However, I will: "The ghosts won't recognize you. Pay the new immigrants twenty-five cents an hour and say we have no unemployment. And of course," Kingston goes on, "tell them we're against Communism. Ghosts have no memory anyway and poor eyesight. And the Han people won't be pinned down."[58] It is the aftermath of the Exclusion Law and the fever of the Red Scare that silenced Chinese Americans. To conceal "the unspeakable" is a strategic response to institutional racism, an act of survival, and not at all an immutable Asian cultural trait.[59]

Failure to inform oneself of Asian American history is frequently coupled with a colonialist benevolence. "Establishing herself [the narrator Maxine] as a talker in opposition to her mother—as American instead of Chinese, a truth teller instead of a liar—makes it possible for her to define herself as separate from her mother," Suzanne Juhasz remarks in her reading of *The Woman Warrior,* "[l]eaving home at this stage means leaving China, and her mother's Chinese way of talking."[60] Sure enough, the mother's immigrant way of lying can hardly be deemed American, while the daughter's acquisition of English has enabled her to depart China—the metaphor is too subtle for me to grasp, for to my literal mind, the narrative protagonist has never been to China—not in the text, not in the author's biographic context, but definitely in the critic's political and cultural geography that all too willingly assigns Asian Americans an alien status. No wonder Juhasz thinks Kingston's command of English commendable, "[i]ts style, as *correct* as it is exquisite, seems to make acceptable to *literary* people the most *sophisticated criticism* in its themes."[61] Well, the hope of salvation for the Asian American female subject lies in the power of English language, or rather, as Juhasz tries to convert us, in sister critic's rescue mission.

What we have here is a tragic repetition, this time in the critical realm, of the exercise of power by American Orientalist discourse. Now, when the West again decides to know the East, the only epistemological vehicle available, it seems, is to automatically assume a speaking part for the East—thou China, still unravished bride of quietness. Gayatri Spivak's critique of Julia Kristeva's wishful representation of China in *About Chinese Women,* I believe, sheds light on the interested positionality of so many of Kingston's feminist critics as well:

> The pioneering books that bring First World feminists news from the Third World are written by privileged informants and can only be deciphered by a trained readership. . . . This is not the tired nationalistic claim that only a native can know the scene. The point I am trying to make is that, in order to learn enough about Third World women and to develop a different readership, the immense heterogeneity of the field must be appreciated and the First World feminist must learn to stop feeling privileged *as a woman.*[62]

The Orientalist nature of scholarship on *The Woman Warrior* also characterizes the male critics with only a slightly different turn of the screw. While the female critics stress their shared gender oppression with Asian American women despite cultural differences, the male critics cannot help deploring the wretched fate of "Chinese women" wrapped in "the double bind that would limit them to the maggot nonidentities of wife and slave."[63] The accusation of the horrifying "village patriarchy" has thus functioned to compromise Western sexism and consolidate the Euro-American male subject. "The violent consequences of the aunt's assertion of her individuality balance in searing intensity the depth of the villagers' commitment to cultural determinism and conformity," Eakin proclaims. "The quest for selfhood, so familiar in the literature of the West, unleashes a rush toward annihilation in this stark and somber tale from the East."[64] He seems to have forgotten the puritan patriarchy that branded the scarlet letter on Hester Prynne and the Creole patriarchy that limited Edna Pontellier's choices to the bottom of the sea. Only in the despotic Orient, as his cathartic reading goes, are men capable of such inhumane cruelty.

When "the attempt to deconstruct the hegemony of *patriarchal* discourses through feminism is itself foreclosed by the emphasis on "Chinese" as a mark of absolute difference," as Rey Chow remarks, and "when the West's 'other women' are prescribed their 'own' national and ethnic identity, . . . they are most excluded from having a claim to the reality of their existence."[65] As Asian American women's oppression is displaced onto their ancestral cultural origin, what the white critical benevolence accomplishes, in addition to elevating the status of *The Woman Warrior*, is precisely the reinforcement of racial and cultural incommensurability between ethnic and dominant populations within the same nation. One is left to wonder if the book's prominence is derived from its occupation of a barbarous periphery away from the civilized metropolis.

Though perhaps politically unconscious, the desire to appropriate by way of assimilation prompts fatally reductive and essentialist readings that have made, to the best of my knowledge, the "No Name Woman" chapter almost *the* canonical elect of *The Woman Warrior*. *The Norton Anthology of Literature by Women*, *The Harper American Literature*, *Crossing Cultures: Readings for Composition*, *The Bedford Reader*, *The Conscious Reader*, and *The Harvest Reader* all choose to anthologize "No Name Woman."[66] Paul Lauter's et al's *The Health Anthology of American Literature* is a notable exception to this pattern.[67] There is not even a single footnote in all these anthologies to reference a date with which Kingston attempts to catch the reader's attention early on. The third sentence of *The Woman Warrior* reads,

> In 1924 just a few days after our village celebrated seventeen hurry-up weddings—to make sure that every young man who went 'out on the road' would responsibly come home—your father and his brothers and your grandfather

and his brothers and *your aunt's new husband* sailed for America, the Gold Mountain.[68]

So, we know that the "no name woman" aunt was just married and did not accompany her groom to America. What we do not know from the text and what I think the editor should have made known is the context that *may have* given rise to the aunt's act of "extravagance."[69] The year 1924 was when the 1882 Chinese Exclusion Act was expanded to exclude all Asians from entry as immigrants, even Chinese alien wives of U.S. citizens.[70] Can we afford to neglect the historical contingency from which Kingston stages her narrative incident, an incident about marriage and estrangement, deviation and discipline that occurred under the shadow of legislative racism against Asian Americans? While not to advocate a view of literature as social documentation, the provision of this historical note could at least prepare the uninformed audience for a more meaningful reading than some free reader response may warrant. The reader deserves this because the editorial decision has screened out the context of the other chapters, which might otherwise have provided a sense of history. The reader would probably be a little more cautious and far less likely to make sweeping judgments about "Chinese repression of women," realizing that behind this atrocious scene of gender oppression is also racial domination that differentiates the various subjects of the nation.

The fact that "No Name Woman" is so frequently anthologized and is probably the only Asian American literature many college students will ever be exposed to, and the fact that unfailingly, my students of American literary survey respond to the chapter as a Chinese story, pose a serious challenge to the reading and writing of Asian American literature that the interpretive history of *The Woman Warrior* has helped highlight. Besides articulating Asian America into the national consciousness and activating the quest for the ethnic anecdote, lore, and myth, *The Woman Warrior*'s enduring contribution lies perhaps just in its foregrounding of critical representational issues that were as prominent in the 1970s as they are pertinent in the 1990s. The differences in the use of geocultural space, generic convention, and gender characterization and the dilemma of individual and collective delineation between the ethnic and dominant cultures that Kingston's debut text intensified not only were strategically engaged by the author in her later works, notably *China Men* (1980) and *Tripmaster Monkey* (1989), they also remain central to the construction and the contestation of the Asian American imaginary. If Kingston has revised her original turn to cultural Asia through "claiming America," her implicit affirmation of such ethnic nationalist models as Chin et al.'s *Aiiieeeee!* has also questioned its nativist and chauvinist lapses. If Kingston has become sympathetic to the ideology of identity politics, her negotiation of internal Asian American differences also recognizes the provisional nature of any representational claims.[71] In the shifting trajectory between the yearning for ancestral Asia and the longing for American national incorporation, the Kingstonian corpus will continue to animate the critical dialogue of nationalism and transnationalism as the contours the United States' culture have become visibly multiracial.

Notes

1.   Hereafter referred to as *WW.* Pagination of the text accords with its Vintage paperback edition (New York: Random House, 1976).

2.   *Roots: An Asian American Reader,* ed. Amy Tachiki et al. (Los Angeles: Asian American Studies Center, Univ. of California, 1971); *Asian American Authors,* ed. Kai-yu Hsu and Helen Palubinskas. (1972; reprint, Boston: Houghton, 1976); *Asian American Heritage: An Anthology of Prose and Poetry,* ed. David Hsin-Fu Wand (New York: Washington Square, 1974); *Aiiieeeee! An Anthology of Asian-American Writers,* ed. Frank Chin et al. (1974; reprint, Washington: Howard Univ. Press, 1983).

3.   Since this essay is not so much concerned with the exegesis of *WW* as it is with its interpretive history, for readers interested in aspects of the book's textual complexity, see an earlier essay of mine, "The Naming of a Chinese American 'I': Cross-Cultural Sign/ifications in *The Woman Warrior,*" *Criticism* 30.4 (1988): 497–515.

4.   Frank Chin, letter to Maxine Hong Kingston, 13 July 1976. Maxine Hong Kingston, letter to Frank Chin, 8 August 1976. Permission to quote the correspondence granted by both authors.

5.   John Okada, *No-No Boy,* (1957; reprint, Seattle: Univ. of Washington Press, 1990).

6.   *WW,* p. 1.

7.   Laurence Yep, *Dragonwings* (New York: Harper and Row, 1975), 1.

8.   China as the choice of fictional site becomes especially interesting if we realize that *The Woman Warrior* is not Kingston's first book but her first *published* book. An excerpt of her earlier manuscript came out as a post–*Woman Warrior* showcase piece, "Duck Boy" (*New York Times Magazine,* 12 June 1977, 54–55, 58, which takes place in a U.S. setting without particular geocultural distinction. The shift from the fictional normality of America to the exoticity of China in *The Woman Warrior* is to me a conscious artistic effort to turn her manuscript into published form.

9.   Gayatri Chakravorty Spivak, "Can the Subaltern Speak?" in *Marxism and the Interpretation of Culture,* ed. Cary Nelson and Lawrence Grossberg (Chicago: Univ. of Illinois Press, 1988), 292–93.

10.   Sui Sin Far (Edith Eaton) in Mayumi Tsutakawa and Alan Chong Lau, ed., *Turning Shadow into Light: Art and Culture of the Northwest's Early Asian/Pacific Community* (Seattle: Young Pine, 1982), 90.

11.   The literary fate of the Eaton sisters, Edith (Sui Sin Far) and Winnifred (Onoto Watanna), may crystallize the inevitable relation between an Asian American author's writing and her presumed cultural legitimacy and spatial belonging. See Amy Ling's *Between Worlds: Women Writers of Chinese Ancestry* (New York: Pergamon, 1990), 21–55.

12.   See *Readers' Guide to Periodical Literature* between 1973 and 1976 for a comprehensive coverage of the topics.

13.   The term "late capital" is from Fredric Jameson's "Cognitive Mapping" in *Marxism and the Interpretation of Culture,* eds, Cary Nelson and Lawrence Grossberg (Chicago: Univ. of Illinois Press, 1988); 347–57. See Paul Ong et al., *The New Asian Immigration in Los Angeles and Global Restructuring* (Philadelphia: Temple Univ. Press, 1994) for an analysis of late capital's

impact on contemporary Asian American demography. See also my *Imagi-Nation: Asian American Literature and Cultural Legitimacy* (forthcoming from Stanford Univ. Press) in which the emergence of "Asian America" was attributed to both the global—the ascent of transnational or late capital and Third World decolonization—and the local—the civil rights movement and the states' renewed commitment to formal equality.

    14.   I am referring to the rise of the "Pacific Rim" discourse, or "Rim Speak." See Arif Dirlik, ed, *What Is in a Rim? Critical Perspectives on the Pacific Region Idea* (Boulder, Colo.: Westview Press, 1993), which includes his essay, "The Asian Pacific Idea in Asian-American Perspective"; see also Michael Omi and Dana Takagi's guest edition of *Amerasia Journal* 21.1, 21.2 (1995), "Thinking Theory in Asian American Studies," which includes, among other significant contributions, Sau-ling Wong's "Denationalization Reconsidered." It is worth noting that Chin et al.'s *The Big Aiiieeeee!* (New York: Meridian, 1991) revises the anthology's original no-no stance to affirm an Asian American cultural symbolic traceable from Asian antiquity. While the editorial change of mind is certainly prompted by the effect of transnational capital in the United States, the subject is beyond the scope of this paper.

    15.   Blackburn, "Notes of a Chinese Daughter," *Ms.,* January 1977, 39.

    16.   Johnson, "Ghosts," *The New York Review of Books,* 3 February 1977, 19.

    17.   Chan, "The Mysterious West," *The New York Review of Books,* 28 April 1977, 41.

    18.   Tong, "Critic of Admirer Sees Dumb Racist," *San Francisco Journal,* 11 May 1977, 6.

    19.   Blackburn, 39, and Johnson.

    20.   Johnson, 20.

    21.   Chan, 41.

    22.   Tong, 6.

    23.   Fong, "An Open Letter/Review," *Bulletin of Concerned Asian Scholars,* 1977: 67–69.

    24.   Wong, *"The Woman Warrior,"* [a review] *Bridge* 6.4 (1978–1979): 46–48.

    25.   Jameson, *The Political Unconscious: Narrative as a Socially Symbolic Act* (Ithaca, N.Y.: Cornell Univ. Press, 1981), 106.

    26.   Elliot's remark is from Gloria H. Chun's paper presented at the Sixth National Conference of the Association for Asian American Studies, New York, 3 June 1989, "Metaphysician of Orientalism: Maxine Hong Kingston." As Elaine Kim notes in *Asian American Literature: An Introduction to the Writings and Their Social Contexts,* the same editorial marketing of Asian American fiction as autobiography also happens in the case of Carlos Bulosan's *America Is in the Heart* (Philadelphia: Temple Univ. Press, 1982), 48.

    27.   Chin, letter to Kingston.

    28.   I am not altogether discrediting poststructural theories of autobiography as self-invention. Rather, I try to emphasize how autobiography as a generic convention functions for minority writers both as an available channel of expression and a constrained form at that. James Olney observes in an analogous situation that "black writers entered the house of literature through the door of autobiography . . . because black history was preserved in autobiographies rather than standard histories" in Olney, ed., *Autobiography: Essays Theoretical and Critical* (Princeton: Princeton Univ. Press, 1980), 15. I might add that in the social construction of literary hierarchy, autobiography has become a peculiarly "ethnic/minor" form.

    29.   Kingston, "Cultural Mis-readings by American Reviewers" in *Asian and American Writers in Dialogue: New Cultural Identities,* ed. Guy Amirthanayagam (London: Macmillan, 1982), 55–65.

    30.   Chin, *The Chinaman Pacific & Frisco R.R. Co.* (Minneapolis: Coffee House, 1988); i–ii.

    31.   It is noteworthy that Chin's reconstruction of *The Woman Warrior's* receptional scene has considerably simplified the camps of opposition as if there were only one community response. The diversity of opinions about the book—some of which we have already sampled—as dictated by gender, class, and professional status is erased in this allegory of his. See also note 51.

32. Chan, 41 and Tong, 6.

33. *WW,* 103.

34. Yep, 10.

35. John King Fairbank, *The United States and China,* (4th ed.) (Cambridge: Harvard Univ. Press, 1983), 163. The usage is also reflected in English book titles such as Carl Crow's *Foreign Devil in Flowery Kingdom* (London: Hamish Hamilton, 1941).

36. Wolfe, "Bok Gooi, Hok Gooi and T'ang Jen: or Why There is No National Association for the Advancement of Chinese Americans," *New York,* 27 Sept. 1971, 35–41.

37. Lentricchia, *Criticism and Social Change* (Chicago: Chicago Univ. Press, 1983), 36, original emphasis.

38. *Aiiieeeee!,* xxii.

39. Tong, 6.

40. Baker, "To Move without Moving: Creativity and Commerce in Ralph Ellison's Trueblood Episode," in *Black Literature and Literary Theory,* ed. Henry Louis Gates Jr. (New York: Methuen, 1984); 221–48.

41. Guoen You et al, ed, *A History of Chinese Literature* (Beijing: People's Literature Press, 1964), 51.

42. *WW,* 243.

43. Ibid, 9.

44. "Cultural Mis-readings," 64–65.

45. John Leonard, "In Defiance of 2 Worlds," *New York Times,* 17 Sept. 1976, C21.

46. Karen Horton, "Honolulu Interview: Maxine Hong Kingston," *Honolulu Today,* Dec. 1979, 49–56.

47. Susan Currier, "Maxine Hong Kingston," in *Dictionary of Literary Biography Yearbook: 1980,* ed. Karen L. Rord et al. (Michigan: Gale Research, 1980), 235–41.

48. Following Kingston, Morrison won the National Book Critics Circle Award in 1977. And after Kingston was given the 1980 National Book Award for *China Men,* Walker obtained in 1983 both the National Book Award and the Pulitzer Prize for *The Color Purple.*

49. Chun.

50. Stephen Talbot, "Talking Story: Maxine Hong Kingston Rewrites the American Dream," *Image (San Francisco Examiner),* 22 June 1990, 6–17.

51. The publication of *The Woman Warrior* signals the beginning of the professionalization of not only Asian American writers but critics as well. In many ways, the categorical viability of "Asian American literature" is currently sustained by the work of professional Asian American writers and critics. Though the contribution of Asian American academic critics to the legitimation of Kingston's debut text is significant, their earlier work was unable to considerably alter the basic critical terms set by the predominantly white academic left, who, in my view, was principally responsible for the book's initial canonization. For this reason, the remaining analysis of *The Woman Warrior*'s interpretive history will concentrate on the work of non–Asian American critics.

52. Charles Kemnitz, "The Hand of Forging Personal Narrative," *Genre* 16 (Summer 1983): 175–89; Victoria Myers, "The Significant Fictivity of Maxine Hong Kingston's *The Woman Warrior,*" *Biography* 9.2 (1986): 112–25; Deborah Homsher, "*The Woman Warrior,* by Maxine Hong Kingston: A Bridging of Autobiography and Fiction," *Iowa Review* 10.4 (Fall 1979): 93–98; Stephanie Demetrakipoulos, "The Metaphysics of Matrilinearism in Women's Autobiography: Studies of Mead's *Blackberry Winter,* Hellman's *Pentimento,* Angelou's *I Know Why the Caged Bird Sings,* and Kingston's *The Woman Warrior,*" in *Women's Autobiography: Essays in Criticism,* ed. Estelle C. Jelinek (Bloomington: Indiana Univ. Press, 1980), 180–220.

53. Linda Morante, "From Silence to Song: The Triumph of Maxine Hong Kingston," *Frontiers* 9.2 (1987): 78–82.

54. *WW,* 194.

55. Ibid., 13.

56. Ibid., 235.

57. Morante, 78, 80.

58. *WW,* 214–15.

59. Ibid., 6.

60. Suzanne Juhasz, "Narrative Technique and Female Identity," in *Contemporary American Women Writers: Narrative Strategies,* ed. Catherine Rainwater and William J. Sheick (Lexington, Ky.: Univ. Press of Kentucky, 1985), 174–89.

61. Juhasz, "Towards a Theory of Form in Feminist Autobiography: Kate Millet's *Flying* and *Sita;* Maxine Hong Kingston's *The Woman Warrior,*" in *Women's Autobiography: Essays in Criticism,* ed. Estelle C. Jelinek (Bloomington: Indian Univ. Press, 1980), 236.

62. Spivak, "French Feminism in an International Frame," *Yale French Studies* 62–63 (1981): 154–84.

63. John Paul Eakin, *Fictions in Autobiography: Studies in the Art of Self-Invention* (Princeton, N.J.: Princeton Univ. Press, 1985), 275.

64. Ibid, 257–58.

65. Rey Chow, *Woman and Chinese Modernity: The Politics of Reading Between West and East* (Minneapolis: Univ. of Minnesota Press, 1991), 163.

66. Sandra Gilbert and Susan Gubar, ed., *The Norton Anthology of Literature by Women: The Tradition in English* (New York: Norton, 1985); Donald McQuade et al., ed., *The Harper American Literature* (New York: Harper & Row, 1987); Henry and Myrna Knepler, ed., *Crossing Cultures: Readings for Composition* (New York: Macmillan, 1983); X. J. and Dorathy M. Kennedy, ed., *The Bedford Reader* (New York: Macmillan, 1985); Caroline Shrodes et al., ed., *The Conscious Reader* (New York: Macmillan, 1985); William A. Hetternan and Mark Johnston, ed., *The Harvest Reader,* 2d ed., (San Diego: Harcourt, Brace Jovanovich 1991).

67. Paul Lauter et al., ed, *The Heath Anthology of American Literature* (Lexington, Mass.: D.C. Heath, 1990).

68. *WW,* 3. My italics.

69. Ibid., 7.

70. H. M. Lai and P. P. Choy, ed., *Outlines of the History of the Chinese in America* (San Francisco: Chinese American Studies Planning Group, 1971), 93; Judy Yung, *Chinese Women of America: A Pictorial History* (Seattle: Univ. of Washington Press, 1986), 42.

71. Kingston's call of "claiming America" is very much a response to the controversy over *The Woman Warrior* and to Chin et al.'s nationalist concerns. See my "*China Men:* Maxine Hong Kingston and the American Canon," *American Literary History* 2.3 (Fall 1990): 482–502 for a related discussion. Although Kingston never explicitly challenged Chin's theory and practice of Asian American literature, *Tripmaster Monkey: His Fake Book* is clearly her improvisational parody and pastiche of Frank Chin, which both affirmed and critiqued her fellow writer's program of culture.

REVIEWS OF *CHINA MEN*

◆

Chinese Ghost Story

FREDERIC WAKEMAN JR.

Although Maxine Hong Kingston's *China Men* is partly about the tense and ambivalent relations between women and men, its main theme is the experience of becoming Chinese-American, a process as filled with risk and ambiguity as the relationship between the sexes. The very title of the novel is calculated with this ambivalence in mind. As Kingston wrote in an essay published several years ago:

> In the early days of Chinese-American history, men called themselves "Chinamen" just as other newcomers called themselves "Englishmen" or "Frenchmen": the term distinguished them from the "Chinese" who remained citizens of China, and also showed that they were not recognized as Americans. Later, of course, it became an insult. Young Chinese Americans today are reclaiming the word because of its political and historical precision, and are demanding that it be said with dignity and not for name-calling.[1]

Kingston's China Men are the protagonists of that effort to become Chinese-American: first as sojourners, then as settlers, and finally as citizens.

Like her first book, *The Woman Warrior,* Kingston's *China Men* is a mixture of myth, history, and recollection. Of these, the myths seem at first the most striking element, and they become the most perplexing. As Kingston herself has admitted, many of the myths she describes are largely her own reconstructions.[2] Often, they are only remotely connected with the original Chinese legends they invoke; and sometimes they are only spurious folklore, a kind of self-indulgent fantasy that blends extravagant personal imagery with appropriately *völkisch* themes.

Yet this sort of self-resurrection is an important way for Kingston to establish a link between her present Americanness and the China of her ancestors' past. Toward the end of the novel, for instance, she inserts a chapter on the legendary Ch'ü Yuan, the third-century BC poet whose suicide by drowning is celebrated in South China by the yearly Dragon Boat festival. To Kingston, the tragic figure of Ch'ü Yuan epitomizes the eternal male

From *The New York Review of Books.* New York: *The New York Review of Books,* 14 Aug. 1980, 42–43. Copyright 1980 by Nyrev, Inc. Reprinted by permission of Nyrev, Inc.

sojourner, longing for home while unable to return. But he is far more for her than just a symbol of exile. By telling his story through a series of successively expanded images, each more ornate than the other, Kingston seems to be trying to enlarge the pathways connecting her self, as the daughter of a Chinese-American laundryman and a Cantonese midwife in Stockton, California, with the high culture of classical China.

To be Chinese, she claims at one point, is to know that culture at birth, without instruction. "All Chinese know this story," her father says of the Ch'ü Yuan legend. "If you are an authentic Chinese, you know the language and the stories without being taught, born talking them." Yet he himself does not speak of the past; he does not even seem authentically Chinese to his own daughter, who tells him:

> You say with the few words and the silences: No stories. No past. No China. You only look and talk Chinese. There are no photographs of you in Chinese clothes nor against Chinese landscapes. Did you cut your pigtail to show your support for the Republic? Or have you always been American?

Her father's sullen silence permits Kingston to claim the right to tell his own story, even if that story is imaginary: "I'll tell you what I suppose from your silences and few words, and you can tell me that I'm mistaken. You'll just have to speak up with the real stories if I've got you wrong." With this special poetic license, she proceeds to portray her father in the first of many guises: the mythical father from China.

Kingston's mythical father—BaBa—is born near Canton toward the end of the nineteenth century. As she imagines his birth in China, Kingston is really remembering the birth of her own brother in Stockton. The two births, hundreds of pages, thousands of miles, and five decades apart in *China Men,* are described in almost identical images:

The Father in China
The brothers balanced the teaks and pines in a stack under their parents' window and climbed it like acrobats. By the time they reached the curved sill, the baby had been born. They saw its foot sticking out of a bundle tied to the hook of the rice scale. . . . They cheered, jumped up and down. " 'Jump like a squirrel,' " they sang. " 'Bob like a blue jay, tails in the air, tails in the air.' A baby is born. A baby is born."

Each of us carried a crate or a stool outside and lined it up on the porch under the window. . . . We climbed up in a row and saw the doctor lift a white bundle like a snowdrop on a hook. A foot stuck out. The baby had been born. He was being weighed. . . . " 'Jump like a squirrel. Bob like a bluejay. Tails in the air. Tails in the air.' " We added our own lines, "The baby's born. The baby's born."

These recurrent images sharpen the mythical quality of Kingston's family history.

After a youthful marriage, the father from China is selected by his parents to train for the imperial civil service examinations. The last traditional exams were held in 1905, and although Kingston's real father would have been far too young to have sat for those, her mythical father takes them. His examination ordeal (which is fancifully described) does not lead to a civil service post, but it does land him a job as the village schoolmaster.

The job is a thankless one, and BaBa's tribulations in the one-room schoolhouse are hilariously described:

> The students ran amok. They stole vegetables from the neighboring gardens; they played war; they staged shows on top of the tables. He tried locking the door on the late boys and got some satisfaction from their shadows bobbing and passing like puppets at the windows, but they worried him when they disappeared. Where did they go? The school looked like a crazy house, like a Sung Dynasty painting of a classroom showing kids putting boxes over one another's heads, drawing cartoons of their teacher, lying on their backs and spinning chairs and tables with their feet.

Frustrated to the point of rage, Kingston's mythical father decides to give up his job, and joins the other China Men of his clan to talk about leaving their village to migrate to America.

Many of these Cantonese "ocean men" (so different from the landlocked northerners) have already crossed back and forth between China and America. Bak Goong (the Great Grandfather of Sandalwood Mountains) is such a heroic "Gold Mountain Traveler." Recruited by an agent of the Royal Hawaiian Agricultural Society, Bak Goong sails for three months locked below deck, where the berths are stacked "like coffins in a death house." Disembarking in Honolulu, he is marched by white overseers into the overgrown back country, where he clears the lush land, plants sugar cane, and harvests the thick stalks before finally returning to his family in China. Another epic figure is Ah Goong (the Grandfather of the Sierra Nevada Mountains), who travels to Gold Mountain (San Francisco) three times. Kingston's descriptions of his construction work on the transcontinental railroad contain some of the most arresting prose in *China Men*.

> Then it was autumn, and the wind blew so fiercely, the men had to postpone the basketwork. Clouds moved in several directions at once. Men pointed at dust devils, which turned their mouths crooked. There was ceaseless motion; clothes kept moving; hair moving; sleeves puffed out. Nothing stayed still long enough for Ah Goong to figure it out. The wind sucked the breath out of his mouth and blew thoughts from his brains. The food convoys from San

Francisco brought tents to replace the ones that whipped away. The baskets from China, which the men saved for high work, carried cowboy jackets, long underwear, Levi pants, boots, earmuffs, leather gloves, flannel shirts, coats. They sewed rabbit fur and deerskin into the linings. They tied the wide brims of their cowboy hats over their ears with mufflers. And still the wind made confusing howls into ears, and it was hard to think.

By the time the railroad over the Sierra is finally finished, Ah Goong has won his American citizenship—if not altogether legally, then quite deservedly. Later, when he returns to Canton after the 1906 San Francisco earthquake, it is in the author's imagination as "an American ancestor, a holding, homing ancestor of this place."

The closer Kingston moves to the present, the more history displaces myth. At first, for example, she tells how the father from China was smuggled to New York in a nailed-down crate, hidden in a ship's hold. But then she quickly adds that "of course, my father could not have come that way"; and she describes how he arrived at Angel Island, across the bay from San Francisco, where he was detained until he could persuade the US immigration authorities that his papers were genuine and that both his father and grandfather had been naturalized citizens.

The historical father becomes part-owner of a laundry in New York, along with three other China Men who spend their salaries on $200 suits, dime-a-dance girls, motorcycles, and flying lessons. This is very much the bachelor's dream world, and it is followed in *China Men* by a brief and powerful retelling of the classical Chinese ghost story about a hauntingly beautiful woman who beguiles a handsome traveler until he loses nearly all memory of his family back home. Eventually, the woman turns out to be the spirit of a noblewoman long dead, and the man is released from her spell to return to his wife.[3] In the same way the father from China turns away from the lure of his three high-living friends, and puts the temptations of bachelorhood behind him after his wife joins him in New York. But as soon as he stops spending time with them, the three partners cheat him out of his share of the laundry. It is then that the historical father and mother leave New York for California, where Maxine Hong Kingston was born.

The author's own childhood memories are present throughout the book, and even though the imagery of the mythical and historical passages is usually vivid, I found myself more affected by the recollections of her San Joaquin Valley childhood in Stockton's Chinatown, which is very different from San Francisco's Chinatown.

> San Francisco Chinatown shows off for the tourists; our Chinatowns blend into the Valley towns and cities. Our businesses and houses are spread out, not concentrated into a few blocks. Yet our communities are more tightly knit. We speak the peasant dialects. We know one another. Gossip gives each person a

reputation. . . . It's not only the older generation which sees differences between the Big City Chinese and the rest of us in Stockton, Sacramento (Second City), Marysville (Third City because it was the third largest in Gold Rush days), Lodi, Locke, Watsonville, Tracy, and other central California towns. My own scholarly friends have complained how the Big City Chinamen refuse to share research work, whereas we Valley Chinamen will help each other get ahead.[4]

Kingston's memories of Stockton are sometimes recollections of older relatives: grand-uncles like Say Goong (Fourth Grandfather) and Sahm Goong (Third Grandfather) who drive a vegetable wagon drawn by enormous black horses. After Say Goong's death, his ghost returns to haunt Third Grandfather, who has to tell it to leave him alone and go back to China. The ghost disappears, but soon Third Grandfather dies as well; and even though Kingston imagines that his ghost might have gone back to China too, the two deceased men have become American ancestors to the relatives left behind: "When their descendants came across the country to visit us, we took them to the place where two of our four grandfathers had had their house, stable and garden. . . . They took pictures with a delayed-shutter camera, everyone standing together where the house had been. The relatives kept saying, 'This is the ancestral ground,' their eyes filling with tears over a vacant lot in Stockton."

Her American father's way is paid from New York to Stockton by a fellow-villager who is now one of Stockton's wealthiest Chinese-Americans. The benefactor is repaid with personal service: Kingston's mother irons his family's clothing and bathes his children; the father manages his gambling house and allows himself to be arrested in place of his patron whenever the house is raided. During World War II, however, the gambling parlor is closed, and BaBa—the American father—loses all drive to work and becomes listless and cranky. He moans and screams in his sleep; in the daytime he sits by himself and curses, ignoring his children. This is the silent father, whom Maxine Hong Kingston has earlier so bitterly addressed: "Worse than the swearing and the nightly screams were your silences when you punished us by not talking. You rendered us invisible, gone."

Desperate for attention, the children become uncontrollably wild, attacking each other physically and goading their father until BaBa bursts out of his torpor and attacks them in a rage. He smashes down a door and beats his daughter with a wire hanger; and, in some inexplicable way, the violence redeems him. Soon afterward he invests in a laundry, and "at last owned his house and his business in America." He is finally the American father his daughter has always wanted: a BaBa who buys her pets, tells her stories, sings her Chinese poetry, and plants for her "many kinds of gourds, peas, beans, melons, and cabbages—and perennials—tangerines, oranges, grapefruit, almonds, pomegranates, apples, black figs, and white figs—and from seed pits, another loquat, peaches, apricots, plums of many varieties—trees that take years to fruit."

The author's Stockton childhood coincided with World War II, and many of her relatives were drafted or enlisted. One even went to China to help fight the Japanese, who looked to her, in the propaganda posters directed against them, like beings from outer space. The Chinese-American GIs, on the other hand, "looked like the good soldiers in the movies," wearing campaign hats and helmets in the snapshots sent back from overseas. After they first returned from wartime service, her uncles and cousins continued to resemble their photographs, seeming very American, and not at all Chinese. "But then they put on their regular slacks and white shirts. Their hair grew out, and their wives trimmed it with home clippers. Their noses rounded out, the bridges receding, and their tight jaws softened. They did not walk from the shoulders like football players and boxers anymore. They started speaking Chinese loud again."

Soon enough there was a new enemy, just as inhuman as the Japanese from outer space: the Communists. The Communists had once been Chinese, of course, but now they were "people who had gone crazy and perverted."

> The Communists were monkeys trying to be human beings; they were pretending to explain and reason, putting on serious faces. They were saying nonsense, pretending they knew the classics when they were not teaching from real books. Communist schools, Communist books, Red art work, Red courts, theaters, customs were almost like real ones but off. The shrewd villagers were not fooled. The Japanese had tortured people for the fun of it; the Communists wanted something else: their monkey civilization. Neighbors informed against one another to prove they were true Communists. The number of people the Communists killed was 60 million. After the uncles were killed, the aunts fled to Hong Kong, Canada, and the United States. That the Communists were holding their distant cousins as hostages did not deter them. "I wish the Japanese had won," my mother said.

Though drawn from childhood memory, this is not only parody. Time and again in *China Men,* Kingston mentions the Chinese-Americans' fear of the Communists, though once when a great aunt returned to Canton after 1950 because she was estranged from her husband in America, Kingston notes that this "was a clue that Red China couldn't have been as horrible as everyone made out."[5] But then the Vietnam war begins, and because the government claims that the Viet Cong's weapons come from China, Chinese-Americans in Stockton fear that they may end up having to fight against the Chinese.

Kingston's last China Man is the brother whose birth is earlier foreshadowed by that of the father in China: "Jump like a squirrel. Bob like a bluejay. A baby is born." Like the mythical father, the brother born in Stockton has a dreadful experience as a schoolteacher that may owe as much to Kingston's own experience teaching English in Hayward, California, as to her powers of imagination.

> His students stole anything. They shot up bowling alleys, and beat up hippies and whores ("Hors Welcome" they painted on their cars). One boy collected German helmets, bayonets, knives ("with real bloodstains"), swastikas, atrocity and Hitler photos, flags, iron crosses, grenades. . . . One boy had three babies by three different girl friends, and persuaded all of them to keep the children; the brother gave him three Doctor Spock books. One student was a vampire boy, who wore a cape and would not go out into the sun. . . . One, Benjie, lowered his heavy head snarling over his papers, peeped and spied over his left arm so nobody could cheat off his poor paper. He held his pencil straight up and down in a fist that stuck out of an unraveling sweater sleeve. His eyebrows jerked; growls came from inside his arms. Whenever his pencil broke, he walked all the way around the room to the sharpener, and wrote *fuck* and *chink* on the blackboards.

As the war in Vietnam intensifies and his own students drop out to enlist, the brother considers evading the draft by fleeing to Canada. But because this would mean leaving America, "the only country he had ever lived in," he instead enlists in the Navy for four years, believing that aboard ship he least risks the danger of having to kill someone.

"A gook [sent] to fight a gook war," the brother sees his tour of duty in the Far East as an opportunity to search for his Asian identity, reversing the direction of his ancestors' quest. As he stops over in the Philippines, in Korea, and in Taiwan, however, the greeting from Asians is always the same: "You're a Chinese American. You're lucky." In Taipei, he feels more at home inside the American military base than on the city streets, where he seems to stand out as a foreigner. At sea in the Gulf of Tonkin aboard the USS *Midway*, he tries to protect his pacifism by keeping himself detached from all the military activity, but in his bunk underneath the roaring rocket launchers, he can feel no separation from the war. Still, even though he flies along on one bombing raid over North Vietnam, he turns down a flattering promotion to flight school and remains a bluejacket. Harder to refuse is an invitation to enter the Monterey Language School—partly because this accompanies a security clearance which certifies "that the family was really American, not precariously American but super-American, extraordinarily secure—Q Clearance Americans." But to learn Vietnamese is to risk becoming an interrogator-torturer, and that he cannot stomach. In the end he rejects this promotion too.

Toward the end of his tour, the brother goes to Hong Kong on R and R, and he decides to look up some of his relatives there. When he goes to the street address given to him by his parents, he finds no one of their name, nor do any of the neighbors know of them. He leaves the presents that he has brought them by a stranger's door, and soon is on a cargo plane, flying home to America and civilian life. Despite the war, he has managed to preserve his pacifism honorably; he has killed no one. But he has not discovered a different and foreign Asian self. Rather his quest has led him to a sharper recognition of what it means to be a third or fourth generation American of Chinese descent. "Chinese Americans talk about how when they set foot on China, even just Hong Kong, their whole lives suddenly made sense; their youth had been a preparation for this visit, they say. They realize their Americanness, they say, and 'You find out what a China Man you are.' "

In the end, then, Maxine Hong Kingston is impelled to transcend her own myths and let her China Men become Chinese-Americans. The myths—which by their very nature mediate the irreconcilable—initially make it possible for her to rediscover an otherwise lost China, and by then summoning it, lay that spirit to rest. Yet precisely because the myths are usually so consciously contrived, her pieces of distant China lore often seem jejune and even inauthentic—especially to readers who know a little bit about the original high culture which Kingston claims as her birthright. Paradoxically, the myths which were ideally intended to aggrandize the history of her family actually draw their authenticity from the tangible evocations of her own childhood. It is the private world of her Stockton relatives—the aunts weeping over a dead ancestor's vacant lot, the sons and husbands driven half-mad by the continual clamor for help from kinsfolk in Canton—that truly commands our attention, and into which we feel privileged to be admitted. Less fanciful and flamboyant than her first book, *China Men* is a much more authoritative personal reflection than *The Woman Warrior.* This is because Kingston is finding a surer voice as an American writer of Chinese descent: the daughter of migrants but not an emigrant herself.

In the final scene of her book, she describes a Filipino scholar telling her and some young Chinese-Americans conflicting and contradictory stories about the Chinese diaspora. By now the myths have become tales to recount, stories to be written. As the Chinese-Americans cluster around the scholar to hear their legends told by another, Kingston senses her own liberation from self-doubt. "Good," she thinks, "I was free to watch the young men who listen." Finally confident of her own identity, she is secure enough to be capable of detachment. "Good," she repeats, "now I could watch the young men who listen."

Notes

1. Maxine Hong Kingston, "San Francisco's Chinatown: A view from the Other Side of Arnold Genthe's Camera," *American Heritage,* December, 1978, p. 37.
2. "The way I keep the old Chinese myths alive is by telling them in a new American way. I can't help feeling that people who accuse me of misrepresenting the myths are looking

at the past in a sentimental kind of way. It's so *easy* to look into the past. It is harder to look into the present and come to terms with what it means to be alive today." Timothy Pfaff, "Talk with Mrs. Kingston," *The New York Times Book Review,* June 15, 1980, p. 26.

3.   Kingston intersperses mythical interludes throughout the book. Some of these passages (which are on the whole less overdrawn than the more florid episodes of *The Woman Warrior*) are not always effective. The coy retelling of the story of Robinson Crusoe (Cantonese: Lo Bun Sun) and Friday (Cantonese: Sing Kay Ng), for example, seemed particularly forced.

4.   Maxine Hong Kingston, "San Francisco's Chinatown," p. 37.

5.   Maxine Hong Kingston has never visited the People's Republic of China herself. "My friends know how many years I have been on the verge of deciding whether or not I really want to apply for a visa to China, a country that may not be there at all, you know. They send me clippings to show how real it is, how benign or dangerous." Maxine Hong Kingston, "Reservations about China," *Ms.,* October, 1978, p. 67.

Ghosts on a Gold Mountain

Clara Claiborne Park

The astonishing books under review[1] are not long, and not at all difficult. A child could read them; children—older children—should. Yet though I shall pack as much as I can into this reasonably long review, I shall be able to convey only a little of their harsh richness. This is an unknown universe, and it is not obvious where to enter it.

I could begin where Maxine Hong Kingston began *The Woman Warrior,* with the story of No Name Woman, her father's sister, who gave silent birth in the pigsty more than nine months after her husband had left for America, whose body was found with the baby's plugging up the family well the morning after the villagers tore up the rice and killed the pigs and chickens and trashed the house and smeared the walls with blood. Her mother told her that story when she began to menstruate. "What happened to her could happen to you. Don't humiliate us. You wouldn't like to be forgotten as if you had never been born." Or I could start with the Woman Warrior herself, Fa Mu Lan, military commander, brilliant swordswoman, defending her people against warlords and bandits—another one of her mother's stories, the other side of the immemorial Chinese denigration of the female. The girl took the old tale for her own, grafting into it her own heroic deeds, so she could forget for a little while that "girls are maggots in the rice" and that it is better to raise geese than daughters. Or I could begin with the bound feet we all know of, on which her grandmother swayed from room to room, delicately touching the wall when the maids (slaves bought at market) were not near to support her. *China Men* begins with another old tale: when, long ago, Tang Ao crossed the ocean, looking for the Gold Mountain, and came to the Land of Women, they captured him, but in turning him into a woman they did not bother with castration. They bound his feet. The little American girl, growing up in Stockton, California, getting all A's in the public school where every thought had to be rethought in a new language, inherited her mother's power to "talk story," to make old tales new, in words almost too immediate to be borne.

From *The Hudson Review* (Winter 1980): 589–95. Copyright 1981 by *The Hudson Review*. Reprinted by permission of *The Hudson Review*.

The old ladies squeezed each foot and broke many tiny bones along the sides. They gathered his toes, toes over and under one another like a knot of ginger root. . . . As they wound the bandages tight and tighter around his feet, the women sang footbinding songs to distract him . . . Every night they unbound his feet, but his veins had shrunk, and the blood pumping through them hurt so much, he begged to have his feet re-wrapped tight. They forced him to wash his used bandages, which were embroidered with flowers and smelled of rot and cheese. He hung the bandages up to dry. . . . He felt embarrassed: the wrappings were like underwear, and they were his.

Or I could put by the woman theme and begin with the ghosts, since they are everywhere; the dead are restless if not tended, and all foreigners are ghosts. The grandfathers left China to live among them. Great Grandfather went to Hawaii, the Sandalwood Mountain, which sends out a sandalwood sweetness which smells, to men who have been crowded below decks three months in a sailing ship, "like a goddess visiting." Rainbows gleamed double there, and there were so many bananas that you didn't have to scrape the peels and eat the scrapings, you could throw them away. But it only looked and smelt like Paradise; he cleared jungle from dawn to dark, in silence and under the whip for a dollar a week for some twenty years before he went back to China. That must have been in the 1850s. The Grandfather who went to the Gold Mountain—America—had a crazy streak. He actually swapped his baby boy for a neighbor's girl. Grandmother made him trade back, leaving the house to teeter after him on little knobs of feet, shoving him ahead of her and holding onto him at the same time. But before that he had spent 20 years in the Sierra Nevada, shoved there too by Grandmother: "Make money," "Don't stay here eating." He, and thousands of other men of China (not china-men) put through the transcontinental railroad, pickaxing tunnels under the hard mountains where the Donner Party had turned cannibal and died. After three years of hammering granite the white demons invented dynamite; it "added more accidents and ways of dying, but if it were not used, the railroad would take fifty more years to finish."

Nitroglycerine exploded when it was jounced on a horse or dropped. A man who fell with it in his pocket blew himself up into red pieces. . . . Human bodies skipped through the air like puppets and made Ah Goong laugh crazily as if the arms and legs would come together again. The smell of burned flesh remained in rocks.

Nobody recorded the number of Chinese dead. You could die from sickness, or frostbite; you could fall from the wicker baskets in which you were lowered thousands of feet to the work site, only the lucky words painted on the baskets to protect you from the mountain wind. Crazy grandfather pissed overboard and shouted "I'm a waterfall"; once, overcome by the beauty of sky and treetops, "he stood up tall and squirted out into space," shouting, "I am fucking the world." When the railroad was finished the white ghosts made speeches: "Only Americans could have done it." True, too, for who had earned America if not those who built it with inconceivable toil and danger? There follows one of those loaded details which announce the difference between mere narrative skill and art:

> A white demon in top hat tap-tapped on the gold spike, and pulled it back out. Then one China Man held the real spike, the steel one, and another hammered it in.

But of course that was not the way the white demons saw it. The Driving Out began in 1863: *China Men*'s seven-page summary of the history of the Chinese Exclusion Laws ought to be required reading in any course in American history; almost all of it will be news to non–Chinese Americans. In a work permeated with the fabulous, there is no breath of the fabulous here. The Rock Springs Massacre. The Los Angeles Massacre. China Men set adrift off Alaska without food or water. But the ancestors of this American—a Berkeley graduate, a teacher of creative writing, someone Like Us, no doubt with dishwasher and formica kitchen—were not massacred or set adrift. Nor did they remain, disappearing into slums where the white ghosts could not recognize them to deport them, since all chinamen look alike. Not settlers but Sojourners, they took their American savings and their stories of the Gold Mountain back to their Chinese village, came again, again returned, until 1924, when Maxine Hong Kingston's father came to stay.

I could begin anywhere in the dissolving chronology of these books where no clear order is apparent, yet every story is disposed with invisible art to resonate and echo. Each of these memoirs unifies its shimmering details in terms of its own experience—female in *The Woman Warrior,* then male in *China Men.* But the unity is fuller: to complete her exploration Maxine Hong Kingston (no one of her names, taken singly, makes a true statement) had to write both books, imagining her way out of the Yin symbol she was born to and into the Yang of masculine experience. The two together complete the circle.

One can enter a circle anywhere. Let it be with the little girl's theory that males feel no pain. To test it, she kicked a boy at school with her heavy shoes, armored with toe-taps. Sure enough, he didn't cry. " 'See,' I told the girls. 'Boys have no feelings. It's some kind of immunity.' It was the same with Chinese boys, black boys, white boys, and Mexican and Filipino boys." And with fathers; her father, BaBa, was silent for days, never wept. "Girls and women of all races cried and had feelings"; men were immune, except to anger. BaBa came at them with coathangers and brooms, striking anywhere, not like the orderly American spanking. He spoke to swear, to call them names: "Dog vomit," "Stink pig," "Your mother's smelly cunt." He said with the words and the silences: "no stories. No past. No China." He had renamed himself Edison when he came to America; the children had lucky American names. "Father, I have seen you lighthearted"—catching dragonflies once, tying threads to them, a toy airplane for each child. But not often. Men have no feelings. *China Men,* dedicated to the men of her family, brothers, husband, son, father, is a journey to set that straight.

He was born "in a year of the Rabbit, 1891 or 1903 or 1915." The name he took when he passed the Imperial Examinations was Think Virtue, a name "not as cerebral as it appears in English," the ideograph for "think" combining "field" and "heart." Think about that for a while in the field of the heart, a linguistic window opening on a universe of meaning. The books are full of things like that. BaBa was different from birth, skinny, with long fingers made for holding pens. It was a peasant family, never a scholar in all the long village generations, but this baby, at his one-month birthday party (girls never had one) was given the Four Valuable Things: ink, inkslab, paper, and brush. His brothers had got only money. "The house was ashine with lights and lucky with oranges." Grandmother sewed him little scholar's caps and scholar's gowns; he didn't work in the fields like his brothers, but practiced handwriting and hummed poems. His brothers wouldn't gamble with him because he memorized the cards; "Poetry Addict!" they taunted, and excluded him from their clubhouse. He walked four days to the city where the examinations were given—the five pages devoted to these must be one of the most evocative historical recreations ever written. He passed them—he was about fourteen. Grown men tried all their lives to pass the Imperial Examinations. "Winning, a scholar would become one of the philosophers who rules China. . . . All things good come to the mandarin scholar." If BaBa had won top honors he would have "flown" to Canton or Peiping. Instead he won the job of village teacher, a boy trying to keep order among unruly boys who cared nothing for learning. It got so bad he couldn't eat. He couldn't repeat the examinations and better his score; though they had been the avenue of advancement for a thousand years, those he had taken were the last ever given. He married and kept at it, but he "did not learn how hard and often students have to be hit to make them polite." When he couldn't stand it any more he escaped to the Gold Mountain.

There he worked in a laundry, morning to midnight, bought into it, sent for his wife, was swindled out of it by Chinese partners with Gold Mountain names, Roosevelt and Woodrow and Worldster. He managed a gambling house (part of his job was to get arrested in place of the owner, but because all chinamen look alike he never got a record), bought a house with savings squeezed from years of working-hours that contemporary Americans are just barely able to imagine, lost his job, at length ended up with his own laundry. The temperature there in summer reached 111 degrees. His daughter, imagining her way into what it was like to take the examinations, writes of the days in which the scholars waited to hear their results. In three sentences she stabs her way into the silence of that angry father.

So he had once had three free days. He spent them talking to the other scholars, making friends, singing, touring the capital. Counting those you spent
walking [Father], you had seven free days.

More than once, MaMa told of a special kind of feast people enjoyed in
China when they had the money. They sat around a doughnut-shaped table
while cooks sawed through the skull of the live monkey clamped in the middle; then they spooned out the brains and ate them. MaMa was a master of
vivid detail: the little girl wanted to cry out "stop it," but she never did. Did
the Chinese really smear bad daughters-in-law with honey and tie them
naked on top of ants' nests? Did the Japanese really cut into a prisoner's side
where he couldn't see it, take out an end of intestine, and tie it behind him
and let him go so that he pulled out his own insides as he ran? It is not that
one becomes immune to cruelty reading these pages; rather one feels that to
go on reading is to consent to join the human condition from which we have,
here on the miraculous gold mountain, so long been exempt. Famine: it is an
old word. Were people in the Cantonese village where BaBa and MaMa
came from really eating clay and bark? When the dogs and cats and slugs
and beetles were gone, was the meat that appeared in the market really the
flesh of babies sold by their parents? In the fifties, in the early years of Mao?
We were alive in the fifties. That's not long ago. We defend ourselves with
incredulity: surely it isn't true, as the grandmother wrote, that children
grow coarse black hairs all over their body when they starve, so the other
things don't have to be true either. Who knows what really went on in
China and what was made up so the emigrants would send money? Yet the
uncles were all dead, that was true; the husband of the aunt who escaped to
San Francisco had really been pressed between millstones. It was a traditional way of execution; revolutions leave some things unchanged. Though
it is not proper for young Chinese to respond to adults as equals, to the
aunt's story the American niece risks the conventional old lady's response:
"Aiya . . . how hard to endure." The words were developed by a culture to
which they were indispensable.

This aunt is not imaginative; the girl likes her "use of exact numbers."
Sixteen hotel-rooms in eight hours is too many to clean when you have high
blood-pressure; MaMa would have said "Ten thousand rooms per second."
"Uncountable. Infinite." So what can one believe? Facts? She doesn't even
know within ten years when her father was born (though unless it was 1891,
the Imperial Examinations, last given in 1905, are fiction too). Chinese adults
talk story, but they do not explain things to children. Playing, the girl jumps
over her brother and is beaten. No one explains what she later learns, that no
female can position herself above a male even for an instant.

What is not explained, securely placed in space and time and logic,
whether hideous or beautiful, takes on the quality of magic, becomes
Romance. MHK has kept this way of talking story; her writing breathes the
child's vision of wonder. The grandfathers in Stockton—brothers of the real

grandfather—have a pile of horse manure taller than a human being, valuable stuff which they bag for presents. It's beautiful too; flies, "green and turquoise-black and silvery blue," hum round it "like excess sparks."

> Say Goong took my hand and led me to a cavernous shed black from the sun in my eyes. He pointed into the dark, which dark seemed solid and alive, heavy, moving, breathing. There were waves of dark skin over a hot and massive something that was snorting and stomping—the living night. In the day, here was where the night lived. Say Goong pointed up at a wide brown eye as high as the roof. . . . "Horse," he said. "Horse."

Then the horses were gone. No explanation. They must have existed; proof is found in the family photograph album, incontrovertible evidence for horses. But another relative, secure in the California fifties with a house and mortgage and a new car, was visited by his mother's ghost, dead of starvation; he had to withdraw all his savings and take her back to China. "Those of us in the first American generations have had to figure out how the invisible world the emigrants built around our childhoods fit in solid America." There are so many ways to tell stories, so many versions to imagine into truth. The American offspring are "always trying to get things straight, always trying to name the unspeakable." "I don't want to listen to any more of your stories," the adolescent girl screams at her mother. "You lie with stories. You won't tell me a story and then say, 'This is a true story,' or, 'This is just a story.' I can't tell what's real and what you make up." Do people really sell girls? Now MaMa says it's a joke. "The emigrants confused the gods by diverting their curses, misleading them with crooked streets and false names"; they confuse their children too.

> I had to leave home in order to see the world logically. . . . I learned to think that mysteries are for explanation. I enjoy the simplicity. Concrete pours out of my mouth to cover the forests with freeways and sidewalks. Give me plastics, periodical tables, t.v. dinners with vegetables no more complex than peas mixed with diced carrots. Shine floodlights into dark corners: no ghosts. . . . Now colors are gentler and fewer; smells are antiseptic . . . Soon I want to go to China and find out who's lying—the Communists who say they have food and jobs for everybody or the relatives who write that they have not the money to buy salt. . . . Did my grandmother really live to be ninety-nine? . . . Do the babies wear a Mao button like a drop of blood on their jumpsuits?

Long ago when MaMa talked story until the children fell asleep, the little girl "couldn't tell where the stories left off and the dreams began." Reading these books, no more can we. But they convince us that this story of "The Making of More Americans" can only be told as fabulous; though *The Woman Warrior*'s National Book Award was for non-fiction, the comparison which comes to mind is not with other memoirs but with a novel, with the super-reality of *One Hundred Years of Solitude*.

Listening to the aunt from China, the girl felt she had nothing to share: "I have no stories of equal pain." America, for all its injustice and exploitation, has been kinder than that, even to Chinese Americans, far kinder to most of us. It is hard, reading these books, not to feel we have paid a price, glad as we must be to pay it. Our colors too seem leached out, by affluence (even the poorest of us), by security (no matter how many anxieties we nurture). These are books to buy, to lend to friends, to give to adolescents in these days of Boat People and Cuban refugees. They are charged with the power of need—the writer's overwhelming need to talk story, to summon art to search out and understand that past in which the fabulous and the true can never be disentangled. But it is finally we who need the book, as Americans, and as Sojourners in a world of wonders.

Note

1. *The Woman Warrior: Memoirs of a Girlhood Among Ghosts,* by Maxine Hong Kingston. Knopf. $10.95. *China Men,* by Maxine Hong Kingston. Knopf. $10.95.

China Men

LINDA KAUFFMAN

Chinese-Americans, when you try to understand what things in you are Chinese, how do you separate what is peculiar to childhood, to poverty, insanities, one family, your mother who marked your growing with stories, from what is Chinese? What is Chinese tradition and what is the movies?

This is as haunting a question in *China Men* as it was in Maxine Hong Kingston's first book, *The Woman Warrior: Memoirs of a Girlhood Among Ghosts,* which won the National Book Award in 1976. Like her ancestors, Kingston is a weaver of fictions, embroidering history, myth, and legend in a remarkably complicated tapestry, deftly intertwining continents, cultures, centuries.

Kingston resembles Faulkner in her creation of a cosmos in miniature. Not only do many of the same characters reappear in both of her books, but they participate in creating facts, legends, and memories, never retelling a story twice in the same way. Thus, much of what seems autobiographical has been imaginatively reconstructed so many times that Kingston's works are best considered as fiction. Like Faulkner, she acknowledges the presence of the past but sees the impossibility of reconstructing the past with factual accuracy; instead she portrays the movement of the heart and the mind from memory to imagination.

Perceiving *China Men* and *The Woman Warrior* as parts of a whole heightens one's sense of the significance and scope of Kingston's achievement. Indeed, she has remarked that she thinks of these two works as "one big book. I was writing them more or less simultaneously. The final chapter in *China Men* began as a short story that I was working on before I even started *The Woman Warrior.*" Not only the same characters but the same motifs and images recur in both books: her themes are exile and wandering; madness, suffering, and betrayal; exploitation and endurance. Her quest is for unity as well as identity; she seeks to connect the separate strains of her experience and heritage by remembering, observing, writing, and listening.

From *The Georgia Review* 35 (Spring 1981): 205. Copyright 1981 by *The Georgia Review.* Reprinted by permission of *The Georgia Review.*

What is particularly brilliant about her technique is that the reader participates in the confusion and frustration which marked her own efforts of comprehension. Chinese, after all, is the "language of impossible stories." She complains to her parents in *The Woman Warrior* that their stories have no logic and that it is impossible to tell whether they are true stories or fiction. "They scramble me up," she says. "You lie with stories." Truth and fiction are equally elusive in *China Men* and the connection between episodes is less apparent. Of her style, she says

> I have come to feel that the myths that have been handed down from the past are not something that we should be working toward, so I try to deal with them quickly—get them over with—and then return to a realistic kind of present. This time I'm leaving it to my readers to figure out how the myths and the modern stories connect. Like me, and I'm assuming like other people, the characters in the book have to figure out how what they've been told connects—or doesn't connect—with what they experience.

It is all connected—from the mythical tale of Li Sao (the man doomed to exile because "people are too corrupt to deserve a man like this") to the story of the pacifist brother who is sent to Vietnam; from the legend of Maui the Trickster (who braids his mother's pubic hair and tries to steal immortality from Hina's womb) to the saga of the Grandfather of the Sierra Nevadas (who dangles over sheer cliffs, chips away at granite to make railroad tunnels, and masturbates while imagining that the valley below is a huge vagina).

Kingston's characters are authentic survivors and eccentrics with remarkably varied obsessions—with words, with nature, with Communism, with toil, with China. She charts her family's exodus from China to New York to Stockton, where her father's gambling and laundry businesses eventually enable him to buy his own home. The descriptions of the Chinese-American community and of her own childhood in the San Joaquin Valley during World War II are particularly moving and memorable.

What is perhaps most remarkable about Kingston's relatives in China and America are their extraordinary imaginative powers. Kingston speaks of going to China to talk to Cantonese, "who have always been revolutionaries, nonconformists, people with fabulous imaginations, people who invented the Gold Mountain. I want to discern what it is that makes people go West and turn into Americans. I want to compare China, a country I made up, with what country is really out there." Just as Kingston invents China, her ancestors invented America—transforming a land of hardship into a land of plenty and so igniting the imaginations of other peasants who in turn became sojourners and sufferers. While constructing the continent—from the cane fields of Hawaii to the railroads of Alaska, they also construct themselves, inventing new names like Worldster or Woodrow or Roosevelt or Edison. They become avid moviegoers, believing that Astaire and Chaplin will teach them how Americans should look and act. In *The Woman Warrior*, similarly, Kingston describes the difference between her Chinese personality and the "American-feminine speaking personality" which she invents to gain acceptance.

Rejection and abandonment are pervasive fears and realities in both books. One of the most poignant stories in *The Woman Warrior* concerns Moon Orchid, Maxine's aunt, who goes mad when her husband becomes a Westerner and abandons her, explaining that he had "turned into a different person. The new life around me was so complete; it pulled me away. You became people in a book I had read a long time ago." In *China Men,* Mad Sao is tormented by the starving ghost of the mother whom he abandoned. Chinese girl babies are abandoned, substituted for Japanese boys; brides are married by proxy to roosters when fiancés go to war or emigrate. Silence and secretiveness become a way of life, as does the fear of deportation, the dread of immigration officials, and the "drivings out" which accompany the completion of every herculean task in which Chinese labor was exploited—from gold mining in the Northwest and harvesting cane in the South to building the transcontinental railroads. (In the South, Chinese were expected to step off the sidewalk as Negroes did when whites passed by.)

As with poetry, Kingston's prose is the language of paradox. Fathers flee from war, the draft, and taxes in China, only to find themselves drafted in world wars and later to see their sons conscripted to fight Asians in Vietnam. Mothers teach daughters that they are both slaves and warriors. Maxine's father claims that all Chinese, if they are "authentic," know certain stories without being taught; they are "born talking them." Kingston both yearns to know and avoids asking her relatives what they suffered and how they endured. She respects their silence but despairs too: "I would never be able to talk with them; I have no stories of equal pain."

Even more paradoxical are her descriptions of cosmic creation and destruction as simultaneous visions: in a photo of the bombing of Hiroshima, she can almost hear the golden music of trumpets and drums, the music of the spheres. The lurching of the earth and the clanging of the poles mark China's changing, "as it does every thirty years in small cycles and every hundred years in large cycles." One of the most dazzling visions of cosmic unity is her great grandfather's, enroute to Hawaii: he sees his thoughts

connected like rivers, veins, roads, ships' lanes. New ideas sparked, and . . . he saw their connections to old ideas. . . . The world's people arranged themselves in parades, palaces, windows, roads, stadiums, attempting to form this bond. These men in the hold were trying to circumnavigate the world. Men build bridges and streets when there is already an amazing gold electric ring connecting every living being as surely as if we held hands, flippers and paws. . . . Everything was true. He was Lao Tse's great thinker, who can embrace opposing thoughts at the same moment.

To achieve such unity in opposition is Kingston's objective—for her readers and for herself. Her vision, finally, is one of affirmation, for after attempting to separate what is peculiar to her childhood, her family, her mother's stories, and Chinese tradition, after trying so hard to distinguish fact from fiction, she discovers the essential unity underlying all experience—Chinese and American, young and old, male and female. She learns, as she says in *The Woman Warrior,* to make her "mind large, as the universe is large, so that there is room for paradoxes." She enlarges the reader's mind as well with these elusive, contradictory, evocative myths and legends and tales which enable us to see creation and destruction at the same time, and to understand why the god of war is also the god of literature. We discover why the Chinese are haunted and why white people are ghosts; we gain a new perspective on the forging of America and on the preservation of the earth. Kingston expands our powers of perception, giving us new insight into the meaning of patience and fortitude by showing us how and why these remarkable men and women endured.

ESSAYS ON *CHINA MEN*

◆

Tang Ao in America:
Male Subject Positions in *China Men*

DONALD C. GOELLNICHT

Maxine Hong Kingston's second (auto)biographical fiction, *China Men,* opens with a brief section entitled "On Discovery," the initial sentence of which runs as follows: "Once upon a time, a man, named Tang Ao, looking for the Gold Mountain, crossed an ocean, and came upon the Land of Women" (3).[1] Tang Ao, emblematic of Chinese male sojourners in America (the Gold Mountain), finds instead the Land of Women, where he is caught and feminized—his feet bound, his ears pierced, his facial hair plucked, his face painted. The closing sentence of this introductory tale states: "Some scholars say that that country was discovered during the reign of Empress Wu (A.D. 694–705), and some say earlier than that, AD 441, and it was in North America" (5). With characteristic interrogation of all her sources, Hong Kingston gives us two possible dates for this mythic event, but the narrator seems certain that the location of the Land of Women "was in North America." Yet, when asked in an interview with Paula Rabinowitz to compare *The Woman Warrior* with *China Men,* Hong Kingston responds: "Historically, of course, the men [of her family in particular, and Chinese male sojourners in and immigrants to America in general] went to a different country without their families, and so they had their adventures by themselves. It was as if they went to a men's country and they had men's stories" (179).[2]

How do we reconcile these apparently contradictory statements? To begin with, contradictory statements, or statements that contest one another, are not antithetical to Hong Kingston's art; they are integral to it.[3] But there is a sense in which no contradiction exists here: historically, only *men* from China were allowed into America for work—usually manual labor on plantations, in mines, on railroad construction, or in fishing; only the wives of a few treaty merchants, of students, and of teachers could enter America freely until 1952, when a provision of the Immigration and Nationality Act enabled "for the first time Chinese women . . . to immigrate under the same condi-

From *Reading the Literatures of Asian American Literature,* ed. Shirley Geok-lin Lim and Amy Ling. Philadelphia: Temple University Press, 1992; 191–212. Copyright © 1992 by Temple University Press. Reprinted by permission of Temple University Press.

tions as men" (*China Men* 158). By then, the restrictive and exclusionary laws instituted by the dominant white culture against the Chinese had emasculated these immigrant men, forcing them into "feminine" subject positions of powerlessness and silence, into "bachelor" Chinatowns devoid of women, and into "feminized" jobs that could not be filled by women.[4] It is no accident, then, that Tang Ao remains helpless to change his fate of becoming a courtesan and that, as they prepare to pierce his ears, the women joke that they are "sewing your lips together" (4), silence being presented as part of the female condition. Thus the "men's country" of the Gold Mountain, the place men went to find fame and fortune, the "country with no women" (54), becomes the Land of Women, a site where a legalized racism turns "men" into "women."[5] In this brief introduction, Hong Kingston has adapted a story from the early-nineteenth-century Chinese novel *Flowers in the Mirror* in order to mythologize the historical and political situation faced by China Men in America during the latter half of the nineteenth century and the first half of the twentieth.[6] (This situation is given a historical, rather than mythic, treatment at the center of the book—a prominent location—in the section entitled "The Laws," to which I will return.)

The significance of the privileged position that the Tang Ao legend occupies at the start of the text cannot, I believe, be underestimated. Like the Fa Mu Lan legend in *The Woman Warrior*, it acts as a kind of controlling myth—treated neither entirely reverentially nor entirely critically—for the rest of the text. Fa Mu Lan, the woman warrior, represents the attempts by women to break out of gendered positions, to cross over into "male" territory. Tang Ao is also involved in a gender crossover, but one representing a "demotion" in gender hierarchies and one forced on him rather than one willingly adopted: no one, it seems, wants to fill the "feminine" gender role.

But I should also observe that "White Tigers" (the story that presents the Fa Mu Lan myth) does not introduce *The Woman Warrior*; "No Name Woman," the story of Maxine's aunt—pregnant by a man not her husband, ostracized, and suicidal—does. The Tang Ao story also has affinities with this opening story of the earlier text. The no-name aunt had been affected by "the rare urge [to go] west [which] had fixed upon our [Maxine's] family, and so [she] crossed boundaries not delineated in space" (*Woman Warrior* 9) by disobeying patriarchy, while Tang Ao "crossed an ocean" to the West and had his gender changed. Just as the no-name aunt is forced into a position of powerlessness and silence, both physically and linguistically (for her indiscretions, she is driven to suicide and denied a name) by the traditions of Chinese patriarchy that deny her existence once she has transgressed its laws, so too Tang Ao the sojourner finds himself forced into a position of powerlessness and silence by the Laws of the Ruling Fathers (the white majority). In this second introductory story ("On Discovery"), the gender inequity of the first ("No Name Woman") becomes intensified through its links to a general situation of racial inequity, as the rest of *China Men* makes clear. The feminization of

Tang Ao acts metonymically for the emasculation of China Men in white America.[7]

To say that Hong Kingston discloses—for her feminist and mainstream white audience—the legalized humiliation and degradation suffered by China Men at the hands of the dominant race is not to say, however, that she wishes simply to recuperate and valorize the traditional Chinese culture, with its base in patriarchal Confucianism, that was undermined by America's exclusionary immigration laws. This is a point that two critics writing on this topic seem to have missed. Linda Ching Sledge, in a valuable early article, points out: "The inversion of sexual roles [in *China Men*] . . . illuminates the internal tensions accumulating in [sojourner] families as a result of the erosion of sex differentiation in the household. The strain on husband, wife, and children as a result of the father's 'emasculation' or failure as provider is clear" (10). She goes on to conclude, however, that Hong Kingston, in the final analysis, gives

> an overwhelmingly heroic account of sojourner family life. . . . Through-out *China Men,* the continuing hold of certain fundamental aspects of the primordial Confucian ideal of family unity, economic interdependence, and mutual help is maintained. . . . Rather than undermining the ancient notion of family accord, the scenes show that faith in the patriarchal family system . . . remains the ideal against which the daughter's [Maxine's] more modern definitions are measured. (13–14)

Alfred Wang also discusses the triumph of Hong Kingston's male protagonists over legalized discrimination and implicitly praises the survival of traditional Chinese culture by linking her *"Men Warriors par excellence"* to "Guan Goong, Liu Pei, and Chang Fei" (27), the military heroes of patriarchal Chinese literature and legend.[8]

The impulse to champion the survival of Chinese American family life in the face of repeated, conscious attempts to destroy it is both understandable and admirable; but Sledge and Wang have fallen victim, I believe, to thinking in binary oppositions: if Hong Kingston lambasts—as she does—the white racists for their behavior and attitudes, then, in her sympathy for the hero-victims, she must be supportive of the traditional family structures that have come under fire. This kind of thinking is anathema to Hong Kingston's feminist argument, which critiques all systems that establish social relationships as hierarchies of power and which is perfectly capable of a both/and approach instead of an either/or one. Hong Kingston can both deplore the emasculation of China Men by mainstream America *and* critique the Confucian patriarchy of traditional family life, as King-Kok Cheung has recognized. Of the Tang Ao story, Cheung writes: "I cannot but see this legend as double-edged, pointing not only to the mortification of Chinese men in the new world but also to the subjugation of women both in old China and in America. . . . The opening myth suggests that the author objects as strenuously to the patriarchal practices of her ancestral culture as to the racist treatment of her forefathers in their adopted country" (240). It is this double-edged antiracist, antisexist sword wielded by the narrator that I wish to examine here.[9]

As mentioned above, one of the most debilitating aspects of the exclusionary acts for Chinese and Chinese American men was the banning of female immigrants: "1924: An Immigration Act passed by Congress specifically excluded 'Chinese women, wives, and prostitutes.' Any American who married a Chinese woman lost his citizenship; any Chinese man who married an American woman caused her to lose her citizenship" (*China Men* 156). The deliberate agenda of using sexual deprivation to prevent any increase in the Chinese American population and to undermine the virility of Chinese and Chinese American men is obvious. Through such discrimination, the "Oriental threat" could be contained by mainstream culture.

The narrator's attacks on the dominant culture's laws against female immigration, and her profoundly sympathetic grasp of the effects of such emasculation on male immigrants and sojourners, emerge clearly in almost every "talk-story." With Bak Goong, the great-grandfather, for example, it manifests itself in his imagined—all these ancestral stories are imagined by the female narrator—biting sarcasm. His comment upon being forbidden to talk while working on the Hawaiian sugar plantation is revealing: "If I knew I had to take a vow of silence, . . . I would have shaved off my hair and become a monk. Apparently we've taken a vow of chastity too. Nothing but roosters in this flock" (100). In contrast, Ah Goong, the railway grandfather, expresses his sense of loss of women through nocturnal fantasies on the myth of Altair and Vega, the Spinning Girl and the Cowboy transformed into stars and allowed to meet only once a year across the bridge of the Milky Way. The pathos of these meditations becomes heartrending: "He felt his heart breaking of loneliness at so much blue-black space between star and star. The railroad he was building would not lead him to his family" (129).

The wielding of such pathos and sarcasm in defense of China Men without women does not, however, prevent the female narrator from injecting her stories with more subtle barbs aimed at the very Confucian life these men long for. For example, in "On Mortality," a story of how a man named Tu Tzu-chun was offered immortality by a Taoist monk if he could pass the test of remaining silent when faced with various "illusions," one of those testing illusions is the threat of becoming a woman: "He heard gods and goddesses talking about him, 'This man is too wicked to be reborn a man. Let him be born a woman' " (120). Thus, in a more extreme form of the Tang Ao myth, Tu changes not only gender position but also his biological sex: "He discovered that he had been reborn a deaf-mute female named Tu." Again, as with Tang Ao, here muteness/silence is held up by patriarchy as an ideal of womanhood: "When she became a woman, her parents married her to a man named Lu, who at first did not mind [her muteness]. 'Why does she need to talk,' said Lu, 'to be a good wife? Let her set an example for women' " (121). This female silence is broken, however, by Tu-as-woman when Lu deliberately injures her child. In a play on the Western myth of the Fall caused by woman, here humanity loses the opportunity to gain immortality because maternal love (Tu-transformed-into-mother) disobeys a patriarchal (in this case monastic Taoist) injunction to silence. But while the Edenic myth presents Eve's disobedience as the cause of human suffering, here Hong Kingston displays maternal love as a superior attribute to immortality; it is an emotion even men (Tu-as-woman) must learn, for this love makes us intensely human, mortal, superior to the gods of patriarchy. Once more, the narrative subverts our expectations about gender roles.

Throughout the text, religion reveals itself as one of the powerful institutions of the masculine symbolic order that entrenches male privilege. Another pillar of this patriarchal structure is the law, in which sexism becomes allied with racism.[10]

"The Laws" section has been rightly praised for its "purely factual" account of the discrimination leveled against the Chinese who came to America, for its accurate record of legal history presented through "substantial documentary material" (Sledge 5–6) that nevertheless stands out as anomalous in Hong Kingston's variegated/multivalent/polyphonous narrative.[11] Yet there is also a sense in which "The Laws" is ironic. Sometimes the irony surfaces bitterly from the facts themselves, as in this juxtaposition: "Though the Chinese were filling and leveeing the San Joaquin Delta for thirteen cents a square yard, building the richest agricultural land in the world, they were prohibited from owning land or real estate" (153). More subtly, though, the section carries an ironic undertone: by imitating the monological voice of authorizing History—the history imposed by the dominant culture that made the laws—this section uncovers both the dullness of this voice and its deafness to other, competing voices, those of the minorities suffering legalized discrimination. This undertone of irony becomes most resonant when Hong Kingston quotes from the exclusionary laws enacted by federal, state, and municipal legislatures against Chinese workers and immigrants, especially when we measure these "laws" against the "invented" biographies of China Men that make up the rest of the text. Paradoxically, the imagined/fictional history proves more truthful than the official version.

There is also irony in the position of "The Laws." It occupies the middle of the book, a centric position that would appear to be one of (legalized) authority; yet this centric authority of American law is subverted and contested by the "eccentric" or marginal, but richly imaginative, stories of China Men that surround it. China Men lament the loss of their centric place when they come to America; but this "eccentric" text itself, in auto-representational fashion, illustrates the power of the margins, despite all the attempts to limit/ eliminate that power.

As Alfred Wang observes: "No other racial group have been subjected to worse *legalized* personal, collective, and sexual deprivation than the Chinese male immigrants between 1868 . . . and 1952" (18). Wang is right to stress the legalized nature of this discrimination, for the law constitutes in many ways the center of the masculine symbolic order, the institution that inscribes and entrenches masculine privilege. The evidence presented here, however, indicates that, Lacanian theories of gender acquisition aside, the law does not encode the same subject position—traditionally a position of power, as in Confucian law as well—for all men. Instead, positions of power are reserved for the Ruling Fathers (men of the dominant group, white men), while men of other racial groups are forced into "feminine" subject positions of "inferiority."

The social and psychological repercussions of the exclusion laws on Chinese and Chinese American men were tremendous, and they have been documented by a number of historians and sociologists.[12] Elaine Kim has pointed out that with job opportunities scarce and women absent in the "bachelor" Chinatowns—ghettoes where Chinese and Chinese American men were forced to live—some of these men ended up, against their will, in traditionally "women's" jobs, as waiters, launderers, servants, and cooks. In "The Father from China" Hong Kingston presents her father and his partners as engaged in their laundry business for long periods each day—a business considered so low and debased that, in their songs, they associate it with the washing of menstrual blood, which links their occupation back to Tang Ao, whose foot-binding bandages smelled like menstrual rags when he was forced to wash them (4). The laundry partners sing as they iron:

> The laundry business is low, you say,
> Washing out blood that stinks like brass—
> Only a Chinaman can debase himself so.[13]
> (63)

At night, these "bachelors" engage in more "woman's work": they cook their own meals and hold eating races, with the loser washing the dishes. The absence of wives is stressed, but this has to do as much with the difficulty of taking on the menial tasks women would usually perform as with a sense of emotional deprivation. Once Brave Orchid—Ed/Baba's wife from China—arrives in New York, the traditional roles resume: she cooks, cleans, and washes for the men. Once again, the female narrator sympathizes with these fathers but also critiques traditional gender roles.

Most criticism is leveled, however, at the dominant racist society. In what appears a deliberate attempt to trap China Men in the stereotypical "feminine" positions it had assigned them, American society perpetuated the myth of the effeminate or androgynous "chinaman," while erasing the figure of the "masculine" plantation worker or railroad construction worker.[14] We are all familiar with the stereotype of the Chinese laundryman or waiter, but few know that the railroads so essential to development in North America were built with large numbers of Chinese laborers, who endured tremendous hardship and isolation in the process, or that Hawaiian sugar plantations were carved out of tropical forests with Chinese labor. Hong Kingston presents a vivid example of one of these racist stereotypes in the figure of Chop Chop, who appears in the military comic book *Blackhawk:*

> Chop Chop was the only Blackhawk who did not wear a blue-black pilot's uniform with yellow and black insignia. He wore slippers instead of boots, pajamas with his undershirt showing at the tails, white socks, an apron; he carried a cleaver and wore a pigtail. . . . Fat and half as tall as the other Blackhawks, who were drawn like regular human beings, Chop Chop looked like a cartoon. It was unclear whether he was a boy or a little man. (274)

"Tall dragon ladies" are not attracted to Chop Chop as they are to the other Blackhawks.

Hong Kingston seeks to redress this wrong of stereotyping and historical erasure, not by a simple reversal of the figure of laundryman/cook and that of railroad laborer/plantation worker, "feminine" and "masculine," respectively, but by a disruption of this gendered binary opposition—as we find in the Tang Ao and Tu Tzu-chun myths—which shows both roles and both job types to entail hardships and rewards. To this end she presents us with a variety of China Men from her family: Bak Goong, her "Great Grandfather of the Sandalwood Mountains," who endured the physical hardships of being a sugar plantation worker in Hawaii but who was also "a fanciful, fabulous man" (110); Ah Goong, her "Grandfather of the Sierra Nevada Mountains," a railway construction worker who risked his life from a suspended basket to set gunpowder charges in the mountains but whose intense loneliness at being a married "bachelor" finds expression in his nocturnal reveries on the myth of the Spinning Girl and her Cowboy (129); and BaBa, her father, the Chinese scholar who becomes an American laundryman. These generations of men are presented in all their pain and dignity.

The trajectories Maxine imagines for BaBa's journey to the West in "The Father from China," be it the legal journey to San Francisco or the illegal one to New York, bear striking resemblances to the life journeys women had to go through in Old China. First, because of the discriminatory American laws, prospective sojourners to the Gold Mountain had to "change" their parentage, had to be "willing to be adopted by Gold Mountain Sojourners who were legal citizens of the United States" (46), just as a girl had to give up her own family and become part of her husband's when she married.[15] This family change for the purpose of illegal immigration also necessitated a change of name for the sojourner—Maxine's father had "unusual luck" in that his "bought papers had a surname which was the same as our own last name" (47)—a situation faced by women upon marriage. And like a Chinese bride who travels to her in-laws' house in a closed palanquin, unable to see where she is going, the father in one version of the immigration story travels by ship in a sealed crate from which his view is almost entirely restricted.[16] As he crosses over to a new world that he cannot control, he suffers the same sense of entrapment, fear, isolation, and apprehension for the future that a bride might experience as she travels to her new life with a man and a family unfamiliar to her.

The experience of powerlessness and humiliation that these "emasculated" China Men must endure becomes emphasized even further by their physical location on a floor below the Chinese women on Angel Island: "Diabolical, inauspicious beginning—to be trodden over by women. 'Living under women's legs' said the superstitious old-fashioned men from the backward villages. . . . No doubt the demons had deliberately planned this humiliation" (55). Once more, the narrator sympathizes with the immigrant men in their humiliation, which they presume to be a plot by the dominant white society, but she also mocks their feelings of superiority over Chinese women.

Once in America, the treatment China Men received at the hands of the dominant culture was remarkably similar to that suffered by women of all races for centuries: they were disenfranchised (142, 155), denied the right to become U.S. citizens; "they were prohibited from owning land or real estate" (153); they had no voice to "talk in court" (142); and they were forced to attend separate schools (156). As the white male order lost some of its legal power over one subordinate group—women—in the late nineteenth and early twentieth centuries, it turned to racial minorities to reassert such privilege. Hong Kingston exposes the injustice of privilege based on either race or gender.

The psychological effects of the dominant society's forcing minority men into "feminine" subject positions are perhaps even more profound, and it is here that Hong Kingston's explorations are especially cogent and incisive. We might expect that, having experienced a form of entrenched legal and personal discrimination based entirely on race, Chinese American men would be sympathetic to, and supportive of, the plight of Chinese American women, who have suffered doubly: as a racial minority and as women crossing between two patriarchal cultures, the traditional Chinese and the modern American. Linda Ching Sledge suggests such rapprochement between the sexes when she claims that "the myth [of Tang Ao] also speaks of the growing equality of the sexes as a result of the male's adventuring into unknown territories" (9). But, while Chinese women do assert their independence in the absence of sojourning men, Hong Kingston shows no acceptance of gender equality by the men. Quite the opposite is indicated: having been ground down themselves by white men, having been forced into "feminine" subject positions, Chinese American men often seek to reassert their lost patriarchal power by denigrating a group they perceive as weaker than themselves: Chinese American women.

Ironically, the strongest male sympathy for, and understanding of, women arises not in modern America but in traditional China, where Maxine's paternal grandfather so desired a daughter after producing three sons that he traded his fourth son, the valuable scholar, for a neighbor's daughter. Within the norms of Confucian society, this act is considered insane, not only by men but even more so by women (15–21).[17] It is the grandfather in China who blames his penis for failing to give him a daughter, thus attacking the symbol of the phallus that constitutes the very center of patriarchal law. The maternal grandfather from China also "was an unusual man in that he valued girls; he taught all his daughters how to read and write" (30). Hong Kingston thus subverts our expectations that life in China would have been more rigidly patriarchal than life in America, perhaps suggesting in the process that Chinese traditions were more rigorously observed by the immigrant community in America out of a sense of nostalgia for the lost homeland.

The father in America, having been forced into "feminine" subject positions as outlined above, lapses into silence—itself a state associated with the "feminine"—breaking that silence only to utter curses against women as a means of releasing his sense of frustration and powerlessness in racist America. The narrator Maxine addresses her father with one of the few facts based on her personal experience in the first half of the narrative: "You were angry. You scared us. Every day we listened to you swear, 'Dog vomit. Your mother's cunt. Your mother's smelly cunt.' . . . Obscenities. I made a wish that you only meant gypsies and not women in general" (12). Maxine then narrates a story of BaBa being tricked by gypsies and harassed by the police, an incident that results in his venting his rage on the women of the family. She traces her father's abuse of Chinese women back to his feelings of emasculation in America: "We knew that it was to feed us you had to endure demons and physical labor. You screamed wordless male screams that jolted the house upright and staring in the middle of the night" (13).

BaBa's simmering rage, as mentioned above, takes two forms: one, the verbal and physical abuse of women (later Maxine relates a memory of her or her sister being beaten by her father); the other, silence. This is not a positive silence but the silence of resignation that signals withdrawal and humiliation, the inability to articulate his own subject position so that he is doomed to the one—that of inscrutable, passive "chinaman"—created for him by the dominant society. It is also a form of silence as abusive power over Chinese American women. As the daughter-narrator observes: "Worse than the swearing and the nightly screams were your silences when you punished us by not talking." Rather than empathize with Chinese women, who have been silenced by the symbolic order of patriarchy for centuries, unable or forbidden to inscribe their own identities, China Men like BaBa seek to punish Chinese women with a silence that denies them a linguistically constituted identity: "You rendered us invisible, gone. . . . You kept up a silence for weeks and months. . . . You say with the few words and the silences: No stories. No past. No China" (14).

In her interview with Paula Rabinowitz, Hong Kingston expresses these same sentiments, but in a light and positive tone, when she says: "In fact, I wrote the characters so that the women have memories and the men don't have memories. They don't remember anything. The character of my father, for example, has no memory. He has no stories of the past. . . . He is so busy making up the present, which he has to build, that he has no time for continuity from the past. It did seem that the men were people of action" (180). Perhaps because this interview was conducted long after the writing of the book, which seems to have had a cathartic effect on Hong Kingston, here we find none of the feminist anger of *China Men,* where the daughter pleads with the silent father: "What I want from you is for you to tell me that those curses are only common Chinese sayings. That you did not mean to make me sicken at being female" (14). Of course, the personal intention of the father in these utterances is not important; the fact remains that the symbolic order of Confucian patriarchy inscribes for women these positions of inferiority, degradation, nonbeing, and BaBa's self-hatred stems from seeing his position in racist America mirrored in the subjection of women in traditional Chinese culture.

To be fair, Hong Kingston does not always present the father as morose and abusive in America. In a temporal reversal that may constitute a deliberate attempt to ameliorate the reader's and narrator's opinion of him, she presents earlier, more attractive memories of the father in the second half of the text, in "The American Father." Here he appears, not as a slave, but as a kind, gentle man who takes time to explain dark, mysterious places (the attic, the cellar with its well) to his daughter. In these early memories, the father emerges, along with the mother, as a hero of endurance, until he loses his gambling house job and deteriorates from the man in "power suits" to the ninety-pound weakling. Sympathy accrues to the father under this new form of "emasculation"—he is no longer the breadwinner—but this sympathy becomes severely compromised when the incident that galvanizes him out of his depression turns out to be a misogynous one: the beating of one of his daughters, either Maxine or her sister, as a means of venting his rage (253). This assertion of male power arouses him from his torpor, and he opens a new laundry; but such a positive result neither justifies his violence against women nor diminishes the fact that women have suffered for centuries what he now suffers.

That BaBa's self-hatred originates in his feelings of identity with Chinese women becomes apparent in Maxine's description of her father as the man "who inked each piece of our own laundry with the word *Center*" (15). In the face of silence, this inscription of the Chinese character *zhong,* center or middle, signifies BaBa's desire to return physically to China, the Middle Kingdom, *Zhong Guo,* but also his desire to reestablish his centric position of masculine authority, to break out of the "eccentric" (15) position of marginality into which China Men have been forced in America but which Chinese women have always occupied in a patriarchal culture.[18]

Ironically, BaBa, in his longing to recuperate his centric position of Confucian scholar—signaled by his calligraphy on the family laundry—fails to recognize the destabilizing power of an eccentric point of view as a place from which to critique the mainstream through subversive tactics, a kind of guerrilla periphery. This is a lesson that his daughter, the narrator, has learned extremely well—as this autorepresentational fiction, written from her double margin with amazing power, attests.[19] With a double irony, though, she uses her marginal vantage point, not only to critique the racist mainstream for its treatment of her forefathers but also to avenge herself on those very forefathers, the malestream, for their sexist treatment of Chinese women.[20] This text emerges, then, as both an act of compassion by the female narrator toward the father and a kind of subversive triumph over him. While he attempts, and fails, to deny her an identity with his imposition of silence, *she* imagines his-story, granting him a linguistically constituted identity in this text. It is, by and large, a positive identity, and she does request that he correct any mistakes she makes in the narrative (15); but his voice never intrudes to correct hers, so that the text, his-story, remains her creation. Thus, feminist subversive strategies prove more effective than the father's worn-out desire to return to male privilege and centric heroism. The father himself, along with other immigrants, seems to have recognized this situation when, on Angel Island, he and the other poets who covered the walls of this institution concluded that they "had come to a part of the world not made for honor, where 'a hero cannot use his bravery' " (55). The desire to employ masculine heroic tactics is there (56–57), but means and opportunities remain nonexistent for these imprisoned men.[21]

Not surprisingly, then, "feminine" strategies of subversion from the periphery, from positions of apparent powerlessness—"the skill of . . . deceits" (60)—are the very ones that brought success to the forefathers in their times of oppression.[22] Bak Goong, for example, finds himself in a "feminine" subject position when the "demon" owners of the Hawaiian sugar plantation impose silence on the laborers: "How was he to marvel adequately, voiceless? He needed to cast his voice out to catch ideas" (100). He rebels first in a direct fashion, singing instead of talking, but this leads to punishment. He then finds success through a form of triumphant deceit in which he speaks indirectly, disguising his words in his cough: "The deep, long, loud coughs, barking and wheezing, were almost as satisfying as shouting. He let out scolds disguised as coughs. . . . He did not even mind the despair, which dispelled upon his speaking it" (104).

Even the coughs cannot dispel the despair completely, however; Bak Goong must eventually join the other China Men in a group therapy session of shouting their desires, concerns, fears into a hole in the earth: "They had dug an ear into the world, and were telling the earth their secrets" (117). Their most intense desire is for "Home. Home. Home. Home." The attempt to fill an orifice with words, to find comfort in mother earth, and the desire for home, the domestic, love, the mother country/culture—" 'Hello down there in China!' they shouted. 'Hello, Mother' "—reveal their psychological and sexual frustration caused by the exclusion laws against Chinese women.

The great-grandfather's shouting incident harks back in the narrative, and forward temporally, to the father's debilitating silence; it also anticipates Ah Goong's even more ingenious solution to the loss and frustration caused by emasculation: he fulfills his sexual desire by "fucking the world" from his suspended basket, setting off seminal explosions (133). Again, the desire to return to the mother is clear. It is a desire shared by Ed/BaBa, who identifies with the wily mother, "the kind parent" (71) in the movie *Young Tom Edison*. In fact, Ed explains to Brave Orchid that "this cunning, resourceful, successful inventor, Edison, was who he had named himself after."

Ed may wish for the cunning of an Edison, but what his forefathers seem to have had in common that he lacks is a strong element of fantasy or the fabulous to mix with their cunning and deceit: "[Ah Goong] did not buy [a lottery ticket for a visiting prostitute]. He took out his penis under his blanket or bared it in the woods and thought about nurses and princesses" (144). The objects remain those of male fantasies, but from the start Maxine associates the ability to fantasize or fabulate with women and with Cantonese: "BaBa became susceptible to the stories men told, which were not fabulations like the fairy tales and ghost stories told by women" (41); "I want to talk to Cantonese, who have always been revolutionaries, nonconformists, people with fabulous imaginations, people who invented the Gold Mountain" (87). The reality of "emasculation" and discrimination on the Gold Mountain has destroyed her father's ability to fabulate, however; he has "no stories" to tell, and he dismisses dreams as fermentation, rot: " 'Fermenting dreams' said BaBa. 'Dreams fermenting.' I heard in his scorn and words how dreams ferment the way yeast and mold do, how dreams are like fungus" (193).

I have said that *China Men* is to some extent an act of revenge on the father; but it is also an act of attempted reconciliation between daughter and father, just as *The Woman Warrior* was an act of reconciliation between daughter and mother. Unfortunately, it cannot match the competing dialogue between mother and daughter that the earlier fiction attained, for the father has no voice; therefore, it must be a pure gift, an act of restoring something he lacks. It is the restoration, though, not of the phallus he feels he lacks in white America but of the imagination America has robbed him of by "defeating" his dreams and by excluding him from its history. In a sense, he does not need a restoration of phallic power: the filial attendance of his children and the attentions of Brave Orchid demonstrate his "masculinity." Furthermore, he has the traditional Confucian solution to securing a place in history: procreation, family endurance, "the making of more Americans." What he needs to be a complete being is his-story, the very gift Maxine tries to give him in this text of her fantasies, her imaginings, her fabulations.

Ironically, there is another sense in which America is the Land of Women for Chinese immigrants: with the absence of men—through sojourning and immigration—from their villages in Guangdong, China, women became independent, controlling their own fate and giving voice to their own stories.[23] Thus, when they are permitted to immigrate to America to join their husbands, it is Chinese and Chinese American women who become the sources of "talk-story" in this new land, the Land of Women. "Talk-stories" have been a source of empowerment for Chinese women; the gift Hong Kingston attempts to give her father is polyphonous fabulation as a powerful form of shared rebuttal to the monological voice of dominant white history, which has attempted to erase Asian American experience. She challenges and disrupts the symbolic order with the semiotic.[24] She thus (re)claims for her forefathers the father land, America, the Gold Mountain they came to conquer, (re)claims this sublime goal not in any masculinist military sense—"The Brother in Vietnam" makes her pacifist ideology clear—but as a word warrior, a Fa Mu Lan of the pen instead of the sword. Unlike Fa Mu Lan, however, she can never return to being the filial daughter. She cannot even afford a return to Chinese legend to discover a figure like the poet Tsai Yen, who acted as the vehicle for tortured reconciliation with her mother and mother culture in *The Woman Warrior.* Instead, reclaiming the Gold Mountain involves putting her faith in the next generation of Chinese American men, "the young men who listen" to the stories of China Men, and whom she watches (308) to see if they have benefited from fabulation as she herself gives up trying to establish the facts of any particular version of how China Men discovered the Gold Mountain. She has given the gift of various fabulous versions of his-story in her text; one suspects that she now listens for the next generation of young men to respond with their own dialogical voices, to lay claim to their America.

Notes

1.   All quotations are from Maxine Hong Kingston, *China Men* (New York: Knopf, 1980); page numbers appear in the text.

2.   Rabinowitz summarizes: "One might roughly say that China is a landscape inhabited, at least in the narratives, by the women and their myths, and the Gold Mountain, America, is really where the men are and that's where history is" (180).

3.   Hong Kingston's description of Bak Goong, her great-grandfather, on opium could apply equally to her art: "Everything was true. He was Lao Tse's great thinker, who can embrace opposing thoughts at the same moment" (*China Men* 95). The experience of crossing between cultures—Bak Goong was sailing from China to Hawaii when he smoked opium—seems to enhance this ability to appreciate multivalent truth.

4.   For a succinct summary of social conditions in "bachelor" Chinatowns and the literary depictions of these Chinatowns, see Kim, *Asian American Literature,* 91–121. Elsewhere,

Kim writes: "Prevented from establishing families in the United States by exclusion and anti-miscegenation laws the Chinese American community was largely a community of aging men with wives in China, to whom they usually sent regular remittances from their laundry and restaurant labor. It was not until 1970 that the balance between the sexes among Chinese Americans approached the American norm" ("Asian American Writers" 53).

    5.   I employ the terms "men" and "women" in this context, not to denote biological sex, but in Kristeva's sense of a subject position in culture and language that can be occupied, at times, by men as well as women. Quotation marks indicate such usage. See Kristeva, "Women Can Never Be Defined."

    6.   I am grateful to Amy Ling for pointing out in a letter to me the origin of the Tang Ao story in "an early 19th century novel by Li Ju-chen, translated by Lin Tai-yi as *Flowers in the Mirror* (Berkeley: University of California Press, 1965). But as Hong Kingston modified the legend of Fa (Hua) Mu Lan, conflating it with the story of the general Yueh Fei, so she changed this story slightly. It was Tang Ao's brother-in-law, Master Lin, who landed in the Country of Women and had all those tortures inflicted on him." The shift in characters does not affect Hong Kingston's major concern, which is that a man experienced this situation.

    7.   Before going further, I should stress that, although Asian American men have been forced into feminine subject positions in work and social situations, there remains a significant area of distinction between their lives and those of minority women in general: men do not usually experience the threat of sexual victimization, of bodily assault, faced in minority women. As Houston Baker points out, such genuine fear of "the [white] patriarch-as-rapist" is a "dramatically foregrounded *topos* of the [black] woman's account" of the "economics of slavery" (54), and similar motifs abound in the narratives of other minority women.

    8.   Hong Kingston does link Ah Goong, her grandfather, and herself as writer-avenger, to Guan Goong: "Guan Goong, the God of War, also God of War and Literature, had come to America—Guan Goong, Grandfather Guan, our own ancestor of writers and fighters, of actors and gamblers, and avenging executioners who mete out justice" (149–50). Ah Goong's triumph, however, is decidedly antimilitary and unheroic: he becomes "a homeless wanderer, a shiftless, dirty, jobless man with matted hair, ragged clothes, and fleas all over his body"; but he also manages to have an American "child of his own" despite the antimiscegenation laws (150–51). His triumph is not military but pro-creative, just as Hong Kingston's vengeance on behalf of her forefathers is literary rather than physical. Once more Hong Kingston disrupts the expectations aroused by our traditional hierarchized binary oppositions.

    9.   A more psychological reading might stress that two allegories of desire collide in this text: the desire for the recuperation of a lost and idealized family structure (a traditional family romance) and the desire for revision of the traditional family structure to enable the daughter's liberation from patriarchy.

    10.   Frank Chin and Jeffery Paul Chan observe: "For the Chinese, [the white majority] invented an instrument of racist policy that was a work of pure genius, in that it was not an overtly hostile expression of anti-Chinese sentiment, yet still reinforced the stereotype and generated self-contempt and humiliation among generations of Chinese and Chinese-Americans, who after having been conditioned into internalizing the white supremacist Gospel of Christian missionaries, looked on themselves as failures, instead of victims of racism. This wondrous instrument was *the law*" ("Racist Love" 71). Chin and Chan make no reference, however, to the misogynous aspects of such legislation; in fact, their own discourse brims with misogynous rage.

    11.   Hong Kingston herself has explained "The Laws" in this way: "The mainstream culture doesn't know the history of Chinese-Americans, which has been written and written well. The ignorance makes a tension for me, and in the new book [*China Men*] I just couldn't take it anymore. So all of a sudden, right in the middle of the stories, plunk—there is an eight-page section of pure history. It starts with the Gold Rush and goes right through the various exclusion acts, year by year. There are no characters in it. It really affects the shape of the book and it might look quite clumsy" (Pfaff 26).

12. See the studies in "Part Two: Assimilation and Sex Roles" of *Asian Americans: Psychological Perspectives,* ed. Sue and Wagner, as well as Reed Ueda, "The Americanization and Education of Japanese-Americans."

13. The sense of debasement here stems not only from the perception that laundry work is "women's work" but also from the knowledge that white society considers this work humiliatingly menial. Paul C. P. Siu, in *The Chinese Laundryman: A Study of Social Isolation,* quotes the attitudes of whites: "My opinion of him [the Chinese American] is quite natural so long as he remains only a laundryman. . . . He is all right as long as he stays in his place and does not try to do too much"; "The Chinks are all right if they remain in their place. I don't mind their working in the laundry business, but they should not go higher than that" (quoted in Kim, *Asian American Literature* 99).

14. Frank Chin and Jeffery Paul Chan point out: "The white stereotype of the Asian is unique in that it is the only racial stereotype completely devoid of manhood. Our nobility is that of an efficient housewife. At our worst we are contemptible because we are womanly, effeminate, devoid of all the traditionally masculine qualities of originality, daring, physical courage, creativity" ("Racist Love" 68). See also Wang 19–20, and Cheung 236–37; Cheung both employs and deconstructs Chin and Chan's argument, drawing out its sexist and homophobic tendencies.

15. In *The Woman Warrior* Hong Kingston quotes traditional Chinese sayings about girls which indicate that their parents consider them to be the potential daughters of their future husbands' families: " 'There's no profit in raising girls. Better to raise geese than girls.' . . . 'When you raise girls, you're raising children for strangers' " (54).

16. A superb recent example of the literal and figurative limitations placed on the view of a traditional Chinese bride is found in the film *Red Sorghum* (China 1987; directed by Zhang Yimou). As the bride travels to her new husband, the camera forces us to see largely from her restricted perspective *inside* the sedan.

17. A classic example of women who have imbibed the values of the Confucian patriarchal system comes in the figure of Mad Sao's mother, who writes from China to her American son: "Why don't you do your duty? I order you to come back. It's all those daughters, isn't it? . . . Leave them. Come back alone. You don't need to save enough money to bring a litter of females. What a waste to bring girls all the way back here to sell anyway" (*China Men* 172).

18. A more clearly sympathetic portrait of a good man's failure to reestablish his centric position appears in Hong Kingston's narration of "The Li Sao: An Elegy," in which Ch'u Yuan the poet "had to leave the Center; he roamed in the outer world for the rest of his life, twenty years. He mourned that he had once been a prince, and now he was nothing. And the people were so blind, they thought he was a wrongdoer instead of the only righteous man left in the world" (*China Men* 256–57). This elegy becomes another parable of what China Men experience when they "go out on the road." Unlike her father, however, Ch'u Yuan managed to retain "his imagination and dreams" (257) in exile.

19. Chin and Chan do not agree with the idea that a minority position of "doubleness" can be a source of empowerment as well as of victimization. They claim that "the concept of the dual personality successfully deprives the Chinese-American of all authority over language and thus a means of codifying, communicating, and legitimizing his experience" ("Racist Love" 76). My own position is expanded in "Father Land and/or Mother Tongue: The Divided Female Subject in *The Woman Warrior* and *Obasan.*"

20. In *The Woman Warrior,* Hong Kingston defines "revenge" as "not the beheading, not the gutting, but the words" (63). The words in *China Men* are all hers. The term "malestream" I have borrowed from Amy Ling, "I'm Here: An Asian American Woman's Response," 152.

21. On the conflicts in Asian American studies created by some male critics' attempts to recuperate a lost "heroic tradition"—conflicts that focus on Hong Kingston's feminist impulses—see Cheung, 241–45.

22. I do not employ "deceit" and "subversion" here with negative connotations; rather, I mean to suggest that such surreptitious avenues to power are usually the only ones open to women in patriarchal societies, and they can be just as effective as direct confrontation. As Emily Ahern observes of gender politics in Chinese culture: "According to the male ideal, power should be exercised by male heads of households, managers of lineages, and community leaders. No wonder the ability of women to exercise power of a very different kind, power wielded behind the scenes, unsupported by recognized social position, is seen as a threat to the male order. No matter how well-ensconced men are in the established positions of power, the surreptitious influence of women remains beyond their capacity to control" (201).

23. Sledge notes: "As historians have remarked, Cantonese women were forced to assume total family governance after the emigration of male villagers to foreign lands. Thus, there arose a strong tradition of womanly self-sufficiency and aggressiveness among Cantonese. Kingston shows the persistence of that tradition among those few Chinese women, like her mother, who were allowed to enter the U.S during the lengthy period of exclusion" (9–10).

24. I use the term "semiotic" here in Kristeva's sense of preoedipal *jouissance,* strong traces of which can be found in "female" language. See Kristeva, *Revolution in Poetic Language,* sec. 1.

Works Cited

Ahern, Emily M. "The Power and Pollution of Chinese Women." In *Women in Chinese Society,* ed. Margery Wolf and Roxane Witke. Stanford: Stanford University Press, 1975. 193–214.

Baker, Houston A., Jr. *Blues, Ideology, and Afro-American Literature: A Vernacular Theory.* Chicago and London: University of Chicago Press, 1984.

Chen, Jack. *The Chinese of America.* San Francisco: Harper and Row, 1980.

Cheung, King-Kok. "The Woman Warrior vs. The Chinaman Pacific: Emasculation, Feminism, and Heroism." In *Conflicts in Feminism,* ed. Marianne Hirsch and Evelyn Fox Keller. New York: Routledge, 1990. 234–51.

Chin, Frank, and Jeffery Paul Chan. "Racist Love." In *Seeing Through Shuck,* ed. Richard Kostelanetz. New York: Ballantine Books, 1972. 65–79.

Chua, Cheng Lok. "Golden Mountain: Chinese Versions of the American Dream in Lin Yutang, Louis Chu, and Maxine Hong Kingston." *Ethnic Groups* 4.1–2 (1982): 33–59.

Goellnicht, Donald C. "Father Land and/or Mother Tongue: The Divided Female Subject in *The Woman Warrior and Obasan.*" In *Redefining Autobiography in Twentieth Century Women's Fiction,* ed. Colette Hall and Janice Morgan. Garland: New York, 1991. 119–34.

Islas, Arturo. "Maxine Hong Kingston." In *Women Writers of the West Coast: Speaking of Their Lives and Careers,* ed. Marilyn Yalom. Santa Barbara: Capra, 1983. 11–19.

Juhasz, Suzanne. "Maxine Hong Kingston: Narrative Technique and Female Identity." In *Contemporary American Women Writers: Narrative Strategies,* ed. Catherine Rainwater and William J. Scheick. Lexington: University Press of Kentucky, 1985. 173–89.

Kim, Elaine H. *Asian American Literature: An Introduction to the Writings and Their Social Context.* Philadelphia: Temple University Press, 1982.

———. "Asian American Writers: A Bibliographical Review." *American Studies International* 22.2 (October 1984): 41–78.

Kingston, Maxine Hong. *China Men.* New York: Knopf, 1980.

———. "Cultural Mis-readings by American Reviewers." *Asian and Western Writers in Dialogue: New Cultural Identities,* ed. Guy Amirthanayagam. London: Macmillan, 1982. 55–65.

———. *The Woman Warrior: Memoirs of a Girlhood among Ghosts.* 1976. New York: Vintage, 1977.

Kristeva, Julia. *Desire in Language.* Ed. Leon S. Roudiez, New York: Columbia University Press, 1980.

———. "On the Women of China." Trans. Ellen Conroy Kennedy. *Signs* 1 (Autumn 1975): 57–81.

———. *Revolution in Poetic Language.* Trans. Margaret Waller. New York: Columbia University Press, 1984.

———. "Women Can Never Be Defined." In *New French Feminisms: An Anthology,* ed. Elaine Marks and Isabelle de Courtivron. New York: Schocken Books, 1981. 137–41.

Ling, Amy. "I'm Here: An Asian American Woman's Response." *New Literary History* 19 (1987): 151–60.

Lyman, Stanford M. *Chinese Americans.* New York: Random House, 1971.

Neubauer, Carol E. "Developing Ties to the Past: Photography and Other Sources of Information in Maxine Hong Kingston's *China Men.*" *MELUS* 10.4 (Winter 1983): 17–36.

Pfaff, Timothy. "Talk with Mrs. Kingston." *New York Times Book Review,* 15 June 1980.

Rabine, Leslie W. "No Lost Paradise: Social Gender and Symbolic Gender in the Writings of Maxine Hong Kingston." *Signs* 12.3 (1987): 471–92.

Rabinowitz, Paula. "Eccentric Memories: A Conversation with Maxine Hong Kingston." *Michigan Quarterly Review* 26.1 (Winter 1987): 177–87.

Siu, Paul C. P. *The Chinese Laundryman: A Study of Social Isolation.* New York: New York University Press, 1987.

Sledge, Linda Ching. "Maxine Kingston's *China Men:* The Family Historian as Epic Poet." *MELUS* 7.4 (Winter 1980): 3–22.

Sue, Stanley, and Nathaniel N. Wagner, eds. *Asian Americans: Psychological Perspectives.* Ben Lomond, Calif.: Science and Behavior Books, 1973.

Tsai, Shih-Shan Henry. *The Chinese Experience in America.* Bloomington and Indianapolis: Indiana University Press, 1986.

Ueda, Reed. "The Americanization and Education of Japanese-Americans." In *Cultural Pluralism,* ed. Edgar G. Epps. Berkeley, Calif.: McCutchan, 1974. 71–90.

Wang, Alfred S. "Maxine Hong Kingston's Reclaiming of America: The Birthright of the Chinese American Male." *South Dakota Review* 26.1 (Spring 1988): 18–29.

Wolf, Margery. "Chinese Women: Old Skills in a New Context." In *Woman, Culture, and Society,* ed. Michelle Zimbalist Rosaldo and Louise Lamphere. Stanford: Stanford University Press, 1974. 157–72.

When the Ghosts Speak:
Oral and Written Narrative Forms
in Maxine Hong Kingston's *China Men*

Mary Slowik

Maxine Hong Kingston begins *China Men,* her history of the Chinese immigration to America, with two peculiar chapters that suggest such a book is not easily written. The first chapter, "On Discovery," is the legend of Tang Ao, a Chinaman who sets off for America, the Gold Mountain, the land of infinite riches. Instead of finding America, he discovers rather the "Land of Women" where, in a grotesque parody of Chinese traditions, his feet are broken and bound, his ears are pierced, he is fed nothing but rice cakes and he enters into female enslavement. So much for discovery. For the Chinaman who thinks he can leave China, any sailing away from China is a sailing into China, its tradition enforced with a vengeance.

Chapter two, "On Fathers," suggests another kind of failed immigration. A young American girl and her sisters are waiting at their gate for their father to come home from work. They rush to greet him when he arrives, only to find out that they have greeted the wrong man, "from the back certainly looking like our father," but not him. Their mother reassures them, and they return to the sidewalk. Their father does finally come, but the chapter leaves us with the haunting image of a man who only from the back looks like the real father, a man easily mistaken. Some Chinese men may have escaped China after all, but if they are as elusive as Chinese fathers are to their daughters, their undertakings might never be known nor understood.

Maxine Hong Kingston places *China Men* in the middle of this gap between generations and countries. Her opening chapters ask two questions: Did the Chinese ever leave China culturally, and if so, can we ever know their story? The way these chapters are written, however, suggests even more difficult problems. At issue is not only a serious break in historical continuity, but the possibility of writing immigrant history at all. "On Discovery" is a folktale, evoking the authority of oral tradition, as it is revered, remembered,

From *Multi-Ethnic Literature of the United States (MELUS)* 19.1 (Spring 1994): 73. Copyright *MELUS,* the Society for the Study of the Multi-Ethnic Literature of the United States (1994). Reprinted by permission.

passed on, but also as it imprisons and ultimately destroys its characters. The first-person narration in "On Fathers," however, suggests a modern novelist's sensibility—isolated, subjective, and skeptical. To join the two stories, Maxine Hong Kingston must find the ground where oral and written traditions meet, where pre-literate and post-literate stories can question and ultimately free each other. That Kingston makes these issues of narrative as much the subject of her book as the history of the Chinese immigrants themselves establishes *China Men* as a seminal study in multi-cultural literature. The dilemmas of Tang Ao and the little girls are to some extent resolved—*China Men* of course has been written. How this happens is the subject of my study.

Let us look more closely at the narrative problems posed by Kingston in the opening chapters of *China Men*. "On Discovery" is not only a story about an aborted emigration, it is also a parable of fixed meanings. In a time outside of time, an omniscient voice speaking with the authority of fairy tale ("once upon a time"), historical document ("in the Women's land, there are no taxes and no war"), and scholarship ("some scholars say . . .") recounts the story of Tang Ao. There is an acknowledged agreement between narrator and audience. Everyone accepts without question the story to be told. The heroes and victims are unchanging in an unchangeable world. Their lives are fated as the story drives them unerringly to their pre-conceived ends. There are no alternatives to this story—for its characters or for its audience. Not only is "On Discovery" about a cultural paradigm gone tyrannical, it is also about a narrative form as enclosed and imprisoning as the story it tells.

On the other side of the self-enclosed omniscience of "On Discovery," however, is the self-enclosed subjectivity of "On Fathers." Although this chapter is particular, personal, and surrounded by the mystery of movement and flux (Participles, "waiting," "hastening," "pressing," replace the tense-less "once upon a time," of "On Discovery."), the story nonetheless doubles back on itself; its ending is its beginning—the children are forever running out to meet the father who retreats from them only to approach again in another guise, only to retreat another time. Despite the particularity of the story and the idiosyncrasy of the speaker, the story's subject is as condemned as the fated heroes of the legends. If all beginnings and endings are known to the omniscient voice, there are no beginnings or endings for the first-person speaker of this father's story, only a condemned "in medias res." And what authority can the child/first person command in order to grab that approaching man by his lapels and ask him who he is? Apparently none, for the mother in the story only concurs that the man was that kind of father easily mistaken and the children can only return to waiting.

The story of Tang Ao and the little girl could be taken as two conflicting but typically post-modern versions of history, both fatally self-enclosed, both representing the polarities of relativity and objectivity. (See Bernstein for a helpful discussion of this philosophical and literary opposition.) "The formulations," Clifford Geertz tells us, "have been various: 'inside' versus 'outside,' or 'first person' versus 'third person' descriptions; 'phenomenological' versus 'objectivist' or 'cognitive' versus 'behavioral' theories; or, perhaps most commonly, 'emic' versus 'etic' analyses" (56). Kingston, however, explores the problem narratively. "On Discovery" is in the hands of an omniscient authority, understanding the full patterns of life and condemning all characters in the story to pre-ordained fates and the audience to silent complicity in the tale. Such authority represents a radically objective point of view. "On Fathers," on the other hand, is the stuff of radical historical and cultural relativism where the ephemeral motion of a present moment and the rich though self-limited "I" preclude any transcendence. There are no larger structures beyond the self-constructed one, so there is no way of seeing above and beyond the present moment into a past radically different from the present. Tang Ao, the prisoner of omniscience, needs freedom from stories with fixed beginnings and endings. The little girl and her sisters, the prisoners of solipsism, need the means to discover these new stories. Both need a history that will connect them. *China Men* is just that history. By overlaying post-modern and pre-modern methods of storytelling, Kingston makes the connections for Tang Ao and the little girl. She also discovers the connections our forefathers have made for us.

The first thing Maxine Hong Kingston does to release both Tang Ao and the young girl from their respective isolations is to take their stories out of the hands of singular narrators and make those stories the possession and invention of the audience. Re-told by many different speakers, stories can carry people like Tang Ao of "On Discovery" back into time with all its unpredictability and introduce the lonely first person, the little girl of "On Fathers," to a group of people to whom she can listen and from whom she can speak. To use the term from oral history (and with apologies to auto mechanics), audience-generated tales can re-link the first-person speaker to a "chain of transmission." Thus, Kingston opens the post-modern story's dilemmas to the pre-modern methods of storytelling.

Very early in the book, Kingston demonstrates how an audience reformulates a story it has heard, re-shaping it across time. In the first section of the book, "The Father from China," Kingston tells of a whipping her uncle received for letting her father, then a baby, play in the rice paddy and destroy the plants. The punishment is a severe beating in front of the rest of the family, a beating that is also witnessed generations later. Notice how complex the audience for this moral lesson is. It involves every member of the family and then the child himself and the generations after him, each interpreting the lesson in his/her own way:

> They took turns hitting him across the back and shoulders, not his head because they did not want to damage his brains.
> "This—will—teach—your—younger—teach—your—younger— brother—to—watch—his—younger—brother," a switch with each word.

They administered what Tu Fu called "the beating by which he remembered his guilt." There was sap in the branch yet. "Thank you, Father and Mother," he said when they were done whipping. BiBi and Ngee Bak stood nearby and watched. The two of them listened, thankful he wasn't the oldest, who has the duty of setting a good example. (We American children heard too, and resolved not to return to China.) (23)

The whipping is a punishment intended for the audience as well as for the miscreant. The mother and father speak words during the beating for the benefit of the brother as he is punished and for his brothers and sisters "nearby," to be heard later by American children, and heard again by Kingston several generations later who is speaking to us, a predominantly non-Chinese audience, even farther from Bibi in time and place. Kingston is pre-eminently post-modern in this passage. As firmly as Harold Bloom, Kingston and the old grandparents understand a story must include all its subsequent interpretations. But the "de-centering" of the text from one self-enclosed story to an interplay of many re-tellings is not meant primarily to displace the narrator nor to demonstrate the many layers of meaning constituting language nor to assert the primacy of the text. For the non-literate subjects of this story, such concerns are moot points. As Walter Ong has pointed out in *Orality and Literacy* (31–33, 146), in oral cultures to which our foreparents belonged, there are no written "texts" attributable to specific authors. Rather, a storyteller or poet tells a story or recites a poem but then "disappears" when the recitation is over. He or she is not preserved in print in libraries or bookstores. In fact, such preservation is not his or her goal because he or she is pre-eminently a public spokesperson, using the full repertoire of oral forms that preceded him or her. Such oral narrators are supreme plagiarists. For them and for Kingston's grandparents, stories are not the formulations of the private, idiosyncratic imagination. They are literally in the public domain to be used skillfully by the public spokesperson.

What we learn from people who take inter-textuality for granted is that stories constitute generational as well as literary continuity. A story has power because ultimately it is not in the hands of the storyteller, but rather in the hands of the audience who actively interprets, re-tells and re-interprets the story generation after generation across time.

Kingston, the twentieth-century writer, is not simply a child in the rice field frightened by the story, however, nor is she a distant relative at the end of the generational line. She is now an adult re-telling that story, making it again immediate—alternating the language with the whip strokes, noting the sap still fresh in the branch, and then placing all the subsequent generations in a dramatic final present moment of the story. Thus, inter-textual reading, for Kingston, is not a kind of sophisticated source study that starts with the last version of the story and works backward. Rather, she recalls the story with urgency, as if witnessing it for the first time. We are once again at the moment of the original event looking forward in time through all its subsequent re-tellings. In this story we are momentarily meeting all fathers, mothers, sons and daughters at once.

Bringing the past into such immediacy is possible for Kingston because, for all the self-consciousness of her story, she, nonetheless, takes on the story-telling mentality of her ancestors. A story is told and remembered only in relation to the immediate demands of life. A story is a moral tale intended to teach a lesson not only with ethical content, but with practical content about family and livelihood crucial to physical and cultural survival. Bibi's story, for instance, tells us how to grow rice, how to organize a family, and how to raise children. It is called forth not simply by literary or ethical concerns, but by immediate, physical concerns. Although the story will not be written down, "published," housed and passed on by bookstores and library systems, it will be remembered and re-told by family members as each generation teaches and learns the art of survival. Even though rice has disappeared and children are allowed more rebellious thoughts, the basic narrative frame will still house our ancestors' voices giving us advice on livelihood and children. Thus, a story breaks out of omniscient self-enclosure because an audience, whose lives are never as final as any story's, continually re-tells and re-interprets the tale, connecting their limited, "first person" experiences to the directives of the oral tradition.

The way the pre-literate audience is allowed to intrude upon the tale, however, is more extensive than the post-literate audience is accustomed to. Whereas the post-literate audience can re-make stories because they are available as written documents, visual structures to be re-shaped, the pre-literate audience understands story as theater, oral performances encouraging "re-acting" in daily life (Ramsay xvii–xxxiii). Out of their extreme need, Kingston, for instance, tells us, the men in China, including her father, are "susceptible to the stories men told [about America, the Gold Mountain], . . . plausible events not fairy tales. . . . In their hunger men forgot that the gold streets had not been there when they'd gone to look for themselves. . . . The hungrier the family got, the bigger the stories, the more real the meat and the gold" (41–42).

Reality and dream fuse for Kingston's father and friends in the character Kau Goong, the uncle who returns with riches from The Gold Mountain on a night the men are ardently "talking story."

> He was . . . an incarnation of a story hero, returning during a night of stories, a six-foot-tall white gorilla with long hair and white eyebrows that pointed upward like an owl's, his mouth jutting like an ape's, saying "Huh! Huh! Here I am," he roared. "I've come back." He threw down his bags. "Help yourselves! Ho!" His sister's relatives scrambled for the gifts. Nobody asked where he had won these prizes. He threw off his coat and unbuckled pistols and silver knives. . . . He was the biggest man in the known world, and there was no law. (40)

By the end of the night the men are preparing to leave for the Gold Mountain.

At issue here is not the post-modern preoccupation with the way words do or do not represent the things they name, but the pre-modern concern with the way people become the characters they perform, a "susceptibility," Kingston tells us, grounded in the exuberance of the imagination, but also in the strain of extreme physical hardship. Performance, however, is not limited to the stage, a physical structure set aside for use at a given time. Rather the "stage" encompasses all the physical settings the actors find themselves in as they improvise the script in their own lives—Angel Island, Hawaii, New York, the Rocky Mountains. In listening to stories, they become the characters in stories and thus accomplish the incredible feat of leaving China with virtually nothing more than their own cleverness to sustain them in a strange and brutal land.

Seeing themselves not as economic casualties, as we might see ourselves if we had to undertake such an immigration, but rather as sojourners to the Gold Mountain, the emigrating Chinese look to the old stories for narrative guidance. Narrative has a cultural and physical usefulness. Mythical stories provide valuable information for humans who wander in profoundly unfamiliar terrain since so many myths are peopled with heroes on strange and dangerous journeys. Becoming hero/actors in such stories, the Chinese sojourners know how to handle the antagonists of the story. Thus, white men and women become "demons" and "demonesses," and require the kind of cleverness and slyness the Chinese mythic heroes use to defeat dragons. One afternoon, in true trickster fashion, the Chinese men continually offer heavily sugared tea to the white "demonesses" who are trying to convert them to Christianity:

> At last the ladies got up one at a time, and everyone knew they were going to the outhouse to piss. Later the men rolled on the floor laughing. Bak Goong told the origin of the joke they'd played: "The Story of Chan Moong Gut and the Gambling Wives," he announced, and clanged his pot-lid cymbals. (113)

The stories also give the sojourners physical and psychological energy. Taking on a larger-than-life script, they find the stamina to survive murderous physical conditions: "One day, like a knight rescuing a princess, Bak Goong broke clear through the thicket" (102). "Like a savage, Bak Goong ran with brands, torching the cane along the border. During the night watching-fires like furry red beasts lurked and occasionally roared" (104). "On New Year's the dragon in its fierce dance undulated like the Pacific Ocean" (108). "It was a recreation to sleep like a winter god" (112).

Even more importantly, the sojourners must find in the strange land the narrative points of reference with their old land. Ah Goong, for instance, lives more easily with his loneliness once he has again discovered the stars, Altair and Vega, the Cowboy and the Spinning Girl, whose narrative connects the sky and the seasons both in America and in China (129).

Story/scripts cannot be too freely improvised, however, for the basic narrative, unaltered in plot and character, becomes the point of contact between the sojourners and all they have left behind. Although the Chinese find in America a world cruelly different from the Gold Mountain, they nonetheless write back home about the wonders of the New World as if the Gold Mountain did exist. The lie is indeed the product of embarrassment and pride. But more essentially, it is an act of loyalty to the imagination and the myth which sustains that imagination and with it the physical survival of the men themselves.

The Gold Mountain story is also used by the wives and mothers to demand faithfulness across time and place. The men must continue to support their people back home. Wealth brings with it obligation. Thus, even when far from the fateful night in China, the Gold Mountain story becomes the place where its audiences, now separated drastically in time and place, still exert their hold on each other.

Kingston herself uses the story's power to obligate an audience in an act of "reverse history," that is, she makes even her most distant fathers listen to her story and dares them to respond. Kingston, in the first chapter, does not sit and wait like the child of "On Fathers," but takes on the "peasant" mind of her mother: "We see a stranger's tic and ascribe motives." Aggressively Kingston starts telling her father's story in an attempt to draw him out: "I'll tell you what I suppose from your silences and few words, and you can tell me that I'm mistaken. You'll just have to speak up with the real stories if I've got you wrong" (15). And if the stories turn out to be like the tale of Tang Ao that opens *China Men,* Kingston has demonstrated the ways an audience can refashion an old parable, while freeing Tang Ao from his self-reflexive shackles and letting him loose in America.

Kingston, however, does not deny the fact that she lives in late twentieth-century America. She is not a grandfather. Invoking an oral narrative authority is not easy. As a historian, she is faced with the breaks in continuity between her time and her grandfather's time. Many of the old stories have been lost, the old China inaccessible, the immigrant Chinese dispersed (in many instances forcibly) once the railroads have been constructed, the mining camps closed. Kingston faces the end of overlapping generations, the death of the listening performer/audiences we have been speaking of.

Furthermore, as a late twentieth-century historian, Kingston approaches her fathers with a faith in language and history more fragile and vulnerable than their own. The two hundred dollar suitcoat and wing-tip shoes are as elusive for Kingston, the historian, as they are for the little girl waiting at the gate in the opening chapters of *China Men.* Unlike her pre-literate fathers, Kingston is trapped by a literate culture. She is *writing* her story, not *telling* it.

Pages of type not the sets of a world-encompassing stage make up her novel. Already distanced by a 1977 copyright, Kingston, the author, is indeed removed from her text in the same way her fathers are "removed" from their history. " 'Writing,' Jacques Derrida says, " 'in the commom sense is the dead letter, it is the carrier of death because it signifies the absence of the speaker . . .' " (Derrida qtd. in Spivak, xl). So, too have the fathers long abandoned the slim pieces of evidence they have left behind.

Yet for Derrida and Kingston, the "dead letter" still bears the imprint of the writer, so that words are never completely meaningful nor completely absurd, but rather are simultaneously strung between absence and presence, meaning and the unmaking of meaning. Both Heidegger and Derrida, Gayatri Spivak tells us in her introduction to Derrida's *Of Grammatology,* teach us that language is a trace structure, effacing meaning even as it presents it. Heidegger and Derrida start, nonetheless, with words as they mean something, the "is" or the "thing" and then they proceed to put the words under question, under an erasure where we can still see them, but only through the X. Thus, every assertion is questionable, every system of meaning vulnerable to doubt (Spivak xvii). Kingston, however, must start with the X, the erasing, the silences of her fathers, the apparent extinctions of her history. And then, while never putting aside her questions, she must move through and with these silences to the words within. She starts with the absences and moves to the presences. Unlike the little girl who politely waits at the gate, Kingston must push the ghosts with the business suits and wingtip shoes towards revealing themselves, the shells of meaning towards meaning.

To do so she finds the places where pre-literate and post-literate understanding of language and history intersect. "Meaning" for pre-literate cultures and for Kingston is not primarily Meaning, the metaphysical, teleological and logocentric centers that Derrida objects to. There is, of course, in pre-literate cultures shamanistic and other ritual languages which indeed point to and even make present the mysterious, unspeakable "gods" which center primitive life. The language that interests Kingston as she discovers her fathers, however, is not primarily religious or philosophical, but rather, the language of immediate and particular experience. Here, Derrida's likening of words to "traces" or animal prints, "spoor," is helpful (Spivak). Although the tiger may be absent, his pawprints can tell much about his physical shape, his pathway through the rocks, what he ate, how he lived. So too the words of Kingston's China fathers as they reveal the particulars of the world within which they live are still heavy with the scent of their speakers and audiences. Their language reveals the "props" in and through which the fathers dramatized their lives.

Thus, Kingston does her homework, not simply examining documents, but also placing herself in the physical locations of her subjects—the Hawaiian cane field, the New York laundries, the Rocky Mountain railroad passes. Then she learns the language by which her fathers knew these locations. In this context, the imagination does not become tangled in the problems of its own perception. Because physical survival is at stake, words prove their own usefulness. They delineate the strange world the immigrants discover so that they can function within it. Skepticism is tempered by physical demand. And the grandfathers survive.

Though Kingston does not discover hidden transcendent meaning, attention to the words required by physical necessity makes the place and time of that earlier life available across vast historical distances. Paradoxically, such immersion in the immediate needs of a past life make what is most strange about that life accessible to us in the present: "Toward the end of *The Woman Warrior* [the book preceding *China Men*]," Kingston explains, "I wrote about the savage barbarians shooting off arrows with whistles on them. I wrote that, and then, not very much later, I saw one of those whistling arrows in a museum. I felt that I created it. I wrote it; and therefore, it appeared" (Rabinowitz 182). Kingston writes about the visit she made to China after she had written *China Men* and *The Woman Warrior:* "I think that I found that China over there because I wrote it. It was accessible to me before I saw it, because I wrote it. The power of imagination leads us to what is real" (Rabinowitz 182).

At her boldest, Kingston literally uses the language of her grandfathers as a kind of footprint, a "trace" to imagine the trace-maker. In writing history, Kingston does not start with a character and then put into his mouth the language he would speak. Rather, she starts with the language as it delineates the immediate environment and lets these details construct the character. Notice, for instance, how the literal meaning of the word for "envy" physically describes a grandfather remotest from Kingston in time and place: "His mouth and throat, his skin puckered all over with envy. He discovered why to be envious is 'to guzzle vinegar' " (18).

Chinese is a language ready-made for such literal use. Because it is a tonal language, voice pitch determines the meaning of the word. It is easy for a single word to have several meanings depending on how the speaker pitches the voice. Thus, Kingston's attention to the particulars of her fathers's experience does not result in an unsophisticated realism. Her fathers's language is not naively representational with simple one-to-one correspondence between word and referent. Rather it is as richly multi-valent as Derrida's language when he is most self-conscious, that is, when he is using the etymology of words and their syllabic makeup to put tail-spins on their meaning. And the Chinese as self-consciously as Derrida delight in such language play and the puns it creates. Note how complex the nominal "toad" is, for instance, in one of Kingston's earliest language lessons. I quote this passage at length because it is one of the most complete lessons in pre-literate Chinese that Kingston offers us:

The black dirt in their yard set off my dazzling shoes—two chunks of white light that encased my feet. "Look, Look," said Say Goong, Fourth Grandfather, my railroad grandfather's youngest brother. "A field chicken." It was not a chicken at all but a toad with alert round eyes that looked out from under the white cabbage leaves. It hopped ahead of my shoes, dived into the leaves, and disappeared, reappeared, maybe another toad. It was a clod that had detached itself from the living earth; the earth had formed into a toad and hopped. "A field chicken," said Say Goong. He cupped his hands, walked quietly with wide steps and caught it. On his brown hand sat a toad with perfect haunches, eyelids, veins, and wrinkles—the details of it, the neatness and completeness of it swallowing and blinking. "A field chicken?" I repeated. "Field chicken," he said. "Sky chicken. Sky toad. Heavenly toad. Field toad." It was a pun and the words the same except for the low tone of *field* and the high tone of *heaven* or *sky*. He put the toad in my hands—it breathed, and its heart beat, every part of it alive—and I felt its dryness and warmth and hind feet as it sprang off. How odd that a toad could be both of the field and of the sky. It was very funny. Say Goong and I laughed. "Heavenly chicken," I called, chasing the toad. I carefully ran between the rows of vegetables, where many toads, giants and miniatures, hopped everywhere. Which one was the toad in my hand? Then suddenly they were all gone. But they clucked. So it isn't that toads look or taste like chickens that they're called chickens; they cluck alike! (165–66).

As a pitched language, Chinese holds disparate meanings together in ways different from English. As the deconstructionists point out, English is a language of metaphor and metonymy. Our system of reference allows things to become other things, or the part to represent the whole. If we allow our language to enter into a centerless whirl of activity, we speak of endless substitutions, words standing for other words. Not so with the Chinese where two pitches cannot be simultaneously sounded. Instead, disparate meanings are held at arm's length but encircled by the word. The toad is not a chicken, nor is he the sky. There is no "is" connecting these things; they are joined but not collapsed together. Simile or analogy or allegory is perhaps the closest English comes to this habit of mind. In allegories, for instance, parallel worlds exist side by side. They can be brought into an alignment which reveals interesting things about each. But they remain basically separate and distinct.

Yet, for all the richness of meaning, notice how silent these language lessons are. As with the deconstructionists, the Chinese are aware of all that words cannot point to. Although Kingston recalling the experience presents a flood of words bringing the experience back in full, lyric, sensuous immediacy, the moment itself is not filled with words. The grandfathers simply offer the world and the language (primarily nominals) by which they know it to their children. Both teacher and pupil share the delight of discovering the particulars of experience as if for the first time. Although such moments suggest that we can experience the world in an unmediated, pre-verbal way, it is, nonetheless, the word "field chicken," a generic noun, that sparks Kingston's memory. Language, particularly the words that connect generations of people, conveys experience across time. Rather than at the beginning of time, innocent perception takes place at the point of historical transition, when generations overlap each other, when the old meet the young.

In this context, language is not an "assumed" inheritance, the kind of imprisoning "given" that deconstructionists must recognize and then destroy. Kingston's grandfathers are not the authorities who demand obedience and then inspire rebellion from their sons, in those cycles of making and unmaking to which Harold Bloom refers. As if already foreseeing their role as ancestors, the old uncles reach out to their children when the child's perception is closest to their own. When Kingston visits Say Goong and his brother, she has a sense of physical immensity—that the world is huge and cannot be seen or understood in its entirety. Neither she nor her uncles have traveled by jet nor ridden trams to mountaintops nor taken speed elevators to seventy-fifth floors where the world spreads at one's feet in all-inclusive patterns of organization. Such industrial omniscience is irrelevant to the child and the uncles. Rather, the world is filled with disparate things, registered side-by-side by a language which delights in unlikely, whimsical combinations. The uncles offer the child this world and the language with which to know it as an act of immediate perception to be repeated every time parents teach their very young children to speak. Thus, language is not an abstract grammar nor is it a voiceless text. Rather, it is a pathway of empty footprints with the lions conjured into presence with each recalled conversation, each repeated story, each inter-generational vocabulary lesson.

When Kingston discovers the analogic language of her fathers, she also discovers a nimbleness of perspective that loosens the omniscience of the old tales which the father/actors are re-living and also complicates the simple first person point of view that imprisons the little girl at the gate. When words can hold disparate meanings simultaneously, real and mythic stories can become parallel in such a way that a speaker can question his audience without undermining it. Kingston's Hawaiian grandfather, for instance, allows both the magical and realistic versions of his experience to exist side by side. He leaps quickly from one to the other when he is faced with an audience which is too self-assured. One night while watching some Hawaiian fishermen, he experiences a profoundly transcendent moment:

> It was either two people or one Hindoo with four arms. He heard music draw out into one long note. The waves going in and out forever was the same as no motion at all. . . . He sat for hours in the exact center of eternity. Then it all started up again; the couple on the water stirred. A fisherman and woman suddenly came out of the sea and walked toward him. "Want to see our catch?" . . . Later when he heard people say they had seen the torches of the dead warriors who walk across the water, he would say, "You saw Hawaiians nightfishing or checking their lobster traps": But when someone said, "Those are the Hawaiians nightfishing," Bak Goong, a fanciful, fabulous man, said, "It may be dead Hawaiian warriors walking." If a human being crossed the path of the walker, he could die on the spot, but Bak Goong said that he knew for a fact that this was not true. (109–10)

Not only is the moment brief, drawn quickly back into the rhythms of ordinary experience, Bak Goong uses the realistic version of his experience· to question a simple faith in the dead warriors returning. Conversely, he uses the religious interpretation of his tale to question the simple realism of Hawaiians nightfishing. He is seeing one kind of reality in and through the frame of the other, without giving one priority over the other.

When Kingston re-tells this experience to us, she also moves nimbly between the magical and the real—almost sentence by sentence this passage shifts between the transcendent and the temporal, the timeless god and the fishermen on the water, the omniscient and the first-person experience. "Time moved at their rate of motion," she asserts, for instance. But lest we get caught up in the eternal, she provides in the next sentence a set of alternative explanations without choosing either: "It was either two people or one Hindoo with four arms." The next sentence returns to the transcendent moment: "He heard music draw out into one long note." The next, the utter transience of the experience, motion held against permanence not by metaphor but by simile: "The waves going in and out forever was *the same as* no motion at all." And so forth through the passage.

There are many other ways Kingston takes on the analogic perspective of her fathers to tell their story. Sometimes even more fully than themselves she sees them as characters in a myth—both more grand and yet more comic than even they could imagine. Take, for instance, her re-working of the primitive fertility story of the sky inseminating the earth. One of her grandfathers is being lowered in a wicker basket over a mountainside to plant dynamite for railroad blastings:

> "One beautiful day, dangling in the sun above a new valley, not the desire to urinate but sexual desire clutched him so hard he bent over in the basket. He curled up, overcome by beauty and fear, which shot to his penis. He tried to rub himself calm. Suddenly he stood up tall and squirted out into space. 'I am fucking the world,' he said. The world's vagina was big, big as the sky, big as a valley. He grew a habit: whenever he was lowered in the basket, his blood rushed to his penis, and he fucked the world." (130)

Here the absurd and profound, the vulgar and elegant are joined together in a comic-serious re-enactment of a creation myth. Surely her fathers would approve of the wonder and laughter with which their great-granddaughter tells the story.

In more complicated ways, Kingston's own life parallels theirs. Like her father whom she recreates as a stowaway nailed in a crate in the hold of a ship, she too has many stow-away experiences. The most vivid of these is when she hides from her "bossy" uncle, Kau Goong, in the dark storeroom under the basement stairs. Such places throughout the novel are claustrophobic interruptions in the flow of time. They are places where visions take place—the grandfather dreams of his many possible futures in the new world, the hiding little girl revels in "useless things like wishes, wands, hibernation." Both the stowaway and the miscreant under the stairs enter into conversation with people who are only partially present—the caretaker in the hold of the ship who is hiding the father, the imaginary cowgirls and cowboys, the "talking men," for the little girl. There are the tense interruptions, more auditory than visual—the calling of the ship's sailor in the hold, the roaring of the bossy uncle. Then, there is the graceful exit through good luck.

At such narrative moments, the novel seems to fold analogically on itself. The voices heard beyond the crate, the visions spun within it seem like an image for Kingston's historical quest, the discovery of the footprints, the traces of words the grandfathers have left behind, the ghosts returning across the gaps in history. Such moments join both Kingston's grandfathers and her own historic quest. Paradoxically, such a quest is possible because of the generational breaks that have left people disconnected and alone, surrounded not by embodied narrators but ghostly footsteps. "I talked to the people whom I knew were not really there," Kingston tells us. "I became different, complete, an orphan" (181). Thus, *China Men* is not an elegiac mourning for loss of meaning nor the ironic exposure of such loss. Rather it is filled with delight and laughter at the ingeniousness of connections which hold things both apart and together.

When applied to the ultimate task the fathers undertake, the founding of an "ancestral home," such laughter becomes proof that the doorstep upon which the little girl sits in "On Fathers" is indeed the home also of her fathers. The particulars of her life are indeed the particulars of the life they founded, the China they discovered and made here. She need not wait for them, they have "founded" her and given her life significance, authority and meaning.

In the middle of *China Men,* Maxine Hong Kingston tells a story which not only complicates Derrida's "trace" in the way we have been discussing, but also gives it the pre-literate power to find and inspire an audience hearing it not immediately but much later in time. The Chinese workgangs have been clearing the Hawaiian jungles for weeks, coughing and dying from the inhaled dust, working morning to dusk with machetes under the bullwhips of overseers. Forbidden to talk, Kingston's grandfather nonetheless mumbles on and on—curses in Chinese, sometimes old stories, sometimes messages to his loved ones far off in China. As long as he can talk, he can survive. Sometimes he "talks story" to those around him. One of his stories is the old tale of the kitty ears.

A king longs for a son and when he at last has one discovers to his chagrin that the baby is born with little kitty ears. Embarrassed, the king decides to keep his son's oddity a secret and so, covers the child's head and never tells anyone. The boy grows into handsome and noble manhood but for the king, "the secret grew large inside his chest and mouth" until he can hold it in no longer. So, he digs a hole in a winter field and shouts the secret of the kitty ears deep into the earth and then covers it over. The next spring when the grass grows, the people hear words in the wind which as the summer progresses become more and more clear: "The king's son has kitty ears, the king's son has kitty ears," to which the people laugh with delight and envy.

Heartened by the tale, the China men in Hawaii the next day plow an enormous hole and lean into it and yell all their unspoken words—they call out to their wives in China, they confess their transgressions with Polynesian women, they cry out again and again, "home, home, home." "They had dug an ear into the world," Kingston tells us, "and were telling the earth their secrets. . . . Soon the new green shoots would rise and when in two years the cane grew gold tassels, what stories the wind would tell." Bak Goong justifies the act: "That wasn't a custom. . . . We made it up. We can make up customs because we're the founding ancestors of this place" (117–18).

And so, words are planted—to be heard at some later time by some future generation. Indeed, they are footprints or traces, as ephemeral as the wind, but they are also rooted in place, making that field ancestral. Though the contact between generations may be broken, the words remain—not in the substance of books but in the substance of physical location. To find that location and listen is to again become an actor/audience hearing and then re-telling/re-living the tale. At such moments the ancestral spirits come very close, the generations again overlap, the ancestral home is created and renewed.

During the time Kingston is searching for her grandfathers's history in Hawaii, she swims to an island called Chinaman's Hat:

> We were climbing along a ledge down to the shore, holding on to the face of the island in the twilight, when a howling like wolves, like singing, came rising out of the island. "Birds," somebody said. "The wind," said someone else. But the air was still and the high, clear sound wound through the trees. It continued until we departed. It was, I know it, the island, the voice of the island singing, the sirens Odysseus heard. The Navy continues to bomb Kaho'olawe and the Army blasts the green skin off the red mountains of O'ahu. But the land sings. We heard something. It's a tribute to the pioneers to have a living island named after their work hat. I have heard the land sing. I have seen the bright blue streaks of spirits whisking through the air. I again search for my American ancestors by listening in the cane. (90)

The tales they tell inevitably take on the accoutrements of print but in *China Men* they also become the revelation possible when narrative as well as familial generations at last have met.

Works Cited

Bernstein, Richard J. *Beyond Objectivism and Relativism.* Philadelphia: U of Pennsylvania P, 1985.

Geertz, Clifford. " 'From the Native's Point of View': On the Nature of Anthropological Understanding." *Local Knowledge.* New York: Basic, 1983. 55–70.

Engendering Genre:
Gender and Nationalism in
China Men and *The Woman Warrior*

LeiLani Nishime

China Men, Maxine Hong Kingston's book on the history of Chinese-Americans, followed close on the heels of the publication of her much acclaimed autobiography *The Woman Warrior.* Kingston has said that she first envisioned the two volumes as one book; yet if we view these books as companion works, then it is curious how differently they represent what might be called the Chinese-American experience (Talbot 12). While the first, most obvious divide may be at the level of gender, as evidenced by the two books' titles, another equally important division takes place at the level of genre. When Kingston allies generic distinctions, i.e., history and autobiography, with particular genders she both explores and exposes that underlying alliance, raising questions about the role genre plays in defining both gender roles and Chinese-American identity. At the same time, she raises questions about the meaning of the public and private in relationship to history and autobiography and how notions of public and private give those genres a gendered status. By locating gender in Kingston's manipulations of genre and mythology and looking at the gendered categorization of generic forms, we can also locate the place of Chinese-American identity in her conception of gender and genre.

Much of the power of these two works lies in Kingston's attempt to intervene in and undermine a "master narrative" of history and identity in America. Although Kingston does skillfully parody and disrupt accepted notions of history and autobiography and destabilize those categories with her introductions of gender and race, her ability to escape the boundaries of genre remains in question.

Perhaps the question that must be asked is: How complete is the connection between genre and the ideology that gave rise to it? Does Kingston's

From *Multi-Ethnic Literature of the United States (MELUS)* 20, no. 1 (Spring 1994): 67–82. Copyright *MELUS,* the Society for the Study of the Multi-Ethnic Literature of the United States (1995). Reprinted by permission.

repetition of these genres, albeit in altered forms, merely contribute to rein-forcing those forms or, as Judith Butler claims, can there be "repetition with a difference?" In other words, as Gayatri Spivak might ask, "Can the subaltern speak?" Kingston never fully escapes genre because she must write within and against the constraints of generic forms in order to comment upon them and manipulate them. If she abandons the forms completely, the cultural res-onances so crucial to her disruption of hegemonic conceptions of Chinese-American identity, gender and history, would be lost, but her adherence to those forms raises questions about her ability to fully subvert or escape the ideologies that inform those genres.

Whether Kingston speaks without being consumed by the "epistemic violence" of her writing tools, namely language and genre, is my central ques-tion. My search is not for Kingston's "authentic" voice hidden within these forms, but an examination of how she engages with and uses these forms to her own ends. By examining Kingston's deconstruction of the opposition between fictional and non-fictional forms, such as autobiography and history, her use of mythology to explore issues of national identity, and her manipula-tions of genre and mythology through the introduction of race and gender, I hope to delineate constraints of genre and the meaning of the subversion of these forms at the intersection of gender and Chinese-American identity.

Looking at the opposition between these two books' genres proves to be no easy matter, as Kingston rarely lets any clear opposition stand. Instead, what was a matter of black and white, autobiography and historiography, slips away into a hazy area where generic boundaries are difficult to define. Although both books blur the boundaries between the two genres, they do not find a common third term, and instead they present examples of two very different approaches to both history and autobiography.[1]

These unstable oppositions are apparent even before one cracks the binding of either book. Although both books now can be found in the fiction or Asian American literature section, the generic distinctions given to them by their publisher betray their earlier distinctions. *The Woman Warrior* falls under the rubric of autobiography while *China Men,* a work of history, is cate-gorized as nonfiction/literature. But the books do not remain within the two distinct genres of autobiography and history, much less maintain their mutual exclusivity. Perhaps some of the loudest uproar over *The Woman Warrior* cen-tered upon Kingston's blurring of the boundary between non-fictional auto-biography and a fictional retelling of her life story. She insists on an eccentric voice, telling her memoirs from a highly personal point of view and making no attempt to "objectively" review her subjective, skewed vision of her world. *China Men* also participates in this transgression of generic boundaries, for this history makes room for fables, myths, family lore and personal accounts as well as official laws and documents. In both cases, Kingston questions and undermines the status of "truth" and "facts" by questioning the concepts of universality and objectivity.

The problem of generic distinctions appears endemic to Asian American literature, since "ethnic histories" almost always threaten the boundaries between genres, because the term is traditionally seen as an oxymoron. In some senses, all minority writing is considered to be always/already autobiographical. Trinh T. Minh-ha reminds us that, "the *minor*-ity's voice is always personal; that of the *major*-ity, always impersonal" (28; original emphasis). Asian American writing, like much minority writing, is perceived as autobiographical in the sense that writing by Asian Americans is "about" their experience as Asian Americans in a way that Anglo-American writing, with its assumption of universality, is never "about" being white. Thus Michael Fisher, despite his otherwise careful reading of several Asian American novels, claims to research "the range or historical trajectory of autobiographical writing within each ethnicity" while unselfconsciously citing clearly *fictional,* non-autobiographical works by Frank Chin and Shawn Wong (202). The history of the dominant, unlike that of the minority, is perceived to be universal or unmarked. An ethnic history, following this logic, is a private, personalized history that cannot transcend to the level of the general and the public.

By blurring the distinction between autobiography and history, Kingston at first appears to be repeating and encouraging a common misreading of writings by Asian Americans as always autobiographical. Donald Goellnicht begins his article on *China Men* saying, "Maxine Hong Kingston's second (auto)biographical fiction, *China Men* . . ." (191), although this book has few "(auto)biographical" markers (for instance, Kingston rarely appears as a character in the novel, and the stories she tells more closely resemble short stories or anecdotes than biographies). Still, this categorization of *China Men* as (auto)biographical rather than historical seems, in fact, to be encouraged by the way Kingston crosses genres in this book. Instead of rushing to shore up the distinctions in Asian American writing between autobiography, fiction and history, Kingston chooses a different strategy. In *China Men* rather than attempting to rid Chinese-American history of the "taint" of the personal or autobiographical, Kingston revises notions of what makes an experience historical, by asking by what standards we decide what can enter into history and the public realm.[2]

Kingston contrasts the "private" (read: non-representative and therefore non-historical) stories of the "Grandfathers" to the official public (read: objective and historical) documents of the time. For example, Kingston follows the story of the "Grandfather of the Sierra Nevada Mountains" with a recitation of the restrictive laws against Asian Americans that basically legalized racism. The chapter, which simply recounts the laws, appears midway through the book, yet, as Goellnicht says, "This centric authority of American law is subverted and contested by the 'eccentric' or marginal, but richly imaginative stories of China Men that surround it" (197). Her juxtaposition of the two versions of history points out the inaccessibility of that official history in comparison with the "Grandfathers'" story. The narrated, and perhaps fictional, stories of the "Grandfathers" allow a more meaningful view of the history of Chinese-Americans and provide a space in which to write the history that had been left out of the exclusionary laws. This use of official documents also emphasizes the fact that the documents are only available in an already interpreted form, and they do not provide a transparent look into the past. They frame the narrative of the Chinese in America by the stories they leave out, stories such as Kingston's. Although the documents masquerade as objective, they are not necessarily more true or real than the history we receive through the Grandfathers' story.

China Men at first appears to be a private family history populated by the narrator's grandfathers, but soon it becomes clear that she has more grandfathers than is biologically possible. While the "Grandfathers" are individual people with their own personalities and personal histories, they also are a type or a generic forefather whose story is representative of many Chinese-American immigrants. Kingston gestures towards a history of Chinese-Americans in America that is beyond her family history, yet the quirkiness of each individual characterization prevents the creation of a single individual who represents the norm of Chinese-American experience. One cannot gauge the authenticity of one's family by measuring how closely one's history conforms to the stories. Kingston tries to create a new definition of history for Chinese-Americans by foregrounding the individuality of the stories, yet the book also documents their role in history as Chinese-Americans.

Homi Bhahba has asked "Whether the *emergence* of a national perspective—of an elite or subaltern nature—within a culture of social contestation, can ever articulate its 'representative' authority in that fullness of narrative time" (295). This difficulty in both being within a "culture of contestation" and trying to speak with authority is reflected in *China Men* by the placement of the "Grandfathers" as both the object and subject of a national identity. While they may be acting as subjects by expanding the definitions of Americanness, they also act as objects of that nationalistic discourse so that they may speak as Americans, thus gaining a "representative authority." Their history cannot be separated from the "public" national history of America. In this way, Kingston simultaneously claims a "representative authority" for her history in the service of creating a space for Chinese-Americans in Anglo-American history while remaining "within a culture of social contestation" by refusing to fall back upon notions of authenticity and origin. The experiences of the book's characters do not stand apart from history, just as what we know as history is caught up in social, cultural, and "private" perceptions. This book asks us to question what facts we deem real and what experiences are "historical" and, in so doing, makes explicit the connection between individual identity and history without reverting to the paradigm of history as a point of origin.

The attack on Kingston over the autobiographical status of her book *The Woman Warrior* is well known. Frank Chin, perhaps Kingston's most well known critic, describes Kingston's transgressions by saying, "[Her] elaboration of this version of history, in both autobiography and autobiographical fiction, is simply a device for destroying history and literature," because Kingston does not "accurately" portray the experience and history of Chinese-Americans (3). To her critics, Kingston violates the commitment to "factuality" that the name autobiography implies and, in doing so, confronts two differing traditions of autobiography. She challenges, on the one hand, the non-fiction appellation of autobiography, and, on the other hand, the anthropological information retrieval concept of ethnic autobiography.

The anxiety over Kingston's book centers upon the role of and expectations for ethnic autobiography. Kingston writes against a tradition of Chinese-American autobiography that gave an ethnographic treatment of Chinese-American society. As Sau-ling Wong says, with a great deal of irony, in "Autobiography as Guided Chinatown Tour," "Ideally, an ethnic autobiography should also be a history in microcosm of the community, especially of its suffering, struggles, and triumphs" (*Multicultural* 258). Autobiography has a long history in Chinese-American writing, beginning with early "conversion" narratives prompted by Christian missionaries, and many of the better selling, earlier works do fit into Wong's pattern.[3] In her article about the reception of her book, Kingston notes the tendency of critics to review her book on the basis of how good a "tourguide" she proves to be, judging her by how well she recreates the "mystery" of Chinatown and how "authentically" she displays its exotica. The concern over Kingston's book relies on a notion of ethnic autobiography as a learning tool for the projected white audience. Kingston's book would seem to be a failure if ethnic autobiography is to be read as a type of ethnography, but her success lies in a reworking of this tradition.

This, then, is the tradition within and against which Kingston is writing. Yet instead of a total rejection of the ethnographic impulse in ethnic autobiography, *The Woman Warrior* does, in many ways, uphold the concept of ethnic autobiography as an exploration of what it means to be a Chinese-American. At the same time, Kingston still insists upon the singularity of her view and does not attempt to speak for all Chinese-Americans nor represent them completely. In the book she admits that she cannot speak for Chinese-Americans because she is not even sure what exactly is *the* Chinese-American experience.

In the book, the narrator's isolation from other members of her community does not allow her to hear the stories of others to provide a scale by which to measure her own experience. The narrator tells us that she could never tell if what she was experiencing was typical of Chinese-Americans or simply a family eccentricity, so that when she leaves her hometown she must read anthropology books about China to look for hints about her life. Her alienation is so complete that she must read books written by outsiders to find out about herself and try to find a self that she can recognize. This ironic situation prevents the protagonist from taking a position of absolute or sole authority on Chinese-Americans or acting as a source of information retrieval, since she learns about Chinatown from books instead of the "ultimate" referent of experience.[4] She cannot act as the symbol or representative of Chinese-Americans for the outsider who wants to learn about the "true" culture of a Chinatown since her experience is so personalized. Kingston must expand the boundaries of ethnic autobiography in order to explore her identity as a Chinese-American and create an alternative authority rather than formulating a complete definition of that identity for the imagined outsider reader.

Kingston also plays with other conventions of autobiography, conventions that are not limited to ethnic autobiography. As I mentioned earlier, autobiography is often assumed to be factual and empirically true. In the book, the clear distinctions between fiction and non-fiction are not made so; what the protagonist recounts as her subjective experience may or may not exist in an "objective" account of her life. Yet the truth of her life is more clearly represented through the fictions she tells since she lives in a world where her own reality is bound up with half truths and fictions. In a telling scene in *China Men,* Kingston and her sister remember the same event completely differently, and they never find out which version was true, yet for each of them her own memory was true. The narrator has had to create her own reality and says, "She [her mother] tested our strength to establish realities" (*Woman* 5). When the protagonist narrates her life, she must include the non-truths that make up her reality; sticking to empirical truth would falsify her experience.

In *The Woman Warrior,* the convention of the singular individual in autobiography is also dismantled, and the author plays with the assumption of the centrality of the individual in autobiography. The typical American autobiography, with *Autobiography of Benjamin Franklin* as its archetypal example, emphasizes the theme of individual struggle and triumph, often in the face of community resistance. *The Woman Warrior* concerns itself less with the individual character of the narrator than with her place within a social structure. In fact, the book's protagonist never actually gets named, questioning the immediate identification of the protagonist with the author and allowing the protagonist to participate in the narrative as a character rather than claiming the ultimate authority of authorship.

The story does not function as a tale of individualism. Rather it details her search for her place within the community and her family and the meaning of her identity as a Chinese-American. The story of the protagonist is intertwined with her relationship with her mother, and *The Woman Warrior* tells the story of the protagonist's mother and is as much a story of her relationship to her mother as it is "about" the protagonist. Kingston, by emphasizing the social aspect of an individual identity, broadens the scope of autobiography to include the constant negotiations with different social structures that make up the shifting ground of ethnicity. As Michael Fischer tells us,

"Ethnicity is not something that is simply passed on from generation to generation, taught and learned; it is something dynamic . . ." (195). Ethnicity, in *The Woman Warrior,* cannot be understood as an individualist experience but has meaning only within a social context. It resides within a social dynamic. The book's protagonist says, "[We] have had to figure out how the invisible world the emigrants built around our childhoods fits into solid America" (*Woman* 6). Ethnicity, and by extension Kingston's identity, is constantly being created through the competing discourses of the emigrant's "invisible world" and "solid America."

A close examination of the function of mythology in *China Men* and *The Woman Warrior* makes clear the breakdown of generic distinctions and the performativity of ethnicity in those books. While Kingston's use of mythology has raised objections from other members of the Asian American community, her manipulations, or distortions, of those myths enable her to question the basic assumptions of the generic forms of history and autobiography. The use of myth helps her to find a way to write Chinese-Americans into American history and to search for her own Chinese-American identity.

As I mentioned earlier, Kingston undermines traditional notions of history by questioning the meaning of objectivity and neutrality in the narrative of history. By inserting Chinese-American mythology and Chinese-American people into Anglo-American history, Kingston does not merely augment the existing history. She also exposes the mythological roots of Anglo-American history, putting its claim to objectivity and truth into jeopardy. Richard Slotkin calls myth "the primary language of historical memory" which functions to "assign ideological meaning to that history" (70). Yet myth, like history, is a symbolic production that acts like a transcendent truth by effacing its ideological use value. In Slotkin's elegant aphorism, "[Myth] transforms history into nature" (80). Myth is the narrative that gives meaning to history, that allows history to function as truth rather than as just another story.

In her story in *China Men* entitled "The Adventures of Lo Bun Sun," an auditory pun on the story of Robinson Crusoe, Kingston exposes the ideological underpinning of the traditional story. Like Robinson, Lo Bun Sun is a shipwrecked pirate, and the story is a familiar one, but the use of a Chinese name is different enough to defamiliarize the story and cast it in a new light. The story depends upon the assumption that the sailor is white, so that it can plug into the myth of the Great White Adventurer civilizing the "native." However, when the two characters are both "natives," the naturalness given to the story by the power of myth is lost, and the story appears both ludicrous and brutal. Kingston's re-visioning of the Robinson Crusoe story demonstrates the ability of myth to naturalize and normalize to such an extent that the gaps and fissures in a story that should mark the fault lines of the "master narrative" are glossed over. The gaps that mark where certain histories were left out disappear behind the familiar myths of Anglo-American history.

Kingston reveals and reopens those gaps by reinstating the Chinese-Americans who were erased from Anglo-American history. She does not reject the notion of a Chinese-American history along with all history but emphasizes its constructed nature. In fact, she uses the American mythology of the West to help her write Chinese-Americans into the history of the frontier. Linda Hutcheon characterizes the postmodern relationship to the use value of the past when she says, "It puts into question, at the same time it exploits, the grounding of historical knowledge in the past real" (92). After showing how mythology enters into history, Kingston does not abandon the project of history but, instead, attempts to create a new mythology for Chinese-American history. Kingston depicts a certain "heroic dominance" in terms of the land. The first job of the character Ah Goong is to fell a redwood and, in the end, he conquers the mountains through which he has to tunnel. Kingston firmly places the Chinese in the American landscape and enumerates the ways in which he has participated in forming and creating that landscape in order to further her goal of "claiming America" and creating a Chinese-American history and identity. It is crucial to note that their part in the building of America is couched in legendary and epic terms, unlike the "factual" empirical tone of traditional history books. Kingston exploits rather than naturalizes the power of mythology in her histories.

The Woman Warrior describes a very different relationship between the female protagonist and mythology than is found in China Men. The former focuses much more narrowly upon Chinese myth rather than exposing the mythology of Anglo-American history. After the short first chapter, Chinese myth forms a frame around the account of a Chinese-American girl's childhood in a small town Chinatown. The mythical figure of Fa Mu Lan, "the girl who took her father's place in battle," haunts the book and her childhood (Woman 24). Like the myths of China Men, the story of Fa Mu Lan offers a chance of escape, not the "China men's" escape from historical obscurity but an escape from the anonymity that is her gender's fate. The protagonist remembers her mother's stories and says, "She said I would grow up to be a wife and a slave, but she taught me the song of the warrior woman, Fa Mu Lan. I would have to grow up a warrior woman" (Woman 24).

Much of the controversy surrounding The Woman Warrior revolves around the issue of Kingston's revision of classical Chinese myth, yet this very revision is the means by which she can write her own history. Through her rewriting of Chinese myth she can include her own voice within a Chinese—and, since she learned these stories from her mother in America, a Chinese-American—tradition. The protagonist of The Woman Warrior inserts herself into the stories of Chinese myth and, thereby, participates in the narrative of the community. She rewrites Fa Mu Lan in such a way that Fa Mu Lan speaks with her voice, and she can identify and recognize herself in the stories of Chinese America and claim a Chinese-American identity. Unfortunately, she is left with the problem of getting others in the community to recognize her version of the myth and confirm her voice and place within the community, a difficulty I will discuss later.

Thus, in the words of Homi Bhabha, Kingston "acknowledges the status of national culture—and the people—as a contentious, performative space of the perplexity of living in the midst of the pedagogical representation of the fullness of life" (307). Kingston negotiates between a fixed, complete, "pedagogical" definition of Chinese-American culture and her lived experience of national identity, an identity that is continually being defined, redefined and "performed." The main character now has a history and a legacy that gives her authority to act as more than a "wife and slave," but, by not effacing her participation in the act of creating that history, she avoids the trap of origins and the trap of biological determinism. So while the main character still "could not figure out what my village was," she was able to carve out a space for herself through the act of narrative by making her "village" the world of Chinese myth (*Woman* 54). Unlike the work done with myth in *China Men*, the protagonist's involvement with myths does not rework Anglo-American history, but, instead tries to find her a place within her family and community not only as an individual but also as a Chinese-American.

The Woman Warrior and *China Men* both challenge assumptions about the nature of history and myth in the Anglo-American tradition, yet their similarities cause their differences to stand out in bold relief. *China Men* subverts notions of a seamless, "factual" history, untouched by either mythology or particularity, in an effort to write Chinese-Americans back into the history of America. *The Woman Warrior* examines and undermines similar concepts, yet the protagonist never succeeds in fully reconciling her gender and her identity as a Chinese-American and never enters into "history" like the "Grandfathers" in *China Men*. Thus, her ability to speak as a national remains threatened, since nationalism is not a quantifiable trait but exists in a fluid relationship to society, and her identity as a Chinese-American is tenuous as long as her place within the community does not allow her view to be as "universal" as any other voice. Her struggle has a different location from the struggle in *China Men*. The two books explore different boundaries between myth and history and the public and the private, highlighting the difficulty of finding an identity that encompasses both nation and gender.

In Sau-Ling Wong's discussion of the intersection of nationalism and gender for Chinese-Americans, she coins the term "ethnicizing gender," contrasting it to gendering ethnicity. The assignation of gendered characteristics according to ethnicity is a familiar trope, but Wong proposes a flip side to this analysis. Instead, the enactment of gender leads to an ethnic labeling. In America a strict gender demarcation of Asian ethnicities as feminine, as opposed to the more masculine "Americans," operates to bind notions of gender to ethnicity and nationalism. In Wong's example of Chinese-American immigrant writing she says, "Thus the characters' actions, depicted along a spectrum of gender appropriateness, are assigned varying shades of "Chineseness" or "Americanness" to indicate the extent of their at-homeness in the adopted land" ("Ethnicizing Gender" 114).[5]

In *China Men* the crossing of the boundaries between the public and private spheres has implications in terms of the gendered connotations of those two terms. The conception of Chinese-American history as essentially private as opposed to the public Anglo-American history also genders that history feminine since the private sphere has long been associated with the female. By bringing the "private" Chinese-American history into the public sphere, Kingston moves its story into the traditionally masculine public sphere of American history. In *China Men,* the claim to a Chinese-American identity and history necessitates this move from the feminine private sphere into the masculine public discourse. Since, in Wong's formulation, American ethnicity, as opposed to Chinese ethnicity, means masculinity, the assertion of the place of the Chinese in America is, by definition, also a move towards confirming Chinese-Americans' masculine "Americanness."

This is not to say that Kingston whole-heartedly embraces a masculine ideal for Chinese-Americans. The ambiguity of her response to this split between a "feminine Chineseness" and a "masculine Americanness" may be best exemplified by *China Men*'s opening chapter, "On Discovery." The short chapter resembles a fairy tale about a man named Tang Ao who sails to the Gold Mountain, which is another name for America, where he is captured and dressed and treated like a woman. At first glance this seems merely to be about the trauma of the feminization of Chinese men who came to America, yet the story also is concerned with the suffering of Chinese females. Tang Ao's ear piercing and painful foot binding were both practices of Chinese women, and the story appears to be as much about the constraints of women's roles as the "emasculinization" of Chinese men in America. Still, despite Kingston's recognition of the pain of fulfilling these gender roles for women, she still celebrates a masculine ideal to counteract the stereotypes of Asian males and to assert their "Americanness." Although Kingston often maintains a playful tone, the irony of aspiring to a masculine ideal that ultimately traps Asian American males cannot seem to overcome the immediate appeal and power of that ideal.

This re-writing of American myth and history to create a masculine, and therefore Chinese *American,* ideal for Chinese men raises difficult questions about the role of Chinese-American women in this new history. While it is true that due to exclusionary laws women were largely absent from early Chinese-American history, the images and terminology that Kingston uses in relation to the land do not leave a space for women trying to find their voice in this history.[6] While one might argue that it is unfair to hold Kingston responsible for articulating a female voice in a book specifically focusing on Chinese-American males, the question remains as to why Chinese-American males and females must speak their history through different genres and with different vocabularies. Kingston, through the character Ah Goong, configures the land as something to be conquered and overcome. He has a highly erotic relationship to the whole landscape and, in one unforgettable scene, is so overcome by the beauty of the scenery that he ejaculates out of a hanging basket into a valley yelling, "I'm fucking the world" (*China Men* 133). This type of language, that sexualizes and feminizes the land and puts it in terms of possession, is characteristic of a great deal of the writing about Western expansionism and the Frontier. Not only is it troubling in terms of the environment, but it raises concerns about finding a place for women when this male centered language underlies Kingston's version of Chinese-American historical myth.[7]

While Kingston treats these visions of Chinese-American masculinity with irony and humor, she does, nevertheless, celebrate them as symbols of Chinese-Americanness. She juxtaposes Ah Goong's view of Chinese men as "pale, thin Chinese scholars and the rich men fat like Buddhas" and the positive ideal of "these brown muscular railroad men" (*China Men* 142). Ah Goong tells himself, "He was an American for having built the railroad" (*China Men* 145). By participating in this visible, public part of American history, by "fucking the world," and by becoming an American masculine ideal, Ah Goong can claim a place as a Chinese-American, but where does that leave Chinese-American women? Perhaps a partial answer can be found in the relationship of a woman to nationalism in *The Woman Warrior.*

In the controversy surrounding *The Woman Warrior,* one of the most often heard accusations charges Kingston with an alliance with white feminism and denying the cause of Chinese-American nationalism. Her detractors read her criticism of Chinese and Chinese-American men as another display of pandering to a white audience and a betrayal of Chinese-Americans, more specifically Chinese-American men. The strong reaction to Kingston's book recalls the injunctions of the ethnicizing of gender described by Wong. Wong analyzes a short story by Yi Li and says, "In Huang's eyes, strength in a Chinese woman is not only unwomanly but tantamount to ethnic betrayal" ("Ethnicizing Gender" 117). Since Americanness translates into masculinity, Chineseness for Huang suggests femininity, and a Chinese woman's deviance from prescribed gender roles connotes an abandonment of femininity and, by extension, Chineseness. Within this logic of ethnicity and gender, *The Woman Warrior* tells the story of a woman who rejects her feminine roles and thereby rejects her identity as a Chinese-American.

The Woman Warrior can be read as Kingston's attempts to reconcile the opposition between feminism and nationalism through her reworking of the genre of autobiography. Jean Franco argues that the study of gendered subjects who exist in the periphery and "off center" forces us to alter hierarchical thinking and "challenges the often unexamined assumptions that yoke feminism with bourgeois individualism" (xi). Kingston does challenge those assumptions and deviates not only from the convention of ethnic autobiography but also from the "bourgeois individualism" of many feminist autobiographies. Rita Felski in *Beyond Feminist Aesthetics* plots what she sees as the usual trajectory of feminist autobiography and relates it to the masculine tradition of the *Bildungsroman*. In feminist autobiography of the 1970s and 1980s, according to Felski, women move from the private to the public sphere and break away from their place in patriarchy, emphasizing "internal growth and self-understanding rather than public self-realization." In contrast, the protagonist in *The Woman Warrior* eventually moves away from the Chinese-American community, "out of the hating range," but her purported goal is always directed towards the community. Her search for self-understanding and for her identity is invested in a recognition by the community since her identity cannot be fully realized outside of a social relationship. By insisting on a feminist view while maintaining the centrality of community, Kingston attempts to link feminism with community and nationalism rather than individualism.

By incorporating issues of nationalism and community into the autobiographical form, Kingston further complicates the public/private divide suggested by that form. Autobiography, often seen as a private form of writing about the individual, seeps into the public arena in *The Woman Warrior* as I noted above. Notions of the public and private shift from those in *China Men*. In *China Men* I defined the public as the Anglo-American discourse as opposed to Chinese-American history that was, by that definition, private. But in *The Woman Warrior,* that world of the private sphere shrinks even smaller. While Chinatown may represent a private world to the "public" world of the American metropolis, in this book Chinatown is the public world that shapes the protagonist's "private" or personal identity. The dichotomy of the public and private becomes even more vexed because of the uneasy place that the protagonist in *The Woman Warrior* occupies within the Chinese-American community. Rather than viewing that community as her private sphere, the community also functions as the public sphere to the much tighter circle of her family. Instead of grappling with Bhabha's question about "representative authority" as an oppositional force within dominant culture, the book's protagonist must struggle with her ability to even speak as a Chinese-American in her own community.

Before the protagonist can participate in the public debate over Chinese-American history, she tries to find "public" recognition as a Chinese-American within her community. Once again she attempts to negotiate this public/ private divide with a manipulation of genre.

Jean Franco tells us that, "nationalism demands new kinds of subjects invested with authority to define the true and the real" (xviii). The protagonist of *The Woman Warrior* attempts to obtain this authority through the interruption of the genre of autobiography with mythology. By interspersing the autobiographical sections with mythology, Kingston stresses the importance of myths in creating the narratives of our daily lives and the necessity of new stories to tell ourselves. Only through a fantastic rewriting of the myth of Fa Mu Lan can the protagonist reconcile the opposition between feminism and nationalism. By rewriting the fable, she creates a Chinese myth that allows her to subvert gender roles and still be a national hero. Through Chinese myths she begins to realize a Chinese-American identity and says, "The swordswoman and I are not so dissimilar. May my people understand the resemblance soon so that I can return to them" (*Woman Warrior* 62).

That recognition never fully arrives so she cannot be "invested with the authority to define the true and the real," and she cannot redefine nationalism along the lines of her invented heroine. As we are reminded by the mother in the first chapter, one does not exist without recognition from the community. "You wouldn't like to be forgotten as if you had never been born" (*Woman Warrior* 5). She remains distanced from Chinatown in a world where, "the colors are gentler and fewer, smells are antiseptic. Now when I peek in the basement window where the villagers say they see a girl dancing like a bottle imp, I can no longer see a spirit . . ." (*Woman Warrior* 238). Still, the last pages perform a fictional resolution, and she tells her mother's story, "The beginning is hers, the ending mine" (*Woman Warrior* 240). She shares a story with her mother and, by writing the ending, she makes it her own and writes herself into a communal myth. In the final utopian moment we can imagine that her story, like the songs Ts'ai Yen brought "back from savage lands," can be understood by her childhood community since "It translated well" (*Woman Warrior* 243).

In the end, Kingston never gives us the ultimate solution to the conflict between nationalism and gender. Despite her attempts to subvert or write alternatives to the many master narratives of Anglo-American history, Chinese-American nationalism, feminist autobiography, and Chinese-American autobiography, among others, she can never completely escape those narratives. While she decenters these narratives and calls into question the gendered assumptions that enable them to function, she still remains inscribed within their discourse and writes in reaction to those discourses. Nevertheless, Kingston's project cannot be read as either a complete failure or a complete triumph. Her manipulation of generic forms opens up a space for her to explore Chinese-American identity and to imagine the different shapes it can take.

Notes

1.   Here I wish to invoke Judith Butler's *Gender Trouble*. Kingston "troubles" and problematizes the categories of genre and, by "making trouble," forces us to reconsider genre.

2.   I am not characterizing Chinese-American communities simply as "private" as I hope to show by my use of quotation marks. Instead, I will argue in this essay that notions of public and private are constantly shifting depending upon a similarly shifting positionality.

3. See Jade Snow Wong's *Fifth Chinese Daughter*, Pardee Lowe's *Father and Glorious Descendant* as popular examples of early Chinese-American autobiography often classified as "tourguides."

4. See Donna Haraway's *Cyborgs, Simians and Women* for a discussion of situated knowledge. She formulates a model of identity that accepts a type of situated knowledge that does not lay claim to any universal knowledge and accepts the subject's inability to know itself completely.

5. Wong talks about the function of these assignments of gender and ethnicity in terms of sexuality, but it would also be useful in analyzing the relationship of genre to gender and ethnic identity.

6. In an effort to keep a steady supply of cheap labor while also preventing the Chinese from settling in America, a series of laws prohibiting the immigration of Chinese women were enacted. These laws were passed to encourage the laborers to eventually return to China or face a future of bachelorhood.

7. See Annette Kolodny's *The Lay of the Land* for an in-depth discussion of the relationship between feminine metaphors of the land and colonialism.

Works Cited

Bhabha, Homi. "DissemiNation: Time, Narrative, and the Margins of the Modern Nation." *Nation and Narration*. Ed. Homi Bhabha. New York: Routledge, 1990. 291–322.

Chin, Frank. "Come All Ye Asian American Writers of the Real and the Fake." *The Big Aiiieeeee!: An Anthology of Chinese American and Japanese American Literature*. Ed. Jeffery Paul Chan et al. New York: Meridian, 1974. 1–92.

Felski, Rita. *Beyond Feminist Aesthetics: Feminist Literature and Social Change*. Cambridge: Harvard UP, 1989.

Franco, Jean. *Plotting Women: Gender and Representation in Mexico*. New York: Columbia UP, 1988.

Fischer, Michael. "Ethnicity and the Post-Modern Arts of Memory." *Writing Culture: The Poetics and Politics of Ethnography*. Ed. James Clifford and George Marcus. Berkeley: U of California P, 1986. 194–233.

Goellnicht, Donald. "Tang Ao in America: Male Subject Positions in *China Men*." *Reading the Literatures of Asian America*. Ed. Shirley Geok-lin Lim and Amy Ling. Philadelphia: Temple UP, 1992. 191–212.

Hutcheon, Linda. *A Poetics of Postmodernism: History, Theory, Fiction*. New York: Routledge, 1989.

Kingston, Maxine Hong. *China Men*. New York: Vintage, 1975.

———. *The Woman Warrior*. New York: Vintage, 1975.

Lowe, Pardee. *Father and Glorious Descendant*. Boston: Little, Brown, 1943.

Slotkin, Richard. "Myth and the Production of History." *Ideology and Classic American Literature*. Eds. Sacvan Bercovitch and Myra Jehlen. New York: Cambridge UP, 1986. 70–90.

Talbot, Stephen. "Talking Story: Maxine Hong Kingston Rewrites the American Dream." *San Francisco Examiner* 24 June 1990, *Image*: 6–17.

Trinh T. Minh-ha. *Woman, Native, Other; Writing Postcoloniality and Feminism*. Bloomington: U of Indiana P, 1989.

Wong, Jade Snow. *Fifth Chinese Daughter*. New York: Harper, 1950.

Wong, Sau-ling. "Autobiography as Guided Chinatown Tour? Maxine Hong Kingston's *The Woman Warrior* and the Chinese-American Autobiographical Controversy." *Multicultural*

Autobiography: American Lives. Ed. James Payne. Knoxville: U of Tennessee P, 1992. 248–79.

———. "Ethnicizing Gender: An Exploration of Sexuality as Sign in Chinese Immigrant Literature." *Reading the Literatures of Asian America.* Ed. Shirley Geok-lin Lim and Amy Ling. Philadelphia: Temple UP, 1992. 111–29.

REVIEWS OF
TRIPMASTER MONKEY
◆

Wittman at the Golden Gate

BHARATI MUKHERJEE

World-class writers like Joyce, Garcia Márquez, Grass and blasphemous writers like Salman Rushdie not only transform our perceptions, they incarnate new realities. Nabokov's *Lolita,* with its incipient love of mall-sprawls, gave us an America very different from Donna Reed's. Now *Tripmaster Monkey* by the homegrown American, Maxine Hong Kingston, whacks into birth an America in which "the common man has Chinese looks," and in which Walt Whitman reincarnates himself as Wittman Ah Sing, a fifth-generation Chinese-American.

Kingston has already given us two extraordinary memoirs of growing up Chinese-American, *The Woman Warrior: Memoirs of a Girlhood Among Ghosts* and *China Men.* The memoirs were, simultaneously, a search (for "roots") and a disclosure (of a new ghetto). In *Tripmaster Monkey,* her brash, punchy, loud-mouthed first novel, Kingston repudiates nostalgia for China and "dukes out" (Wittman's favorite phrase) the critics' insistence on ghettoizing American writers with Asian names. We're neither "exotic" nor "inscrutable." Wittman, a poet and playwright, "had been tripping out on the wrong side of the street. The wrong side of the world . . . His province was America. America, his province." The woman-warrior has yielded place to the writer-samurai. Writing is an act of military aggression. The unequivocal goal is conquest.

Though Wittman is a writer, this is no conventional rendering of the artist as a young man. Wittman is a werewolf, a shape-changer. He is the Monkey of Chinese legends, a tripper through 72 reincarnations, a savior, a discoverer of Inner Truth (Inner Truth is Wittman's Chinese byname). He is also the monkey-suited child of showbiz parents with absurd names, a Berkeley graduate, a closet-beatnik, a war-resister, a loner and drifter, a would-be reformer, a casual lover, an impulsive bridegroom and, most of all, a young man angry in the tradition of Frank Chin, another California writer.

Wittman's mission is to "spook out prejudice," and he finds prejudice everywhere: in the movies (remember Lon Chaney, Peter Sellers, Jerry Lewis and more with taped-up eyes?); in literature, especially in Kiplingesque accounts of Chinatown and in the orthography of ethnic speech ("Mark Twain's insultingly dumb dis and dat misspelling and apostrophying"); in institutions where bureaucrats routinely demand proof of citizenship from Asian-Americans. Wittman's enemy is as much the white writers who make Ming of Mongo and Confucius speak in the third person as it is Mr. and Mrs. Potato Head. "They're taking the 'I' away from us," Wittman accuses. Stop the linguistic emasculation, Kingston crusades.

A crusader demands a pulpit. The contemporary American conventions of story telling restrict and "sicken" Kingston/Wittman. *Tripmaster* is so *bloated* with talk-stories, myths, dreams and desires, history and trivia, anecdotes, jokes and indictments that it is only nominally a "novel." Wittman is "a stand-up tragic" in the tradition of stand-up comics. He slips on his "hallucination glasses" and "jumps reality to reality like quantum physics." The imaginary waterfalls and battlefields of the Monkey Kingdom assume the solidity of recognizable cities such as Oakland and Berkeley. Time takes on the pleated flexibility of an accordion.

New visions require a new vocabulary. Rushdie transforms the English language when he describes Bombay coffee ships in *Midnight's Children* or movie billboards in *The Satanic Verses*. Kingston does well enough, but doesn't quite pull off a Rushdie. Here's Kingston on North Beach: "Oh, the smell of the focaccia ovens—O Home. A florist with white moustachios jay-walked through traffic with armsful of leonine football chrysanthemums. Behind glass, at the all-day-night place on the pie-wedge corner, poets, one to a table, were eating breakfast. The Co-Existence Bagel Shop was gone. The old guys, *Seventh Seal* knights, had played chess with Death and lost. The Bagel shop, Mrs. Smith's Tea Room, Blabbermouth Night at the Place—all of a gone time."

In place of passion-infused language, we get cockily allusive one liners, such as "Daedalate the line-up from cow to mouth, and fill up your life." Of course, Kingston crams her paragraphs with references to literature and films for a purpose: Wittman the artist has been formed by the West, not the East. Still, there's a "get it? get it?" quality to the prose that's annoying. The stand-up comic goes for every joke, no matter how silly: "How is a minority poet a minor poet? You might make a joke on that?" or "Do Jews look down on men who use bobby pins to hold their yarmulkes on?"

There are some outrageously hilarious (more or less conventionally rendered) scenes in the Toys Department of a large store. Wittman is definitely a sales assistant to avoid! And those readers who, in spite of Kingston's admonition, look to her books for revelations about Chinese American ghettoes, will be rewarded. Wittman's relatives are not self-effacing laborers. They are flamboyant dancers, magicians, professional beauties with names like Ruby Long Legs, Zeppelin Ah Sing, Dr. Woo and the Flora Dora Girls. They outsmart immigration officials; they survive. Their children grow up to wear black leotards or cowboy boots, sip cappuccino in Berkeley cafes, and cringe at the sight of Fresh off the Boat families in polyester pantsuits spitting sun-flower seeds on sidewalks.

Tripmaster Monkey is a remarkable display of wit and rage. When Wittman invites you, "Fellow tripper, come through the night, come home," heed his invitation. And when he adds the "not every last one of us who trips out of a Friday night makes it back home," heed, too, the caution.

Manic Monologue

Anne Tyler

Maxine Hong Kingston's many admirers will probably be surprised to learn that *Tripmaster Monkey* is billed as her first novel. Her first? What about *The Woman Warrior?* What about *China Men?*

Well, true, those may have read like novels, with their daring leaps of language and flights of imagination; but they were actually nonfiction—the former a study of the women in her family, the latter a study of the men. They were full of poetry, but they were based upon the facts of Chinese immigrant life in this country.

So this is, indeed, her first honest-to-goodness novel: a great huge sprawling beast of a novel, over 400 pages densely packed with the rantings and ravings and pranks and high jinks of one Wittman Ah Sing, a young Chinese-American (but how he would hate that term! Correction: American) rattling around San Francisco at some indeterminate point in the early 1960s. Just a year out of Berkeley, Wittman divides his time between writing poetry and clerking in a toy department, and when we first meet him he's considering suicide, but in such animated and slapdash terms that he doesn't have us worried for a moment.

A few of Wittman's mottoes are: "Better to be dead than boring," "Always do the more flamboyant thing," and "Do something, even if it's wrong." You see where all this could lead—and it does. Wittman's life is anything but dull. During the course of this novel, which encompasses just two months or so, Wittman gets fired for staging a pornographic scene between a Barbie doll and a battery-operated monkey, marries a virtual stranger in an impromptu ceremony performed by a mail-order minister, and produces a marathon play whose cast consists of nearly everyone he's ever met. And that's just the plot's stripped skeleton. There's much, much more, all of it related in his own highly exclamatory interior voice:

> At noon, Wittman got up and walked his bathroom gear, including his private roll of toilet paper, down the hall. He walked in on a woman, who scolded him

From *The New Republic* 200 (17 Apr. 1989): 44–46. Copyright 1989 by *The New Republic,* Inc. Reprinted by permission of *The New Republic,* Inc.

from her throne, "Who do you think you are, haw, boy? Haw, boy?" As he stepped out—her own fault, she hadn't locked the door—she called him some of the many Chinese words for "crazy"—"Saw! Deen! Moong cha cha! Ngow! Kang!" So many ways to go bananas. Kang, the highest degree of nuts. "Too late, he's gone kang." He returned to his room and pissed in the sink. "There comes a time in life when everybody must take a piss in the sink—here, let me paint the window black for a minute."

Many of Wittman's most impassioned monologues, private or public, have to do with his resentment of the way white Americans perceive him. Why, he wonders, do readers always assume a character is white unless they're told otherwise? (" 'Dear reader, all these characters whom you've been identifying with—Bill, Brooke, and Annie—are Chinese—and *I* am too.' The fiction is spoiled. You who read have been suckered along, identifying like hell, and find out that you've been getting a peculiar, colored, slanted p.o.v.") And why, he asks his theater audience, do white Americans always focus immediately upon his Chineseness?

"Let this be the last time anyone says or hears the following: 'Where do you come from?' I deign to retort, 'Sacramento,' or 'Hanford,' or 'Bakersfield,' you don't get the sarcasm, do you. 'How long have you been in the country?' 'How do you like our country?' 'Fine,' I say; 'how do *you* like it?' 'Do you speak English?' Particularly after I've been talking for hours, don't ask, 'Do you speak English?' The voice doesn't go with the face, they don't hear it. On the phone I sound like anybody. I get the interview, but I get downtown, they see my face, they ask, 'Do you speak English?' Watch, as I leave this stage tonight after my filibuster, somebody's going to ask me, 'You speak the language?' "

Tripmaster Monkey is a novel of excesses—both the hero's and the author's. Wittman careens through the story with that oversupply of manic energy often found in bright, idealistic, not-yet-mellowed young men; and Kingston describes his adventures in a style equally manic, equally energetic. If we didn't know better, we could imagine this book had been written by, say, a 23-year-old newly graduated college student.

Sometimes this is dazzling. How does she do it? we marvel. Where, for instance, does she find the vitality to embark upon a minutely detailed five-page description of what a roomful of high and contact-high party guests sees while staring at a blank TV screen? How has she managed to summon the youthful quirkiness, the youthful sense of limitless time and entirely idle curiosity, that allows Wittman to delight in the reflection of his own naked crotch as distorted by the handguard of a fencing sword? Or, for that matter, the youthful cruelty with which he surveys his fellow human beings? "*Her* turn to talk about *her* kiddie-hood," he reflects during a supposedly tender first date with a girl he's long admired. Children disgust him ("We have a lost child, a lost bleeding child found unconscious, possibly dead, in the Toy

Department," he imagines announcing when mothers park their offspring in his place of employment), and the sight of a recently immigrated Chinese family infuriates him:

> The whole family taking a cheap outing on their day off. Immigrants. Fresh Off the Boats out in public. Didn't know how to walk together. Spitting seeds. So uncool. You wouldn't mislike them on sight if their pants weren't so high-water, gym socks white and noticeable. F.O.B. fashions—highwaters or puddle-cuffs. Can't get it right. Uncool. Uncool.

But at other times the effect is exhausting—much as if that 23-year-old had taken up residence in our living room, staying way too long, as 23-year-olds are wont to do, and wearing us out with his exuberance. The myths and sagas are particularly tiring. Wittman loves to tell lengthy stories that possess the grandiosity and the meandering formlessness common to folk legends. It's hard to believe that his friends, who tend to be as frenetic as Wittman himself, would sit still for what amounts to hours of this. Certainly the reader has trouble doing so. After a while, the merest mention of Liu Pei or Sun Wu Kong, the Monkey King, is enough to make our eyes glaze over.

No, what keeps us with *Tripmaster Monkey* (and we do stay with it, wholeheartedly) is not the larger-than-life sagas that Wittman finds so compelling but the tiny, meticulously catalogued details that fill his quieter moments. Just listen to the jumbled conversation of his mother and aunts as they play mah-jongg, or watch the hilarious lengths to which his father will go to save money, or observe Wittman's extended, gently humorous encounter with an elderly applicant in the Unemployment Office. When he lists the outward signs of a disintegrating marriage (the shrimp shells rotting on the dinner table, the off-the-hook telephone lost among the dirty clothes), or when he announces his resolutions for self-improvement ("decant the catsup . . . wash coffee cup between usings. . . . Peel an orange into the garbage bag, okay, but then walk a ways off, don't slurp over the bag"), the miracle is that we are riveted to his words no matter how long they go on. These passages refuel us; they remind us how infinitely entertaining everyday life can be when it's observed with a fresh eye.

Chinese, American, Chinese-American—Wittman is all three, whether he likes it or not, and the reader benefits. That Wittman is Chinese gives his story depth and particularity. That he's American lends his narrative style a certain slangy insouciance. That he's Chinese-American, with the self-perceived outsider's edgy angle of vision, makes for a novel of satisfying complexity and bite and verve.

Demons and Warriors

Caroline Ong

Tripmaster Monkey is Maxine Hong Kingston's new, long-awaited work of fiction after her first two bestsellers, *Woman Warrior* and *China Men*. Thematically, Kingston has not drifted far from her previous concerns with cultural assimilation and the loss of roots in a displaced community like her own, but where the first two books focused on the generation gap, *Tripmaster Monkey* takes a view from the inside out, that of a central character who cannot free himself from the web of his heritage.

Kingston's protagonist is again an American-born Chinaman, Wittman Ah Sing, son of Zeppelin Ah Sing and Ruby Long of Sacramento. Set in the early 1960s, the novel uses the drug and beatnik culture of the San Francisco Bay area as a backdrop to Wittman's existentialist *Angst*. A dropout from Berkeley, a conscientious objector and draft-dodger, a welfare-scrounger, a frustrated poet-playwright and an unfilial son, Wittman is fated, cursed (or perhaps blessed) by his Chinese middle name Joang Fu (meaning "inner truth"), to seek but never find "truth" and "reality." He has a visionary dream of himself as the "present-day U.S.A. incarnation" of the Monkey God of Chinese mythological history, whose contemporary mission is twofold: to restore pride and dignity to an oriental heritage no longer valid for an American-born generation of Chinese and Japanese youth who consider themselves as Americans (no prefix attached), and to regenerate a sense of community among those lost amid the predominantly White culture of America.

Named after Walt Whitman, the great soul poet of America, the Chinese Wittman, a self-professed "fool for literature," seems to spend his entire waking life tripped out not on any of the mind and reality-altering drugs abundant in San Francisco in the 1960s, but on words and language, fictions and histories, handed down from his cultural past despite their irrelevance to the world he lives in. Surreal, fantastic, and at times bordering on the incomprehensible, *Tripmaster Monkey* takes the reader inside Wittman's head for a view of the moment-by-moment, day-to-day existence of one who often conflates dream with reality, by materializing a mythical imagery of demons and

From *Times Literary Supplement*. London: *Times Literary Supplement*, 15 Sept. 1989: 998. Copyright 1989 by the *Times Literary Supplement*. Reprinted by permission of the *Times Literary Supplement*.

warriors. In the down-and-outs and street people of the city, in his friends and family, he thinks he sees other mythological figures reincarnated; but they are trapped in the bodies of those who refuse to believe in these facets of themselves. In spite of these preoccupations, Wittman manages to do as ordinary people do. He gets fired from his job as sales assistant in a large toy shop, falls in unrequited love, visits his parents, gets married, and even manages to write and stage an epic Chinese play, *The Romance of the Three Kingdoms.*

Kingston's command of language and imagery is nowhere more apparent than when Wittman is not in control of the material things and emotional trips in his life. But there is a self-indulgence in the way she contrives increasingly bizarre situations to show off her character's exuberant love for words and literature. To relieve the tedium of a bus ride across town, Wittman reads Rilke's *The Notebooks of Malte Laurids Brigge* aloud to his fellow-passengers trapped in the locked bus. Much of the novel, in fact, reads like the workings of a mind on a drug-induced psychedelic trip. This is a description of breakfast at daybreak:

> Sky poured pink through the windows. Everyone floated in pink air—spun sugar, spun glass, angel's hair, champagne. . . . Is it a time of year—a season of rose air? The crew in the lightbooth has flipped on the pink gels, and tinted all the stage and the men's and women's faces. It seemed you could float out the window on the strange atmosphere. . . .

Yet Kingston takes great pains self-consciously to situate herself amidst this abundance of language. The chapters end with editorial comments like "Our monkey man will live—he parties, he plays—though unemployed. To see how he does it, go on to the next chapter," and "A reader doesn't have to pay more money for the next chapter or admission to the show if there's going to be a show, you might as well travel on with our monkey for the next while." This omniscient narratorial voice exposes the flimsy underpinnings of The Tripmaster Monkey's delusional Monkey-God fantasies. Perhaps this explains the book's rather puzzling subtitle, "His Fake Book."

This book will both delight and disappoint. Readers who enjoyed Kingston's dazzling use of dream imagery in her earlier works will be enthralled by the rhythms set up by her extremely loose narrative style, which weaves back and forth between imaginative brilliance and ironic reality. But the way in which she ultimately controls and resolves this counterpoint is somewhat contrived. Many of her characterizations seem to start out as satirical caricatures. Ruby Long, Wittman's mother, used to be the showgirl Ruby Long Legs (pronounced "Looby Long Legs" by the Chinese audiences) in a revue called The Wongettes, and his father Zeppelin (the dirigible) Ah Sing, in fulfilling the dream of all Chinese who come to the Golden Mountain (the Chinese name for San Francisco), writes a newsletter called *Find Treasure,* which features an abandoned mine each week. At the end of the book, they remain amusingly ridiculous, and we are no nearer understanding their middle-class lives and middle-American values, despite Wittman's attempts to assemble in his play all these caricatures of Chinese/Japanese idiosyncrasies. The fact that Wittman's epic drama is such a resounding success also seems much too convenient; after all, it has to succeed in order to save our hero from turning into a long-haired "bum-low" in the eyes of the very community that he wants to "save."

ESSAYS ON
TRIPMASTER MONKEY

◆

Clashing Constructs of Reality:
Reading Maxine Hong Kingston's
Tripmaster Monkey:
His Fake Book as
Indigenous Ethnography

PATRICIA LIN

A postmodern artist or writer is in the position of a philosopher: the text [s/]he writes, the work [s/]he produces are not in principle governed by preestablished rule, and they cannot be judged according to a determining judgment, by applying familiar categories to the text or to the work. Those rules and categories are what the work of art itself is looking for.

—Jean-Francois Lyotard

It has been close to fifteen years since Maxine Hong Kingston first published *The Woman Warrior: Memoirs of a Girlhood among Ghosts.* In the ensuing years, the work has been both praised and censured. In one of the first critical essays on the work I had suggested that the form within which Kingston chose to frame her story was very much in keeping with the vision and agenda of the postmodern writer (Lin-Blinde 1979). Then, as it is today with her most recent work, *Tripmaster Monkey: His Fake Book,* any attempts at reading Kingston require a revision on the part of the reader's assumptions about literary genres, authorial voice, and the question of veracity—particularly as her works pertain to "truthful" or "accurate" representations of Chinese Americans (Wong 1988). Attention to form as a structure of knowledge as well as a principle for organizing experience, in other words, is a requisite activity in any attempt at understanding a cultural projection of postmodernism such as Kingston's new work (Connor 5; Fischer 208–13).

From *Reading the Literatures of Asian American Literature,* ed. Shirley Geok-lin Lim and Amy Ling. Philadelphia: Temple University Press, 1992, 333–48. Copyright 1992 by Temple University Press. Reprinted by permission of Temple University Press.

The Woman Warrior was and still is categorized (and hence read) as an "autobiography" even by otherwise sophisticated readers and critics. This generic label continues to lend itself to readings that are locked into the expectations associated with autobiographies, including the demand that Kingston's accounts of her family's history and Chinese American reality adhere to some determinable measure of truth. Interviews of Kingston's mother have been undertaken to "prove" that the writer had in fact misrepresented events in the family's history, as well as distorting Chinese American culture. Kingston's detractors who claim that she has distorted the Chinese American experience (Chan 1977) have similarly responded to the ideological precepts inherent in the autobiographical form. Their contentions are that there are uncontestable truths about Chinese Americans. Any experience that deviates from a set of given parameters about the Chinese American experience does not conform to the truth-telling mandate of the autobiography and is thus fictive, that is, an untruth. There is of course a circularity to this logic: if autobiography (as a mechanism for organizing and retelling the life of an individual) delimits what can be regarded as "truth," it does so by setting up the sort of "truth" that necessitates excluding what cannot be accommodated. The "truth" which emerges is hence the kind of truth that Nietzsche saw as possible only through the "lies" of exclusion.

On the cover jacket of *Tripmaster Monkey* we are discreetly told in small print that the work is a "novel" and on the inside flap the publishers announce that "this is Maxine Hong Kingston's first work of fiction." As with *The Woman Warrior* the rush to delineate Kingston's new work within recognizable formal boundaries threatens to minimize some critically important aspects of *Tripmaster Monkey*. More significantly, the failure to recognize *Tripmaster Monkey* as something both more and less than a novel deprives the work of a place among the representative voices of the postmodern era. Furthermore, the narrow definition assigned to Kingston's most recent work detracts attention from the crucial recognition that ethnic Americans, by virtue of their hybridized experiences as identified by critics of postmodernism such as Baudrillard, Jameson, and Lyotard, in a sense have always carried the essential germ of the postmodern (Baudrillard; Connor; Giroux; Gitlin; Jameson 1983, 1984a, 1984b; Lyotard; Newman). Specifically, their experiences identify them as persons at the intersections of contested cultural codes and discourses who are uniquely positioned and enpowered to undertake what new anthropology terms the task of the "indigeneous ethnographer (Clifford 9).

Within the last decade anthropologists have grappled with the privileged status of the Western world's most characteristic discursive modes including the discourses of science, philosophy, and literature. Rejecting the authority and rhetorical stance to represent those deemed "primitive," "without culture/history," or "pre-literate," new ethnography mirrors the postmodern condition in its efforts to represent the multiplicity of human existence using a much wider range of discourses than the approved scientific, textual, and empirical approaches of "the classic norms of social analysis [that] have eroded since the late 1960's" (Rosaldo 28). "Writing reduced to method: keeping good field notes, making accurate maps, 'writing up results' " (Clifford 2) have given way to a postmodern ethnography that is

> a cooperatively evolved text consisting of fragments of discourses intended to evoke in the minds of both reader and writer an emergent fantasy of a possible world of commonsense reality, and thus to provoke an aesthetic integration that will have a therapeutic effect. It is, in a word, poetry—not in its textual form, but in its return to the original context and function of poetry, which, by means of its performative break with everyday speech, [evokes] memories of the ethos of the community. (Tyler 125–26)

The argument for reading *Tripmaster Monkey* as an ethnographic enterprise of the postmodern era rather than as a novel is based on the premise that it "anthropologizes" rather than novelizes the United States. In other words, ethnography exposes the constitution of everyday or taken for granted realities—unlike the novel, whose representations of reality are meant to simulate the actual. The lenses through which both Kingston and the book's protagonist Wittman Ah Sing view the world around them, and to which the reader in turn is subjected, are in effect those which defamiliarize the familiar. "Letting it all come in"—as Wittman puts it (4), uncensored and uneditorialized by some internalized authorial voice—becomes one of the work's central tropes for the multilayered postmodern condition: a condition that challenges us with its contradictions, discontinuities, repetitions, and complexities. Correspondingly, the ethnographic enterprise is the reflexive attempt to talk about the inconsistencies of life in the latter third of the twentieth century.

The complexities are particularly evident in the person of Wittman Ah Sing. A fifth-generation native Californian of Chinese American ancestry, he is a descendant of a great-great-grandfather who arrived in the New World on the Nootka, a boat "as ancestral as the Mayflower" (41). (Nootka Sound off British Columbia was the first settlement of Chinese in North America.) With this, his claim to American nativism is established, even though as a Chinese he and his family are part of a community historically disenfranchised in American society. The contradictions are further heightened by the fact that, unlike many native Chinese Americans who are descended from laborers who arrived in the United States in the nineteenth century, Wittman is able to trace his lineage to a long line of actors and entertainers. Instead of coming in search of gold during the Gold Rush, Wittman's folks came to California "to play . . . [staging] plays that went on for five hours a night, continuing the next night, the same long play going on for a week with no repeats" (250). He himself was "born backstage in vaudeville" and kept in a theatrical trunk with "wall paper lining, grease paint, and mothball smells, paste smell" (13). His mother, a Chinese American showgirl, was a "Flora Dora girl" named Ruby Long Legs. She was part of a roadshow known as Dr. Woo and the Chinese Flora Dora Girls that traversed the United States "boogie-woogying and saluting right through World War II" raising money for war bonds. His father, who has the unlikely name of Zeppelin Ah Sing, was a "Stagedoor Johnny" who was later incorporated into the roadshow, first as a backstage electrician then an onstage emcee.

The personal history is an overly familiar one in American lore. It resonates comfortably with stories about the early lives of others in American entertainment history—"The Seven Little Foys," a fifties movie starring Bob Hope, for instance, depicted the itinerant life of vaudevillian Eddie Foy and seven of his children who were part of his family act. Likewise, the popular song "Born in a trunk at the Princess Theatre/in Pocatello, Idaho" clearly reaffirms the American tradition that there is an innateness to being an entertainer. In Wittman Ah Sing's case, a note of dissonance is struck by the fact that the players in his story are Chinese. The comfortably familiar and well-entrenched "born in a trunk" story is thus "defamiliarized," if we are to use Shklovsky's term (Lemon and Reis 4), giving us a decentered, double vision of the story: from this perspective we see the historical exclusion of the fact that Chinese Americans too have been part of America's theatrical and vaudeville lore.

The disjunctured, decentralized perspective is an important characteristic of postmodernism. In an era where material artifacts and information proliferate and bombard the senses it becomes humanly impossible to trace things to single causes and "truths," much less to be able to reach back to points of origins. The dictum of the era is the impossibility of the new, namely that there are no new stories, ideas, or constructs left to be made since all things that can be said or done have so been done. Jameson in his critique of postmodernism thus identifies *pastiche* as the only interpretive mode that remains possible. As a mode, it capitalizes on the "already made" by borrowing, even plagiarizing, and repeating bits and pieces of other works wholesale with little or no commentary. Through this "metareferencing," that is, the placement side by side of two fragments of a work, each work is flattened and emptied of its specific contents, thus blurring the distinctions between past, present, and future (Jameson 1983, 117). In the postmodern era, what is finally left for the artist is the task of re-presenting representations. No "realism" or "realistic" representations are possible, Jameson adds, once we become conscious that "we seem condemned to seek the historical past through our own pop images and stereotypes about the past, which remains forever out of reach (Jameson 1983, 118).

What is actually going on in postmodernism and informing Kingston's *Tripmaster Monkey* is the recognition that we, like Wittman Ah Sing, all arrive in an "already made" world. This is a world (as we have increasingly been made aware of since the sixties) that is preinhabited and defined by mythologies, stereotypes, and cultural constructs, all of which have equal though arbitrary claims on our lives. For Wittman Ah Sing, who graduates during the Vietnam era from the University of California, Berkeley with a major in English literature, his own life becomes a converging point of pre-scripted texts and clashing cultural constructs. These textual and cultural constructs occupy a "polyphonic space," where they offer an interplay of voices from a range of different sources that shape and actualize Wittman's existence.

From the opening pages of *Tripmaster Monkey* the reader is moved along with Wittman from one pre-written text to another. Rilke's *Malte Laurids Brigge* is tightly interwoven into the contextual ground of Wittman's life to the point where it forms a prescription or template for Wittman's existence. Like Malte Laurids, Wittman is an aspiring writer. They are about the same age (Rilke/Malte Laurids was twenty-eight when he arrived in Paris in 1902; Wittman is a year out of college), both adrift in busy metropolitan cities. The extensive excerpts of *Malte Laurids Brigge* that appear in *Tripmaster Monkey,* as well as the obvious parallels between Malte Laurids and Wittman, underscore the point that lives are dictated by preexisting textual scripts, thus undermining the question of either the uniqueness or privileged status of identity. In contrast to the novelistic determinants vis à vis character and its development, we find that Wittman is less a signifier of human typology than a locus for the recovery of prior texts, codes, and representations. As a Chinese American, however, Wittman's scenario is also the unique rendezvous point of numerous classical Chinese texts such as Shih Nai-An/Lo Kuan Chung's *Shui Hu Chuan* (variously translated as *The Water Margin, The Water Verge* and *All Men Are Brothers*); Wu Cheng-en's *Hsi Yu Chi* (translated as *Monkey, Tripitaka,* and *Journey to the West*); and various other works from the Chinese classical canon including *The Three Kingdoms* and *The Dream of the Red Chamber.*

Significantly, Kingston uses Monkey (Sun Wu Kong) as Wittman's choice of an alter ego: "I am really," he says, "the present-day U.S.A. incarnation of the King of the Monkeys" (33). In the Chinese classic, Monkey springs *sui generis* from a stone egg. On a dare from other monkeys in the forest he penetrates a water fall and discovers an edenic world. For his bravado he is made king of the monkeys and leads the other simians into the new kingdom. Monkey later seeks immortality by entering a monastery and acquires the Taoist/Zen-like name, "Aware of Emptiness." He masters the art of seventy-two transformations, which allows him to change his size and appearance, perform diverse magical acts, as well as cover great distances at a single leap. In the best known part of *Hsi Yu Chi,* Monkey accompanies the somewhat befuddled monk Tripitaka on a journey west to India to find the Buddhist scriptures. The details of *Hsi Yu Chi,* and particularly the figure of Monkey, are used contextually with Rilke's *Malte Laurids Brigge,* to elucidate both the meaning of Wittman's artistic pursuit and characteristic postmodern awareness, namely the "awareness of emptiness" where all things deemed "true" or "real" are fundamentally human-made constructs. As such, nothing really new can be invented and the work of the artist lies simply in the rearrangement of prefabrications in such a manner as to simply suggest the new. As would-be writer and playwright in the postmodern sixties, Wittman's fate is not to invent but to retell stories and stage an epic based on ancient established Chinese stories. He is, like Monkey, a trickster since his tale-spinning and dramatic renditions of something old are enterprises requiring manipulations and "magical" transformations of reality to produce a sense of novelty. "[In] all magic acts," Wittman muses, "you have to cheat, the missing step is cheating" (17).

Like Monkey, the postmodern man Wittman has no origins to which he can make absolute claims. His parents both defy traditional definitions of parenthood, and he has a mysterious grandmother he is not sure is in fact his grandmother. As a fifth generation Chinese American, he feels no connections to the large numbers of recent Chinese immigrants: "What did he [Wittman] have to do with these foreigners? With F.O.B. emigres?" he wonders (41). Deracinated from those with whom he shares nothing except national origins, he is ostensibly free through the trickery of disguise, change of costume, hair length, and beard to take on whatever appearances or forms he chooses from the range of prototypes that he, as a Chinese American, is able to avail himself from both the Euro-American and Chinese reservoirs of culture and history. As a product of Berkeley in the sixties, however, Wittman opts for the appearance of "a Chinese hippy." His wardrobe consists of a grab bag of used mismatched clothes: a blue pinstriped suit ("of some dead businessman," 44) bought for five dollars from the Salvation Army, a green shirt and tie, and Wellingtons. Neither the suit nor the shirt and tie match and the outfit clashes incongruously with his long hair. The effect, he hoped, would be "an affront to anybody who looked at him" (44). Defiance of cultural norms is obvious at one level, but the deliberate combination of mismatched articles of clothing suggests a transformational magic at work—namely, the creation of a new if bizarre look salvaged from oddments and discards. Self-creation through costume changes as well as cosmetics and surgery is clearly linked to the fictive and fluid status of identity in postmodern society. As a late twentieth century "trip master" (i.e., one skilled at manipulating halluncinations, if we are to use the sixties coinage for "trip"), Wittman stands for the constituted self that is eclectic, ephemeral, and an empty signifier moving from one theater of action to another without serious engagement in the actualities. Disengagement through disguise becomes a means of both challenging and transcending social and cultural boundaries and norms: one can be anyone one wants through a change of outfits, yet costumes which hold their own signified meanings can also be made to signify something other than what they were originally intended to signify. Specifically, the banker's suit that Wittman wears with his hippy hair-do and Wellingtons no longer signifies the wearer's profession or social standing, placing its wearer instead in another realm or "theater" of society.

However, because he is racially Chinese and clothed irrevocably in "this-color wongsky skin," Wittman still wears the "uniform" that marks him as marginal in white America. In this society that essentially has not or will not catch on to the arbitrariness of externals as a basis for hierarchical ordering, Wittman (alias the individual "Aware of Emptiness," particularly of empty signifiers) is nevertheless helpless despite his insights.

The Monkey parallelism is brought home in this instance as Wittman's Chineseness resonates with the fact that Monkey, despite his considerable magical prowess, was often at the mercy of both humans and the gods who could not transcend their experience of him as a simian. Tripitaka, Monkey's Buddhist master, for instance, tricks him into putting on a gold band around his head. This band becomes a device to control Monkey, for in the event Monkey does not act in accordance to Tripitaka's wishes, the Buddhist monk mutters a prayer and the band squeezes around the monkey's head causing him to writhe in agony until he promises to conform. Kingston uses instances from the *Hsi Yu Chi* to suggest Wittman's vulnerability, in an episode where his "showbiz" parents actually treat him as a monkey when he is a child. In one episode, while his father Zeppelin plays a hurdy-gurdy, little Wittman, dressed in an outfit actually meant for a monkey complete with opening for a tail, collects donations from the audience. But it is this reduction to animal status that enables Wittman to function as the subversive factor in terms of whatever undesirable circumstances he finds himself. Thus, in both *Tripmaster Monkey* and *Hsi Yu Chi* the interplay of vulnerability versus obvious empowerment suggests the paradox where it is the very appearance of powerlessness that ultimately enables Wittman and Monkey to master both their environments and those around them, to be a "trip master."

The American pop-culture counterpart to this paradox is "Superman" and in one scene Wittman actually merges the two myths. "Listen Lois [Lane]," Wittman tells an astonished date, " 'underneath these glasses'—ripping the glasses off, wiping them on his sleeve . . . I am really" and here he interjects the Chinese myth that he is the Monkey King rather than the expected Superman (33). The side-by-side placement of Superman and Monkey serves to demonstrate the arbitrariness in cultural choices about the constitution of heroism as well as to present the potential that this offers to Wittman Ah Sing and Everyman to reconstitute their own personae after whatever images of heroism they choose. In America, which has a culture that de Tocqueville saw as resembling the marketplace jamboree, a powerful alien from Krypton can thus hide out in a busy metropolis as mild-mannered, bespectacled Clark Kent until the demands arise for him "to leap tall buildings in a single bound," as well as display supranormal abilities in the service of good over evil. Likewise Wittman Ah Sing, the incarnation of Monkey, is capable of pole-vaulting into the skies and leading his band of heroes into battle against the "havoc monster" and so represents another entry into the postmodern cultural marketplace of unlikely heroes.

Wittman's dream, however, is to stage an already-written text—the Chinese classic *The Water Verge*. To Wittman the ultimate "trip" or constituted scenario is one where the boundaries between what is conventionally agreed upon as "real" merge with fictional reality. The dualistic enterprise at work in Wittman's project is to write both within the dramatic constructs as well as against them; by doing so he exposes the fictive, that is, the man-made and self-enclosed staginess of traditional drama. The spike of its contrived nature, Wittman thus tells his Caucasian lady love, his play nevertheless "continues like life" (169).

The play eventually includes his friends, various sundry denizens of his neighborhood, and his mother's band of now-retired, elderly, former show-girls who perform a reprise of their World War II showgirl routine. *The Water Verge* or *Shui Hu Chuan,* upon which Wittman's play is loosely based, is an epic with a hundred and eight characters; thirty-six of them are major characters and seventy-two of them are minor ones. The characters are all victims of a corrupt system and are forced to live their lives as fugitives and outlaws. Wherever possible, these outlaws take on evil government officials, and a la Robin Hood and his band, plunder the rich to help the poor and the oppressed. Although the *Shui Hu Chuan* is set in thirteenth-century China, it resonates thematically with the social protests and counterculture movement of the time during which Kingston's work is based. For Wittman, restaging the *Shui Hu Chuan* is a means of protesting the war in Southeast Asia: "Our monkey, master of change staged a fake war, which might very well be displacing some real war" (306). Wittman, however, cannot claim this protest as his own "voice"—that protest is already embedded in the authorial voice of the writer of the *Shui Hu Chuan* and the only way that Wittman the postmodern playwright can claim preeminence is by repeating an existing text.

In one of Jorge Luis Borges' short stories, "Pierre Menard the Author of Don Quixote," Pierre Menard, the principal character, actually wants to write the work *Don Quixote,* that is, to commit an act of textual repetition. To this end, Pierre Menard initially considers actually becoming Cervantes but eventually rejects this scheme as being less interesting than writing *Don Quixote* by being Pierre Menard himself. The point of Borges' fable, Alicia Borinsky explains, is to suggest the idea of authorship/authority as "the production of voice" and to raise questions about how this voice is extended in its discourse (Borinsky 92). In rewriting *Don Quixote,* Pierre Menard used the archaic Spanish version of Cervantes and, according to Borinsky, "re-enacted Cervantes"—in other words, he used Cervantes' discursive mode since he, Mennard, cannot be Cervantes and hence cannot create an original work.

A similar situation presents itself to Wittman Ah Sing, who as an American of Chinese descent must "re-enact" writers from both the Euro-American and Chinese canon since he receives the discursive voices from both traditions. In both *Tripmaster Monkey: His Fake Book* and "Pierre Menard, Author of Don Quixote," the underlying message is that since claiming authorial authority over one's own life is an impossibility, the only artistic and hence independent claim that either Wittman or Menard can achieve is through their visibly proclaimed presences in the reenactment of prior discursive voices. Thus, while Cervantes and Lo Kuan Chung, the writer of the *Shui Hu Chuan,* are rendered invisible by virtue of their authorial positions, Wittman and Menard are visibly evident because of their repetitive activities as artisans or makers of artificial texts (hence in Wittman's case his "fake" book).

In Pierre Menard's case, Borinsky even notes that "Menard's work [his rewritten *Don Quixote*] is considered to be superior to the original *Don Quixote* because it is a higher level of artifice" (Borinsky 92). Its patent artificialness stands in contrast to the original *Don Quixote* which Menard describes as a "spontaneous work" written "à la diáble, swept along by inertias of language and invention" (Borinsky 92).

In the case of Wittman Ah Sing, the additional level of artifice through repetition functions as a device for the evocation and attempt to locate something quintessentially identifiable as "Chinese Americaness," or as Michael M. J. Fischer puts it, the attempt to claim "a voice or style that does not violate one's several components of identity." This is an identity that is "an insistence on a pluralistic, multidimensional, or multi-faceted concept of self . . . a crucible for a wider social ethos of pluralism" (Fischer 196). As such, both Kingston and, by extension, Wittman engage in repetitions of other literary texts, as well as extensive excavations and inventorying of received cultural lore. The "fakeness" of *Tripmaster Monkey* lies in the trickery with which the word "book" is used. It is a literal book in its material sense, but a nonbook in terms of the received understanding that Western civilization has come to understand the meaning of the word. It is a "fake" book in that it is not a source of original thought, but rather itself a repetition and catalogue of other textual, experiential and cultural constructs.

In his essay "The Fantasia of the Library," Foucault identifies the same activity on the part of Flaubert, particularly in his final book *Bouvard et Pecuchet.* Foucault identifies this work as "a book produced from other books" (Foucault 105), an encyclopedia of human attempts at achieving permanence through textual means. Bouvard and Pecuchet, after ten years of living by everything they have read, commit themselves instead to the task of simply copying every book in existence including their own. By previously believing and acting on what they had read or heard about. Bouvard and Pecuchet, according to Foucault, believed "immediately and unquestioningly in the persistent flow of discourse" (Foucault 107). In contrast, their repetition and inventorying of books, objects, and experiences allowed them to *become* the things they copied "because to copy," according to Foucault, "is to do nothing; it is to be the books being copied" (Foucault 107). Furthermore, in the repetition of inventories, Bouvard and Pecuchet are incorporated into the continuous movement of textual repetition that stretches on for as long as humans exist.

As a twentieth-century Californian, Wittman (notwithstanding his Chinese racial origin) is a cultural by-product of scenarios from books as well as movies. These movies represent another discursive source that is projected not only onto the rear screen of Wittman's own life but also at times provides the actual formulae by which he goes about pursuing a course of action. The reflexive interaction between Hollywood's creations and human life is characteristically evident. "The movie marquees," Wittman notes, "seemed to give titles to what was going on—*Mondo Cane, The Trial, Lord of the Flies, Dr. No, Manchurian Candidate, How the West Was Won* . . . not educational films but big-bucks full production-values American glitz movies" (70).

Movies also provide Wittman with ontological reference points or parallel narratives to his own life. The Steinhart aquarium, for instance, exists through its referential reality in *The Lady from Shanghai* starring Orson Welles and Rita Hayworth. While making love with his Caucasian wife, Taña, Wittman's thoughts and conversation are fragmentary evocations from movies such as *Far from the Madding Crowd* and *Hiroshima Mon Amour* (155). When they go on an excursion to Reno at the Washoe County Courthouse, Wittman and Taña sit "on the steps that Marilyn Monroe had walked down after her divorce in *The Misfits*" (209). Later they eat at a restaurant "famous for boarding the cast and crew of the *Gold Rush*." (212).

The search for ethnic authenticity is also referenced against an inventory of Hollywood's representations and misrepresentations.

> Films of the '50s did not use Blacks "so Russ Tamblyn . . . the gangleader with kinky hair indicates Blackness . . . like Leslie Caron with her wide mouth as Mardou Fox in *The Subterraneans* is supposed to be Black. George Peppard as Jack Kerouac, also as Holly Golightly's boyfriend in *Breakfast at Tiffany's*. Mickey Rooney with an eye job and glasses as Holly's jap landlord, speaking snuffling bucktoof [sic] patois. The leader of the Sharks [in *West Side Story*] is . . . George Chakiris. Greek Danish Puerto Ricans of the East Coast. (71)

Asian Americans, particularly those in the acting professions, are themselves manipulated by Hollywood to conform to the movie industry's perceptions about what they ought to look like or how they are supposed to behave. Nanci Lee, the object of Wittman's true love, is told at auditions that she does not look "oriental" and that she "doesn't sound right" in regard to Hollywood's expectations of how Chinese women are supposed to look or sound. Her Chinese physical characteristics are deemed aberrant in terms of white American standards, while working as an extra in both a movie and a television show, a makeup artist attempts to give her "an Irish nose," and another remarks that "there's just so much we can do about those eyes" (24). "History" Wittman notes, "is embodied in physical characteristics" (213); many characteristics identified as being Chinese (at least in American history) are constructs manufactured by Hollywood and perpetuated in society as signifiers of inferiority. For Wittman, the reclamation of Chineseness necessitates abandonment of the trappings affected by Chinese women in order to look more "desirable" in American terms. In his monologue to his audience after the performance of his play, Wittman exhorts the actresses to "take off their false eyelashes, to go bare faced and show what we look like" (312). Even worse than cosmetic attempts at defacing Chineseness, he adds, are plastic surgery and orthodontics. New beauty, he promises, can be discovered only by voiding white America's definitions of beauty, and his pronouncement, "I declare my looks—teeth, eyes, nose, profile—perfect" (314), represents both self-affirmation and the reclamation of what he terms the "lost I" (91). Specifically, the "lost I" refers to Hollywood movies where historically Chinese people are repeatedly presented as being unable to use the pronoun "I" to represent self as subject. Instead, Chinese characters over several decades of movies are made to say "me no likee," or "me name-um Li'l Beaver," reducing them to the level of passive objects rather than active subjects (318). Hollywood's linguistic incapacitation, however, can be rectified through remembrance of the historical roots of the word for "I" in the Chinese language—an ideograph that depicts the "I" as "I-warrior . . . the same whether subject or object, 'I-warrior' whether actor or the receiver of action" (31). Thus self-retrieval, and particularly the retrieval of a self-as-subject, emerges as a central thread in *Tripmaster Monkey*. It is a project that is even more significant for ethnic populations such as Chinese Americans, who live under the the the encumbering weight of representations that others have fashioned about them.

Ultimately, the act of self-retrieval from amidst a morass of prefabricated representations is accompanied by rejection of the idea that there is finality or permanence of any text, truth, or representation. The transformational "monkey power" that informs *Tripmaster Monkey* suggests that "there is no 'complete' corpus of First Time knowledge, that no one . . . can know this lore except through an open ended series of contingent, power-laden encounters" (Clifford 8). To this end, *Tripmaster Monkey* transcends the protocols and demands of the novel in that it challenges the ideology of textual authority as well as textual finality. Within the work, Wittman's task is to effect the "power-laden encounters" between various cultural and literary constructs, and to orchestrate the juxtapositions between imaginative and lived experience so as to discover relevant meanings. As the "writer" of *Tripmaster Monkey*, Maxine Hong Kingston extends the continuum of making meaning not through use of the totalizing strategies of the novel but through deliberated disjunctions of language and texts. Less novelist than ethnographer, she performs the postmodern ethnographic role of producing a "cooperatively evolved text consisting of fragments of discourse" (Tyler 125).

Unlike traditional fiction the fantasy evoked by the ethnographic enterprise, according to Tyler, does not entail a locus of authorial judgement outside the text, but rather, as in *Tripmaster Monkey*, allows an interjection of judgements and perspectives derived from several authorial voices and discourses which by turns compete and harmonize with one another (Tyler 125–26). Within a space that permits a "dispersed authorship" both writer and text share a tentative status. Hence, gleaning the authenticity of *Trip-*

master Monkey lies in comprehending its re-presentation, rather than represen-tation, of reality. Its irresolutions signify a mediative abatement that needs to be understood as representative of the tentative status of artists and their cre-ations. This abatement is different from "the willing suspension of disbelief" that has heretofore been required of the reader of the traditional novel. Within the novelistic pact between writer and reader, the reader is promised "truths" only for as much as s/he is willing to countenance the boundaries established by the single authoritative author. Within the space of "dispersed authorship," however, the irresolutions set up by the divergent voices offer a proliferation of possible scenarios that enable reality to ultimately be "trans-formed, renewed, and sacralized" (Tyler 125–26).

Works Cited

Baudrillard, Jean. *Simulations*. New York: Semiotext(e), 1983.

Borinsky, Alicia. "Repetition, Museums, Libraries: Jorge Borges." *Glyph* 2 (1977): 88–101.

Chan, Jeffery Paul. "Jeff Chan, Chair of San Francisco State Asian American Studies, Attacks Review." *San Francisco Journal*, 4 May 1977.

Clifford, James. "Introduction: Partial Truths." In *Writing Culture: The Poetics and Politics of Ethnography*, ed. James Clifford and George E. Marcus. Berkeley, Calif.: University of California Press, 1986. 1–26.

Connor, Steven. *Postmodern Culture: An Introduction to Theories of the Contemporary*. Cambridge, Mass.: Basil Blackwell, 1989.

Fischer, Michael M. J. "Ethnicity and the Post-Modern Arts." In *Writing Culture: The Poetics and Politics of Ethnography*, ed. James Clifford and George E. Marcus. Berkeley, Calif.: University of California Press, 1986. 194–233.

Foucault, Michel. *Language, Counter-Memory, Practise: Selected Essays*, ed. Donald F. Bouchard. Ithaca, N.Y.: Cornell University Press, 1980.

Giroux, Henry A. "Modernism, Postmodernism and Feminism." *Postmodernism, Feminism and Cultural Politics*, ed. Henry A. Giroux. New York: State University of New York Press, 1991. 1–59.

Gitlin, Todd. "Postmodernism Defined at Last." *Utne Reader* July/August (1989): 52–61.

Jameson, Fredric. "Postmodernism and Consumer Society." *Anti-Aesthetic: Essays on Postmodern Culture*, ed. Hal Foster. Port Townsend, Washington: Bay Press, 1983. 111–18.

———. "Postmodernism or the Cultural Logic of Late Capitalism." *New Left Review* 146 (1984a): 53–92.

———. "Periodizing the Sixties." *The Sixties without Apology*, ed. Stanley Aronowitz et al. Min-neapolis: University of Minnesota Press, 1984b. 178–215.

Kingston, Maxine Hong. *Tripmaster Monkey: His Fake Book*. New York: Alfred Knopf, 1989.

Lemon, Lee and Marion J. Reis. *Russian Formalist Criticism: Four Essays*. Lincoln: University of Nebraska Press, 1965.

Lin-Blinde, Patricia. "The Icicle in the Desert: Perspective and Form in the Works of Two Chi-nese American Women Writers." *MELUS* 6:3 (1979). 51–71.

Lyotard, Jean-Francois. *The Postmodern Condition: A Report on Knowledge*, trans. Geof Bennington and Brian Masumi, Minneapolis: University of Minnesota Press, 1980.

Newman, Charles. *The Postmodern Aura: The Act of Fiction in an Age of Inflation*. Evanston, Ill.: Northwestern University Press, 1985.

Rosaldo, Renato. *Culture and Truth: The Remaking of Social Analysis.* Boston: Beacon Press, 1989.

Tong, Benjamin R. "Critic of Admirer Sees Dumb Racist." *San Francisco Journal,* 11 May 1977.

Tyler, Stephen A. "Post-Modern Ethnography: From Document of the Occult to Occult Document." In *Writing Culture: The Poetics and Politics of Ethnography,* ed. James Clifford and George E. Marcus. Berkeley, Calif.: University of California Press, 1986. 122–40.

Wong, Cynthia Sau-ling. "Necessity and Extravagance in Maxine Kingston's *Woman Warrior.*" *MELUS* 15:1 (1988). 3–26.

Bee-e-een! Nation, Transformation, and the Hyphen of Ethnicity in Kingston's *Tripmaster Monkey*

ISABELLA FURTH

Near the end of Maxine Hong Kingston's *Tripmaster Monkey: his fake book,* a linked pair of acrobatic twins somersault across a stage. Played by two Americans, one of Japanese ancestry, one of European, both wearing one green velveteen suit, Chang and Eng the Double Boys are both separate and conjoined, neither fully unified nor fully distinct, and expressible only by the grammatical impossibility of the plural singular pronoun (t)he(y). As an individual(s), (t)he(y) find loneliness and identity equally impossible, and their/his (un)solitary (un)doubleness extends to the culture (t)he(y) inhabit. Adopting green velvet and the surname of a battle of the American Revolution, (t)he(y) are included in the practice of cultural signification: (t)he(y) marry, get drafted, attend parties and get drunk. Simultaneously, (t)he(y) are debarred from it, relegated to a marginal world of Black women, yellow men, and freak show exotica. Assaulted by the audience and jailed for the ensuing riot, (t)he(y) berate the crowd through the bars:

> "We know damned well what you came for to see—the angle we're joined at, how we can have two sisters for wives and twenty-one Chinese-Carolinian children between us. You want to see if there's room for two, three bundling boards. You want to know if we feel jointly. You want to look at the hyphen. You want to look at it bare." (*TM* 293)

The hyphen, the mark that simultaneously conjoins and separates, is a central trope of multicultural theory, yet it is seldom more central than it is in the discussion of Asian-American writers. It adheres to Asian immigrants with particular tenacity, for one; whereas for most European immigrants the hyphen drops out after a generation, it remains with citizens of Asian extraction like Kingston's hero Wittman Ah Sing even unto the fifth generation born on U.S. soil, a mark of Otherness and of the persistent failure to inscribe

From *Modern Fiction Studies* 40, no. 1 (Spring 1994): 33–49. Copyright © 1994 by The Johns Hopkins University Press. Reprinted by permission of The Johns Hopkins University Press.

the Asian American fully within the limits of American discourse. The valorization of the hyphen, along with the imposition of a "model minority" paradigm and the highly eroticized attitude towards encounters in which "East meets West," is, Wittman argues, a dissimulation of the fact that "They want us to go back to China where we belong" (307). The putatively unitary and stable American "They" invoked by Wittman both fetishizes and rejects the more ambiguous and indeterminate (t)he(y) of Chang-Eng, doubled by his/their hyphen.

Kingston has long written against this practice of masking exclusionary politics with the rhetoric of inclusion, calling (as Wittman does in *Tripmaster Monkey*) for Americans of Chinese ancestry to call themselves unhyphenated "Chinese Americans" and so to reject the exoticizing implication that, for the racially Asian, both sides of the hybrid ethnic/national equation have equal weight. Yet in spite of the efforts of writers like Kingston to circumvent the hyphen, to return "Chinese" to the status of adjective, the case of Chang-Eng shows how the marks of separation are clung to, fetishized, and commodified. The current market for "ethnic fiction" is booming, as audiences clamor to see the hyphen, to see it bare and "authentic," and simultaneously to see it bracketed and contained, thrown into the freak show prison of exoticism.

From a critical standpoint, one need only turn to the critical discussion of Kingston's earlier semi-autobiographical works to see this fetishization of the mark of separation from *soi-disant* "mainstream culture." Again and again, Kingston is treated as a native informant and ethnographic source, as her critics attempt to valorize the "truth" of her ethnic experience and to discard the rest as "decoration" that, in the words of one critic, "fills in the gaps when accurate information is not available" (Neubauer 22). The persistent effort to authenticate Kingston's work by reducing it to a straightforward reference to some sociologically verifiable ethnic reality brings to mind Salman Rushdie's acerbic observation that " 'Authenticity' is the respectable child of old-fashioned exoticism" (67).

Kingston's dilemma, and that of any "ethnic" writer, is to negotiate between the pull of an essentialism that reduces the author to a representative member of a specifically marked (usually racialized) society, and that which attempts (equally impossibly) to erase the marks of difference and hold all works of literature up to a "higher" standard of "objective artistic truth" (a paradigm that usually manages to designate the works of non-white writers "extracanonical" and hence "intrinsically" inferior). She is given a choice, in effect, between an exclusionary inclusion (being admitted, but only as a marked commodity), and an inclusionary exclusion (being admitted only if deemed "worthy" by virtue of having suppressed her particularity and made herself indistinguishable from the "mainstream"). In either case, the hyphen dominates the transaction, in the first case as mark of bondage and separation, of being tethered yet kept at a distance; in the second case as scar, mark of the wound of a difference that must be excised if the discourse is to be accepted. Writing oneself out of this dilemma is extremely difficult; as Wittman discovers in *Tripmaster Monkey,* there is always a great temptation to "make a move when [one] should be upsetting the chessboard" (107). For Kingston's trap is only in part one of critics and their misreadings; it is also the trap of textuality itself. Inscription by nature tends towards the static and totalizable: "The story will remain as printed for the next two hundred years," Kingston said in a 1983 interview. "[W]hat would be wonderful would be for the words to change on the page every time, but they can't" (Islas 18). The text's apparent stasis, its illusory transparency, makes it susceptible to ethnographic totalization, and allows it to be catechized according to its adherence to the "women's lib angle . . . the Third World angle, the *Roots* angle" ("Mis-readings" 55) as these angles are presented through the lens of a fallacious standard of the "authentically Oriental."

In *Tripmaster Monkey,* Kingston has frustrated the all-too-common critical tendency to totalize and anthropologize her work, and has fulfilled her stated goal to "keep ambiguity in the writing all the time" (Islas 18). A measure of her success can be found in the reviews of *Tripmaster Monkey,* which have been almost schizophrenic in their inconsistency. The novel is "hilarious," or it demonstrates "the funniness of grimaces, not of humor" (Tyler 46); its language is passionate, or "the words on the page fail to convey feeling" (Pollard 41). Wittman's one-man show is "dazzling," (Gerrard 28) or it is "inappropriate and redundant" (Wilhelmus 151). The degree of critical dislocation reaches absurd proportions: The *New York Times* reports on April 14th that *Tripmaster Monkey* is a multivocal text: "everyone in this book . . . turns out to be a non-stop monologuist dispensing Chinese 'talk-stories,' drug induced fantasies, family memories, [and] ridiculous riffs about the lost 'tradition of fatness' and the sensitivity of elephants' trunks" (Kakutani C30). Ten days later another *Times* reviewer complains that Wittman's voice drowns out everything: "Nobody else gets a word in edgewise, not if Wittman can help it" (Schrieber 9). Indeed, even the physical book itself manages to confound the critics—Anne Tyler can call it "a great huge sprawling beast of a novel, over 400 pages densely packed with the rantings and ravings and pranks and high jinks of one Wittman Ah Sing" (45), while Tom Wilhelmus reassures his readers that *Tripmaster Monkey* is "not long," weighing in at a slim 340 pages (150). Significantly, the novel has yet to be treated in academic and professional journals, a surprising absence given that it was published nearly five years ago.

The consternation and confusion that greeted the publication of *Tripmaster Monkey* and the deafening silence from scholarly literary journals begs the question: What rough beast is this de-hyphenated monkey? The irreducibly physical text (there are 340 clearly numbered pages in my paperback edition) nevertheless manages to break its boundaries and resist attempts at totalization and theorization. Kingston's highly allusive (not to mention elusive) text minimizes its own transparency and attempts to escape the common, comfortable but restricting binaries of a one-to-one correspondence between text and anthropo-sociological subject. Perspectives shift, narratives multiply, significations oscillate through multilingual puns, and the straightforward, stable equation balanced on a hyphen is revealed as a reductive appropriation. Kingston's model of ethnicity, nationality and textuality is unstable, and defies the hyphen; it is instead a constant series of negotiations and changes. In it, the hyphen can also become the "magic pole . . . that the King of the Monkeys keeps hidden behind his ear" (*TM* 32), a magical implement that shifts from toothpick to giant's staff, an axis of transformations, negotiations, and subversions.

At the same time, however, the hyphen is not utterly transcendable: even in their multiplicity, the generative and non-totalizable spaces of the novel constantly return to and coalesce around the hyphens and scars that determine the racialized body. This essay traces the permutations and paradoxes of transforming pole and scar, of nation, ethnicity and wound, and the attempt to create a textuality of nation and identity that can modify, if not transcend, the exclusionary bondage of the hyphen. Such an escape from hyphenation and its reductive doubling can take place not through a retreat into unity but through an embracing of multiplicity. Uncomplicated identity and wholeness are revealed in *Tripmaster Monkey* as impossible fictions; rather than a body or a nation that is stable, self-sufficient, and impregnable, Kingston envisions a world of constant transformation and flux.

The hyphen exists in a space between words, linking them as well as establishing their separation. Yet the space within which the hyphen itself operates is charged with potentiality. Kingston's drive to eliminate the hyphen and escape from the ethnic writer trap, the limitations of a static text, and the reductions of the totalizable self, leads her to explore this new, disjunctive space through the creation of Wittman Ah Sing, her infuriating, excessive, manic hero. There is no "Real" Wittman; like his namesake, he is large and contains multitudes. He cannot be read in terms of hyphenation, dualities, or oppositions—comprising disparate bits of all fictions, all nations, all narratives in an ever-transforming frenzy of speech and gesture, he occupies and embodies a radically disjunctive and paradoxical space. His quest cannot be read as a stable Enlightenment narrative of self-discovery, nor as the classic "hyphenated American's" narrative establishment of a stable identity. Authentic-hipster-San-Francisco-aficionado-playwright-dutiful-son-working-stiff-impulsive-lover-sexist-pig: Wittman's hyphens expand and multiply to connect *all* terms, to keep them all in play at once. Yet simultaneously they undercut one another; his self-malleability is mirrored by the often contradictory permutations of the multitude of narratives in which he is enmeshed. His pretensions and self-constructions are constantly undermined, his elaborately crafted streetwise cool evaporates as his "Chinese giggle" erupts, and his would-be seductions are subverted as the objects of his desire steal his lines and resolutely refuse to play the role he has imaginatively scripted for them. Even the narrator steps in on Wittman's self-creation to point out his failings and inconsistencies, or to utter a simple "Shut up, Wittman." There is no stability, equality, or balance in Wittman's ethno-national equation; his self seems constituted not around a fixed and fixating hyphen, but in and around a radically untotalizable space.

Indeed, Wittman's "space" is quite literally indeterminate: the geographical and temporal scene of the novel cannot be established firmly. The 1960s—a time, the epigraph announces, "when some events appeared to occur months or even years anachronistically"—slide into all times. The novel throngs with Edens and Apocalypses, from the Big Bang of Wittman's imaginary suicide in the opening paragraph and the origin myths of the Monkey King, to the end of the world in a nuclear deluge, and beyond. Likewise, the physical San Francisco becomes an infinitely malleable locus—large enough to contain the universe and a cast of billions, or reduced to a single jittering pixel on a snowy TV screen.

This malleability of the national chronotrope, its refusal to be totalized, aligns Wittman's quest for a nation with that disjunctive, internally liminal structure of nationality posited by Homi Bhabha in his essay, "DissemiNation." Instead of locating the sociological solidity of the nation in imaginative participation in a synchronous narrative of national unity, Bhabha posits national identity as a disjunctive and instantaneous space, a spatial and temporal break that disrupts the generation of a stable national narrative. Linear models of space and time are dislocated, and national identity comes to be in the untotalizable gap between the poles of the pedagogical, sedimentary historical narrative and the performative praxis of everyday life, which takes place everywhere at once. In such a disjunctive space of signification, the individual must be figured multiply. The people are, according to Bhabha,

> a complex rhetorical strategy of social reference where the claim to be representative provokes a crisis within the process of signification and discursive address. We then have a contested cultural territory where the people must be thought in a double-time; the people are the historical "objects" of a nationalist pedagogy, giving the discourse an authority that is based on the pre-given or constituted historical origin or event; the people are also the "subjects" of a process of signification that must erase any prior or originary presence of the nation-people to demonstrate the prodigious, living principle of the people as that continual process by which the national life is redeemed and signified as a repeating and reproductive process. The scraps, patches, and rags of daily life must be repeatedly turned into the signs of a national culture, while the very act of the narrative performance interpellates a growing circle of national subjects. (297)

The nation is constantly coming to be through the action of its own internal marginality, as "counter-narratives of the nation . . . continually evoke and erase its totalizing boundaries" (300). The "doubling" of the people that

Bhabha describes differs from the restrictive doubling of the hyphen, for it replaces the stability of the pedagogical with the flux of the performative, which "introduces a temporality of the 'in-between.' . . . The boundary that marks the nation's selfhood interrupts the self-generating time of national production with a space of representation that threatens binary division with its difference" (299).

Wittman's Great American Play, like Kingston's Great American Novel, is a performative act that defies binaries through just such an enactment of "internal liminality." At the outset of *Tripmaster Monkey,* as Wittman seeks entry into the national identity, an "I" unmarked by the hyphen, he finds himself in a landscape that can only be traversed, not inhabited. The instantiating image of the novel is one of dispersal: Wittman's own imaginary suicide, when "his head breaks into pieces that fly far apart in the scattered universe" (*TM* 3), underscoring the impossibility of a unitary identity such as he seeks. As Wittman continues to traverse the park, he is swept up in a vortex of the marginal, as the city's human detritus cross his path on their "sorry feet" (4), vomiting, panhandling, spitting seeds, cursing, and leaving behind traces of their passing in paint and vomit and half-chewed food. The impossibility of a textual compendium of this marginal space at the heart of the city provokes Wittman's lament (which he lifts from Beckett) on the absence of a resting space in which to formulate a stable, pedagogical identity: "I can't go on, I go on" (7). A stable sense of self, a totalizable, unhyphenated "I," cannot be formed here, and the provisional "I" that laments must continue in its search for self-definition.

In his search for such a space of national and personal signification, Wittman takes his own narrative on the road, reading Rilke to his fellow passengers on the crosstown bus, and imagining a career (the first of many occupational fantasies) as a professional reader on the Southern Pacific, matching texts with the landscapes being traversed. And as Wittman traverses Northern California, the traces of his passing are gathered up into an overwhelming narrative of excess. *Tripmaster Monkey,* like the play that concludes it, describes an attempt to match a text with the landscape it traverses. In the quest for a narrative adequate for his own internal landscape, Wittman can only create one by combining and recombining the vast unformed quantities of narrative he encounters. From a dynamic of intersection and passing on, *Tripmaster Monkey* becomes a narrative of involution, of turning the various times of the multiple narratives of the city, of the state, of the nation, and of all nations, into a performative praxis which explodes the boundaries of time, space, textuality and narrative and which regenerates the national identity. Marginal and tangential narratives appear and reappear—as a red plastic bull in a shopping cart and a "cuntless bitch" being abused by its owner are returned into components of the play's generation—and almost every character Wittman encounters is eventually caught up and returned in its performative torrent. His provisional "I" becomes a multiplicity of "I's" transcending the reductive doubling of the hyphen, the Monkey King's aria from *Journey to the West:* "I. I. I. I. I. I. I. I. I-warrior win the West and the East and the universe" (*TM* 319).

In its fusion of Chinese history and epic with tales of the American West, as well as of the Chinese West and all the figures past and present who have appeared thus far, Wittman's play erupts out of the boundaries set for it by the conventions of historical and cultural signification. Its critics, the arbiters of boundaries, are (like Kingston's own) confounded by the play's excesses and struggle to reassert the hyphen in their readings: " 'East meets West.' 'Exotic.' . . . 'Snaps, crackles and pops like singing rice.' 'Sweet and sour.' " (307). Yet the play manages to subvert these readings, not by eliminating the hyphen but by going beyond it: instead of presenting a stable, unitary vision, the play embraces a protean, unquantifiable one, which cannot be apprehended from any individual perspective. "As in real life, things were happening all over the place. The audience looked left, right, up and down, in and about the round, everywhere, the flies, the wings, all the while hearing reports from off stage. Too much goings-on, they miss some, okay, like life" (298). The ragtag and improvisational play, and its growing and ever-more-included audience become the signs of a national culture constantly exceeding its own bounds. The negotiation between the pedagogical and the performative is held together by a logic of excess. The hopeful possibilities of this generative and ever-expanding community are discussed at a party Wittman attends in the first half of the novel: "Here we are, miraculously on Earth at the same moment, walking in and out of one another's lifestories, no problems of double exposure, no difficulties crossing the frame. Life is ultimately fun and doesn't repeat and doesn't end" (103). There is no constriction in this model, no doubling, just crossing and recrossing, as the multiple narrative spaces and times are drawn together in the disjunctive and non-totalizable space of Wittman's play.

Yet these crossings and recrossings are predicated on an ultimate reassertion of the hyphen. They tend to coalesce around stable loci, where the multiply vectored tangents of cultural signification are contained and converted into a narrative of national unity. Spatially, such loci are often highly determined lines of linkage and controlled transit: tunnels, crosswalks, bridges and doorways where "los immigrantes go in . . . to become citizens" (178). The stability of the pedagogical narrative of national unity depends on "a continual displacement of its irredeemably plural modern space" into a sameness of time that "turn[s] Territory into Tradition, . . . the People into One" (Bhabha 300). The Golden Gate Bridge enacts just such a process of coalescing the plurality of San Francisco into a tradition of unity (as The San Francisco *Chronicle* put it on the occasion of the fiftieth anniversary of the opening of the bridge, it bears "a surging sea of humanity straddling the quiet waters of the Bay" [25 May 1987, A]).[1]

Wittman's San Francisco is a space attempting to be free of the hyphen, yet the span of the Golden Gate Bridge stretches across it: as a suicide leap, to be passed over in travel and passed under in immigration, sign of both gateway and exclusion. Wittman drives across the bridge, sits under it, contemplates throwing himself from it, passes beneath it, yet is fundamentally excluded by it from the overwhelmingly binary rhetoric of national unity. "I can't wear that civil-rights button with the Black hand and the white hand shaking each other. I have a nightmare—after duking it out, someday Blacks and whites will shake hands over my head. I'm the little yellow man beneath the bridge of their hands and overlooked" (*TM* 307–308). Wittman is trapped beneath the hyphen, marked by his racialized body, anchored to the discourse of national unity, yet excluded from it.

For in spite of all its unfettered promise, the putative unity engendered by the involution of narrative is itself based on a profound scarring; the hyphen is inescapable, for it is bound to the racialized body. Tempting as it is to believe that in some multicultural utopia there are "no problems of double exposure, no difficulties crossing the frame," the generative space of party and play intersects with that of a wound specific to and characteristic of the racialized body. The party appears to present a scene of infinitely malleable interpretation, as when Wittman and others read the nonsense of a snowy television screen as a series of fantastic fluid images that differ from viewer to viewer but can be described with a common vocabulary (" 'Wow,' 'Oh, wow,' 'Do you see what I see?' 'Beautiful, yeah' " [94]). Yet just at this point, when it seems that "the party was getting somewhere, fluxing and flowing okay" (105), its dehyphenated space is invaded by the "Nazi anthropology" of essentialist racial politics, and the conversation turns to Asian eyes and, inexorably, to their mutilation. A Japanese American classmate of Wittman's announces her plans for cosmetic surgery: "I'm going to have my single lids cut, and a line sewn in. The plastic surgeon . . . will remove some of the fatty tissue and the lid will fold better. Double up" (107). The mark of Asian identity is a doubling scar, the mark of which is fetishized and commodified. Even Yoshi "soon-to-be Doctor Ogasawara" becomes aware of the problematics of this mutilating self-inscription. " 'They—they don't like eyes like ours. We don't find my kind of eyes attractive. We like eyes that. . . . We like eyes like his. . . . Oh, *you* know. *You* know what I mean' " (107). The scar on the eyelids both writes Yoshi into the system of national identity, and simultaneously cuts her out of it. It doubles her, while denying the possibility of either identity as valid—and more devastatingly, it reduces her to an impossible, totalizable, hyphenated and scarred duality, one with no access to a pronoun save an appeal to the totalizing "You." Even Wittman, in spite of his vows, is implicated in this dialogue of facial/racial mutilation and totalization: " 'I don't have much of a bridge,' " he says apologetically (106), and finds himself once again tied to the discourse of the hyphen and the scar.

That which is "typically Asian" is figured as a physical dismemberment, a marking through excision: eye surgery, sidekicks in movies being "shot, stabbed, kicked, socked, skinned, machine gunned, blown up" (324), Buddha-shaped aftershave bottles with twist-off heads, jokes about vaginas running sideways, "slitty" eyes, and, lurking always behind the scenes, the gash, in all its obscenely reductive horror.[2] Indeed, in the United States, the category of Asianness itself is a dismemberment, both radically inclusionary and radically exclusionary, having been created by the United States immigration authorities to better classify and exclude the workforces that had been imported in the late 19th and early 20th centuries. The category of "Asian" excises the particularity of language, nationality, history and legend, and reassembles the once individuated Chinese, Korean, Vietnamese, Malaysian body and text as an amorphous, indifferent, alien mass, one to be identified and excluded on the basis of racial marks inscribed on its surface.

Viewed in this light, Wittman's move towards the multiple, metaphysical space of the play becomes more complex. The moment that inspires Wittman to attempt to formulate a space from the disparate vectors of marginality is the prospect of an Asian American woman's mutilation. To defend the aspiring actress from cosmetologists, to prevent her mouth from distorting in the lacerating language of self-hate as she derides yet must acknowledge and accept the mainstream's vision of the "ching-chong Chinaman," he announces that he will write a play for her and " 'make of my scaffold, a stage" (30). But beyond its attempt to displace the wounds inflicted on the bodies of Nanci Lee and Yoshi Ogasawara, Wittman's play also displaces the most egregious example of the dismemberment of Asian bodies: the Vietnam War.

For all its extremity and its centrality to the time, Vietnam is strangely absent from *Tripmaster Monkey*. The "War" that erupts periodically in this novel is always deferred, becoming instead the Second World War, or the second century War of the Three Kingdoms, or a draft that must be dodged. Yet the particularity of *this* war, while it may be displaced, can never be fully suppressed. Vietnam lurks behind the novel and the play, forming their half-spoken center, and manifesting through its excessive absence the truth of the destruction of Asian bodies on *both* sides of the conflict. The moment of its most explicit emergence, erupting "unpaired, singular in the isolation of the sky," takes place at the exact center of the book:

> Too low in the sky came a black warplane. Its two winglights glared in the bright day. Its flat belly had hatchdoors—for bombs to drop out. The plane was the shape of a winged bomb. That humming and roaring must have been underlying everything for some time. It had no insignia, no colors, no markings, no numbers. It hung heavy in air. . . . Wittman started the car, and drove fast to get out of there. But the plane came back around, skulking around and around. The sky seemed not to have enough room for it. (177)

The "evil plane" forms the center around which the narrative organizes itself. Its humming and roaring *have* been underlying everything for some time; they have in fact informed the entire novel. At this juncture between the two halves of the narrative—between San Francisco and Sacramento, between single life and marriage—the war's unspoken forces erupt in a total absence of identifying marks. The war-plane is negative space, an unmarked absence, yet it is an absence that marks the wound around which all else is structured. A bomb-shaped mark of excision, the plane traverses the sky and anchors the space of the wounds of war, just as the Golden Gate Bridge traverses and anchors the space of the city.

The hyphen is also the mark of a wound, one inflicted in the process of signification that takes place in cultures and in wars. In her analysis of the structure of pain, Elaine Scarry examines the referential instability of the wounded body. Physical pain, she argues, is inexpressible, destroying world and self and language, and so reducing the individual to pure body. This objectification makes the process of physical signification highly malleable. The wound is an unstable referent, and as a result pain can be translated into power, made to serve any agenda. War performs a similar action of turning wounds to the service of an ideological framework, but on a much larger scale. The wound on a soldier's body is in and of itself empty of reference, but is given meaning by its juxtaposition with symbolic elements that reinscribe the system of belief at stake in the conflict. So while the action of war is to reinforce a sense of national identity, a national ideology or narrative, what is striking, according to Scarry, is "the extreme literalness with which the nation inscribes itself in the body" (112).

This inscription of the nation on the body is infinitely flexible: the wounds on both sides of the conflict can be used to substantiate the validity of the "victorious" belief. Further, the precariousness of this belief is itself the motivating factor for war; wars occur when pedagogical narratives of nationality have come into question. Scarry observes that "when the system of national self-belief is without any compelling source of substantiation other than the material fact of, and intensity of feeling in, the bodies of the believers (patriots) themselves then war feelings are occasioned. That is, *it is when a country has become to its population a fiction that wars begin,* however intensely believed by its people that fiction is" (131). This anxiety about the "reality" of the pedagogical narrative leads to a need to inscribe its "truths" on the bodies of its and other people, to gain power and instantiate itself through the massive infliction of pain.

Just such an instantiation through pain occurs in *Tripmaster Monkey:* "People who've seen the evil plane and heard it forget to do anything about it when they get back. Its dull blackness and noise are somehow subliminal, and cause helplessness and despair. They just want to hurry and get to their people" (*TM* 177). Through its scarring inscription, the war sends people to *their people,* reinforcing the discursive formation of nationality, turning Territory into Tradition. War is a dark inverse of the play that forms community by ever widening the boundaries of its internal liminality, for war forges a community based on the body and the violence perpetrated upon it. Much as the nuclear blast Wittman sees in the snowy television screen fuses a baby to its mother's back, the war fuses separate individuals into a doubled singularity, welds the present to its past and cements a narrative of national unity by precluding any chance of existence beyond the bond that joins and separates. "We are all hibakushas," *Tripmaster Monkey* tells us (111), and this is true, for the wars that have cemented our narration of nation have acted by operating on our bodies and fusing us together as a People. For us to gather a sense of national identity, to be able to say "we," we must be hibakusha, survivors of the atomic blast. We must have suffered the national wound and bear its meaningful scar.

The Vietnam war was enacted in the name of an American national fiction (that is, we must all prevent Communist expansion in Southeast Asia and so make the world safe for democracy), and worked to inscribe and reify that fiction on bodies of various human beings. The national fiction at stake in *Tripmaster Monkey* is a fiction of Asianness that wounds, hyphenates, inscribes and exoticizes. The nation is constructed around the wounds of the incorporated Other: in American English, Vietnam is both a country and a conflict— the nation and the war are indistinguishable. The nation of Vietnam is made equivalent to the wounds inflicted within its borders, and this wound undergirds the American narrative of national identity. Wittman's dilemma is that in order to write himself into the narrative of American nationality, he must participate in this global, political, personal and linguistic mutilation; he must organize himself around a wound that automatically excludes him from the narrative he seeks to join. The hyphen appears here inscribed in flesh, as the wounded Asian body signifies doubly: its wounds mark its exclusion from the American identity that is identified as white, yet to the extent that the narrative identity of America is equivalent to the wounds inflicted by its wars, Wittman and others like him are like Chang-Eng: "as human as the next American man" (293).

The dilemma appears insuperable, and the initial alternatives to this duality quickly prove inadequate. One can simply refuse to participate in any dialogue at all and retreat into the fiction of stable and inviolable self-hood: the impregnable body of the "cuntless bitch" of the first chapter seems to figure such an option. The lean, taut, brown body of the dog is a totally self-sufficient integrity, without ingress or egress, but it is yanked along by a chain. It "wears a shame look on its face, and its legs [bend] with straint" (6). Wittman's initial insulation (until he decides to "let it all come in" [4]) manifests just such a desire to insulate himself from the wounds inscribed on his body through nationality and race.

But absolute repudiation of the hyphen through retreat into unitary identity proves impossible; instead, Wittman addresses himself to the flux-

ional, wounded world, the world that is "splitting up" and placing "the dying
. . . on the Asian side of the planet [and] the playing—the love-ins and the
be-ins—. . . on the other, American side" (306). He demonstrates the horror
of sustaining such a division, of distancing and exoticizing wounds and war
while keeping them accessible and using them to formulate identity, through
the play's depiction of the fate of Chang-Eng. After Chang Bunker dies, his
twin lives on for a time:

> The remaining brother pushes at the dead one, runs without getting anywhere,
> and says: *Now it was there. Now it grew out of me like a tumor, like a second head, and
> was so big. It was there like a huge, dead beast, that had once, when it was still alive,
> been my hand or my arm.* Eng dies too after several days of sympathy and fright.
> (294)

Rather than trying to reinscribe the division between the dying half and the
living half, Wittman allows "picnickers and fighters [to] take to the same
fields" (306). The multiply hybrid play displaces some real war, bringing it
into the side of play, as well as allowing some play to enter the space of war.
The play's infinite transformations, the crossings and recrossings involuting
into new discursive boundaries, are predicated on wounds, yet the transformations are the only means of bringing re-generation and healing to those
wounds and healing the divisive hyphenation of the planet. The play must be
both generative space and wound; the hyphen must be both scar and magic
staff.

Through his play's involuted actions of multiple marginality, Wittman
links the two halves, using the Monkey King's pole of transformations—
which both is and is not a hyphen—to generate representations of loss and
pain. He brings the dying to the playing side of the planet, and vice-versa, as
he "vocalesed a wail of pain that a dad might cry who'd given his only kid to
his country. His eyebrows screwed toward each other, and his mouth was bent
into the sign for infinity. Some audience members laughed" (309). With the
stereotypical cry of the hyphenated Asian-American—"Aieeeee!"—Wittman
inscribes the wounds of racial identity into the space of American identity,
allowing the negotiation to continue unchecked and indeterminate.

In order to fully resist the war, in order to "save the world from the
Bomb," one must internalize that war; the violence of the wound is the only
way to open the performative rupture of nationality. Wittman demonstrates
this with his suggestion that he serve as a "human detonator":

> We implant the detonator inside a human chest. The only way the President
> can get at the red button is to tear a man open. He has to reach inside the chest
> cavity with his own hands, and push the button with his personal finger-
> print. . . . I volunteer to be the one holding the detonator. It would be better
> to put it inside the chest of a little kid, but, I'll be the fail-safe detonator. . . .
> I'm signing up with you. Fail-safe detonator. That's what I'll be. (242)

The image allows Wittman to literally internalize the wounds of war that inscribe him and exclude him; by becoming war, he can subvert it, and open a space where such literal and gruesome national inscriptions are impossible. This conflation of wounding and generation pervades *Tripmaster Monkey*. The initial, violent explosion of the novel, Wittman's head, with its "blood, meat, disgusting brains, mind guts" that scatter across the universe, is the violent opening of the space in which the narrative of national identity can be enacted. Even after the dispersal, "the mouth part of his head remain[s] attached," and the negotiations between the discourse of the hyphen and the discourse of the play, between the racialized body and the performative space of identity, can continue.

When nations are both generative non-totalizable space and wounds, when hyphens are both scarring tethers and axes of transformation, how can we avoid the confusion of Chang-Eng, baffled by the very notion of identity? Or, to return to the question of critical reception that opened this essay, how can we read this text when our only choice is to misread it? Wittman provides a hint in his final, despairing monologue about the failure of his marriage, as he faces the inescapable fact that the protean love he had thought would allow him to be completely understood can never exist. At the close of his monologue, Wittman chronicles his marriage's descent into a wilderness of shrimp shells, gnawed bones, cat shit and mold. Yet even as he recounts his failure, "out of all that mess of talk, people heard 'I love you' and 'I'll always love you'. . . . They took Wittman to mean that he was announcing his marriage to Taña" (339). The chronicle of disintegration into an utterly degraded physicality is transformed into a wedding feast.

It is this inadvertent but inescapable blessing of misreading that finally provides us our clues for approaching *Tripmaster Monkey*. Our only choice is to misread this novel; our only choice is also our only chance. A totalizable system of reading will always be inadequate and reductive, but we can build a new unhyphenating discourse if we internalize the violence of these misreadings and transform them through a consistent application of generosity. In a 1989 interview in *The New York Times Magazine*, Kingston herself provides a hint for her readers. "The omniscient narrator is a woman. . . . She's always kicking Wittman around and telling him to do this and that and making fun of him. . . . She's Kuan Yin, goddess of mercy" (Loke 28).

Rigor and generosity, power and mercy. . . . We must negotiate, negotiate, and keep negotiating, between the wound of our identity and the shifting pole that scars across it and allows it to heal.

Notes

    1.   The nostalgia that brought upwards of 800,000 people to the bridge to celebrate its fifty years of signification as the symbol of San Francisco provides a concrete example of the

precarious nature of the tradition-building process Bhabha describes. At the height of the celebration, doubts arose about the bridge's ability to support the masses of people crowding on to it, so many that the span actually flattened. A hastily convened panel of structural engineers concluded that since the bridge hadn't actually collapsed at that point, it probably wouldn't; still, as ever increasing numbers of subjects are interpellated into this discourse of nation and region, the seams in the forging of discursive unity begin to show in a very physical sense.

2.   Needless to say, this figuration of in/exclusion is heavily gendered. One might at this juncture point to the proliferation of confessional "abused concubine" tales among Chinese American women writers—the reinscription of the wound can be seen as the empowering voicing forth of the marginalized, but also as a reification of the fetishized wound—the gash. This debate has become a focal point for critics of Asian American literature as they wrestle with gender politics and their impact of the pragmatics of publication.

Works Cited

Bhabha, Homi K. "DissemiNation." *Nation and Narration*. Ed. Homi K. Bhabha. London: Routledge, 1990. 291–322.

Gerrard, Nicci. "Wittman Ah Sing." *The New Statesman and Society* 2.64 (25 August 1989): 28.

"The Great Party." *The San Francisco Chronicle*. 25 May 1987: A.

Islas, Arturo. "Maxine Hong Kingston." *Women Writers of the West Coast: Speaking of Their Lives and Careers*. Ed. Marilyn Yalom. Santa Barbara: Capra, 1983. 11–14.

Kakutani, Michiko. "Being of Two Cultures, and Liking and Loathing It." *The New York Times* 14 April 1989: C30.

Kingston, Maxine Hong. "Cultural Mis-readings by American Reviewers." *Asian and Western Writers in Dialogue: New Cultural Identities*. Ed. Guy Amirthanayagam. London: Macmillan, 1982. 55–65.

———. *Tripmaster Monkey: his fake book*. New York: Vintage/Random House, 1989.

Loke, Margaret. "The Tao Is Up," *The New York Times Magazine* 30 Apr. 1989: 28.

Neubauer, Carol E. "Developing Ties to the Past: Photography and Other Sources of Information in Maxine Hong Kingston's *China Men*." *MELUS* 10.4 (1983): 17–36.

Pollard, D. E. "Much Ado About Identity." *The Far Eastern Economic Review* 145.30 (27 July 1989): 41–42.

Rushdie, Salman. *Imaginary Homelands: Essays and Criticism 1981–1991*. New York: Granta/Penguin, 1991.

Scarry, Elaine. *The Body in Pain: The Making and Unmaking of the World*. Oxford UP: 1985.

Schreiber, Le Anne. "The Big, Big Show of Wittman Ah Sing." *The New York Times Book Review* 23 April 1989: 9.

Tyler, Anne. "Manic Monologue." *The New Republic* 17 April 1989: 44–46.

Wilhelmus, Tom. (Untitled book review). *The Hudson Review* 43.1 (1990): 149–151.

Parody and Pacifist Transformations in Maxine Hong Kingston's *Tripmaster Monkey: His Fake Book*

A. Noelle Williams

There is a subversive laughter in the pastiche-effect of parodic practices in which the original, the authentic and the real are themselves constituted as effects.
—Judith Butler, *Gender Trouble*

The epigraph might have easily been written to describe the technique of Maxine Hong Kingston's *Tripmaster Monkey: His Fake Book*. In fact, the quote comes at the end of Butler's book-length critique of feminist politics which assumes that a universal identity is necessary for effective political action. This insistence on a "real" or "authentic" unifying definition of women overlooks (or perhaps, underemphasizes) the social, cultural and economic differences that combine with gender in the shaping of women's experiences. Judith Butler asserts that feminism should not insist on the need for articulating a foundationalist frame (the preoccupation with defining an essential and thus unifying characteristic for all women) prior to political action, but rather, should recognize that gender identities are constructed through political practice. An equally divisive monologism can be seen in the identity politics practiced by many within ethnic communities. One need only look as far as the debate spawned by Kingston's *The Woman Warrior* to see how individuals can get caught between two such unifying groups and find themselves not doubly represented but, rather, twice denied individual identity and agency.

Parody, through its ability to question notions of the real or authentic, can be read as a defensive mechanism in *Tripmaster Monkey,* protecting the text from the antagonisms provoked by Kingston's earlier work and, beyond that, as a positive gesture towards healing the rift between the various com-

From *Multi-Ethnic Literature of the United States* (*MELUS*) 20, 1 (Spring 1995): 83–100. Copyright *MELUS,* the Society of the Multi-Ethnic Literature of the United States (1995). Reprinted by permission.

munities with which Kingston and her work is connected. This essay will explore Kingston's use of parody in confronting the conflicting desires of individuality and community by focusing on how it works to question and subvert monologic constructions of identity pertaining to her male protagonist, Wittman Ah Sing. It will also examine her use of parody not only as a tool for dismantling foundationalist notions of identity and community but as a model for building an inclusive community that is made up of individual identities rather than in opposition to an individual's identity.

I am using parody in the sense of a form of mimicry or imitation which, while requiring a degree of similarity to be recognized in connection with the thing parodied, also contains the imperative for difference, something distinguishing it from the object of the parody.[1] The seemingly paradoxical coexistence of similarity and difference, imitation and originality, commonality and uniqueness is at the heart of Kingston's novel. This definition of parody is informed by Judith Butler's concept of gender parody which "does not assume that there is an original which such parodic identities imitate. Indeed, the parody is of the very notion of an original" (138).

In this concept of parody, the act of mimesis asserts a relationship or membership in a tradition with the thing copied even as it questions the authenticity or "original" status of the thing copied. This essay will analyze parody on the textual plane of *Tripmaster Monkey* but will also rely on the work of Judith Butler in terms of her analysis of identity formation to analyze the politics of Kingston's parodic practices and their relationship to community formation. To discuss the text in terms of community, one must first place the novel within the context of the reception Kingston's work has received in its several reading communities.

The feminist community has largely embraced Kingston's work. Yet many within a predominantly white readership have appropriated *The Woman Warrior* as a catalogue of sexism in Chinese and Chinese-American culture. In her essay "French Feminism in an International Frame," Gayatri Spivak describes the trap that Western-trained feminist academics often fall into when they think about women in a cultural context different from their own as "a web of information retrieval inspired at best by 'what can I do for them?'" Through a discussion of Kristeva's *About Chinese Women,* Spivak describes an orientalist, colonizing tendency of some feminists to appropriate and essentialize the experiences of women of other cultures for their own ends—either as epitomic martyrs of male oppression or, in the case of Kristeva, as possessing some imaginary pre-patriarchal history (135).[2]

In "Come All Ye Asian American Writers of the Real and the Fake," Frank Chin notes a process similar to that described by Spivak in its orientalist, colonizing effect:

> Misogyny is the only unifying moral imperative in this Christian vision of Chinese civilization. All women are victims. America and Christianity represent

freedom from Chinese civilization. In the Christian yin/yang of the dual personality identity crisis, Chinese evil and perversity is male. And the Americanized honorary white Chinese American is female. (26)

When gambling and prostitution arose in the enforced bachelor societies
of America's Chinatowns, this behavior was mythologized as inherent in an
"inscrutable" Chinese character (rather than as an outcropping of harsh and
biased exclusion laws) and was used as further reason to discriminate against
Chinese and (as Chin points out) by Christian missionaries quick to vilify
things connected to a "foreign" culture and religion.[3] As many have noted,
mainstream stereotypes of Asian Americans have caused great tension
between the sexes, positing the Asian man as, in Elaine Kim's words, "asexual
and the Asian woman as only sexual, imbued with an innate understanding of
how to please and serve" (Cheung 236). The intersection of this racist stereotype with dominant gender stereotypes has given Asian women an ironically
privileged status above their male counterparts. While Asian women are
viewed as "real" women due to their assumed passivity, Asian men are seen as
unmanly, even emasculated, due to the same racist stereotype. Chin and his
colleagues are attempting to reassert Asian American manhood through a
revival of the Asian martial heroic tradition. While these Asian American
male authors and critics (most notably the editors of the *Aiiieeeee!* anthologies:
Chin, Jeffery Chan, Lawson Inada and Shawn Wong) expertly analyze the
racial stereotypes in mainstream views of Asian American males, they leave
unquestioned the gender stereotypes that are demeaning to both sexes within
their community. King-Kok Cheung states,

> While these Asian American spokesmen are recuperating a heroic tradition of
> their own, many women writers and scholars, building on existentialist and
> modernist insights, are reassessing the entire Western code of heroism. While
> feminists question such traditional values as competitive individualism and
> martial valor, the editors seize on selected maxims, purportedly derived from
> Chinese epics and war manuals, such as "I am the law," "life is war. . . ." (237)

This search for authentic representations of Asian masculinity has given
a special urgency to the search for an authentic cultural tradition. Frank Chin
blasts Kingston, among other writers, for faking Chinese myth and experience. He asserts that a real or original body of Chinese culture exists which
has been passed on, complete and unadulterated, to Chinese-Americans.
Alterations of the tradition come not from any natural process of change
through time but through ignorance or willful faking.[4] This denial of the
individual and unique imprints that successive storytellers leave in the fabric
of myths bears an eerie resemblance to the racist stereotypes of Chinese culture which Chin confronts elsewhere in his essay. For instance, Chin cites this
passage of Houston Stewart Chamberlain's *Foundations of the Nineteenth Century* (1910) to show how stereotypes have often been printed as fact by racist

writers: "the uneventful humble existence of countless millions . . . who disappear in the night of ages, leaving no traces" (10). This ideal of an unchanging monolithic Chinese culture is equally dangerous to individual expression and agency whether it comes from Asian Americans or white racists. Further, to posit a uniform cultural identity for Chinese nationals and Chinese-Americans is akin to seeing no difference between Japanese nationals and Americans of Japanese ancestry during World War II. Both entail a paranoid denial of American identity due to ethnic origin.

In a recent essay on art and the ethnic experience, Sau-ling Wong describes the way in which the mainstream critical and commercial success of *The Woman Warrior* has led some Asian American critics to accuse Kingston of selling out her own culture. Citing Jeffery Paul Chan and Benjamin R. Tong as two who view Kingston as a mistranslator of Chinese terms who purposefully warps the reality of Chinese-American culture in order to sell to white tastes, Wong writes:

> Implied in all such accusations of "selling out" is the premise that a definitive version of an ethnic group exists, one which it is the ethnic writer's moral responsibility to present. . . . Presumably, this definitive version would represent the given ethnic group in a favorable light, purged of annoyingly "unique" features, and free of useless fantasy which diverts attention from the sordid facts of oppression in American society. (4)

The ethnic writer must contend with two seemingly contradictory claims according to Wong: one, the artistic imperative to express an individual and specific experience, the other, the equally important need to express solidarity with those suffering from similar oppressions (5). Yet the latter need for solidarity does not necessarily require uniformity. In fact, a requirement of uniformity can actually be used to deny artistic recognition to ethnic writers whose viewpoints do not fit easily into mainstream cultural stereotypes of the ethnicity. In "Cultural Mis-readings by American Reviewers," Kingston cites samples from the two-thirds of reviews she received of *The Woman Warrior* which, she relates, measure both the book and its author "against the stereotype of the exotic, inscrutable, mysterious oriental" (55). One reviewer, Bernice Williams Foley of the *Columbus Dispatch*, wrote that the family relationship represented by the text is "atypical" of Chinese families she has observed in New York City and Cincinnati, and that the author rebels against the cultural sensibilities which the reviewer had "always sensed" in the "business friends" and "servants" she came into contact with while living in China. The reviewer finally judges the book as one which is not "likeable" ("Cultural Mis-readings" 58). The work is judged as a failure not because it does not live up to the artistic imperative to express a unique viewpoint, nor because it does not exhibit solidarity with other racially oppressed Asian Americans, but because it is not uniform with one white person's notion of what being Chinese means.

Regardless of its reception by its various readerships, much of Kingston's storytelling questions and often undercuts Western stereotypes of Chinese misogyny. Even in her first book-length work, Kingston is already using the slippery language of complicitous critique and other postmodern devices that she will later perfect in the postmodern parody of *Tripmaster Monkey*. In *The Woman Warrior*, when the young Kingston finally explodes with all her complaints against her culture, it is her mother (rather than her father) who undercuts her statements.

> "You can't even tell a joke from real life. You're not so smart. Can't even tell real from false. . . . I didn't say you were ugly."
> "You say that all the time."
> "That's what we're supposed to say. That's what Chinese say. We like to say the opposite." (202–203)

The narrative constantly questions our ability to distinguish the real from the fake and indeed even the existence of a "real" uniform to all experiences. The narrator herself qualifies her own narrative by stating, "I continue to sort out what's just my childhood, just my imagination, just my family, just the village, just movies, just living" (205). Kingston utilizes all the devices available to the postmodern artist to express an experience that, while it has many connections to her community, is uniquely her own. Her narrative refuses to assert the individual experience it expresses as common and uniform to all within her community(ies). Linda Hutcheon defines some of the techniques or characteristics of postmodernism as "the form of self-conscious, self-contradictory, self-undermining statement," elements of the ironic and subversive with a "commitment to doubleness, or duplicity" and self-inclusive critique (1). In *Tripmaster Monkey*, Kingston uses the devices of postmodernity to protect her text from the quick, essentializing mis-readings that her work has suffered in the past from both the Asian American and feminist communities as well as critics from "the mainstream." But how does one get beyond the struggle between individual artistic expression and the need for community solidarity?

> "How do you reconcile unity and identity?" "Oh, you dear brave man," said a perfectly beautiful girl, who laughed a wonderful laugh. Wittman wished that he too were spiritually far enough along to ask such an advanced question. (*Tripmaster Monkey* 105)

A random party guest poses this question which is at the heart of Kingston's novel. *Tripmaster Monkey* attempts to guide its protagonist through the dilemma of reconciling unity and identity and on to enlightenment. While protecting her from appropriation, Kingston performs a healing, pacifist act between two of her subject positions. Rather than telling a woman's story, enumerating a list of grievances against the patriarchy of the mainstream as well as her own ethnic community, her novel relates the experiences of an Asian American man who, nevertheless, finds a degree of feminist enlightenment in the course of the novel. The novel is not only a feminist text but also an exploration of Asian American manhood and an assertion and affirmation of community.

The novel can be described as a parody or imitation of the sixteenth century Chinese classic *The Journey to the West*, by Wu Ch'eng-en, which details the life of the Monkey King and his search for enlightenment and aid in obtaining Buddhist scriptures from India. This is not parody or mimicry in the narrow sense of a mockery of the thing copied but rather, as in Gilles Deleuze and Felix Guattari's idea of the book and the world, an "aparallel evolution," two separate entities that simulate yet distinguish themselves from each other (10).[5] The mimetic relationship between the two novels is an example of the side of parody which is not just destructive and mocking of its predecessor but affirming of an existing tradition and of the text's membership in that tradition (even as it separates itself from that tradition by asserting its uniqueness).[6]

The novel's full title, *Tripmaster Monkey: His Fake Book*, signals the text's mimetic connection to the classic tale yet it is more than that. As Deleuze and Guattari put it, "At the same time, something else entirely is going on: not imitation at all but a capture of code, surplus value of code, an increase in valence . . ." (10).[7] That is, Kingston is also using this title to signal the existence of another signification that has grown out of the interplay between her text and its Chinese predecessor. In *The Journey to the West*, the pilgrims first receive scriptures that are blank and which they believe to be false. When the pilgrims return to request the real scriptures from Buddha, Buddha responds:

> "As a matter of fact, it is such blank scrolls as these that are the true scriptures. But I quite see that the people of China are too foolish and ignorant to believe this, so there is nothing for it but to give them copies with some writing on." (Ch'eng-en, *Monkey* 287)

Kingston is "capturing the code" of the classic and creating a new (or "surplus") meaning by the juxtaposition of the two works. The title is not only a playful allusion to the controversy over Kingston's use of classical myth in her work but is in many ways a defense of her work. The title is not simply an apologetic disclaimer but, when a reader is able to hear Buddha's words echoing in the background, it becomes a powerful critique of those who claim knowledge of what is real and what is fake and who assert the permanence of those categories. The Monkey King is given the religious name "Wu-k'ung" after he first realizes his own impermanence and goes to search for enlightenment and immortality. The name has been translated as "Aware-of-Vacuity" (Waley) or "Awake-to-Vacuity" (Yu). Anthony Yu notes that this name recalls the Buddhist concepts "which point to the emptiness, the vacuity, and the unreality of all things and all physical phenomena" (Yu 38). The two narratives form a kind of collaboration in their mimetic relationship. Kingston's text extends and disseminates the agenda of the original narrative (Buddhist/Taoist teachings), while at the same time using this content of the narrative to its own ends of asserting the ultimate unreality of monologic constructions of identity and experience (and of defending the text against critics such as Chin). The fake or copy no longer signifies faulty or unenlightened but reinvents itself as the real that only the enlightened can appreciate.

The four hundred and some year old Monkey shares many character traits with Kingston's protagonist. Wittman and Wu-k'ung are both arrogant but artistic spirits in search of enlightenment and a better way to express their talents. On the way to this goal, they both must endure blows to their dignity regardless of their superior talents and often due to their status as outsiders (Wittman in a world dominated by whites, Monkey in a world dominated by humans). Yet it is ultimately through a collaborative, communal effort that the protagonists of the two novels achieve their own individual goals.[8] Again, it can be said that the classic is reterritorializing Kingston's replication of it—The Journey to the West's lesson of achievement through collaboration is reinscribed through the twentieth century novel. The narrative affirmation of achievement through collaboration is expressed through the collaborative product of parody.

Kingston herself can be said to be performing a collaborative act in the creation of her parodic art. Kingston borrows significations not only from her Chinese tradition, but from the tradition of her English medium and other artistic traditions as well. After Wu Ch'eng-en, the second most alluded to author within the pages of Tripmaster Monkey is perhaps James Joyce. The tide of Joyce's visible influence flows into the text particularly when the young artist, Wittman, is discussing his own artistic imperatives, or when the narration follows Wittman and his thoughts through the streets of San Francisco.[9] The way Kingston uses Journey to the West as a template for her English novel echoes the way Joyce uses the Odyssey for his Ulysses and may also be seen as Kingston's affirmation of Wu Ch'eng-en as worthy of membership in the canon of classic authors who are allowed to transcend linguistic boundaries. Kingston's frequent references to European authors is not just a celebration of certain authors but is an assertion of the collaborative, changing nature of American art. Her allusions serve to reinscribe authors from Rilke to the writer of the The Water Margin as sources of American literature rather than foreign to it. Her use of both Asian and European sources may be seen as an attempt to find a kind of geographic center among two of American literature's many influences. It also subverts the idea of a single linear "real" American tradition—of an "original" and an other. It replaces exclusionary ideas of tradition created in uniformity with one of tradition created in multiplicity.[10]

Wittman's story rejects the notion that one has to be either Chinese or American (or, by extension, either a feminist or a Chinese-American), and that these two loyalties must be constantly battling one another to claim the individual's identity. Instead, various identities need to coexist peacefully within the same individual for any of the unities the individual forms with various communities to be affirming rather than stifling. Often, communities utilize tropes of martial alliances in which individuals bond together in a war against the rest of the world—a world which may contain people with equal claims to affinity with individuals within the community. Kingston proposes tropes of marriage. As in Judith Butler's ideal for coalition politics, identity and, in turn, community become fluid, rather than fixed, through parody.

Wittman and Taña parody the notion of an alliance that is unchanging and monolithic when they take their marriage vows atop Coit Tower. Immediately following the vow to forsake all others as long as they both shall live, Taña asks Wittman if it is his first marriage (163). The very spontaneity of this marriage of two people who met the night before gives it an allegorical cast (like that of many other incidents in the novel). The subversion of the concept of marriage as an eternally identifying act (rather than an instance of temporal and performative identity) continues when Wittman and Taña go to Sutro's. "For the rest of their lives, they could say, 'That marriage, I spent my honeymoon at Sutro's' " (166). This episode is an example of parody's power to subvert conventional experience's claim to an unchanging and uniform reality. Yet the commitment of marriage is not undercut but reaffirmed (and reterritorialized). In fact, marriage becomes an allegory for how to live one's life.

The narrator acts as a kind of spiritual guide, always keeping a little ahead of Wittman and his spiritual development. Yet often the narrator's voice and Wittman's interior monologue seem to overlap and become indistinguishable from one another at instances of Wittman's spiritual enlightenment. After the Universal Life Church minister pronounces, "Those whom God hath joined together, let no man put asunder," the voice sighs, "O lovely peaceful words. What if I were to think in that language? I would not have the nervous, crimpy life that I do" (164). This voice goes on to define the "way to make a life" at the chapter's close, where the narrator characteristically speaks directly to the reader (as does the narrator of *The Journey to the West*). This enlightened voice valorizes the need for vows and the commitment they entail, a commitment to the ideals behind the formation of community rather than to any one manifestation of the community in time: "To keep the old promises that are not broken, though the people break. To be a brother, a friend, a husband to some stranger passing through" (164). This commitment to community is also not meant to exclude its members from maintaining ties outside the community. As Wittman notes, "He'll have to tell Taña that he won't have a marriage that makes friends feel left out" (272).

In a passage that bears a striking resemblance to Frank Chin's explanation of "The Ballad of Fa Mulan" as an expression of the Confucian ideal of marriage, Wittman tells Taña a version of *The Romance of the Three Kingdoms* which focuses on the marriage of Lady Sun and Liu Pei. She marries "the famous old warrior" and becomes "his partner, martial and marital" (172). The couple joins when the bride disarms herself. Later, Liu Pei, facing "the utter paranoia of marriage," puts his life in Lady Sun's hands. Both egos become mortally vulnerable at the moment of admitting love for the other. Frank Chin describes the ideals of Confucianism as, "All behavior is strategy and tactics. All relations are martial. Marriages are military alliances" (6). One might apply this to communities which struggle together against oppression. To a point, the novel seems to accept and replicate this ideal but then Kingston reminds us of the implications of using the metaphors of war instead of peace—her parody asserts its difference, deterritorializing the Confucian model. The narrator subverts Wittman's tale of a wife who acquires her husband's swordfencing abilities by commenting:

> Wittman thought that with this story he was praising his lady, and teaching her to call him Beloved. Unbeknownst to him, Taña was getting feminist ideas to apply to his backass self. (175)

Like the story of Fa Mulan, which the Woman Warrior used to empower herself in her struggle against the oppression of patriarchal tyranny, both Confucian and Christian, as well as racial tyranny, Lady Sun's deadly martial skills can be used against her own husband as well as her husband's enemy (which, in this case, happens to be her brother). The attacks by some Asian American critics on Kingston's feminism have been described as analogous to domestic violence in its displacement of pressures from outside of the community onto those within the community.[11] If identity is performative and both identities and thus communities are constantly changing and reforming, is it wise to use tropes of war (killing, destroying) in describing political action when an individual might have an alliance along ethnic lines one day and gender, class, sexuality, or race the next?

Wittman's relationship with the Japanese-American Lance and the looming presence of the Vietnam War serve as backdrop to his tale of martial alliances. During the party, Wittman asks Lance if he remembers beating him up when they were in grammar school together (117). Lance does not remember any violence he perpetrated against a "lone Chinese." Instead, Lance begins telling his wife and Wittman, his "best friend," about his own personal memories. "You had to admire the guy's daring; he was not afraid to declare, 'You are my best friend.' And disarm you" (122). Here, as in the tale of Lady Sun and Liu Pei, expressing one's emotions is a more powerful force than martial weaponry in disarming an opponent. In its odd coincidence and drug-tinged logic, this story takes on a mythic or allegorical feel. How could they have become friends after such a beating, and how could Lance have forgotten about it? Kingston (in "Cultural Mis-readings") exhibits a sense of wonder similar to what readers of this passage feel. After relating how some

Caucasians said, "It doesn't matter," when she noted that a picture of Japanese women in front of Mt. Fuji had been used to illustrate a magazine excerpt
of her "No Name Woman" chapter, she remarks parenthetically:

> And yet, if an Asian American movement that includes Chinese, Japanese, Fil-
> ipinos is possible, then solidarity with Caucasian Americans is possible. I for
> one was raised with vivid stories about Japanese killing ten million Chinese,
> including my relatives, and was terrified of Japanese, especially AJAs, the only
> ones I had met. (61)

In Lance's dual role as both friend and antagonist, Kingston offers us
both reality and hope—the realities of ethnic antagonisms and the hope of
formulating alternatives to belligerent modes of relating to others. When
Wittman, leading his friends in an improvisation of *The Three Kingdoms,* casts
Lance as the warrior, Liu Pei, Lance balks. Lance puts forth alternatives to
warfare. When Wittman, as the god of war, Gwan Goong, exclaims, "Nothing flabbergasts like explosives," Lance's alternative, once again, involves personal revealment and expression of emotion as a form of power: "No guns.
No bombs. . . . Defense—nudity as camouflage, bare skin and hair blending
into nature. Nudity also works as offense; I've scared off Seventh-Day Adven-
tists and Mormons by answering the door naked" (143). Their improvisation
of the *The Three Kingdoms* becomes a parody of warfare. Bare skin rather than
armor is now an attribute of a warrior. The act of uncovering becomes an act
of power in itself.[12]

In the text's anti-war message a tide of signification from *The Journey to
the West* can be seen washing back into the text, reterritorializing it. The Monkey King almost aborted the entire trip that led to his (and China's) ultimate
enlightenment at its very beginning due to his violent tendencies. When he
agrees to return to his master after their disagreement on how to deal with
their enemies, Monkey is punished (Ch'eng-en *Monkey* 132–37). Later, after
he matures somewhat, Monkey, master of transformation and replication,
turns himself into a young woman in order to subdue her husband, a monster
who later becomes a follower, not through force but through the monkey's
abilities of artifice and mimicry. Even in *Tripmaster*'s predecessor, parody is not
only powerful but spiritually acceptable *and* expedient, whereas violence is
neither.

Wittman and his friends' rendition of the Oath in the Peach Orchard
similarly questions our notions of what heroic action entails. What are the
options open to young men "yearning for glory while hiding from the draft"
(139)? How can these young men achieve the traditionally manly attributes
of these military heroes, such as glory, heroic achievement, fortitude, valor,
and comradeship, without involving themselves in the senselessness of war?

After the three "swear to be brother," Wittman follows with the traditional "In war, we will fight side by side." But Lance parodies and subverts

this with the improvisation, "Wherever we find a sit-in, we'll sit. A salt march along the coast? We'll march. A spinning wheel, we'll spin" (144). A refusal to act martially is not a failure to act and certainly not a failure to be masculine. In his references to Gandhi, Lance proposes alternative forms of revolution (to the kind of destructive mass killing described a half-page earlier in the communizing of China); and in doing so, he proposes alternative forms of masculine action.[13] The admirable attributes of warriors are preserved, yet the notion of these attributes as authentically or originally connected to warfare is subverted. The possibility for valorous action is not denied to pacifist males but rather extricated from traditional associations with warfare. Values such as courage and comradeship are resurrected in a pacifist frame. Instead of a military strategy, the Peach orchard oath is emphasized as a creation of family, a taking of vows.

"How do unrelated people get together? They get married" (143). When Lance asserts that their foreign policy should be "We want to marry you," he is replacing the realm of war with the realm of the family, turning the martial into the marital. This shift from a traditionally masculine realm to a traditionally feminine realm should not be read simply as a privileging of the feminine over the masculine. As Virginia Woolf wrote,

> It is fatal to be a man or woman pure and simple; one must be woman-manly or man-womanly. . . . Some collaboration has to take place in the mind between the woman and the man before the act of creation can be accomplished. Some marriage of opposites has to be consummated. (108)

The parody works on several levels. While the domestic sphere has come to signify a feminine sphere, domestication cannot be equated with emasculation. Why is it that when women become warriors, it is seen as empowering yet, when men exhibit peaceful attributes, such as tenderness, it is so often seen as a sign of weakness?[14] Kingston is reclaiming the familial as a (necessarily) androgynous sphere. The parody questions the concepts that identify bellicosity as an inherently masculine attribute and tenderness or nurturing as inherently feminine. Kingston's parody (via Lance) preserves the qualities men such as Frank Chin are looking for in their resurrection of the heroic Asian tradition yet still questions the gender stereotypes that so many painful stereotypes were built on. The two categories cross boundaries of sex and mix within individual consciousness. Lance and Wittman's improvisations provide a glimpse into the as yet utopian world Judith Butler theorizes:

> An open coalition, then, will affirm identities that are alternately instituted and relinquished according to the purposes at hand; it will be an open assemblage that permits of multiple convergences and divergences without obedience to a normative telos of definitional closure. (16)

This description (which could be used to describe the play of signification between two texts in a parodic "assemblage" or relationship) can be used
as a possible summary of Kingston's political agenda in *Tripmaster Monkey*.
She is asserting the need for greater freedom in the way we define our identities in order to create greater possibilities for coalition and agency. Like Butler, Kingston is asserting the need for community action over community definition. Yet affirming gender roles as mobile rather than fixed has a down
side. Kingston brings the momentary euphoria of the peaceful improvisation
back to earth by parodying the myth of women as natural pacifists while getting in a self-conscious dig at her earlier work.

> Unfortunately for peace on Earth, the listening ladies were appeased, and
> Lance had run out of plowshare ideas. Nanci and Taña and Sunny and Judy
> thought that if they were allowed to play war women, they were liberated. The
> time of peace women, who will not roll bandages or serve coffee and dough-
> nuts or rivet airplanes or man battleships or shoot guns at strangers, does not
> begin tonight. (148)[15]

The language of the text points out the martial tendencies that are present in everyone. In the above passage, the polysyndeton of "and . . . and . . .
and" emphasizes the number of women who are appeased and supportive of
war and its narratives, while the polysyndeton of "or . . . or . . . or" emphasizes the many forms that support can take. At one point during his improvisation in Lance's kitchen, Wittman asks "Why the totalitarian armies that
even I, a pacifist person, helplessly see on laughing gas and carbogen?" (137).
Later, the narrator states, "We'll do anything for lighting, die for it, kill for it"
(302). To save his people, the monkey must first purge his community of the
desire for war—the desire for the beauty of explosions and the desire to set
records of the most killed (144). At the same time, the monkey must preserve
those aspects of war which bring communities together in common projects,
common bond. When Wittman introduces Taña to the ladies who "rescued
China and won World War II," he vows to make other outlets for their communal creative talent: "I have to make a theater for them without a war"
(189–90).

The ability to form communities is continually valorized. References to
West Side Story and *Romeo and Juliet* run throughout the novel. These can be
seen as examples where the marital is offered in place of the martial as a solution, a familial bonding in place of violent continuation of division. Yet, when
Wittman watches *West Side Story,* it is the community of the gangs that he
notices (71–72). He considers it an American trait to be individual, "tribeless," which the gangs try to overcome and the employment office videos
push (246).

> Anybody American who really imagines Asia feels the loneliness of the U.S.A. and suffers from the distances human beings are apart. Not because lonesome Wittman was such a persuader but because they had need to do something communal against isolation, the group of laststayers . . . organized themselves into a play. (141)

Wittman's journey towards enlightenment can be seen as a search for a community bound by Chinese ideals but which can allow for the American ideal of individuality.[16] He is not interested in the kind of community that dictates individual identity but in a unity without uniformity. Like the Chinese-Americans at the toy show whom Wittman first perceives as a monolithic group only to recognize their individual uniqueness in their hair color, Wittman is trying to create a community that is neither uniform nor stagnant in a particular time period. It is the word "black" for Chinese hair and the myriad ways of describing "blonde" which define individuals within a community that make identity hard to reconcile with unity, not the idea of unity or community itself. The power of words must be transformed into working towards community rather than against individual identity. As the example of a marriage shows, community can encompass supposed opposites.

Wittman closes his play by revealing himself. His marriage becomes part of the play as well. He speaks to Tañatía in the audience, "I'll do one-half of the housewife stuff. But you can't call me wife. You don't have to be the wife either" (339). Any notion of authentic or original gender roles is subverted. Instead, identities are derived from practices but are never constant or inherent. Naming as a fixing of identity is no longer recognized.

When Wittman uses his play to bring his community together, he is drawing on Gwan Goong's help as the god of literature rather than war. At the opening of the novel, Wittman separates himself from the "F.O.B.s" he sees on the street. By the end, Wittman learns to embrace the various segments of his community. To find an outlet for his individual artistic expression, Wittman is dependent on his community as audience (and for venue). Wittman's art form is ideally suited for the kind of community that he needs to create. It requires individuals working together and it allows for improvisation among individuals rather than keeping to a rigid norm, and, thus, is performative. The experience is not uniformly repeatable. In addition, the fireworks and lights of the war story provide an outlet for people's martial desires without the damage the other meaning of theater of war entails. His staging of *The Three Kingdoms* becomes a kind of catharsis, cleansing the community of its martial tendencies.

> Our monkey, master of change, staged a fake war, which might very well be displacing some real war. Wittman was learning that one big bang-up show has to be followed up with a second show, a third show, shows until something takes hold. He was defining a community, which will meet every night for a

season. Community is not built once-and-for-all; people have to imagine, practice, and re-create it. . . . Blasting and blazing are too wordless. (306)

Finally, it is the laughter and the words which are more powerful than
bombs. In a time when America is at war with a part of Asia, Wittman finds
the tools of the pacifist, such as artistic parody and its embodiment of replication and difference, to be more powerful than the weapons of the warrior for
reconciling the diverse aspects of the Asian American community.

In *Tripmaster Monkey*, Maxine Hong Kingston's work evolves from her
earlier transformation of the feminine into the warlike to the much more difficult (and more beneficial) task of transforming the masculine into the peaceful and gentle through art and specifically parody. By asserting the heroism of
pacifism (and attacking the dominant perception of the pacifist as *passive-ist*),
Kingston defends both her feminine and Asian American communities. She
unites her multiple identities in this action, transforming destructive mainstream constructions of the feminine as passive and thus weak and of the
Asian male as the passive and thus emasculated other.

Her book, like Wittman's play, ends with Wittman's marriage being celebrated by firecrackers and drums. The place of division and warfare is sup-
planted by the act of bonding and community. Kingston's art not only uses
parody as a tool in the effort to purge us of our martial impulses but also uses
parody as a model for reconciling individual identity with communal unity. It
is a model of how to build a community based on multiplicity rather than
uniformity.

Notes

1.   This definition of parody has much in common with Henry Louis Gates's description of "Signifyin(g)" in his account of another trickster monkey. Gates's analysis of the Afro-
American literary tradition focuses on relationships of "repetition and revision" which are
"inherent in parody and pastiche" (110).
2.   Spivak is referring to Western approaches to Third World women, but the problem
she describes has an analogous relationship to the way feminists have contextualized
Kingston's American autobiography.
3.   Wives of Chinese Americans were forbidden to apply for entry to the U.S. by the
1924 Immigration Act. It was not until 1946 that the wives and children of Chinese-
Americans were allowed to enter as "non-quota immigrants." The quotas for people with more
than fifty percent Chinese blood allowed into the U.S. was set at 105 a year until well into the
era of Communist rule in China. See Him Mark Lai, Genny Lim and Judy Yung, *Island: Poetry
and History of Chinese Immigrants on Angel Island, 1910–1940* and parts of Kingston's own *China
Men* among other sources for further details.
4.   Chin compares the unchanging, timeless quality of Chinese myth and literature
and its significance for Chinese-Americans to European traditions: "Losing touch with England
did not result in English whites losing touch with the texts of the Magna Carta or Shakespeare"
(3). While it might be difficult to find Anglo-American college students who could describe

the significance of both the Magna Carta and *The Winter's Tale* to test this assertion, it should not be hard to find many who would confidently define Disney's Jiminy Cricket as a main character in the classic (Italian) fairy tale, *Pinocchio.*

5.   Henry Louis Gates divides the concept of Signifyin(g) into two forms: the "motivated" or critical, which he calls parody, and the "unmotivated," that which is a replication without a negative critique, which he calls pastiche. I have opted to use an extended definition of parody to fit both these categories, because I mean to emphasize the phenomenon of a single text—or phrase—being at the same time affirming of one tradition/antecedent and critical of another (tradition or aspect of the tradition being affirmed), rather than the separateness of these two categories.

6.   An example of this from the English tradition would be the way Alexander Pope's work pays homage to Virgil and Homer even as it uses their styles and devices to mock certain subjects (including literary devices).

7.   They are describing their de/reterritorialization concept and the way a mimetic assemblage creates multiple significations, rather than merely duplicating a prior code.

8.   In *The Journey to the West,* the Monkey King follows Tripitaka (Hsüan-tsang), a human priest, along with other followers at the request of Kuan-yin. This is both penance for past wrongs and, ultimately, the path to heavenly reward.

9.   Just in case her readers miss the similarity with Joyce's descriptions of Dublin, Kingston playfully inserts the verb "to daedalate" (67). This also serves as a signifier of her own artistic imperative to make things difficult or intricate as a defense against oversimplification, uniformity and essentialism.

10.   Deleuze and Guattari term linear constructions "arborescent" or treelike and argue that they are inherently hierarchical (15–17). Perhaps Kingston's remapping of her "Journey In the West" (which she, via Wittman, explicitly discusses on 308) is what D. and G. are getting at when they state that "directions in America are different. . . . India is not the intermediary between the Occident and the Orient, as Haudricourt believed: America is the pivot point and mechanism of reversal" (19).

11.   I am grateful to Professor Shirley Lim for this remark.

12.   One might compare the idea of *revealment* as act of power to Kingston's explanation of revenge in her self-revealing autobiography, *The Woman Warrior:* "The reporting is the vengeance—not the beheading, not the gutting but the words" (53).

13.   The narrator later remarks, "What's crazy is the idea that revolutionaries must shoot and bomb and kill, that revolution is the same as war" (305).

14.   Kingston provides us with a hilarious send up of this tendency in one striking moment when the narration enters Taña's consciousness: "Taña thought about complimenting Wittman on how nice and soft his penis was. But he was such a worrier over masculinity, he'd take it wrong. . . . Taña saved up her acclaim" (157).

15.   King-Kok Cheung cites an interview with Kay Bonetti in which Kingston states that it was the publisher who named her first book "The Woman Warrior" (243).

16.   His search for Popo can be read as an allegory of this search.

Works Cited

Butler, Judith. *Gender Trouble: Feminism and the Subversion of Identity.* New York: Routledge, 1990.

Ch'eng-en, Wu. *Monkey: Folk Novel of China.* Trans. Arthur Waley. 1943. New York: Grove P, 1958.

————. *The Journey to the West.* Trans. Anthony C. Yu. Chicago: U of Chicago P, 1977.

Cheung, King-Kok. "The Woman Warrior versus The Chinaman Pacific: Must a Chinese American Critic Choose between Feminism and Heroism?" *Conflicts in Feminism.* Eds. Marianne Hirsch and Evelyn Fox Keller. New York: Routledge, 1990. 234–51.

Chin, Frank. "Come All Ye Asian American Writers of the Real and the Fake." *The Big Aiiieeeee!* Ed. Jeffery Paul Chan, Frank Chin, Lawson Fusao Inada, Shawn Wong. New York: Meridian, 1991. 1–92.

Deleuze, Gilles and Felix Guattari: *A Thousand Plateaus: Capitalism and Schizophrenia.* Minneapolis: U of Minnesota P, 1987.

Gates, Henry Louis, Jr. *The Signifying Monkey: A Theory of African American Literary Criticism.* New York: Oxford UP, 1988.

Hutcheon, Linda. *The Politics of Postmodernism.* New York: Vintage International, 1989.

Kingston, Maxine Hong. *The Woman Warrior.* 1975. New York: Vintage International, 1989.

———. "Cultural Mis-readings by American Reviewers." *Asian and Western Writers in Dialogue: New Cultural Identities.* Ed. Guy Amirthanayagam. Hong Kong: Macmillan, 1982. 55–65.

———. *Tripmaster Monkey: His Fake Book.* 1987. New York: Vintage International, 1990.

Spivak, Gayatri Chakravorty. *In Other Worlds.* New York: Methuen, 1987.

Wong, Sau-ling Cynthia. "Necessity and Extravagance in Maxine Hong Kingston's *The Woman Warrior:* Art and the Ethnic Experience." *MELUS* 15.1 (1988): 3–26.

Woolf, Virginia. *A Room of One's Own.* New York: Harcourt Brace Jovanovich, 1929.

Yu, Anthony C. Introduction. *The Journey to the West.* By Wu Ch'eng-en. Trans. Yu. Chicago: U of Chicago P, 1977. 1–62.

Cross-Cultural Play:
Maxine Hong Kingston's,
Tripmaster Monkey

Jeanne R. Smith

"All the world's a stage, and all the men and women merely players"
—William Shakespeare

"Somehow, we are going to solve the world's problems with fun and theater.
And with laughter"
—Maxine Hong Kingston

Much of the current debate in multiethnic literatures focuses on the basic
dilemma of where and how to talk about ethnic works in the American literary canon. Though the works of many ethnic women writers share formal features often associated with postmodernism, or with *écriture feminine*—disrup-
tions, breaks, loose ends, multiple voices and perspectives—neither of these
theoretical approaches seems entirely appropriate to their politically engaged
art, which seeks to upset hierarchies not just out of an interest in language or
an inherent philosophical "feminine" dislike for binary oppositions, but for
specific, racially and ethnically grounded political purposes. Discussing the
lack of *ennui* in ethnic women writers' works, which question language, form,
and narrative in otherwise postmodern ways, Maxine Hong Kingston
explains that "words aren't the only thing that's important. . . . Toni [Morri-
son]'s and Leslie [Silko]'s and my aliveness must come from our senses of connection with people who have a community and a tribe."[1]

Mikhail Bakhtin's conception of the multivocal, dialogic novel and his
recognition of various points of view within and outside of a language or culture make him useful to critics of ethnic literature. Bakhtin's work coincides
nicely with ethnic literature partly because he locates the seeds of the novel in
oral forms: the street songs and parodies of the medieval itinerant stage and
public square.[2] Yet writers like Kingston, Louise Erdrich, Toni Morrison,

This essay was written specifically for this volume and is published here for the first time by permission of the author.

Leslie Silko, and Alice Walker derive their oral-based forms from much more immediate sources than the medieval public square: they draw on the rich, varied, and ongoing oral storytelling traditions of Chinese American, Native American, and African American cultures.[3] Ethnic literatures grow out of diverse literary and oral traditions and respond to histories, aesthetic practices, and cultural values both within and outside the Western critical tradition. Part of the difficulty in locating a single theoretical approach adequate to ethnic writers arises from the global roots of their work. Paula Gunn Allen describes the sheer multiplicity of clashing worlds that constitutes the everyday experience of contemporary ethnic writers:

> It is not merely biculturality that forms the foundation of our lives and work . . . it is multiculturality, multilinguality, and dizzying class-crossing from the fields to the salons, from the factories to the academy, or from the galleries and groves of academe to the neighborhoods and reservations.[4]

Such a multifaceted world view renders restrictive, monolithic theoretical approaches irrelevant. Any discussion of multicultural work necessarily demands culturally specific, flexible, border-crossing analysis, a critical method for which we have no established model. Fortunately, ethnic novelists offer a solution: the best way to learn how to talk about their work is to listen to the writers themselves. Contemporary ethnic American women writers do not live lives of quiet desperation on whaling ships or in custom houses; they teach and speak at universities, they give interviews and write essays clarifying their approaches to their own art. Many create fiction that theorizes in its play on conventions and its weaving of alternative, non-Western viewpoints.[5]

Maxine Hong Kingston's novel *Tripmaster Monkey* provides an excellent example of a contemporary author creating theory with her fiction. Many ethnic texts intrinsically rework a stereotypical "American" identity and culture by questioning the centrality of the white male perspective. With *Tripmaster Monkey*, Kingston goes a step further to challenge the possibility of placing exclusive ethnic labels on her work. Playfully and irreverently mixing Chinese novels and legends, canonical American and British literature, Beat generation poetry, and pop culture, Kingston depicts America as a chaotic, multilingual, many-layered world of colliding and overlapping cultures. A profoundly cross-cultural text, *Tripmaster Monkey* makes it abundantly clear that despite university departments and social programs, our world does not divide into neat academic categories. Kingston's novel radically critiques the traditional ways we label and divide literature and people, defying conventional classifications to broaden our conception of American culture.

Kingston's work has always focused on cross-cultural negotiation. From *The Woman Warrior*'s personal exploration of a bicultural identity, to *China Men*'s revisionist versions of history, Kingston's writing claims and defines a multicultural America. In *Tripmaster Monkey,* her first work of fiction,

Kingston turns her focus to the dilemma of the creative artist, who must negotiate among competing cultural claims to find a visionary art form adequate to his (and her) experience of America. Although the genre-crossing quality of Kingston's work blurs the distinction between fiction and nonfiction, the differences between them suggest why Kingston focuses more sharply on theoretical issues of the place and function of art in *Tripmaster Monkey.* Kingston herself distinguishes between the relative limitations she felt in *The Woman Warrior* and *China Men,* given the responsibility she felt to living people and actual events. As Kingston has explained, working in a fictional mode allows greater freedom and thus greater potential for visionary expression: "For fiction, we fantasize about what we would like to happen: [In *Tripmaster Monkey*] I am making what I would like to happen happen."[6] In other words, Wittman's cross-cultural play in *Tripmaster Monkey*—both in the theater and in his everyday interactions—provides the way and the means for Kingston's playful theorizing. The two senses of *play* suggested here are connected. Simultaneously countering stereotypes of Asians as serious and asserting a long and vibrant theatrical tradition, *Tripmaster Monkey*'s narrator reminds us that "the difference between us and other pioneers, we did not come here for the gold streets. We came to play."[7]

    Tripmaster Monkey chronicles the creation of a new artistic consciousness: Wittman Ah Sing, alternately tortured and joyous, brilliant, infuriating, self-conscious, effusive, generous, and self-centered, struggles to integrate the diverging strands of his own life by channeling his superabundance and rage into a flexible, sprawling, communal art form. Wittman's play provides a formalized public space in which to explore race, culture, gender, literature, and ethnicity in direct, nonconfrontational ways. Kingston's attention to every aspect of the play's production, from its initial inception to his search for a venue to rehearsals, performance, and critique, speaks for her interest in the artist's craft and his or her role within the community. During the course of the novel Wittman develops, produces, and critiques his own play, in a grand celebration of theater that constitutes Kingston's ideal vision of a democratic, community-building art form. As Kingston has commented, "Somehow, we are going to solve the world's problems with theater. And with laughter."[8]

To develop a truly cross-cultural art form and establish Wittman's multicultural heritage, Kingston re-creates Wittman's cultural milieu through a vast network of overlapping allusions. An English major at Berkeley in the sixties, Wittman is steeped in Shakespeare, Spenser, Swift, Defoe, Woolf, Joyce, Rilke, Cervantes, Beckett, Hawthorne, Whitman, Dickinson, Melville, Thoreau, Twain, Fitzgerald, Ginsberg, Kerouac, and countless others, as well as in American popular culture and Chinese classic works like *The Water Margin, Journey to the West, Red Chamber Dream, Romance of the Three Kingdoms,* and *I Ching.* The verbally explosive novel is packed with both high- and low-brow allusions, from Yeats and Tolstoy to James Dean, Marilyn Monroe, *West Side Story,* Batman, King Kong, the Lone Ranger, and Chang and Eng. Often, Kingston upsets the cultural hierarchies: "Four years of Chaucer and Shakespeare, Milton, and Dickens, Whitman, Joyce, Pound and Eliot, and you shoot me right through the heart with Robert W. Service," Wittman says of his poetry-reciting girlfriend (*Tripmaster Monkey,* 113).

Wittman is also a modern American incarnation of the Monkey King of Chinese legend, whose adventures were crystallized in Wu Ch'eng-en's sixteenth-century novel *Journey to the West.*[9] Kingston's creation of a cross-cultural trickster, whose "seventy-two transformations" enable him to move in different arenas and tell stories across the world, is crucial to her redefinition of American culture as globally rooted, flexible, and always changing.[10] Typical of her inclusive approach to cultural heritage, Kingston is quick to emphasize that *her* Monkey trickster is an all-American hero: "Listen, Lois," Wittman tells Nanci, "underneath these glasses . . . I am really: the present-day U.S.A. incarnation of the King of the Monkeys" (*Tripmaster Monkey,* 33).

Wittman shows his versatility not only in the book's encyclopedic allusiveness but also in the dizzying inventiveness of his language. We begin to appreciate the myriad strands that make up his cultural milieu simply in the effort to keep up with him. Consider, for example, this excerpt from his one-man "stand-up tragic" show at the end of his play, when he is handed a banana by an audience member:

> " 'Is this a dagger which I see before me, the handle toward my hand?' " said Shakespearean Wittman. "No, it's a banana. My pay? Thank you. Just like olden days—two streetcar tokens, two sandwiches, one dollar, and one banana—pay moviestar allthesame pay railroad man. Oh, I get it—top banana. Thank you. Ladies and gentlemen of the Academy, I thank you. Hello. Hello. Nobody home in either ear. I feel like Krapp. I mean, the Krapp of *Krapp's Last Tape* by Ah Bik Giht. He wears his banana sticking out of his waistcoat pocket. I'm going to wear mine down in my pants. Have you heard the one about these two oriental guys who saved enough money for a vacation at the seashore? . . ." (*Tripmaster Monkey,* 315)

With this verbal riff on the banana (which he also recognizes as a racial insult: "If I were Black, would I be getting an Oreo? If I were a red man, a radish?" [*Tripmaster Monkey,* 315]), Wittman interweaves Shakespearean drama and the theater of the absurd, Hollywood, American idiom, the racist jokes of standup comedy, and the dialect of a Chinese railroad worker.[11] Such unlikely convergences, which uneasily coexist in Wittman's cultural vocabulary, form the particolored background of Kingston's experimental "play" on multiculturality.

Verbal profusion defines the narrative texture of *Tripmaster Monkey,* in which language often overshadows plot or character. The novel's richness is not merely a display of linguistic virtuosity, however. To describe Wittman's experience adequately, the novel creates an American vernacular language that mixes elements of various social worlds in which Wittman moves—from tripping "hippy-dippies" to slick retail advertising campaigns, from his mother's swift, clacking mah-jongg table to his father's gruff poker group, from Mrs. Chew's warnings about "molly-see-no-cherries" to the bureaucratic platitudes of the unemployment office. Wittman clearly connects language to culture and recognizes its power to preserve and define: " 'Fu-li-sah-kah Soo.' He said 'Fleishhacker Zoo' to himself in Chinese language, just to keep a hand in, so to speak, to remember and so to keep awhile longer words spoken by the people of his brief and dying culture" (*Tripmaster Monkey*, 6). As Kingston's attention to fleeting speech patterns implies, "American" language constantly evolves and changes with new waves of incoming speakers and must remain flexible to accommodate diversity. Preserving immigrant dialect is a complicated issue: Wittman's nostalgia immediately follows a particularly contemptuous discription of "F.O.B.'s" (Fresh-Off-The-Boats). Wittman is much more willing to play with the language of new Chinese Americans in his own head than he is to associate with them. Opening his mind and his new American theater to *all* newcomers is one of the things Wittman has to learn to do during the novel.

Kingston's interest in inventing a new American language places her, as she puts it, "in the tradition of American writers who consciously set out to create the literature of a new culture. Mark Twain, Walt Whitman, Gertrude Stein, the Beats all developed an ear for dialect, street language."[12] Writing in the tradition of creators of culture, Kingston offers a solution to the great dilemma of cross-cultural exchange: how to communicate in a world where so many cultural contexts collide. The dialect, or street language, of *Tripmaster Monkey* is as diverse, many-layered, multivoiced, variable, and conflicted as American culture itself. Kingston most clearly defines her philosophy when describing a conversation between Wittman and PoPo, his Chinese (pseudo) grandmother:

> Wittman's English better than his Chinese, and PoPo's Chinese better than her English, you would think that they weren't understanding each other. But the best way to talk to someone of another language is at the top of your intelligence, not to slow down or to shout or to talk babytalk. You say more than enough, o.d. your listener, give her plenty to choose from. She will get more out of it than you can say. (*Tripmaster Monkey*, 267)

Readers of *Tripmaster Monkey* also have "plenty to choose from," and benefit from a narrative that refuses to talk down or oversimplify. Her allusive, excessive, explosive language, which is also Wittman's, creates a new American idiom. We come away from the novel with a broadened, thickened sense of what constitutes American culture.

In addition to theorizing a new, cross-cultural language, *Tripmaster Monkey* focuses attention on the making of a multicultural American artist. Kingston has suggested that Wittman is partially modeled after her brothers, her son, and playwright Frank Chin, and her often critical feminist narrator (a version of Kuan Yin, Goddess of Mercy) chides and corrects Wittman throughout the novel.[13] Yet his growth as an artist also allows Kingston to explore her position as a Chinese American writer. Like his creator, Wittman was born in 1940, grew up in the Chinatown section of a small city near San Francisco, and graduated from Berkeley with an English major in the early 1960s.[14] Just as Kingston notes that "majoring in English interfered with my writing," she warns Wittman, "the fool for books . . . to swear off reading for a while, and find his own life" (*Tripmaster Monkey*, 164).[15] Kingston also draws a parallel between her career and Wittman's, noting that both start out as poets and move to more social art forms.[16]

Through Wittman, Kingston presents one dilemma that any nonwhite American writer faces: to address race essentializes and restricts, and to ignore it erases his difference and identity. When Wittman sits down to work on his play, he

> . . . whammed into the block question: Does he announce now that the author is—Chinese? Or, rather, Chinese-American? And be forced into autobiographical confession. Stop the music—I have to butt in and introduce myself and my race. "Dear reader, all these characters whom you've been identifying with—Bill, Brooke, and Annie—are Chinese—and *I* am, too. . . . 'Call me Ishmael.' See? You pictured a white guy, didn't you? If Ishmael were described—ochery amber umber skin—you picture a *tan* white guy." (*Tripmaster Monkey*, 34)

Wittman's solution is the revue-style play with an integrated cast: "he didn't need descriptions that racinated anybody. The actors will walk out on stage and their looks will be self-evident" (*Tripmaster Monkey*, 34). Wittman's inclusive vision of the theater radically upends traditional racial boundaries: "As playwright and producer and director, I'm casting blind. That means the actors can be any race. Each member of the Tyrone family or the Lomans can be a different color. I'm including everything that is being left out, everybody who has no place" (52).

By insisting on a multiracial cast, Wittman explicitly revises the Eugene O'Neill and Arthur Miller classic American theatrical tradition with its "typical" white American family, refusing also to replace it with an all–Chinese American cast. Wittman's project is revolutionary not only in its mixing of races but in its refusal to link race with character. Any human being, he suggests, can inhabit the life of any other. Like Wittman, Kingston also opens her cast of characters to people of all races. Because she is a novelist rather than a playwright, her representation of race must remain on the printed page, conveyed with words rather than sound and image. However, by creating a character painfully sensitive to the workings of race and gender in virtually every human interaction, she sensitizes her reader to the constant negotiations inherent in both public and intimate exchange.

Through Wittman, Kingston openly negotiates a place within the American canon. When asked about the political agenda of her art, Kingston explains, "I am creating part of American literature. . . . The critics haven't recognized my work enough as another tradition of American literature. . . . There has been exclusion socially and politically, and also we have been left out of literature. . . . I was claiming the English language and the literature to tell our story as Americans."[17] Wittman's politics of inclusion stem from the historical exclusion of Chinese Americans from real or perceived citizenship. His multiracial rather than exclusively Chinese American approach to literary demographics challenges conventional binary oppositions that have often excluded Chinese Americans: "I have this nightmare—after duking it out, someday Blacks and whites will shake hands over my head" (*Tripmaster Monkey*, 308). Claiming her own literary roots in Whitman, Hawthorne, Twain, William Carlos Williams, Gertrude Stein, and Virginia Woolf, Kingston also aligns her hero with canonical American authors.[18] In chapter 1, Wittman brings Nanci into a bookshop, hoping she'll see his just-published work on the shelf and be impressed, recalling (the narrator reminds us) F. Scott Fitzgerald's vain attempt to impress Sheilah Graham in bookstores across L.A. (*Tripmaster Monkey*, 21). Later Wittman offers to show Nanci "like Emily Dickinson secret poems in the false bottom of my Gold Mountain theater trunk," and compares his raggedy-shoed father to "Huck's Pap" (29, 276).

Although mixing such cultural icons as Emily Dickinson and the Gold Mountain sometimes appears effortless, Kingston shows Wittman struggling with an American identity drawn from global roots. Eager to prove his "Americanness," he is wary at first of tapping the full range of his cultural sources. Like Kingston, who admits that "I come to my Chinese roots very tentatively," Wittman wrestles with the question of how to draw on China.[19] After staying up all night inventing adventures as a traveling storyboatman in China, Wittman wakes up to realize that "he had been tripping out on the wrong side of the street. The wrong side of the world. What had he to do with foreigners? With F.O.B. [Fresh-Off-The-Boat] emigres? Fifth generation native Californian that he was. . . . His province is America" (*Tripmaster Monkey*, 41). Kingston interrupts his musings with an episode from *Journey to the West*, which both offers implicit interpretation of the story and illuminates Wittman's difficulties:

> It's all right. Wittman was working out what this means: After a thousand days of quest . . . Monkey and his friends, Tripitaka on the white horse, Piggy, and Mr. Sandman, arrive in the West. The Indians give them scrolls, which they load on the white horse. Partway home, Monkey, a suspicious fellow,

unrolls the scrolls, and finds that they are blank scrolls. "What's this? We've been cheated. Those pig-catchers gave us nothing. Let's demand an exchange." So, he and his companions go back, and they get words, including the Heart Sutra. But the empty scrolls had been the right ones all along. (*Tripmaster Monkey*, 42)

Kingston's interjection of this story at a moment of crisis in Wittman's identity as a writer suggests parallels between Wittman's quest for the right subject and Monkey's quest for the sacred scrolls, stories yet unwritten. But because he has arrived in America, another "West," the blank ones are the right ones: Wittman lives in a new place that demands new writing. As he learns to incorporate and update a vast array of cultural sources, Wittman takes up his storyboatman role with more confidence: "Yes, the music boat has sailed into San Francisco Bay, and the boatman is reunited with his troupe. Write the play ahead of them to include everyone and everything" (*Tripmaster Monkey*, 277).

To write his play, Wittman must create a community to participate in and appreciate it. Aside from occasional moments of connection, *Tripmaster Monkey*'s first six chapters sardonically chronicle Wittman's alienation and the breakdown of community on every level. As Kingston has commented, "Our culture is disappearing and our communities are always disappearing."[20] Wittman considers suicide on page 1 of *Tripmaster Monkey*, quits a pointless job, and picks fights with his mother, his friends, and strangers in scathingly funny scenes. As Jennie Wang observes, the human alienation suggested by references early in the novel to Hamlet, Ishmael, and Bartleby "mark only [Wittman's] beginning, not his end."[21] With Wittman's movement from alienation to community, Kingston critiques and revises individualism as the American ideal: "An American stands alone. Alienated, tribeless, individual. To be a successful American, leave your tribe, your caravan, your gang, your partner, your village cousins, your refugee family that you're making the money for, leave them behind . . . Wittman [had] wanted a tribe since he was a kid" (*Tripmaster Monkey*, 246–47). By the end of the novel, Kingston has seemingly drawn out the isolatoes and loners of American literature's traditional canon.

> We are in a show palace on the frontier. We have come down out of the ice fields of the Sierras and the Rockies and the Yukon, and up from Death Valley. . . . The evening . . . seemed endless because time is like a dragon that curls and smokes. Trappers, hunters, prospectors, scouts are spending their earnings to see fellow human beings. . . . (*Tripmaster Monkey*, 296)

In Kingston's dramatic revisioning, the frontiersmen of Melville, Twain, Dana, Parkman, Cooper, Hemingway, and Faulkner cheer themselves by the communal fire of Wittman's play.

In addition to revising the American canon, Kingston rewrites Chinese American literary and immigration history.[22] She tells the story of a group of "Pre-Americans" who gambled on the *I Ching* and crossed over to a new country, creating a new Chinese American literary tradition.

> A company of one hundred great-grandparents came over to San Francisco during the Gold Rush, and put on epic kung fu opera and horse shows. Soon the City had six companies—not those six business companies—six theater companies. . . . We played for a hundred years plays that went on for five hours a night. (*Tripmaster Monkey*, 250)

Wittman's task, his "right livelihood," is to remake that theater (250).

For Wittman, life itself is performative. He even describes his birth as a stage opening: "I saw: all of a sudden, curtains that rose and rose, and on the other side of them, lights, footlights, and overheads. . . . Rows of lights, like teeth, uppers and lowers, and the mouth wide open laughing . . . I was inside it standing on the tongue" (*Tripmaster Monkey*, 16). For this young man born to talk, writing a "play that continues like life" is only an extension of his natural abilities (169). Yet even with his transformative Monkey powers, Wittman still reels at the backstage quick-changes contemporary American life demands. As he remarks at a strobe-lit dance, "we are blushing chameleons, ripping through the gears of camouflage trying to match the whizzing environment" (109). Painfully self-conscious, Wittman often worries over the impression he makes, inviting Nanci Lee out on a date partly to find out what people thought of him in college. Nanci's remembrance of him as quiet and conservative, when "he had talked for four years, building worlds, inventing selves," convinces him he needs a more visible stage (19).

As Wittman often reminds us, "we make theater, we make community" (*Tripmaster Monkey*, 261). An impromptu rehearsal of his play in the early-morning wreckage of a party reveals the thrust toward connection behind Wittman's theatrical impulse, and behind Kingston's art: "Not because lonesome Wittman was such a persuader but because they had need to do something communal against isolation, the group of laststayers . . . organized themselves into a play" (141). Theater, and its importance to community solidarity, has been an ongoing concern in Kingston's work. The last chapter of *The Woman Warrior* tells of Kingston's grandmother's love for the traveling theater companies in China. She would buy up large sections of seats, braving bandits' attacks to have the whole family with her: "I don't want to watch the play all by myself. How can I laugh all by myself? I want everybody there. Babies, everybody."[23] *China Men* contains a more private performance that underscores the communal function of theater, in the singing and crying ritual performed before her mother's wedding:

> The women punctuated her long complaints with clangs of pot lids for cymbals. The rhymes made them laugh. MaMa wailed, her eyes wet, and sang as

she laughed and cried, mourned, joked, praised, found the appropriate old songs and invented new songs in melismata of singing and keening. She sang for three evenings. The length of her laments that ended in sobs and laughter was wonderful to hear.[24]

The bride's lament, a litany of anger, sorrow, and hope, gives formal voice to the women's joys and frustrations and provides a forum, however limited, for cultural critique. Just as Kingston's autobiography creates a communal sense of self by giving voice to the many women who make up her family and community, Kingston's first fictional work envisions a communal art form by giving voice to the many elements within that community. In *Tripmaster Monkey* Kingston's choice of theater, perhaps the most democratic of art forms, for her experiment with cross-cultural expression allows her to theorize a discursive space that permits interaction, struggle, and exchange.

Wittman Ah Sing's play, which he formulates and produces during the novel, and to which he formally invites the reader, comprises the book's final third. A description of Wittman's writing of his play becomes an accurate description of the novel's plot:

> He spent the rest of the night looking for the plot of our ever-branching lives. A job can't be the plot of life, and not a soapy love-marriage-divorce—and hell no, not Viet Nam. To entertain and educate the solitaries that make up a community, the play will be a combination revue-lecture. You're invited. (*Tripmaster Monkey*, 288)

Like Wittman, Kingston clearly aims not only to entertain but also to educate her readers on the ethics and the aesthetics of inclusion, and to gather a community that preserves the individuality of its members.

Rather than attempting to present a monolithic front (and similar to the structure of the novel), the play as "revue" encompasses a diversity of perspectives. Such a flexible form, Kingston reminds us, is "as ancient as Chinese opera and as far-out as the theater of spontaneity that was happening in streets and parks" (*Tripmaster Monkey*, 141). Theatrical productions intrinsically create community, as they demand the participation and cooperation of author, director, actors, and audience. The play can only be a success, Kingston insists, with "lots of holes for ad lib and actors' gifts," ensuring a democratic, multivoiced presentation in which everyone has his or her say (279). Kingston extends this democratic sense of authorship to her own fiction: her acknowledgments printed at the end of *Tripmaster Monkey*, thanking individuals for specific stories, ideas, and images that contributed to the work, lend it the same sense of communal effort. By giving thanks and credit, for example, to "JAMES D. HOUSTON for the fool-for-literature's reading list" and "STEPHEN SUMIDA for the four-act play," Kingston shows that her own fiction is an accretion of stories and anecdotes invented and borrowed from friends, family, and acquaintances (341). As if to emphasize the equally public and personal roots of anyone's experience of American culture, Kingston follows these individual acknowledgments with a second layer, a copious list of permissions from publishing houses, movie producers, record companies, and journals for the collage of cultural artifacts that are sprinkled throughout the pages of her work.

Like the novel's encyclopedic allusions, its huge cast of characters, verbal side trips, and talk-story forays produce a novel of interruptions, juxtapositions, and miscommunications. Yet rather than creating a sense of chaos or incoherence, the novel maintains its vision of unity in multiplicity. Charley Shaw's description of the movie *The Saragossa Manuscript* illuminates the novel's aesthetic of diversity. Charley explains that after watching the movie, made up of layers of interconnecting stories, he realizes that "I can follow anybody into a strange other world. He or she will lead the way to another part of the story we're all inside of" (*Tripmaster Monkey,* 103). Inspired by this description, *Tripmaster Monkey*'s narrator comments, "Here we are, miraculously on earth at the same moment, walking in and out of one another's lifestories, no problems of double-exposure, no difficulties crossing the frame. Life is ultimately fun and doesn't repeat and doesn't end" (103). This healing vision unifies the divisiveness that Wittman senses everywhere. The seemingly infinite story versions presented in the novel form a cohesive whole, much like the "solitaries" who make up a community.

However, far from idealizing community as an easy solution, Kingston emphasizes the difficulties involved in creating and maintaining a cohesive community that preserves the individuality of its members. When Wittman meets an elderly factory worker at the unemployment office, he is responsible for steering her through the bureaucracy and for listening to her stories. "See what you have to put up with if you want to have community?" the narrator warns. "Any old Chinese lady comes along, she takes your day, you have to do her beckoning. The hippy-dippies don't know what they're in for. They couldn't take Communitas" (*Tripmaster Monkey,* 231). Suggesting the current conflicts within the Asian American literary community, Wittman's friend Lance interprets the invitation to his play as a challenge, bringing his own gang and his own script to the rehearsal. Kingston's ideal of multivoiced presentation comes not without a struggle. Despite Wittman's love of "Communitas," Siew Loong literally has to knock Wittman out to convince him to "let him have his say" (279).

Kingston specifically links the power of art to community building:

> Wittman was learning that one big bang-up show has to be followed up with a second show, a third show, shows until something takes hold. He was defining a community, which will meet every night for a season. Community is not built once-and-for-all; people have to imagine, practice and recreate it. (*Tripmaster Monkey,* 306)

The idea that community must be continually imagined, practiced, and re-created reiterates its dynamic, transient status and highlights the artist's active role in creating it. As Toni Morrison has commented on her own role as artist, "If anything I do isn't about the village or the community or about you, then it is not about anything" ("Rootedness," 344).

If art is to create community, it must somehow step through the fourth wall of the theater to involve its audience. Wittman aims to produce "an enor-mous loud play that will awake our audience, bring it back," recalling Thoreau's effort to "wake my neighbors up" with *Walden* (*Tripmaster Monkey*, 277).[25] He envisions a feast ceremony that will unify actors and audience: "Audience participation—they eat and they're sworn in in this blood cere-mony that will change everyone into a Chinese" (145). When the fire depart-ment roars in to quell the play's finale fireworks, Wittman gets his wish, as the audience joins the show:

> On cue—the S.F.F.D. was bringing the redness and the wailing. The audience ran out into the street. More audience came. And the actors were out from backstage and the green room, breaking rules of reality-and-illusion. Their armor and swords were mirrored in fenders, bumpers, and the long sides of fire trucks. The clean clear red metal glorified all that was shining. (*Tripmaster Monkey*, 303)

Wittman turns this fiasco into a celebration and a victory, artfully orchestrat-ing the chaos as a part of the act. The fire department's arrival enhances the drama and creates more audience and therefore a larger potential community.

Much like her fictional playwright, Kingston directly addresses her audi-ence, often ending chapters with invitations to read on: "A reader doesn't have to pay more money for the next chapter or admission to the show. . . . you might as well travel on with our monkey for the next while" (*Tripmaster Monkey*, 268). Kingston's invitations to her reader emphasize the novel's affinity with oral performance and echo a similar device in *Journey to the West* and other classic Chinese novels. She underscores our relationship to the fic-tional theatergoers and challenges us to consider our own role in this story-telling performance. Wittman begins his "One-Man Show" on the third night by castigating his reviewers. His tirade restates—in more colorful lan-guage—Kingston's own frustrations with reviewers of *The Woman Warrior*, published in "Cultural Mis-readings by American Reviewers." Having explained in "Cultural Mis-readings" that "to say we are inscrutable, mysteri-ous, exotic denies us our common humanness," Kingston has Wittman reiter-ate more angrily in *Tripmaster Monkey*, "I am so fucking offended. . . . Do I have to explain why 'exotic' pisses me off, and 'not exotic' pisses me off? They've got us in a bag, which we aren't punching our way out of" (308).[26] Despite Kingston's sense of frustration that such explanations are necessary, her inscribed critique of stereotyped reviewing educates her critics about how (not) to respond to her novel, forestalling future misreadings of her work.[27] Kingston also implicitly addresses her own critics when she overturns Grand Opening Ah Sing's fears that Wittman's play will be "bad advertising" for Chinese American culture: "Oh, stop looking over your shoulders, why don't you?" (286).

Wittman's and Kingston's critiques of reviewers clarify the dangers of relegating ethnic criticism to the cultural sidelines, as an interesting but peripheral subfield to "real" American studies. Wittman recognizes the colonizing effects of even positive exoticized criticism and finds he must educate his fellow artists:

> 'East meets West.' 'Exotic.' 'Sino-American theater.' 'Snaps, crackles and pops like singing rice.' 'Sweet and Sour.' Quit clapping. Stop it. What's to cheer about? You like being compared to Rice Krispies? . . . They sent their food critics. . . . They wouldn't write a headline for *Raisin in the Sun:* 'America Meets Africa.' They want us to go back to China where we belong. They think that Americans are either white or Black. . . . 'Twain shall.' Shit. Nobody says 'twain shall,' except in reference to us. We've failed with our magnificence of explosions to bust through their Kipling. I'm having to give instruction. There is no East here. . . . All you saw was West. This is The Journey *In* the West. (*Tripmaster Monkey,* 308)

Wittman, like Kingston, demands recognition as an American artist, creating an American art form. In creating and defining a Chinese American community, both emphasize not exclusivity but interchange across cultures. Likewise, Chinese American art forms interweave many cultural elements, adding to the ongoing, multifaceted dialogue and exchange that comprises American culture.

If we are truly to recognize American literature as multicultural, we need to reconceptualize American cultural studies as, in the words of Betsy Erkkila, "a radically comparative field of studies in which a diversity of cultures, languages, practices, and theories encounter and interact with one another across the borders."[28] Just as Kingston's choice of a Chinese American female goddess narrator radically critiques the Anglo-American white-male-god narrative tradition, reminding us that neither point of view is "neutral," literary criticism can unsettle our comfortable views of the world by considering the many conflicting perspectives present in contemporary American literature. Pointing the way for ethnic literary studies today, *Tripmaster Monkey* playfully expresses a new vision of American culture, weaving the diverse, postmodern, multivoiced strands of contemporary life, confronting outrageous contradictions, and making art out of them.

Notes

1. Maxine Hong Kingston, "Eccentric Memories: A Conversation with Maxine Hong Kingston," interview by Paula Rabinowitz, *Michigan Quarterly Review* 26, no. 1 (1987), 184.

2. Mikhail Bakhtin, *The Dialogic Imagination,* ed. Michael Holquist, transl. Caryl Emerson and Michael Holquist (Austin: University of Texas Press, 1981), 400. Of course, Bakhtin himself does not escape a limited viewpoint; his discussion of social languages in literary forms completely ignores factors such as gender or ethnicity—elements that nevertheless take part in any speaking position.

3. Bonnie TuSmith's valuable study, *All My Relatives: Community in Contemporary Ethnic American Literatures* (Ann Arbor: University of Michigan Press, 1993), is one excellent example of the recent trend toward more culturally aware critical approaches.

4. Paula Gunn Allen, " 'Border' Studies: The Intersection of Gender and Color," in *Introduction to Scholarship in Modern Languages and Literatures,* ed. Joseph Gibaldi (New York: Modern Language Association, 1992), 305.

5. For more extensive treatment of fiction as theory, see Barbara Christian, "The Race for Theory," *Feminist Studies* 14 (1988), and more recently, Betsy Erkkila, "Ethnicity, Literary Theory, and the Grounds of Resistance," *American Quarterly* 47, no. 4 (1995): 563–94. Examples of important critical essays by ethnic fiction writers include Toni Morrison's "Rootedness: The Ancestor as Foundation," in *Black Women Writers (1950–1980): A Critical Evaluation,* ed. Mari Evans (Garden City, N.Y.: Anchor Press, 1985), 339–45; and "Unspeakable Things Unspoken, The Afro-American Presence in American Literature," *Michigan Quarterly Review* 28, no. 1 (1989): 1–34; as well as Kingston's "Cultural Mis-readings by American Reviewers," in *Asian and Western Writers in Dialogue: New Cultural Identities,* ed. Guy Amirthanayagam (London: MacMillan, 1982), 55–65. Malini Scheuller discusses this issue specifically in reference to Kingston in "Theorizing Ethnic Subjectivity: Maxine Hong Kingston's *Tripmaster Monkey* and Amy Tan's *The Joy Luck Club,*" *Genders* 15 (1992): 72–85. Some contemporary ethnic women writers, like Paula Gunn Allen and Gloria Anzaldúa, are equally well known as authors and critics. See, for example, Allen's " 'Border Studies' " or Anzaldúa's *Borderlands/La Frontera: The New Mestiza* (San Francisco: Aunt Lute Foundation, 1987).

6. Kingston, "Eccentric Memories," 187.

7. Kingston, *Tripmaster Monkey* (New York: Vintage, 1989), 249. All subsequent references to *Tripmaster Monkey* will be cited parenthetically. Connecting humor and performance in an interview, Kingston comments that "quite often I feel forced to write against the stereotype. . . . Chinese and Chinese Americans are the most raucous people: they laugh so much, they're telling jokes, and they're always standing up and performing for one another. . . . Being able to laugh and to be funny—those are really important *human* characteristics, and when we say that people don't have those characteristics, then we deny them their humanity" (interview by Shelley Fisher Fishkin, *American Literary History* 3, no. 4 [1991]: 788).

8. Kingston, interview by Marilyn Chin, *MELUS* 16, no. 4 (1989–1990): 61.

9. See Wu Ch'eng-en, *Monkey,* transl. Arthur Waley (London: Allen and Unwin, 1942), and Anthony C. Yu, transl. and ed., *The Journey to the West* (Chicago: University of Chicago Press, 1977).

10. For more extensive discussion of the trickster's importance in Kingston's work and in contemporary American literature, see Jeanne R. Smith, *Writing Tricksters: Mythic Gambols in American Ethnic Literature* (Berkeley: University of California Press, 1997).

Kingston's discussion about the young man who danced in front of the tanks at Tien An Men in 1989 clearly illustrates the global terms in which she views family and community relations: "Yue Fei the Patriot and Chu Ping of the Dragon Boat Races are his ancestors. His ancestors are also Thoreau, Ghandi and Martin Luther King, Jr. His relatives were with him, too, and they include all of us on whose behalf he was braving a way of peace" ("Violence and Non-Violence in China, 1989," *Michigan Quarterly Review* 29, no. 1 [1990]: 67).

11.   This verbal riff corresponds nicely to Debra Shostak's reading of the novel's subtitle, *His Fake Book,* as a reference to a jazz musician's prompt book used for improvisations ("Maxine Hong Kingston's Fake Books," in *Memory, Narrative, and Identity: New Essays in Ethnic American Literatures,* ed. Amritjit Singh, Joseph T. Skerrett Jr., and Robert Hogan [Boston: Northeastern University Press, 1994], 239–40).

12.   Kingston, letter to David Leiwei Li, quoted in Li's *"China Men:* Maxine Hong Kingston and the American Canon," *American Literary History* 3, no. 2 (1990): 496.

13.   Kingston mentions her narrator's resemblance to Kuan Yin, the Goddess of Mercy who supervises Monkey's journey to the West, in several interviews.

14.   Nicholas Koss notes the congruence in Wittman's and Kingston's birth years: "Wittman was born in the year of the Dragon, which would have been 1940, since Wittman was a newly graduated young man in the early sixties" ("Will the Real Wittman Ah Sing Please Stand Up?: Cultural Identity in *Tripmaster Monkey: His Fake Book,*" *Fu Jen Studies: Literature and Languages* 26 [1993], 49, n. 15).

15.   Kingston, interview with Susan Brownmiller, *Mademoiselle,* March 1977, 211.

16.   Kingston, interview with Chin, 61.

17.   Kingston, "Eccentric Memories," 183.

18.   Kingston has cited these writers as influences in interviews with Rabinowitz and Fishkin.

19.   Kingston, interview with Chin, 65.

20.   Kingston, interview with Fishkin, 786.

21.   Jennie Wang, *"Tripmaster Monkey:* Kingston's Postmodern Representation of a New 'China Man,' " *MELUS* 20, no. 1 (1995): 111.

22.   For more specific exploration of Kingston's revision of Chinese American history, see Robert Lee's *"The Woman Warrior* as Intervention in Asian-American Historiography," in *Approaches to Teaching "The Woman Warrior,"* ed. Shirley Geok-lin Lim (New York: MLA, 1991), 52–63; Li's *"China Men:* Maxine Hong Kingston and the American Canon"; and Shostak's "Maxine Hong Kingston's Fake Books."

23.   Kingston, *The Woman Warrior* (New York: Vintage, 1989), 207.

24.   Kingston, *China Men* (New York: Knopf, 1980), 31.

25.   "I do not propose to write an ode to dejection, but to brag as lustily as chanticleer in the morning, standing on his roost, if only to wake my neighbors up." Epigraph to Henry David Thoreau's *Walden, or Life in the Woods,* ed. J. Lyndon Shanley (Princeton: Princeton University Press, 1971).

26.   Kingston, "Cultural Mis-readings," 57.

27.   For an alternative reading of this passage, see Isabella Furth, "Bee-e-een! Nation, Transformation and the Hyphen of Ethnicity in Kingston's *Tripmaster Monkey," Modern Fiction Studies* 40, no. 1 (1994): 33–49. She emphasizes the text's ambiguity and resistance to any stable, totalizing reading.

28.   Erkkila, "The Grounds of Resistance," 589.

Index

♦

The Volume Editor

◆

Dr. Laura E. Skandera-Trombley is a professor of American literature, vice president of Academic Affairs, and dean of the faculty at Coe College. She is vice president of the Mark Twain Circle of America and served as executive director of the Northeast Modern Language Association from 1994 until 1997. She is a reviewer for the National Endowment of the Humanities and has been elected to the International Association of University Professors of English. Dr. Skandera-Trombley also serves on the editorial board for *Studies in American Humor.* Her biography, *Mark Twain in the Company of Women*, was published by the University of Pennsylvania Press in 1994 and republished in paperback in 1997. *Choice* selected *Mark Twain in the Company of Women* as one of the outstanding academic books of 1995. Dr. Skandera-Trombley contributed to *Nineteenth-Century American Women Writers,* an edition chosen by *Choice* as an outstanding book of 1997. She is coeditor of *Epistemology: Turning Points in the History of Poetic Knowledge* (1986) and a special edition of *The Mark Twain Journal* "Women and Mark Twain Biography" (Summer 1998). Dr. Skandera-Trombley has published numerous articles in scholarly journals, including *American Literary Realism, College Literature, The Mark Twain Journal,* and *Biography,* as well as an essay on humor in *The Paris Review* and an afterword on *The Diaries of Adam and Eve* in the Oxford Mark Twain edition (1996). She has lectured on American literature in England, Mexico, Canada, Germany, and China. Her current project is an edition of Isabel Lyons' memoirs on Mark Twain.

The General Editor

◆

Dr. James Nagel, J. O. Eidson Distinguished Professor of American Literature at the University of Georgia, founded the scholarly journal *Studies in American Fiction* and edited it for 20 years. He is the general editor of the Critical Essays on American Literature series, published by G. K. Hall/Macmillan, which now contains more than 130 volumes. He was one of the founders of the American Literature Association and serves as its executive coordinator. He is also a past president of the Ernest Hemingway Society. Among his 17 books are *Stephen Crane and Literary Impressionism; Critical Essays on* The Sun Also Rises; *Ernest Hemingway: The Writer in Context; Ernest Hemingway: The Oak Park Legacy;* and *Hemingway in Love and War,* which was selected by the *New York Times* as one of the outstanding books of 1989 and which has been made into a major motion picture. Dr. Nagel has published more than 50 articles in scholarly journals and has lectured on American literature in 15 countries. His current project is a book on the contemporary short-story cycle.